PIETY AND POLITICS

RICHARD JOHN NEUHAUS, one of today's foremost authorities on religion and politics in contemporary society, is the director of the Rockford Institute Center on Religion and Society in New York City and is editor of *The Religion and Society Report*. An ordained Lutheran pastor, he is the author of ten books including *Christian Faith and Public Policy* (1977), *The Naked Public Square* (1984), and *Dispensations: The Future of South Africa as South Africans See It* (1986).

MICHAEL CROMARTIE is a research associate and director of Protestant studies at the Ethics and Public Policy Center. He received his B.A. from Covenant College and an M.A. from the American University in Washington, D.C. He is the editor of *Gaining Ground: New Approaches to Poverty and Dependency* (1985).

PIETY AND POLITICS

Evangelicals and Fundamentalists Confront the World

Edited by
Richard John Neuhaus
and
Michael Cromartie

ETHICS AND PUBLIC POLICY CENTER

THE **ETHICS AND PUBLIC POLICY CENTER,** established in 1976, conducts a program of research, writing, publications, and conferences to encourage debate on domestic and foreign policy issues among religious, educational, academic, business, political, and other leaders. A nonpartisan effort, the Center is supported by contributions (which are tax deductible) from foundations, corporations, and individuals. The authors alone are responsible for the views expressed in Center publications. The founding president of the Center is **Ernest W. Lefever.**

Library of Congress Cataloging-in-Publication Data

Piety and politics.

Bibliography: p.
Includes index.
1. Evangelicalism—United States—History—20th century. 2. Fundamentalism—History—20th century. 3. Christianity and politics. 4.United States—Church history—20th century. I. Neuhaus, Richard John. II. Cromartie, Michael. III. Ethics and Public Policy Center (Washington, D.C.)
BR1642.U5P55 1987) 277.3'082 87-19942
ISBN 0-89633-107-5 (alk. paper)
ISBN 0-89633-108-3 (pbk. : alk. paper)

Distributed by arrangement with:
University Press of America, Inc.
4720 Boston Way
Lanham, MD 20706

3 Henrietta Street
London WC2E 8LU England

Printed in the United States of America.

Ethics and Public Policy Center
1030 Fifteenth Street N.W.
Washington, D.C. 20005
(202) 682-1200

Contents

PART THREE: WHAT OTHERS SAY

Preface

NOT SINCE THE so-called Scopes Monkey Trial in 1925 have American Evangelicals and Fundamentalists received so much public attention as they are getting in the mid-1980s. They have emerged from a half-century of exile from the mainstream of American life every bit as controversial as they were when William Jennings Bryan was defending the Genesis story of creation against the teaching of evolution in Tennessee public schools.

Today their churches are growing, their colleges and universities are expanding, and their political influence is increasing. Their electronic evangelists such as Pat Robertson and Jerry Falwell reach millions of Americans. They are praised, criticized, misunderstood, and feared. All this is in sharp contrast to the half century of ostracism and ridicule they endured in all "respectable" circles of public discourse—the mainline Protestant churches, the academy, the prestige media, the scientific community, and both major political parties.

During their exile, while mainline Protestant churches developed an activist "social gospel," Evangelicals and Fundamentalists continued to preach the "old-time Gospel." They established churches, schools, and communications networks that attracted and nurtured millions of adherents who were committed to theological certainty in a society more and more given to skeptical uncertainty. These efforts were quietly sustained for six decades and enabled them to reassert their influence with vigor in various areas of public life during the past decade.

What burst into public consciousness before the 1980 elections had thus been developing for a very long time. For decades it had been assumed, with some justice, that these people were politically and socially quietist, leaving political concerns to "the world" while they focused their attention on the world to come. Now a sizable number of them have become unabashedly political, striving to re-establish what they believe to be the traditional but abandoned moral foundations of American public life.

The new political involvement of the Evangelicals and Fundamentalists has evoked strong and occasionally alarmist reactions. Many other church leaders and the secular media have declared that the involvement of the New Christian Right in national elections is only a momentary aberration in American life, a blip on the national screen. Those who believe that these "moral majoritarians" will soon go away are, we believe, mistaken. The new public assertiveness of conservative religion is likely to increase rather than decrease in the years ahead.

Until recently, many social theorists assumed that, as a society undergoes rapid change, particularly in technology, education, and science, it inevitably becomes less religious and more secular in outlook. More recently, a compelling alternative thesis has emerged. It holds that, as the modern phenomena of rationalization, specialization, and bureaucratization occur, the need for an overarching "meaning system" becomes more urgent. This analysis suggests that as Americans move deeper into what Max Weber termed "the iron cage" of modern life, questions about the enduring *meaning* of life will become irrepressible for more and more people. Such questions are religious in essence, and Evangelicals and Fundamentalists are among the religious groups most eager to answer them.

The sociological evidence is there to be analyzed by all. It shows that Americans are an incorrigibly religious people, and that an overwhelming majority of them believe that both individual and social morality derive from revealed religion—that is, the Judeo-Christian tradition. Consequently, the relation between private faith and public policy—between religion and politics—is being explored, and advanced, with vigor.

Republican Party leaders have estimated that from 15 to 20 per cent of the delegates to the party's 1988 national convention will belong to the Evangelical and Fundamentalist Christian movement. A *Washington Post* editorial stated that "viewed in terms of power within a political party, and disregarding ideology, the muscle of the Christian right in the GOP is roughly parallel to the power of the AFL-CIO or the National Education Association within the Democratic Party." But as significant as that comparison is, it represents only part of the story. For as historian Timothy L. Smith has written, the "evangelical mosaic or kaleidoscope" includes not only a diversity of denominations but also Christians from the political right, left, and center. In 1985 the *Wall Street Journal* carried a front-page report entitled "Radical Evangelicals Are Gaining Influence Protesting U.S. Policy." The article described the "growing and increasingly influential group of evangelicals whose conservative theology has led to radical—some would say leftist—political action."

Most media interest has been focused on the Christian Right and its concerns, with little attention to the influence of the "radical evangelicals" or the "evangelical left." Moreover, the major media have viewed Evangelicals and Fundamentalists primarily in political terms, without trying very hard to understand their theological and historical roots.

This three-part anthology places the Evangelicals' and Fundamentalists' political resurgence within its proper theological and historical context. It includes representative essays by Evangelical leaders from all points of the political spectrum. Each essay is preceded by a brief introduction, called "Focus," that defines its main themes and relates complementary and opposing selections to one another.

Part One examines the historical development and theological perspectives of Evangelicals and Fundamentalists.

In Part Two, Evangelical and Fundamentalist leaders speak for themselves. Broad theological agreement does not necessarily lead to political agreement; readers will note the varying political positions drawn from common convictions.

In Part Three, outside observers comment on the movement. Here, too, the accounts of the Evangelical resurgence in politics and its prospects are varied, as are the perspectives on the theological and political future of the movement.

The amount of published material on this subject is large and growing rapidly. The editors have provided a short bibliography as a reliable guide for further study.

We are grateful to the authors and publishers represented here for permission to reprint these twenty-six essays, many of which have been shortened to avoid unnecessary repetition. The editors alone are responsible for the selection of essays and for the introductions.

We would like to thank Kerby Anderson for his help at an early stage in the production of this volume. Ken Myers made several very important suggestions. David A. Bovenizer, associate editor of the Ethics and Public Policy Center, provided invaluable editorial assistance in transforming these manuscripts into a well organized book. Center interns Jenise Jones, Clifford Frick, and William Meyer provided timely assistance.

We are also grateful for the patient encouragement of Ernest W. Lefever, president of the Ethics and Public Policy Center.

The great promise of this newly assertive religious movement is renewal of the moral legitimacy of the democratic experiment, including, most importantly, the moral imperative of religious freedom. The promise, to be sure, is attended by many problems, but democratic renewal demands the widest possible participation in open debate. The exclusion of religiously based arguments from that debate, producing what one of the editors has called the "naked public square," is an unnatural and failed experiment in our public life. The naked public square is a very dangerous place. In it there is no religious imperative toward the good, nor any religious or ultimate inhibition against evil.

We offer this anthology with the hope that it will stimulate thoughtful discussions in both religious and other circles. We believe that a vigorous debate will enable religious and political leaders to make better decisions concerning the always complex relationship between religious convictions and public policy.

Richard John Neuhaus, Director
The Rockford Institute Center on Religion and Society
New York

Michael Cromartie
Ethics and Public Policy Center
Washington, D. C.

Part One

Background and Origins

1. *What the Fundamentalists Want*

By RICHARD JOHN NEUHAUS

Focus

Richard John Neuhaus was one of the first major ecumenical leaders to describe sympathetically "what the Fundamentalists want." Pastor for seventeen years of a black and Hispanic Lutheran church in New York City, and an advocate of civil rights reforms in the 1960s, Neuhaus manifests none of the disdain towards Fundamentalists expressed by many mainline clerics and others. He believes that the public resurgence of fundamentalist Christianity is good both for Christianity and for America, because it returns to the national discourse a huge bloc of citizens previously estranged from what Neuhaus calls "the public square."

He observes: "The country cousins have shown up in force at the family picnic. They want a few rules changed right away. Other than that they promise to behave, provided we do not again try to exclude them from family deliberations."

Fundamentalists may have exaggerated the strength of their new political involvement, but "they are not going back to the wilderness" of banishment, or self-imposed exile, from national life. They were aroused to renewed social and political responsibility by a series of events, especially the Supreme Court's ban on school prayer and legalization of abortion-on-demand. The resurgence proves that, despite assumptions to the contrary, "a majority of the American people had not consented'' to the transformation of personal and social morals since the mid-1960s. This transformation, which has been most evident in the ''sexual revolution,'' was primarily the work of the courts, the media, and the ''northeasternliberalestablishment,'' which is, to Fundamentalists, Neuhaus notes, ''one word.'' This analysis may be usefully compared with those by Nathan Glazer (selection 15) and William Bennett (selection 24).

Richard John Neuhaus, a Lutheran pastor, is director of the Center on Religion and Society in New York City and the author of many books on religion and politics, among them *The Naked Public Square* (Eerdmans, 1984), and *Dispensations: The Future of South Africa as South Africans See It* (Eerdmans, 1986).

DISTINGUISHED SOCIAL ANALYSTS, surveying the complexities of our religious, cultural, and political situation, have offered their considered judgment that: "The Falwells are coming! The Falwells are coming!" The less distinguished have joined in sounding the tocsin, and the alarm is getting louder. We can expect it to get louder still. If alarm is our only response to the public resurgence of religion in American life, there is reason for alarm. Yet among those who speak for the knowledge class, alarm has been the dominant, in some cases the only, response to date. It has been more reaction than response; reaction to alleged reactionaries, and therefore reactionary twice over.

Jerry Falwell, Ed McAteer, Gary Jarmin, Pat Robertson, Jimmy Swaggart, Jim Robison, Tim LaHaye—they are, so we hear, out to take over America and establish a theocracy in which all who disagree will be, at best, second-class citizens. But surely, we may think, nobody really believes such alarmist nonsense. Nonsense or not, reports of the great terror that is upon us are raising millions of dollars in fund appeals by Planned Parenthood, the American Civil Liberties Union, the National Organization for Women, Norman Lear's People for the American Way, and others who claim to believe that the religious Right is the greatest peril to American democracy since Joe McCarthy. Whatever else the religious Right may be, it is a bonanza for its opponents. And if its opponents are right about the "whatever else" the religious Right may be, the money is well given and well spent in warding off the threat.

Thus full-page advertisements in prestige newspapers inform us that the religious Right is determined to abolish the no-establishment clause of the First Amendment, impose its fundamentalist morality upon all of us through law, put politicians in our bedrooms, censor what we may read and see, and then, for good measure, blow up the world in order to force history's denouement in the final act of Armageddon. Truth to tell, it is possible to find statements by leaders of the religious Right who in spasms of sermonic excess have suggested that they intend to do all these

Reprinted by permission from *Commentary,* May 1985.

unpleasant things, and more. But they should not be caricatured by their hyperbolic lapses any more than they should caricature their opponents as friends of pornography, incest, pedophilia, drug-tripping, and treasonous opinion, although, truth to tell again, many of their opponents are on friendly terms with some or all of these. I have been warned that, by not taking at face value some of the more bizarre statements issuing from the religious Right, I am making the same mistake made by those who brushed aside the "hyperbole" of the Brown Shirts. For solemn reasons, no reference to the Third Reich should be dismissed lightly. For the same solemn reasons, the experience of the Third Reich should not be trivialized by such facile reference. But I do believe that those who compare our situation to that of the Weimar republic or the religious Right to the Nazis have fallen victim to polemical heat prostration.

'Christian America'

"When I hear the words 'Christian America' I see barbed wire," a notably liberal Reform rabbi tells me. I do not doubt him, but then he and a surprising number of others have a curious view of, among other things, Christianity. In this view the high points, sometimes the only points, of two millennia of Christian history are the blood curse upon the Jews, the Crusades, the Inquisition, and the Holocaust. This way of telling the Christian story is not unlike telling the story of America exclusively in terms of Salem witch-hunts, Indian massacres, slavery, the Ku Klux Klan, and alleged preparations for a nuclear first strike. Both stories, while highlighting some important truths, profoundly distort the tales they would tell.

Those who are most vocally anxious about Christian America usually have a special kind of Christian in mind. They do not worry about people who "happen to be" Lutheran, Episcopalian, Methodist, Catholic, or whatever. Even less worrisome are people who add that they happen to be whatever they happen to be "by background." These are the liberally acculturated who do not let their religion stick out or get in the way of living like normal people. They are, as Mort Sahl said of Adlai Stevenson, the sort of people who believe in the "Ten Suggestions" and who would—

were they members of the Ku Klux Klan—burn a question mark on your lawn. With Christians like that, Christian America is no problem. But then there are those other Christians who do not just happen to be but really are. And what they really are frequently carries an off-brand name, such as Independent Baptist, Holiness, Pentecostal, or Assemblies of God.

Many of us have never actually met one of these people, and almost nobody we know has ever actually met one, but there they are, millions of them, "out there." And we are inclined to think that we know all about them. In a recent interview Norman Lear explains how People for the American Way got started. After leaving the television comedies, "I was planning to write a film called *Religion,* because I was fascinated with the use of religion as a tax dodge by so many people who become ministers in order to write off a chunk of their living expenses. In order to prepare, I started watching how the reverends were functioning on television . . . and very quickly became concerned about the way they were mixing politics and religion." Lear goes on to suggest that the television evangelists are less interested in religion than in gaining political power. At the same time, he is outraged because they believe that "only those who accept a particular version of Jesus Christ as their savior will go to heaven and all others will go to hell." "In some profound way that we never shake, even Jews—and of course Christians—believe that good people go to heaven and bad people go to hell," says Lear.

Norman Lear is also in this respect typical of the reaction of many to the religious Right. They cannot make up their minds whether these television evangelists are religiously sincere or not. Even more troubling, they cannot decide whether it would be better if the evangelists were sincere. Ordinarily, sincerity gets a gold star in the kindergarten of contemporary culture, but not when sincerity is "divisive" in its violation of the rules of a pluralistic society. It is worth noting too that in a film titled *Religion* the subject was to be, of course, religious charlatanism.

For the image of Elmer Gantry runs deep in American elite culture and is now frequently and variously invoked in reaction to the religious Right. The leaders of the religious Right are said to be playing upon a nostalgia for an America that never was, but there is nostalgia too among critics who have revived the cast of villains from the 1920s. After the intellectual fads and passions of intervening decades, the world has become simpler again. Our sense of superiority is assured as we take our stand once more with H.L. Mencken against the "booboisie," the Victorians, Puritans, Yahoos, and rednecks, the benighted denizens of Gopher Prairie (now Virginia Beach) and Winesburg (now Lynchburg). Perhaps even the Left Bank and Greenwich Village will come back and, by the inadvertent grace of Jerry Falwell, it will again be possible to be a bohemian.

But such nostalgic fantasies are dispelled as we are recalled to the sure knowledge that this is not the way things were supposed to be in the future that is our present. Etched upon the mind of every educated American is Mencken's acidly brilliant derision of William Jennings Bryan in the company of his "rustic gorillas," utterly discredited and limping off the Tennessee stage to a timely death. There is more than one "teaching of contempt," and this one most of us learned well. But now some of us are no longer so certain, Broadway notwithstanding, that we understand who sowed the wind and who is reaping the whirlwind. Something has gone radically wrong with the script of modernity. We tell ourselves that this religious Right, indeed the more general phenomenon of religion bursting-out all over, is atavistic, a temporary malfunction in the ordering of time. Until we recognize that it is the certitudes of Clarence Darrow which now seem pitiably quaint, while the future is claimed by "high-tech" religious communicators who style themselves the American Coalition for Traditional Values. Little wonder that sectors of our cultural leadership show every sign of having gone into cultural shock.

Religious America

In fact, this new situation is not so new. The American people have always been determinedly, some would say incorrigibly, religious. What is new is the public recognition of this fact and the debate over the problems that attend it. To put it differently, what was thought to be a private and therefore eminently ignorable reality is spilling over into the public arena in most inconvenient ways. The spillover, or inundation, as some would have it, has been most visibly occasioned by the emergence of the religious Right. As it happens, on the map of American religion, politicized Fundamentalism is a minority phenomenon. This minority, however, has kicked a tripwire alerting us to the much larger reality of unsecular America. As in 1962 Michael Harrington alerted public opinion to the forgotten minority of "The Other America," so the religious Right has thrown open the closet door to expose the beliefs, fears, and aspirations shared by an overwhelming majority of Americans of almost every description.

In high schools and colleges across the country students are reading textbooks that state in a taken-for-granted manner that America is, or is rapidly becoming, a secular society. If religion is mentioned at all, it is said that people once found answers to their problems in religious teaching, but, of course, that is no longer possible in "our increasingly secular and pluralistic society."

Yet the proposition that America is, or is becoming, a secular society has everything going for it except the empirical evidence. The proposition is tied to a two-part dogma which has exercised an intellectual hegemony for nearly two hundred years. The dogma states that as people become more enlightened (read, more educated), religion will wither away. The second part of the dogma states that, to the extent religion endures, it is a residual phenomenon that can be hermetically sealed off in the "private sphere" of life, safely removed from the public arena where, by the canons of secular "rationality," we debate and decide the ordering of our life together. This is a hypothesis about historical development. As such it is subject to historical confirmation or falsification. At least in America, it has been historically falsified.

Survey research does not tell the whole story, but it tells an important part of it. It matters little whether one consults Gallup, Roper, or some other study; on some questions the answers are as close to unanimity as allowed by margins of error. For example, 94 per cent of the American people profess belief in God, 88 per cent say the Bible is the inspired word of God, 90 per cent identify themselves religiously with a specific Christian denomination or as Jews, 89 per cent of us say we pray regularly, and so forth. Why do some otherwise thoughtful people go on insisting that there is no frame of reference for a moral consensus among the American people? With near unanimity Americans say that morality is derived from the Jewish and Christian traditions (the Bible, the Ten Commandments, the Sermon on the Mount, the teachings of the Church, etc.). There is in fact a shared world of moral reference, a common vocabulary, that can be drawn upon in public discourse.

I said that with "near unanimity" Americans believe that moral judgment is derived from our Jewish and Christian traditions. The problem is with the "near." The civil libertarian immediately, and rightly, asks about those who dissent from that view—the religiously indifferent, the atheist, the declared "secular humanist,"as well as the Buddhist or Muslim.

The Middletown Study

For one answer, we can turn to the massive "Middletown III" study of Muncie, Indiana, directed by Theodore Caplow of the University of Virginia and sponsored by the National Science Foundation, which is pertinent to the question both of religious resurgence and religious tolerance. In *All Faithful People* (University of Minnesota, 1983), Caplow and his colleagues demonstrate that, contrary to the expectations of Robert and Helen Lynd who did the original Middletown study in the mid-20s, the people of Muncie are dramatically more religious today than they were then. Comparisons of the Muncie data with national surveys convincingly show that Muncie is not an exception on this score. Of course one can be skeptical about the authenticity, however defined, of this religiousness; survey research cannot search the interstices of the human heart. But it can measure the social reality. It can measure what people say they believe (for example, in Muncie 97 per cent say the Bible is inspired and 86 per cent "have no doubt" about the divinity of Jesus). It can measure churchgoing, rites of passage (marriages, funerals, etc.) under religious auspices, the time and money given to religious purposes, and numerous other facts of behavior. The farther back we go in time the less scientifically rigorous are the data, but on the evidence available Caplow thinks it reasonable to conclude that Americans are more religious today than they were, say, a hundred years ago.

Studies such as Middletown III have caused a remarkable turnaround among social theorists who had supposed there to be a necessary connection between increased modernity and increased secularization. As Peter L. Berger, arguably America's premier sociologist of religion, remarked at a recent conference, the evidence had been accumulating for some years, "but the Caplow study has put the final nail in the coffin of the theory that modernity means secularity."

On the question of tolerance, Caplow says that, "In a liberal perspective, these findings are almost too good to be true." But rechecking and rechecking again only reinforces the conclusion that, as the people of Muncie have become more religious, they have also become more tolerant. "We cannot turn up a group whose religious chauvinism comes anywhere near the level that was normal in 1924," Caplow reports. In this connection it is important to note that the research includes the fundamentalist Christians who are thought to be least tolerant of others. Of this "extraordinary ecumenicism" Caplow ventures the suggestion that "such a situation may never before have existed in the long history of Christianity." A clear and positive correlation between religious commitment and religious tolerance would seem to turn the conventional wisdom on its head.

Caplow offers several speculations on "why Middletown people are so reluctant to lay down the law or to expound the prophets for the benefit of their neighbors." One reason, Caplow suggests, is that religious people tend to think they are in the minority. They believe "the stereotyped misreading of social change" promulgated by television and other media which persuades them that religion is weaker than it is. The result is that "Devout Christians in Middletown, like happily married couples there, regard themselves as exceptional; surrounded by people just like themselves, they think they stand quite alone."

Another explanation is that the people of Middletown believe it is wrong, *morally* wrong, for anybody, and most especially for the state, to mess around with other people's souls. In other words, it is the will of God that we be tolerant of those who disagree with us about the will of God. Respect for those who believe differently or do not believe at all stems not from religious indifference but from religious commitment. If this interpretation is correct, it is very good news indeed for the future of religious freedom in America.

Fundamentalist Doctrines

The public resurgence of religion is hardly limited to Fundamentalism, but Fundamentalists are the main focus of the public debate. The key leaders of the American Coalition for Traditional Values (ACTV—pronounced "active"), for example, are Fundamentalists. This does not mean that all Fundamentalists support the religious Right, and it certainly does not mean that the religious Right is exclusively Fundamentalist. Many, perhaps most, Fundamentalists still adhere to the maxim that was almost universal among Fundamentalists only a few years ago: "Religion and politics don't mix." Jerry Falwell of the Moral Majority was eloquent in arguing that proposition against Martin Luther King, Jr. and other clergy in the civil rights movement. The pattern in the media and elsewhere is to use the term Fundamentalist in a careless way that refers to anything we deem religiously bizarre or fanatical. Thus journalists refer to Islamic fundamentalists and polemicists compare Jerry Falwell with the Ayatollah Khomeini. The pattern reflects intellectual laziness mixed with an unseemly measure of bigotry.

Fundamentalism derives its name from *The Fundamentals,* twelve paperback books issued from 1910 to 1915 which received enormous circulation. Written by conservative American and British writers, these books constituted a frontal assault upon religious "modernism." Modernism, in turn, was the confident liberal doctrine that there is an almost perfect congruence between God's will and the inevitable progress of civilization, especially American civilization. The Fundamentalists believed that this was a false religion and that most of the Protestant churches in America had sold out to it. (It is of more than passing interest that, while today millions of Americans call themselves Fundamentalists, almost nobody calls himself a modernist.)

In its early years Fundamentalism had some formidable intellectual leadership. For instance, J. Gresham Machen, professor of New Testament at Princeton Theological Seminary, made an impressive case in *Christianity and Liberalism* (1923) that religious liberalism was in fact not Christianity but a new religion that, while using Christian symbols and language, replaced faith in God with faith in humanity and historical progress. Most Fundamentalists boiled their case down to insistence upon five "fundamentals": the inerrancy of Scripture (the Bible contains no errors in any subject on which it speaks); the virgin birth of Jesus (the Spirit of God conceived Jesus in Mary without human intervention); the substitutionary atonement of Jesus Christ (on the cross he bore the just punishment for the sins of the entire world); his bodily resurrection; the authenticity of the biblical miracles; and pre-millennialism.

The last point touches on the question of, among other things, Armageddon, a question which erupted in, of all places, the 1984 presidential campaign. All orthodox Christians believe in the return of Jesus in glory and the establishment of the kingdom of God as the consummation of history. Some Christian groups are pre-millennialist, others are post-millennialist, and some do not take a position on the question. Both post- and pre-millennialists believe there will be on earth a thousand-year-reign of perfect peace, justice, and harmony with God's will. Pre-millennialists believe that Jesus will return first and then there will be that millennium; post-millennialists say the millennium will be established first and then Jesus will return in glory. The debate turns upon the interpretation of some marvelously obscure passages in the prophets Daniel and Ezekiel and the last book of the Christian Scriptures, Revelation.

In the past it was generally thought that pre-millennialist Christians would be politically passive, because there wasn't much point in trying to change the world before Jesus returns to set everything right. The important thing was not social reform but saving individual souls. At the end of the last century, before the Fundamentalist-Modernist split was formalized, evangelist Dwight L. Moody set forth the pre-millennialist thesis: "I look upon this world as a wrecked vessel. God has given me a lifeboat and said to me, 'Moody, save all you can.'" Post-millenialists, on the other hand, were avid social reformers, eager to put the world in order, establish the millennium, and thus hasten the return of Jesus. (The more modernist among them thought the last point to be an inspiring metaphor not to be taken literally.) But today the most aggressive political activism is being pushed by pre-millennialists.

The change is causing considerable consternation within the

fundamentalist world. Fundamentalism is magnificently fissiparous. The local churches jealously protect their independence from any larger association. Leaders can cooperate in groups such as ACTV and the Moral Majority because, it is repeatedly emphasized, they are not religious but political organizations. If non-Fundamentalists worry about what Fundamentalists say about them, it is as nothing compared with what they routinely say about one another. Bob Jones (of Bob Jones University) has declared that Jerry Falwell is the greatest instrument of Satan in America today. While they are partners in a moral crusade, off the platform one partner does not hesitate to announce that one or more of the other partners is surely going to hell. That God will not hear their prayers is the least of it. The public platform and the pulpit platform engage two quite different worlds of discourse. The Moral Majority advertises and carefully nurtures its support from Catholics, Jews, and non-believers. But membership in the Moral Majority, it is made unmistakably clear, is not to be confused with membership in the company of the truly saved.

Jews and Fundamentalists

Jews are notably and understandably interested in their part in Fundamentalist scenarios for the End Time. These scenarios are closely linked, of course, to the Fundamentalists' impassioned support for the state of Israel. They involve the Rapture, Armageddon, the final war with the Soviet Union, and other items of high drama which cannot delay us here. Suffice it to say that, while all orthodox Christians say Jesus will return, most Fundamentalists are "dispensationalists" who derive from "Bible prophecy" a quite precise blueprint and timetable for the return. There are, they believe, dispensations or ordered events and time periods predicted in the Bible. Jews are critical to the final act. There is considerable confusion over whether this means that the Jews will finally be converted to Christianity. The alternative way of putting it, which is increasingly accepted, is that Jews will be fulfilled in their Jewishness in welcoming their long-awaited messiah, who will turn out to be Jesus of Nazareth. He will not be the "Christian" messiah but most definitely the Jewish messiah, as he has been the Jewish messiah for Christians all along. As one rabbi has told me, "I can't get exercised over this dispute. If and when all this happens, we will see whether the one who comes is coming for the first time or the second time. I only hope that when we meet we'll be glad to see one another."

Christians of all persuasions have had a difficult time finding a secure theological place for living Judaism. There is little problem with the Jews of the Hebrew Scriptures (the Old Testament, as Christians say) and dispensationalists have an important role for Jews in the End Time, but Judaism between the biblical prophets and the eschaton is something of an anomaly. Today this may be changing as Christians are reflecting in a new way upon Paul's explorations (Romans 9 through 11) into the "mystery" of living Judaism and what it means that God will never break His covenant with the people of Israel. Fundamentalists too are increasingly insistent that this mystery means that the nation that blesses the Jews will be blessed and the nation that curses them will be cursed. It is less a sense of guilt over the Holocaust—which is viewed as something perpetrated by other people in a distant land—than of Divine purpose that gives Judaism and the state of Israel such a special place in the Fundamentalist world view.

Of course some Jews protest that it is demeaning to be fitted into a theological system to which they do not subscribe. This, I believe, may be a mistake. Acceptance of Jews, which means also resistance to anti-Semitism, is better secured when it is religiously grounded. Some Jews take a more pragmatic view in welcoming fundamentalist support for Israel in particular. Irving Kristol recently noted, "It is their theology, but it is our Israel." To that sage observation I would add that Israel is more firmly supported *because* it is their theology and not simply their prudential geopolitical judgment.

An 'Aggressive Defense'

If a previously apolitical pre-millennialist Fundamentalism has now turned in an activist direction, Fundamentalist leaders did not just get together one day and decide to go political. They felt, and they feel, that they are responding to an assault upon their religious freedom. As Seymour Martin Lipset has put it, their activism may be viewed as an "aggressive defense." Their defense is against what they perceive as governmental actions dictated by the "secular humanists" in control of American public life. Ten years ago, before the religious Right was a major factor, Leo Pfeffer (then of the American Jewish Congress) saw the dynamic that would produce this response. "Matters which have long been considered private," he wrote, "are increasingly becoming the concern of government." He added, "The thirst for power is a potent force even in a democracy, and the state will be tempted and will yield to the temptation of seeking to exercise dominion over religion for no other reason than because it is there."

There were several flashpoints that contributed to the political activation of Fundamentalism. Of enormous importance was the outlawing of prayer in the public schools in the early 1960s. These court decisions sent a seismic shock that traveled far beyond the worlds of Fundamentalism. Whatever one may think of the merits of school prayers, their removal was understandably seen as a major step toward the secularization of public space. An incorrigibly and increasingly religious society simply does not understand why children cannot publicly acknowledge God in the classroom, nor why, as another court ruling determined, the Ten Commandments cannot be posted on the classroom wall.

As important as these court rulings were, the religious Right was activated by the increasing aggressiveness of the Internal Revenue Service and other government agencies in "interfering" with the free exercise of religion. During the 1960s and 1970s the IRS moved in the direction of treating tax exemption for religion as a tax subsidy. The reasoning here is that money exempted from taxation is in fact a governmental expenditure, and what the government spends the government should control. It is again understandable that Fundamentalists, and not only Fundamentalists, believe that implicit in this reasoning is a massive, even totalitarian, expansion of state control over religion and other exempt forms of voluntary activity. Moreover, Fundamentalists in particular found themselves in collision with state educational authorities over the control of their Christian day schools. They believe, rightly or wrongly, that some state requirements for the certification of teachers and curricula exceed any legitimate public purpose and threaten to dissolve the religious distinctiveness of the alternative education they have elected for their children.

In discussing the "assaults" that sparked the defensive reaction of the religious Right, I have not mentioned the 1973 *Roe* v. *Wade* decision and abortion on demand. It is generally acknowledged that abortion was not that important in the generating passions of the religious Right. Until a very few years ago it was merely included in the catalogue of our society's "decadence," along with drugs, pornography, homosexual activism, and an exploding divorce rate. Today, of course, the limiting of abortions (or, as they prefer, the protection of unborn life) is high on the agenda of the religious Right, and of many millions of Americans who in no way identify with the religious Right.

What Else Do They Want?

Even those who try to understand the religious Right sympathetically find themselves asking, "Yes, but what else do they want?" One useful answer is ACTV's list of ten issues in its campaign to "restore traditional moral and spiritual values" to American life. The list includes prayer and Bible reading in public schools, a "pro-life" amendment (or some other instrument for overruling *Roe* v. *Wade*), legal restrictions on pornography, an end to state "harassment" of Christian schools, resistance to feminist and gay-rights legislation, increased defense spending, and terminating social programs that, it is believed, only increase the dependency of the poor. Even some of the committed opponents of the religious Right might concede that most, if not all, of these items are legitimate issues for debate in a democratic society. Yet many people are alarmed, for they thought that all these issues had been "settled." Only now has it become evident that, at least on some of these issues, a majority of the American people had not consented to the settlement.

Leaders of the religious Right have expressed surprise at what they view as the hysterical reaction to their enterprise. Jerry Falwell and some others increasingly try to calm the reaction by expressing devotion to the rules of liberal democracy (yes, *liberal* democracy) and by distancing themselves from the anti-democratic theocrats who are attracted to the cause. Falwell and others are publicly insistent that they are not advocating an officially "Christian America." Beneath the public gloating over their triumphs recent and portending is evidence of a deep insecurity about the power they are believed to possess. These people are not accustomed to being viewed with such intense fear and loathing. With loathing, yes. During their half-century in the religious, cultural, and political wilderness, Fundamentalists knew that they were the object of deepest contempt, and that knowledge reinforced their determination to have nothing to do with the "principalities and powers" of the American establishments. But the sensation of being feared is something new. They find it hard to believe that the "northeasternliberalestablishment" (one word) could be so easily intimidated, as some who are of that establishment may also find it hard to believe. Finding it hard to believe, some of us try to persuade ourselves of what it is almost impossible to believe, namely, that the religious Right and the conservative trend of which it is part are but a passing aberration and tomorrow morning we will wake up to discover that America has returned to "normalcy."

The activist Fundamentalists want us to know that they are not going to go back to the wilderness. Many of them, being typical Americans, also want to be loved. They explain, almost apologetically, that they did not really want to bash in the door to the public square, but it was locked, and nobody had answered their knocking. Anyway, the hinges were rusty and it gave way under pressure that was only a little more than polite. And so the country cousins have shown up in force at the family picnic. They want a few rules changed right away. Other than that they promise to behave, provided we do not again try to exclude them from family deliberations. Surely it is incumbent on the rest of us, especially those who claim to understand our society, to do more in response to this ascendance of Fundamentalism—and indeed of religion in general—than to sound an increasingly hysterical and increasingly hollow alarm.

2. *The Evangelical Worldview Since 1890*

By James Davison Hunter

Focus After a half-century in eclipse, the worldview of conservative Evangelicalism has regained cultural and political significance in American life. In this essay, James Davison Hunter traces the complex theological, cultural, and political trends that led, first to the eclipse, and, then to the remarkable resurgence mounted in recent years by Christian Fundamentalists and Evangelicals.

While mainline Protestant churches accommodated their teaching to the progressive politics of the early twentieth century and fashioned a "social gospel" to address contemporary issues, conservative Protestants withdrew from the mainstream of religious, social, and political life. To sustain their convictions in these circumstances, Fundamentalists and Evangelicals created an extensive network of churches, colleges, periodicals, and, more recently, radio and television programs. In doing so, the conservative Protestants—now commonly called Fundamentalists or Evangelicals (the two terms, Hunter explains, are not always interchangeable)—fostered a vibrant subculture. When the cultural and political crises of the 1960s and 1970s shook many Americans' faith in their institutions, this conservative network, representing a bewildering array of personalities and programs, burst into national consciousness.

Is the Evangelical "revival" as widespread and potent, especially in the political arena, as many of its leading proponents insist? Hunter reserves his judgment, but he provides the historical background for understanding the Evangelical movement and its future prospects. Hunter concedes that Evangelicalism by no means represents the primary worldview in America today, but he argues that Evangelicals, though still "a cognitive minority," have emerged as "a socio-cultural majority" whose views will have an impact on all Americans.

James Davison Hunter, an assistant professor of sociology at the University of Virginia, is author of *Evangelicalism: The Coming Generation* (University of Chicago, 1987), and *American Evangelicalism: Conservative Religion and the Quandary of Modernity* (Rutgers, 1983).

TRADITIONAL HISTORIOGRAPHY ON American Evangelicalism is dominated by several pervasive but unsubstantiated themes. One such theme is that Evangelicalism has always been a working-class and lower middle-class "agrarian protest movement centered in the South," incited and maintained by "ill-taught stump preachers or demagogues."[1] Another theme, which provides the basis for the first, is that Evangelicalism as a form of religious worldview has little historical relation, and so bears little resemblance, to eighteenth- and nineteenth-century American Protestantism. The historical background of contemporary American Evangelicalism, it is thus maintained, can be adequately understood by reference to its "beginnings" in the tumultuous decade of the 1920s, and a series of events that followed.

Yet careful treatment of the phenomenon of Evangelicalism reveals the inadequacies of this understanding. My principal thesis is that what is now known as contemporary American Evangelicalism is, first, a socioreligious phenomenon rooted historically in the mainstream (not the sectarian margin) of the nineteenth-century American Protestant experience, and, second, that Evangelicalism has been shaped by—and in reaction to—the symbolic and structural constraints of modernity—a process that began well before the sensationalism of the 1920s. A more suitable starting point than the 1920s for evaluating Evangelicalism is the period many scholars believe was perhaps the acme of American Protestantism. Also, the appropriate emphasis of the study of Evangelicalism is the development of the Evangelical worldview as a response to modernizing changes in American society and culture.

Nineteenth-century Protestant orthodoxy, or "Evangelicalism" as it was then called, was not just one religious worldview among many. In the direct line of succession from the colonial religious temper and the First and Second Great Awakenings, Protestantism's ethical and interpretive system, formally institutionalized within the denominational structure, was unquestionably predomi-

---

nant, not only in the religious life of America, but in the broader culture. The nineteenth-century Evangelical held the core religious beliefs of reformational orthodoxy to be normative for American society: an individuated conception of personal salvation mediated by Jesus Christ, the role of the Bible as the sole authority in religious and spiritual matters, and the need for obedience to the sovereign will of God in vocation and personal and family life. In addition, Evangelicals were convinced of the superiority of the Christian (which always meant "Protestant") faith.

Central to the religious life of the nineteenth-century Evangelical was the revival. An important mode of religious renewal in Protestantism during the eighteenth century, revivalism increased in vitality through most of the nineteenth century until it became one of the central cultural ornaments of the period. Beginning with the Second Great Awakening in 1800 to 1802 and its follow-up after the War of 1812, large-scale revivals can be traced through the late 1820s, the era of Charles G. Finney (1825–1835), the revivals between 1837 and 1857, the layman's revival of 1858, and the revivals of Dwight L. Moody (1870–1892). Revivalism, which found expression in most of the denominations, largely accounted for the unity of style and substance of Protestant life during this period.[2]

A distinct though not unrelated element of the nineteenth century Evangelical worldview was the Protestant ethical orientation expressed in ascetic self-discipline—chastity, temperance, frugality, industry, and pragmatism. This ethical orientation was especially important in the spheres of work and commerce, and spawned a widespread optimism about the future of mankind.

Theological and ethical elements woven together formed the basic fabric of the dominant worldview of this period of American history. This worldview found its primary social support in the small towns of mercantile America. But the theological and ethical elements were not equally represented; differences of emphasis were sometimes major, depending on such variables as region and class.

America as the 'New Israel'

Another important aspect of this tapestry was the widespread belief that America was a nation set apart for a divine purpose.

America was seen as the "new" Israel possessed of a covenant with God. Americans were the chosen people, entrusted with the responsibility of establishing a "righteous empire" or a Christian commonwealth. To be sure, these convictions derived to a considerable extent from the historical precedent of Europe, where the concept of Christian civilization had been firmly rooted since the fourth century. The nineteenth-century American Evangelical could scarcely view society as striving to be anything else. In addition, the larger part of the immigrating population consisted of dissenting Protestant groups. America was a place where these groups could escape social, economic, and often physical persecution. The biblical metaphor of being led from captivity to a land of possibility and fortune was therefore bound to be a recurrent feature of American folklore, especially during migrations of the nineteenth century.

Although nineteenth century American society was committed to the principle of separation of church and state, and also to voluntarism as the means of sustaining religion, the notion of the quest for a Christian America was, nonetheless, institutionalized. Local, state, and federal governments, dominated in the main by people who shared this conviction, were structured to encourage its ascendancy within American culture. Industry and commerce were also dominated by those of this mold. The result was the establishment of a uniquely Protestant style of life and work (and therefore, worldview) in American society, even among non-Protestants. Christianization also occurred in the educational system, especially at the lower levels. Public schools functioned to socialize large elements of the population with the values and expectations of mainstream Evangelical America. Indeed, even conversion at a revival often served as a rite of passage by which the recent immigrant could enter the American mainstream.

Yet the vision of the Christian empire went beyond the political boundaries of the United States. The vision was of the Christianization of the entire world. Even as late as 1890, Lewis Stearns declared:

> Today Christianity is the power which is moulding the destinies of the world. The Christian nations are in the ascendant. Just in proportion to the purity of Christianity as it exists in the various nations of Christendom is the influence they are exerting upon

> the world's destiny. The future of the world seems to be in the hands of the three great Protestant powers—England, Germany, and the United States. The old promise is being fulfilled; the followers of the true God are inheriting the world.[3]

Where the interpretive view of the nineteenth century American Evangelical played an important role in the legitimation of American imperialistic initiatives, the Christian missionary effort played a central role. As several social and historical commentators have maintained, the "thought of Puritan theocracy" established in the United States and worldwide "is the great influential fact in the history of the American mind."[4]

On all of these points, there was widespread consensus. A number of more specific beliefs and ideas were less generally held. Three of these general religious themes are discernible in nineteenth century Evangelicalism. One was constituted by the Reformed, or Calvinist, heritage, whose doctrinal emphasis was the absolute sovereignty of God in both individual and historical affairs. Human efforts in history occurred only through divine Providence, and human ability played little if any role in personal salvation. Heaven was a gift of God to those he foreordained to receive grace. This heritage also tended toward a postmillennial view of history. Corresponding to the Reformed emphasis on right doctrine was the practical emphasis on educational training and development of the intellect. The Confession of Faith and the Catechism of the Westminster Assembly were taught to Presbyterian and other Reformed youth. Memorization of the Shorter Catechism at an early age was common. A third emphasis was ecclesiological. Related to the distinct Reformed theological tradition was a strong church structure, a trait which had important consequences later in the century. It was out of this general tradition that nineteenth century American revivalism developed.

The Impact of Millenialism

A second major theme was *millennialism.* As one historian points out, America in the early nineteenth century was "drunk on the millenium."[5] As with most religious beliefs, Christian eschatology in the early part of the nineteenth century was not formalized in a theological system, nor was it clearly defined in terms of any specific Protestant tradition. There were a variety of beliefs concerning the end of times. The postmillennial view optimistically maintained that the stage was being set in the present era for a thousand-year reign of peace and justice (spoken of in the Book of Revelations) after which Christ would return. Premillennialism, by contrast, anticipated the dramatic bodily return of Christ on earth only when the degenerating effects of man's sinful rebellion against God had reached its utter depths. The Second Advent would signal the end of sin and death, vanquish Satan, and inaugurate a peaceful kingdom lasting a thousand years. Divine judgment would then follow.

The postmillennial and premillennial views of history existed side by side in most denominations in mid-nineteenth century America, though postmillennialism was clearly predominant before the Civil War. Premillennialism, however, was gaining increasing acceptance.[6] Though premillennial views were widely discredited as a result of the sectarian Millerites, who donned ascension robes in anticipation of the Second Advent in 1844, those holding such views organized loosely into a movement toward the end of the century, published periodicals, and held annual conferences.

In time, the premillenarian movement became associated with dispensationalism, a theological system popularized in the nineteenth century by a Church of Ireland expatriate, John Nelson Darby. Dispensationalism stressed not only a premillennial eschatology, but a unique historiography in which human history was classified into specific historical eras, or "dispensations," each dominated by a prevailing principle. Each dispensation ends in conflict, divine judgment on those who rule, and the introduction of a wholly new era. Dispensationalism eventually tended toward an Arminian (free will) as opposed to a Calvinistic (deterministic) approach to salvation. The adoption of premillennialism by the dispensationalists further solidified millenarianism as a recognizable movement. As the movement grew in size, it also gained in respectability. By the end of the nineteenth century, dispensational millenarianism had become perhaps the dominant religious theme in conservative Protestantism.

A third theme in the religious tapestry of nineteenth century

America was an emphasis on holiness. Emerging from the Wesleyan tradition, the holiness movement emphasized sanctification by the Holy Ghost. Many of its adherents considered spiritual perfection to be attainable. The movement's dominant influence was the Keswick (England) association, whose leaders taught that perfection could be approximated only through constant fillings of the Holy Spirit.

Each of these themes, though distinct, influenced each other in significant ways. Doctrinal factions and theological disputes (especially those on the nature of the millennium) were of importance not only to church leaders, but to growing numbers of church people. In spite of this diversity, the strength and unity of the doctrinal character and religious demeanor of the nineteenth century worldview—so emphatically conservative Protestant—could be taken for granted as normative. But, though Protestantism entered the period just before the turn of the century with this good measure of stability, it also displayed signs of stress in its monopoly influence on American culture.

The Disestablishment of Protestantism

Toward the end of the nineteenth century, the perplexing realities of modernization imposed themselves with increasing intensity. The social and economic problems associated with industrialization and urbanization, including, for example, crowded and inadequate housing, the factory system, a changing family structure, and increasing crime and suicide rates, could no longer be ignored. Contributing to this social upheaval was the religious and cultural pluralism of the unprecedented influx of Irish and Italian (Roman Catholic) and Eastern European (Jewish) immigrants. Among the Protestant leadership, there was at first a widespread recognition of these problems and the threat they posed to Protestant hegemony, but there was also widespread confidence that the trends could be accommodated. As Robert Handy has written, "it was believed that good intentions and an abundance of zeal would with God's help be adequate to handle the difficult problems."[7] This confidence soon gave way to anxiety and discontent with traditional understandings and solutions for such problems. The discontent adumbrated a formal split in American Protestantism, and ended the cultural monopoly of conservative Protestantism in America.

Pressure was also coming from the university. From the time of Friedrich Schleiermacher in the late eighteenth century, intellectuals in Europe, and to a lesser extent in the United States, had been grappling with the issues posed by modern rationality and religious pluralism, and thus with the modern worldview. The resolution of these pressures by the theological community had involved a general accommodation signaled by, among other things, the progressive abandonment of supernaturalism and the relativization and equalization of all religious belief systems. For the general clergy and the man on the street, these intellectual trends had little if any consequence until the end of the nineteenth century, when rumors of the theological accommodation began, in Nietzsche's words, "to reach the ears of men."

The 'Social Gospel'

The general response to these pressures was gradual, just as the building of pressure had been gradual. The response first appeared among clergy. While there was still a unilateral effort among all Protestants in missions, and also the reform of such social vices as intemperance, prostitution, and profanity, increasing numbers of the Protestant clergy began to advocate a "New Christianity" and a "new theology." These new ideas were based on the purported inadequacies of their predecessors. As Walter Rauschenbusch, a late nineteenth-century advocate of the New Christianity put it, "when I had begun to apply my previous religious ideas to the conditions I found, I discovered that they didn't fit."[8] Largely a composite of two closely related movements—the "Social Gospel" and "Cooperative Christianity"—the New Christianity was an attempt to deal with the growing perplexities of modern life in what its advocates believed to be a creative and responsible manner. Advocates of the Social Gospel repudiated an individuated conception of moral and social ills in favor of an interpretation resulting from social, political, and economic realities over which the individual apparently had little or no control.[9] Correspondingly, these advocates saw the basis of social reform not so much in the revival—where, so they believed, the "hearts of men would be purged from sin"—as in the modification of the structural conditions related to social maladies. Providing the basis of authority for such a perspective was the Bible—as viewed almost exclusively as a guide for social reform.

Though the first articulation of the Social Gospel could be traced to the 1870s in the works of Washington Gladden, Walter Rauschenbusch, Robert Ely, and, later, Josiah Strong, it was not until the 1890s that the Social Gospel gained force and respectability in major denominations. This respectability became evident in both the popularity of Social Gospel literature, and the rise of new organizations such as the Brotherhood of the Kingdom, the Department of Church and Labor of the Presbyterian Church's Board of Home Missions, the Methodist Federation for Social Service, and the commission on the Church and Social Service. The publication of such documents as the Social Creed of the Churches also attested to Social Gospel influence.

A second feature of the New Christianity was a movement in Protestantism known as "Cooperative Christianity." A number of attempts had been made to unify church bodies on a broad scale, for example, the Evangelical Churches of Christendom in 1900, and the National Federation of Churches and Christian Workers in 1901. But it was not until 1908, with the founding of the Federal Council of the Churches of Christ in America (the FCC) that these efforts achieved enduring success. As a national interchurch agency, the FCC was to function as the effective means by which social and political reform could be organized by the Protestant churches. The interfaith cooperation marked by the founding of the FCC also represented a move toward interfaith toleration and ecumenism.

Formal theology was an interest generally unsuited to the tastes of the nineteenth century American Evangelical. Even among ecclesiastical leaders and intellectuals, academic theological inquiry was not pursued with the vigor and depth it received in Europe, particularly in Germany. Princeton Seminary was, of course, a notable exception. By the turn of the century, however, American interest in formal theology was on the rise. Out of this interest emerged a "new theology." As a movement in intellectual circles, the new theology functioned to legitimate many of the ideological and structural changes occurring within the church at large. In addition, the new theology advocated a synthesis of the major scientific findings within Christian thought (Darwinism and social Darwinism most notably), as well as a social—often brazenly naturalistic—interpretation of the biblical writings.

The New Christianity and the new theology of the 1890s were by no means popularly embraced by the majority of American Protestants. These changes took hold among church leaders and intellectuals primarily in the urban regions of the Northeast, where the processes of modernization were especially accelerated and the social and economic effects of modernity were most visible. Thus, these changes represent only part of the activity within Protestantism during this period.

The Defenders of Orthodoxy

In the 1890s, the majority of Protestants embraced traditional orthodoxy, and from the ecclesiastical leadership there emerged a loosely organized movement dedicated to defending orthodoxy against what were deemed the pernicious doctrines of the New Christianity. The movement derived its structure and direction principally from the premillennialists—men such as Dwight L. Moody, A. J. Gordon, James Brookes, Arno Gaebelein, Charles G. Trumbull, Arthur T. Pierson, Rueben Torrey, and C. I. Scofield—and to a lesser extent from the Princeton Calvinists—men such as Archibald Alexander Hodge, Charles Hodge, and B. B. Warfield. Like the New Christianity and the new theology, this movement was also centered in the urban areas of the Northeast.

Though most of the members of this orthodox movement shared a concern for the problems of industrialization and urbanization, they never proposed a concept of extensive social reform. This proved to be something of a shift in policy, inasmuch as nineteenth century Evangelicalism typically emphasized a balanced concern for the spiritual and social needs of individuals. This shift, which has been labeled "The Great Reversal," was largely a result of the decline in the influence of postmillennial traditions and the rise of the premillenarian influences in the denominations as a whole. In any event, one of the few successful attempts by conservative Evangelicals to deal directly with problems of the time was conducted by the Salvation Army, an imported offshoot of British Wesleyanism. In the main, however, conservative Evangelicals reacted in keeping with their premillennial eschatology with a sustained pessimism toward the period. This reaction derived from their view that the trials of the age were evidences of humankind's total depravity, and of the approaching Second Coming of Christ and the end of time. Thus, Evangelicals' preoccupation was with the salvation of individual souls. The archetypal Evangelical social ministry became the "rescue mission," whose goal was to "rescue" people from the sin and degradation of the general culture. Though there was not nearly as much energy and enthusiasm behind mass revivalism at the end of the nineteenth century as earlier, revivalism still showed signs of vitality. Moody's revivals continued into the early 1890s and were followed by the mass evangelism of the extravagant ex-baseball player Billy Sunday. Missions also continued to be dominated by Evangelicals. The important Student Volunteer Movement is a notable example.

Advocates of traditional orthodoxy typically suspected anyone outside of their camp of apostasy. This was especially true of proponents of the New Christianity. What troubled conservatives about the Social Gospel in particular was not the new movement's endorsement of social concern, but the Social Gospel's emphasis on social concern to the seeming exclusion of the spiritual dimensions of faith. Thus, conservatives feared the growing popularity of the New Christianity as a threat to the apostolic faith. Conservatives considered the defense of the divine authority of the Bible as their primary task. They generally reasoned that, if they successfully defended the doctrine of the Bible as the inerrant and infallible Word of God, they would maintain an adequate basis for dismissing all erroneous teachings. Yet, a fully integrated theology of biblical authority did not exist in Protestantism during the major part of the nineteenth century, as Ernest Sandeen has shown:

> What did exist was a great deal of popular reverence for the Bible, the eighteenth-century literature defending the authenticity of the scriptures and providing "evidences" of their supernatural origin . . . and an apologetic stance which had conditioned defenders of the faith to respond to any challenge to the Bible with the cry "heresy."[10]

The Princeton Calvinists

A systematic theology defending the infallibility of the Bible was therefore articulated primarily through the efforts of the Princeton Calvinists Hodge and Warfield. Their doctrine of the Scriptures was intellectually complementary to the hermeneutic literalism of the dispensational millennialists, and therefore served to provide literalism with intellectual credibility.

Conservatives established other lines of cognitive defense. One was higher education. Before the 1880s almost all higher education was controlled by Protestant denominations, and the primary vocation of colleges and universities was to train ministers, teachers, revivalists, and the like. Thus, institutions of higher education were bastions of Evangelical unity and strength. After the 1880s, however, a trend toward the secularization of higher education began. Religion departments, segregated from other academic departments, were formed, and an increasing number of secular courses of study (the sciences, in particular) were introduced. Compulsory chapel was discontinued. In response, Bible institutes and colleges emerged with the expressed intention of training ministers, missionaries, and lay people for the defense and extension of the central doctrines of Christian faith. These institutions included Moody Bible Institute in Chicago, the Northwestern Bible Training School in Minneapolis, the Bible Institute of Los Angeles, the Toronto Bible Training School, and the Philadelphia Bible Institute. Frequent conferences, such as the Niagara Bible Conferences, the American Bible and Prophetic Conference, the Northfield Conferences, the Old Point Comfort Bible Conference, and the Seaside Bible Conference, became an institutionalized feature of conservative Protestant life. As another means of shoring up the cognitive defense of Evangelical faith, scores of periodicals dedicated to propagating orthodox views were established. Among them were *Waymark in the Wilderness, Prophetic Times, American Millenarian and Prophetic Review, Bible Champion,* and *Watchword and Truth.*

The Fundamentals

These efforts by conservatives to protect orthodoxy from the influence of the New Christianity eventually proved inadequate.

By the 1910s, the majority of Protestant ministers and theologians had abandoned the conservative position as indefensible. The accommodating forces in Protestantism had not been contained, and conservatives had encountered difficulties in effectively organizing. The conservatives were beset by an old leadership without competent replacements, and they were preoccupied with a variety of doctrinal disputes. The future of the conservative Evangelical tradition in America was therefore uncertain. In spite of these perplexities, however, conservatives in 1910 launched a major effort to regain cognitive control of Protestantism through publication of *The Fundamentals*.[11]

Sponsored by two wealthy conservative Protestant businessmen, the twelve volumes (containing ninety articles) of *The Fundamentals* were designed to check the spread of the New Christianity. They systematically covered doctrinal issues relating to the inerrancy of the Scriptures (the doctrine of inspiration, archaeological confirmation of bibilical stories, and the refutation of higher criticism), other Christian doctrines (the existence of God, the historicity of Christ, the nature of the Holy Spirit, the personal premillennial return of Christ, and the nature of the Christian life), commentary on the need for missions and evangelism, and finally, refutations of other religious systems (including Mormonism, Christian Science, spiritualism and Roman Catholicism). Though *The Fundamentals* was widely dispersed among church leaders, it was generally ignored by the academic community. The series' net accomplishment was dubious; at best, it provided only a pause in the decline of conservative power in the Protestant denominations.

In retrospect, it is now clear that the period from just before the turn of the century through the end of World War I was decisive for American Protestantism. By 1919, it was clear even to the man on the street that a bifurcation had arisen in American Protestantism. On the one hand were the purported defenders of Protestant orthodoxy, now disparaged as "Fundamentalists" after the publication by that title. On the other hand were the "Modernists," advocates of the New Christianity and the new theology who had initiated innovations in Protestant belief that were allegedly more attuned to the progressive spirit of the times. As a carry-over from the nineteenth century, the conservative forces had enjoyed wide popular respect and support, and maintained their status as a cognitive majority, while the liberalizing forces slowly emerged to become a recognizable if minority movement through the first decade of the twentieth century. By 1919, however, not only had this split widened, but popular support for the two sides had begun to reverse. Conservative forces had plainly lost the intellectual esteem of the American people, and the progressive ideas of liberalism were making incremental gains within the mainline churches.

In reviewing this chronology of events, one can understand that the New Christianity and the new theology capitulated to the cognitive constraints of modernity at two levels—the popular and the intellectual. The distinguishing characteristic of the popular capitulation was a shift in emphasis from the spiritual to the social and practical. The spiritual needs of humankind were to be treated not necessarily as paramount, but as one set among many. This shift indicated a growing doubt concerning the plausibility and viability of an essentially spiritual interpretation of human experience, as opposed to a more rational, naturalistic perspective. More than a tacit capitulation to the cognitive constraints of religious pluralism, the fledgling ecumenism of the New Christianity also marked a devaluation from the spiritual (the quest for doctrinal purity) in favor of a cooperatively based social reformism.

The new theology also provided an intellectual legitimation for the liberalizing changes in Protestantism. But in its own right, the new theology (higher criticism and the like) also signaled an intellectual capitulation to the cognitive constraints of modern scientific rationalism—the desire to make sense of the biblical literature in light of modern philosophical rationalism, and the desire to make "reasonable" the Christian worldview. The New Christianity and the new theology must, therefore, be understood as direct responses to the cognitive constraints imposed by the modernization process—responses that were intended to make Christianity more compatible with the rising modern worldview.

Were the Early Evangelicals Orthodox?

In examining the conservative movement in Protestantism, one must ask: Were the Evangelicals really defending the apostolic faith and reformational orthodoxy? All too often, this question goes unanswered. Actually, the answer is not so apparent; in fact, the opposite is closer to the truth: Though most conservative Protestants may have intended in the last decades of the nineteenth century to defend American Protestant orthodoxy, it is evident that, by 1919, they espoused something of a variant of it. How did this change come about?

If the New Christianity was a conciliatory response to the cognitive pressure of modern institutional structures and processes, Fundamentalism is a reaction to modernity. On the one hand, Fundamentalism—as an aspect of Evangelicalism—was a reaction to calamities associated with industrialization and urbanization. The postmillennialist vision of a "world growing better and better" became untenable to many conservatives; the premillennialism view of a "world growing worse and worse" was much more plausible to them. Indeed, premillennialism as a cognitive response to modernity not only came to dominate late nineteenth century conservative Protestantism, but also came to determine much of the movement's later character. On the other hand, Fundamentalism was a reaction to the modern worldview as represented by theological modernism. Conservative forces in the nineteenth century had no significant quarrel with institutional changes; neither did the earlier Baconian view of science, or even the modern secular worldview, pose any serious threat to conservative Protestant hegemony in the culture at that time.[12] It was when the presence of the modern worldview became internal to Protestantism in the form of modernism that the threat became imminent. In response, conservative forces defended those aspects of orthodoxy that they regarded as absolutely fundamental: the infallibility of Scripture, the deity and historicity of Christ and his mission, personal salvation as the paramount concern for every person, evangelization of the world, and, finally, the bodily return of Christ. The result of the militant concentration on these themes in Evangelical theology and teaching—to the exclusion of the social dimensions of faith—was a modification of the historical faith instead of apostolic or reformational orthodoxy itself. The labeling of conservatives as Fundamentalists was, then, an accurate indication of this inner transformation of nineteenth-century Evangelicalism.

Not only did liberals reconstruct their belief system during this period, the majority of conservatives did so as well, though perhaps in less drastic terms. From this period on, these two major factions of American Protestantism must be understood in their respective relations to modernity. On the one hand, the liberalizing forces in Protestantism were a direct response—an adaptation—to the cognitive pressures posed by modern institutional processes. On the other hand, the very character of Fundamentalism arose from its reaction to the worldview of modernity in what was considered the new age's most seductive and pernicious expression: modernism.

The Entrenchment of Fundamentalism

The religious transformation that began before the turn of the century culminated in the 1920s in what is now remembered as the Fundamentalist-Modernist controversy.[13] This controversy was fought, not between but within denominations, notably Baptist and Presbyterian. The issues had already been defined. Fundamentalists considered liberals, or Modernists, heretical in theological orientation. The liberals had allegedly abandoned the true Christian faith for an adulterated version informed by new scientific discoveries and hypotheses, especially Darwinian evolution. New methodologies, such as the higher criticism of Scripture, and the new reductionist interpretations of religious reality—the psychology and sociology of religion—were other factors. Liberals, meanwhile, caricatured Fundamentalists as rude, anti-intellectual, and obscurantist in theological orientation and presentation. Fundamentalists were accused of defending an antiquated interpretation of the Bible and religious experience on the basis of noisy dogma, not sound reasoning.

The formal beginning of the controversy was the establishment of the World's Christian Fundamentals Association (WCFA) in the summer of 1919. Composed primarily of millenarian dispensationalists of the urban Northeast, the organization was committed to preserving the great truths of the faith, for, as they put it, the

"Great Apostasy was spreading like a plague throughout Christendom."[14] As such, they also vigorously denounced the FCC, evolution, and anything else that hinted of modernism. The WCFA began with tremendous enthusiasm. Its influence was especially great in the South, for the views promulgated by the WCFA were compatible with Southern conservatism, individualism, and biblicism. Though its influence in publicizing Fundamentalist perspectives and solidifying Fundamentalist support was at first significant, the WCFA soon began to falter. The tenor of the organization was separatist and sectarian. Within a few years, the organization collapsed for lack of popular support.

Another major event in the Fundamentalist controversy was prompted by a Harry Emerson Fosdick sermon entitled "Shall the Fundamentalists Win?" This sermon became perhaps the most well known of an increasing number of diatribes against Fundamentalism and served to unite the Modernists against the Fundamentalist protest. Fosdick's sermon had particular reverberations in the Presbyterian denomination, not only in church's ecclesiastical hierarchy, but in seminaries. The major issue for church authorities was how to deal with the growing number of liberal theologians and ministers. Though initially the church's policy was to require ministers to conform to traditional Calvinist doctrines or face church discipline, pressure was mounting for ecclesiastic and theological tolerance toward liberals. J. Gresham Machen, one of the leaders of the conservatives from Princeton Seminary, defined the situation as a contest between two logically incompatible religions within denominations, and suggested that the liberals leave the Presbyterian denomination. Just the opposite occurred. Church authorities adopted a policy of tolerance; in response, the conservatives, led by Machen, left the Presbyterian denomination and established Westminster Theological Seminary in Philadelphia. Similar, though less significant, debates and ruptures occurred in the Methodist, Episcopal, and Church of Christ denominations, especially in the North.

Another aspect of the controversy concerned missions. Geographically isolated from the "contaminating" effects of modernism, the mission field was still largely dominated by conservatives through the turn of the century. By the 1920s, however, liberals had gained in number.

Darwinism and Prohibition

The final source of controversy, which had its greatest impact outside of Protestantism proper in the general culture, was the rising popular acceptance of what were considered non-Christian beliefs. To Fundamentalists, the most pernicious was the teaching in the public schools of Darwin's theory of evolution. Between 1921 and 1929, thirty-seven anti-evolution bills, all supported by Fundamentalists, were introduced in twenty state legislatures. The most famous case was the highly publicized Scopes trial in 1925. In a trial at Dayton, Tennessee, two prominent lawyers, Clarence Darrow and William Jennings Bryan, faced each other in a legal dispute over Tennessee's antievolution laws, and whether a public school teacher, John Scopes, could teach evolution in spite of them. The outcome is well known. Bryan, arguing for the Fundamentalists and against Scopes, won the legal case. Public opinion, however, was clearly in favor of Darrow, who made mocking sport of the Fundamentalist's crusade. In the end, Fundamentalism was discredited by the event.

The one issue on which there was agreement between Fundamentalists and Modernists was Prohibition. After years of frustrated attempts, a united coalition of Fundamentalists and Modernists succeeded in passing the Volstead Act and the Eighteenth Amendment to the Constitution prohibiting the sale of alcohol.

The many events of the Fundamentalist-Modernist controversy marked a culmination in the tensions within Protestantism that had existed for the preceding three decades. Parallel with the general unpopularity of the Protestant-initiated temperance movement, which had reached its peak with Prohibition, the prestige of American Protestantism in general had fallen to unprecedented depths by the 1920s. Protestantism had succumbed to such indecencies as name-calling and backbiting; indeed, the chief preoccupation within Protestantism during this period was with internal strife. Though the ideal of a Protestant empire in America had not been abandoned, it was no longer actively pursued. The revocation of the Volstead Act in 1933, and the drastic decline of foreign missions, signaled the end of empire building.

The 1920s also saw an overall decline in the plausibility of the Protestant worldview for the man on the street. A process that had begun in intellectual circles, and among church leaders and clergy, had finally percolated to the level of everyday life. Increasing numbers of Americans consciously repudiated the beliefs of conservative Protestantism in favor of the new liberalism. Significant numbers also repudiated Christianity in general. In the course of roughly thirty-five years, Protestantism had been moved from cultural domination to cognitive marginality and political impotence. The worldview of modernity had gained asendency in American culture.

Changing Values and Credit

Another trend that mitigated the plausibility of the traditional Protestant worldview for the common man was, as Daniel Bell has shown, the "invention of mass-consumption."[15] A central ornament of the nineteenth century worldview was an ethical system that esteemed the personal virtues of industry, thrift, discipline, and sobriety, and eschewed the vices of excess, indolence, unruliness, and indulgence. Mass consumption, however, is predicated on mass production of goods by technological innovations in the economy. Mass consumption was justified in American culture by the discovery of instant credit:

> The greatest single engine in the destruction of the Protestant ethic was the invention of the installment plan, or instant credit. Previously one had to save in order to buy. But with credit cards one could indulge in instant gratification. . . . The Protestant ethic had served to limit sumptuary (though not capital) accumulation. When the Protestant ethic was sundered from bourgeois society, only the hedonism remained, and the capitalist system lost its transcendental ethic.[16]

Installment buying, as Bell also pointed out, allayed the old Protestant fear of debt. Through the turn of the century, temperance remained the abiding symbol of the Protestant ethic in America. The revocation of laws of prohibition symbolized Protestantism's final dissolution as a unifying ethic in American culture.

Thus, on virtually all fronts, Protestantism as a whole suffered a loss of both prestige and plausibility. This development was much more disquieting for Fundamentalists than for liberals, primarily because of Fundamentalists' intransigence on the question of the supernatural. The conservative Protestant worldview, whose dominant interpretive characteristic was the immediacy of the spiritual in everyday life, suddenly evoked curiosity as a bewildering oddity.

Another important reason for the extreme cultural dislocation of conservative Protestants in general and Fundamentalists in particular was the uninhibited brashness of their social demeanor and the aggressive bellicosity with which they proffered or defended their beliefs. The Fundamentalists, especially, resented the now-dominant influence of the modern worldview in America. The pervasive pessimism of their premillennialism only contributed to this attitude. Indeed the Fundamentalists were convinced that the emerging modern worldview signaled the inevitable downfall of human thinking and therefore was a sign of the imminence of the Second Coming of Christ.

By the end of the 1920s the conservative Protestant conflict with the worldview of modernity, initially represented by Modernism and later by the modern or secular scientific enterprise (with evolution as its symbol), was essentially decided. The stage for the next several decades had been set. Fundamentalism, which had derived its unique identity from this conflict, had lost in its effort to maintain dominance within Protestant denominations and also within American culture. This loss resulted in the further loss of the credibility of the conservative Protestant interpretation of life, and tarnished its collective identity. In the coming years, Fundamentalism would have to cope with the pejorative stereotype established by the media during the Scopes trial. After the 1920s, Fundamentalism remained, in the mind of the man on the street, and as a facet of the cultural imagination, a sectarian fringe of American Protestantism.

Depression: Economic and Spiritual

Corresponding to the colossal economic depression of the 1930s, there was, as Martin Marty and others have noted, a spiritual depression in American culture. Protestantism was particularly affected. What actually seems to have occurred is that Protestantism continued to decline spiritually. The difference was that this period was much quieter than previous ones. This is unusual, because under conditions of extreme economic and social deprivation, one typically anticipates a forceful resurgence of religious commitment. Indeed, some church leaders of the 1930s hailed the economic collapse for precisely this reason. They reasoned that the hardship men experienced would drive them back to God, so the church would thrive again. Though the economic depression and World War II fostered a general conservatism (in theology the result was neoorthodoxy), a large-scale revival of religion in the culture never came about. Signs of renewal were periodic and relatively unpredictable. Commenting on this state of affairs, Robert Handy has observed:

> Revival in the old pattern simply did not materialize. Revivalism as it had been developed through the nineteenth and into the twentieth centuries had been in the context of a civilization understood to be Protestant in a general sense. Much of its power was drawn in fact from its community nature and from its confident assumption that in calling men to God it also enlisted them directly in the forces which strengthen the Christian character of a civilization. To answer the call was important, therefore, both for the individual and for society.[17]

Revival had previously been facilitated by the close association that existed between religion (Protestantism) and the rest of society, but the modern processes of institutional differentiation and segmentation slowly severed that institutional association. In response to pressures brought about by these institutional changes, the quest to establish a "Christian America" had been abandoned. The sacred covenant had been broken. Religion had been sequestered and formally placed in a contractual relation to society: it was to perform only institutionally specific duties. As such, religious renewal in the general culture was rendered much more difficult. Indeed, religion was becoming a private matter, and therefore, even were a religious renewal to occur, it would have little if any institutional support.

In this situation Fundamentalists were confined to the lower and lower middle classes of the rural and only recently industrialized South. They did not remain dormant, but became increasingly entrenched as a cognitive minority. The frustration and dissatisfaction among conservative Presbyterians that ended in the split in Presbyterianism in 1929 foreshadowed the dominant trend in Fundamentalism during the 1930s: the "independent" church movement. The choice was between remaining in what were considered apostate denominations where maintaining a strict orthodoxy would be difficult, or withdrawing from those denominations and becoming independent. Cognitive purity is always easier if shielded from contaminating forces, a fact that Fundamentalists readily acknowledged. The Bible Presbyterian Church, the Bible Protestant Church, the Independent Fundamentalist Churches of America (drawing from several denominations), and many smaller independent churches that remained unaffiliated all emerged during this period. Holiness, Pentecostal, and Adventist groups also proliferated. Many smaller conservative (confessional) denominations were also drawn to Fundamentalist principles: the Evangelical Free Church, the Missouri Synod Lutheran, and the Christian Reformed were the most important. Denominations in the Anabaptist tradition also responded positively, and included the Evangelical Mennonites and the Evangelical Friends. These groups, in addition to a strong cohort of Baptist and Methodist churches, constituted the major institutional base of Fundamentalism after the 1920s.

Fundamentalists Hold Their Ground

In the context of the Great Depression, Fundamentalism, among all religious groups, suffered least. The pessimism of Fundamentalist premillennial eschatology was compatible with the socioeconomic conditions Fundamentalists experienced in everyday life. The Great Depression was in their view a sign of God's vindictive punishment on an apostate America, and also a sign of Christ's imminent return. Their nearly exclusive orientation toward spiritual salvation was also compatible with the deprivation they experienced. Personal salvation and the variable degrees of holiness attainable by the believer served as compensations for the privileges denied him in the social and economic spheres.[18]

Accordingly, religion in general was being relegated to the private sphere. In the 1920s, the Lynds, in their study *Middletown,* remarked: "In theory, religious beliefs dominate all other activities in Middletown; actually, large regions of Middletown's life appear uncontrolled by them."[19] Eight years later, in *Middletown in Transition,* they observed that the gap had grown even wider: religious thought and practice were, in the minds of most Middletown citizens, unrelated to other spheres of life:

> The gap between religion's verbalizing and Middletown life has become so wide that the entire institution of religion has tended to be put on the defensive; and the acceptance of a defensive role has tended to mean that it is timid in jeopardizing its foothold in the culture by espousing unpopular causes, when they appear in the economic order, in questions of world peace, and in the elements of contradiction in local institutions.[20]

These tendencies to privatization also occurred within Fundamentalism. Revivals remained the staple of Fundamentalist churches. Next in importance to "being saved" was the quest to conform to a rigorous private morality oriented exclusively around avoiding the sins of worldly amusements: playing cards, dancing, gambling, drinking, movies, and swimming with members of the opposite sex. Conformity to these strictures not only differentiated the Fundamentalist from "the world" (that is, the modern world), but provided evidence to others in the community of the Fundamentalist's salvation.[21] The orientation of this ethic attests to the reality that the Fundamentalist's experience in the church bore little relevance to his experience in the world of work. It also points out the fact that, in these circles, economic prosperity and other forms of public success were no longer the main indices of divine favor, as they had been to colonial-Puritans and nineteenth century Evangelicals.

At the same time, there is evidence that Fundamentalists resisted the pressures of privatization, especially in the political sphere. They were, to be sure, the last remnants of nineteenth century Evangelicalism to interpret American history in terms of a nation in covenant with God. Revivalist Billy Sunday, in his final years, continued to speak for Fundamentalism by publicly defending the American way of life. To him (and to most other Fundamentalists), this view meant patriotic adherence to the ideals of the Republican party and nineteenth century laissez-faire capitalism, and also a repudiation of Communism—found, they believed, in the New Deal, the American Civil Liberties Union, the Democratic party, atheism, evolutionism, modernism, the Federal Council of Churches (FCC), and the Social Gospel. The opinion was widely held that, if certain trends were not reversed by virtue of a sweeping revival, the world would surely meet destruction. Though rarely, if ever, organized into a viable political force during the 1930s, Fundamentalists were nonetheless seldom ambivalent or silent about political views on current events and trends.

Recognizing that collective survival depended on an organizational unity, Fundamentalists came together in the fall of 1941 and established the American Council of Christian Churches (ACCC). The ACCC was a logical culmination of the independent church movement, and analogous to the FCC, which now represented what was considered mainstream Protestantism. As such, the ACCC was designed to bear witness to "the historical faith of the church," including:

> the full truthfulness, inerrancy, and authority of the Bible, which is the Word of God; the holiness and love of the one sovereign God, Father, Son and Holy Spirit; the true deity and sinless humanity of our Lord Jesus Christ, His virgin birth, His atoning death, "the just for the unjust," His bodily resurrection, His glorious coming again; salvation by grace through faith alone; the oneness in Christ of those He had redeemed with His own precious blood; and the maintenance in the visible church of purity of life and doctrine.[22]

The ACCC was also explicitly designed to be a separatist organization for churches and denominations that had denounced modernism and disavowed affiliation with the FCC "in the darkening days of apostasy." Thus, Fundamentalism was still defining itself in reaction to modernity—in protest against the dominance of the modern worldview.

The Resurgence of Evangelicalism

Soon after the ACCC was established, a group of moderate Fundamentalists came together to explore the possibility of establishing another national Protestant organization that "was determined to break with apostasy," but would be "no dog-in-the-manger, reactionary, negative or destructive type of organization." It would also "shun all forms of bigotry, intolerance, misrepresentation, hate, jealousy, false judgment and hypocrisy."[23] In the spring of 1942, therefore, the National Association of Evangelicals (NAE) was formed.[24] There was complete unity between the ACCC and the NAE in matters of doctrine, but they differed in matters of policy. Membership in the ACCC was exclusive: no members of the FCC were allowed to participate. Membership in the NAE was more inclusive: selective membership for affiliates of the FCC was permitted. These membership policies suggest the overall difference of attitude between the two theologically conservative groups. While the ACCC held a rigid "no cooperation, no compromise" attitude toward differing theological traditions, the NAE held the more conciliatory attitude of "cooperation without compromise." Indeed, these attitudes applied also to the groups' respective approaches to American culture. Though as a result of these policy differences the two groups often shared intemperate hostility toward one another, together they constituted the dual alignment of conservative Protestantism in America for the next three decades.

The 1950s and 1960s were, without question, the most economically prosperous in American history. The appearance of a pseudo-aristocracy was attainable for an increasing number of Americans, and a brash materialism came to dominate private life. A respectable hedonism made possible by economic growth was institutionalized as a normative expectation in the mainstream culture. Through this period, and in this context, a general religious renewal took place. Church membership in the United States grew from 43 per cent in 1920, to 47 per cent in 1930, to 49 per cent in 1940, to 57 per cent in 1950, to 62 per cent in 1956, and to 63 per cent in the early 1960s. As Martin Marty notes:

> After the American religious depression of the 1930s and the preoccupations of World War II, it became clear that by around 1950 many Americans were in a settling-down mood. They needed a means of justifying their complacencies, soothing their anxieties, pronouncing benedictions on their way of life, and organizing the reality around them. Millions turned to religion, and Protestantism profited from the return to religion.[25]

The preoccupation of mainstream Protestantism during this time was with modern religious pluralism.[26] Since 1908, when the ecumenical FCC had been formed, little had been accomplished in unifying American Christianity, yet cultural pluralism had become even more commonplace and therefore had to be addressed by the churches. In 1948, the international ecumenical movement founded the World Council of Churches (WCC). Two years later, the FCC was reconstituted into a more ecumenical structure with the founding of the National Council of Churches of Christ in the United States (NCC). Both the WCC and NCC sought to go beyond Protestantism to include Eastern Orthodoxy and even Roman Catholicism. Thus, the pluralist interpretation of American life—wherein all religious traditions stood on equal ground—was being established in the mainstream of American culture. Interreligious "dialogue" (a religious détente) became the fashion of the day. The ideological justification for this (as in 1908) was the unity of God's church for the ultimate goal of establishing God's kingdom on earth through progressive social policies. Clearly more was at stake, however: the aggressive ecumenism of mainstream Protestantism marked not only a continued yielding to the cognitive constraints of modern cultural pluralism, but implied a recognition of the market character of religions in competition for the "interest, allegiance, and financial support of potential clientele." Ecumenicity rationalizes and civilizes competition as does the process of cartelization in the secular economy.[27]

Through the late 1950s and early 1960s there was widespread optimism in America about the social and political efficacy of the church in a world confronting acute needs. Ecumenicity had caught hold in Roman Catholicism under Pope John XXIII, signaling progress toward unity between Protestantism and Catholicism in efforts to establish the kingdom of God on earth. The optimism in mainstream Protestantism was sustained by the continued influx of liberal Protestant churchgoers. Liberal Protestant theology, meanwhile, was undergoing drastic changes. Theological notions such as the "death of God" and the "secular city" as the workshop of God became popular. The gospel message, and also the identity and role of the church, were redefined in secular, humanistic terms. True spirituality was defined as the forthright accommodation to the worldview and "life-styles" of modernity. Yet the theological innovations of the early 1960s turned out to be little more than the further cognitive contamination that accompanies dialogue with different religious traditions, and especially with the naturalism of the modern worldview. The worldview of mainstream Protestantism and liberal theology actually became the forthright religious legitimation of modernity.

Opposing Ecumenism and Communism

Conservative Protestantism also had fared well with the postwar rise of social and political conservatism. Its organizations became more cohesive, and its policies became more deliberate. Fundamentalists and Evangelicals alike reacted sharply to the ecumenical initiatives of mainstream Protestantism. Most of all they feared the rise of a superchurch that, as the Bible prophesied, would be established in the last days. The ecumenical movement and its many organizations were, they believed, the precursors of this universal church. Their criticism was unrelenting, but their reaction went beyond words. Several days before the constituent assembly of the WCC in 1948, Carl McIntire, president of the ACCC, assembled a delegation of Fundamentalists in the same city—Amsterdam, The Netherlands—and established the International Council of Christian Churches (ICCC) to counter the WCC. McIntire took full advantage of the assembled media to publicize Fundamentalist grievances with liberal Protestantism. Similar protests were repeated through the 1950s whenever the WCC or its constituent national councils met.

The militancy of Fundamentalism during this period was focused in anti-Communism.[28] National sentiment was decidedly conservative on this issue, largely because of the unsettling nature of Soviet initiatives in Eastern Europe (the "Cold War"), and the swelling nationalism in Asia. The notion of an internal conspiracy designed to subvert governments to Communism seemed plausible; Fundamentalists McIntire of the ACCC-ICCC, Edgar Bundy of the Church League of America, and Billy James Hargis of the Christian Crusade therefore came to the fore in the anti-Communist crusades of the early 1950s. The relationship between the two movements was, to be sure, symbiotic. Of particular concern to Fundamentalists was the alleged infiltration of Communism into the church, so they centered their attacks on the NCC and the WCC as apostate, un-American, pro-Communist, and treasonous ecclesiastical organizations. The formula was simple: liberalism is socialism, and socialism is the first phase of Communism. On several occasions throughout this period, Fundamentalists held exposés of prominent WCC and NCC leaders to attempt to substantiate their allegations.

Evangelicals Sustain a Subculture

The more moderate "neo-Evangelicals," though sympathetic with the Fundamentalists, were critical of the manner in which many Fundamentalist activities were conducted, and therefore avoided direct involvement. The neo-Evangelicals channeled most of their energies into the reconstruction of a strong subcultural infrastructure. A prime example was their effort to reestablish a stable foundation of popular support through evangelism. Religious radio programs such as the "Back to the Bible Hour," "The Children's Gospel Hour," "The Hour of Decision," "Radio Bible Class," and "Old Fashioned Revival Hour," and religious radio stations such as WMBI, KUCA, KUGA, and WMUU proliferated.[29] Evangelical television programming also got its start at this time with "Youth on the March," "Sermons from Science," and "Man to Man." Youth evangelistic organizations such as Youth for Christ, the Miracle Book Club, the American Soul Clinic, Inter-Varsity Christian Fellowship, and others provided, among other things, alternative forms of teenage entertainment. All of these efforts were successful. The most forceful influence, however, was the evangelistic fervor of evangelist Billy Graham. His crusades in Los Angeles, Portland, Boston, Columbia, South Carolina, and New York, between 1949 and 1957, were overwhelmingly successful, not only in "saving souls," but in making the premillennialist Evangelical worldview palatable to the mainstream of American culture again.

Neo-Evangelicalism grew in other ways as well. With the establishment of the NAE came the formal involvement of many conservative denominations in the Reformed-Confessional tradition. Thus, Evangelicalism gained new denominational strength. In addition, Bible institutes, Evangelical liberal arts colleges, and Evangelical seminaries were founded to educate increasing numbers of new Evangelicals. The Christian day school also surfaced as an alternative to primary and secondary public education. This movement gained notable momentum when legislative efforts to provide for "released-time" religious education in public schools (permitting students to voluntarily receive religious education during school hours on school property) were defeated in several states.

Preserving the Faith on Rational Grounds

There was also substantial growth in Evangelical scholarship. After the 1920s, few conservative Protestant thinkers in America were taken seriously in intellectual circles. After World War II, great efforts were made to reverse this trend. Evangelicals repudiated anti-intellectualism in favor of a scholastic attitude dedicated to preserving the essentials of Evangelical orthodoxy on thoroughly rational grounds. Thus, neo-Evangelical scholars attempted to deal with modern rational thought on its own terms. Evangelical "apologetics" became the main intellectual activity; in the process, certain concessions were made. Neo-Evangelical scholars also became sensitive to the social import of their faith. Slowly there arose formal efforts at developing direction for Evangelical social thought. The result of these "clarifications," and of the insistence that Evangelical doctrines could be rationally defended, was that the religious orientation of Evangelicalism gained a new measure of credibility in American culture.

Several periodicals emerged to serve the rising number of educated Evangelicals. *Christianity Today, Eternity, Youth for Christ Magazine, His,* and *Christian Life* were popular, and there were scholarly journals such as *Journal of the Evangelical Theological Society, Gordon Review,* and the *Journal of the American Scientific Affiliation.* Evangelical publishing houses profited from this expansion in both number and in size.

Thus, in virtually all ways, the neo-Evangelicals—now called Evangelicals—were successful in forming a subcultural foundation. Applying the interpretive framework of this research, it can be averred that Evangelicals had established lines of cognitive defense from which to withstand the cognitive onslaught of modernity, and within which the meaning system of conservative Protestantism could plausibly be maintained. Conservative Protestantism in Evangelicalism had by the end of the 1950s also clearly outgrown its insecurities as a cognitive minority. Indeed, it had successfully shed the stigma of being a religious sect, and had come to enjoy a central place within the mainstream of American culture. Nothing better illustrates this achievement than the celebrity status accorded Billy Graham.

The Sixties and Seventies

The trends established within conservative Protestantism in the 1950s continued through the 1960s and beyond. Widely discredited by its association with McCarthyism, Fundamentalism continued its hard-sell campaign against liberal theology, ecumenicism, and Communism. This, together with revivalism, constituted Fundamentalism's exclusive orientation. As a result, Fundamentalism appealed primarily to the rural lower classes. Evangelicalism, however, continued to extend its popular and institutional base of support and also its influence in American society. Evangelicals maintained their alliance with political conservatism—evidenced in their support for the Goldwater presidential campaign in 1964. Evangelicals also maintained close association with higher echelons of political power, struggled to reinstitute prayer and Bible reading in public schools, questioned the civil rights movement, and generally supported American involvement in the Vietnam War. The exceptions to this conservatism were the much-publicized "Evangelical hippies," or "Jesus people," factions: these maintained, as did their secular counterparts, a fairly well-defined, Left-liberal political orientation.

From the end of the 1960s through the mid-1980s, mainstream Protestantism has remained ecclesiastically stable and theologically subdued; yet, to the delight of conservatives, mainstream Protestantism has experienced a drastic decline in popular support. Membership in, and attendance at, mainstream churches have dwindled. The worldview of mainstream Protestantism has, from all indications, shown signs of cognitive impotency in the culture. By contrast, conservative Protestantism has continued to build strong and stable institutions. Evangelicalism showed clear signs of a resurgence by the early 1970s. Beginning with the rise of the "Jesus People" in the mid-1970s, the Evangelical resurgence peaked in 1976 with the media spectacle of the "born-again" movement, the election of Evangelical Jimmy Carter to the presidency, and the designation of 1976 as the Year of the Evangelical. Whereas conservative Protestantism had previously maintained a relatively low profile, it had by 1976 become the object of public attention. Suddenly, it was acceptable, and even socially desirable, to become a born-again Christian—an Evangelical. Celebrities such as President Nixon's former aide Charles Colson, rock star Eric Clapton, pornographer Larry Flynt, and political expatriate Eldridge Cleaver were making headlines talking about their conversion experiences. Within Evangelicalism, confidence had grown to such an extent that, by the mid-1970s, Evangelical leaders such as Bill Bright could boldly predict the evangelization of the United States by 1980 and the evangelization of the world by 1984.

A Real or Illusory Revival?

Whether the resurgence of Evangelicalism in the 1970s was a genuine religious revival or simply a media-encouraged (or media-constructed) revival is difficult to say. There was a significant stirring within conservative Protestantism, and it subsided only toward the end of the decade. Throughout the resurgence, and to date, up to this writing, Evangelicalism has maintained close association with "middle-brow" American culture. Normally, this has meant the quiet affirmation of everyday American middle-class life patterns—and, in extreme cases, an aping of the glitter and pageantry of Hollywood.

Of special significance is the dissolution of the distinction between Fundamentalism and Evangelicalism as a result of the Evangelical resurgence. This is not to say that there is no longer any diversity among conservative Protestants. Clearly, conservative Protestantism has been, and remains, a polymorphic and heterogeneous group, not only in its religious dimensions, but in structural and cultural dimensions as well. What is different, as a result of the Evangelical resurgence, is that the policy differences that precipitated the bifurcation in Fundamentalism in the 1940s are no longer rigidly institutionalized. Although there are clear remnants of the "1920s Fundamentalism" still to be found within conservative Protestantism (the ACCC and ICCC, Bob Jones University, and Hargis and his Christian Crusade), these no longer represent a formidable cultural and political force. By and large, this militant faction of the tradition has been brought into mainline Evangelicalism. This may be due to the reality-defining capacities of the media, specifically through their labeling of all conservative Protestants as Evangelicals.

A Sociocultural Majority

Perhaps the best description of American Evangelicalism during the period between 1943 and 1982 is offered by Martin Marty: Evangelicalism has remained a cognitive minority but has emerged as a sociocultural majority. The core elements of the Evangelical meaning system remain as they were in the beginning of the century. Along with the standard tenets of Christian orthodoxy, these include the Bible as the infallible Word of God, the deity and historicity of Jesus Christ, and a personal relationship with Jesus Christ. Issuing from this is the duty to evangelize all humankind for Christ (which typically means the Evangelical faith and experience), belief in the personal (typically premillennial) Second Coming of Christ, and the individuated conception of personal, social, and institutional problems, i.e., the sinful heart and mind of the individual as the root cause of all human ills. On these beliefs Evangelicals are, in the main, intransigent. Consequently, in a world in which the secular is deemed normative, such beliefs are considered to be tolerably deviant, if not intolerably divisive. At the same time, Evangelicalism is firmly representative of the American middle class, which is dominant in American society. For this reason Evangelicalism has gained widespread public acceptance. How can this be possible?

One could hypothesize that Evangelicals have made concessions to modernity. With the growing plausibility of the modern worldview resulting from the extension of the modernization process in American society came an increased pressure to accommodate. The founding of the NAE marks the point in the history of American conservative Protestantism at which yielding to those pressures began—the point at which a more positive and constructive, or perhaps a more conciliatory, approach to modernity was taken. Efforts to develop a rational apologetic for Protestant orthodoxy, and to establish stable institutional structures within the Evangelical community, are evidences of the accommodation. Evangelicals embraced modern technology and modern (middle class) forms of cultural expression for the same reason. Thus, Evangelicals have succeeded in establishing lines of cognitive defense—but not without some sacrifices.

This conciliatory approach to modernity can also be seen in more subtle terms. From its earliest times, Fundamentalism (as a variant of nineteenth century Evangelical Protestantism) defined itself in opposition to the worldview of modernity as the latter was expressed in theological Modernism. The presuppositions and concepts of the modern worldview were understood to be sinful, and its emerging predominance in American culture was seen as a sign of the end of human history. Being distinct from the world—the modern world—was thus very important for Fundamentalists; it remains important in conservative Protestant circles. Yet until the early 1940s, this separatism was defined exclusively in negative terms; in other words, the worldview of modernity was held to be so utterly sinful that it should be abhorred and avoided at all costs. After the 1940s, however, there emerged a growing trend toward defining separatism more positively; in other words, the worldview of modernity might be sinful, but one must prove at all costs the superiority of Evangelicalism. This approach has required Evangelicals to be involved in modern society and their involvement has had important implications for the character and vitality of the Evangelical worldview.

Notes

1. Ernest Sandeen, *The Origins of Fundamentalism* (New York: Fawcett, 1968), p. 26.
2. Robert Handy, *A Christian America* (New York: Oxford University Press, 1971), p. 29.
3. Ibid., p. 121.
4. Daniel Bell, *The Cultural Contradictions of Capitalism* (New York: Basic Books, 1976), p. 56.

5. Donald Dayton, *Millennial Views and Social Reform in Nineteenth Century America* (Unpublished Manuscript: Northern Baptist Theological Seminary, 1980).

6. Ibid., pp. 94, 152, 163f.

7. Robert Handy, *A Christian America* (New York: Oxford University Press, 1971), p. 143.

8. Martin Marty, *Righteous Empire* (New York: Dial, 1970), p. 185.

9. Ibid.

10. Ernest Sandeen, *The Roots of Fundamentalism* (Chicago: Chicago University Press, 1970), p. 106.

11. Willard Hudson, *Protestant America* (Chicago: University of Chicago Press), 1961, p. 148.

12. Donald Dayton, *Millennial Views and Social Reform in Nineteenth Century America* (Unpublished Manuscript: Northern Baptist Theological Seminary, 1980).

13. George Marsden, *Fundamentalism and American Culture* (New York: Oxford University Press, 1980), p. 192.

14. Ernest Sandeen, *The Roots of Fundamentalism,* p. 243.

15. Daniel Bell, *The Cultural Contradications of Capitalism.*

16. Ibid., p. 21.

17. Robert Handy, *A Christian America*, p. 208.

18. Listen Pope, *Millhands and Preachers* (New Haven: Yale University Press, 1965), p. 86.

19. R. S. Lynd, and H. M. Lynd, *Middletown* (New York: Harcourt, Brace, 1929), p. 4.

20. R. S. Lynd, and H. M. Lynd, *Middletown in Transition* (New York: Harcourt, Brace, 1937), p. 193.

21. Ibid.

22. Louis Gaspar, *The Fundamentalist Movement* (Paris: Mouton, 1963), p. 23.

23. James Murch, *The Growing Super-Church* (Cincinnati: National Association of Evangelicals, 1952).

24. Farley Butler, "Billy Graham and the End of Evangelical Unity" (Dissertation Abstracts International 37: 4429–4430A).

25. Martin Marty, *A Nation of Behaviors* (Chicago: University of Chicago Press, 1976), p. 256.

26. Ibid., pp. 244–254.

27. Peter L. Berger, "A Market Model for the Analysis of Ecumenicity." (*Social Research* 30(1), 1963), p. 85.

28. Gary Clabaugh, *Thunder on the Right* (Chicago: Nelson-Hall, 1974).

29. Data collected on the growth of the religious news media as reported in the *New York Times*, January 28, 1971.

3. *The Evangelical Denomination*

By GEORGE MARSDEN

Focus

In spite of their perplexing diversity, American Evangelicals share a core of common beliefs that unite "born-again" Christians of all denominational traditions. George Marsden suggests that Evangelicals constitute a denomination because "among Protestants the lines between Evangelical and non-Evangelical often seem more significant than do traditional denominational distinctions."

The reasons for this unity within diversity are many. Principal among them, Marsden believes, is that Evangelicals have fashioned a "transdenominational community" through such institutions as independent churches, colleges, magazines, and programs of evangelism. The proliferation of radio and television programs in recent years has contributed greatly to this trans-denominational bond.

As members of a "movement" that they trace to the apostolic age, Evangelicals in America share, Marsden points out, "common heritages, influences, problems, and tendencies." Though their historical experiences have rendered them skeptical of all institutions, even ecclesiastical ones, Evangelicals maintain what Marsden calls "a conscious fellowship, coalition, community, family, or feudal system of friends and rivals who have some stronger sense of belonging together."

Marsden observes that, "On one side of Evangelicalism are black Pentecostals, and on another side are strict separatist Fundamentalists such as at Bob Jones University, who condemn Pentecostals and shun blacks. Peace churches, especially those in the Anabaptist-Mennonite tradition, make up another discrete group of Evangelicals. Nonetheless, once we recognize the wide diversity within Evangelicalism, we can properly speak of Evangelicalism as a single phenomenon."

George M. Marsden, a professor of American Church history at Duke University Divinity School, is author of *Fundamentalism and American Culture* (Oxford University, 1980).

THE GREATEST CONCEPTUAL challenge in an anthology of this sort is to say what Evangelicalism is. The issue can be clarified by asking whether Evangelicalism is not a kind of denomination. Evangelicalism is certainly not a denomination in the usual sense of an organized religious structure. It is, however, a denomination in the sense of a name by which a religious grouping is denominated. This ambiguity leads to endless confusions in talking about Evangelicalism. Because Evangelicalism is a name for a religious grouping—and sometimes a name people use to describe themselves—everyone has a tendency to talk about it as though it were a single, unified phenomenon. The outstanding Evangelical historian Timothy L. Smith has pointed out the dangers of this usage. Smith has remarked on how misleading it is to speak of Evangelicalism as a whole, especially when one prominent aspect of Evangelicalism is then usually taken to typify the whole. Evangelicalism, says Smith, is more like a mosaic or, suggesting even less of an overall pattern, a kaleiodoscope.[1] Most of the parts are not only disconnected, they are strikingly diverse.

So on one side of Evangelicalism are black Pentecostals, and on another are strict separatist Fundamentalists, such as at Bob Jones University, who condemn Pentecostals and shun blacks. Peace churches, especially those in the Anabaptist-Mennonite tradition, make up another discrete group of Evangelicals. Their ethos differs sharply from that of the Southern Baptist Convention, some fourteen million strong and America's largest Protestant body. Southern Baptists, in turn are different from those Evangelicals within the more liberal "mainline" Northern churches.

Each of these predominantly Anglo groups is, again, very different from basically immigrant church bodies like the Missouri Synod Lutheran or the Christian Reformed, who have carefully preserved Reformation confessional heritages. Other groups have held on to heritages less old but just as distinctive: German Pietists and several Evangelical varieties among Methodists preserve tradi-

Reprinted by permission from William B. Eerdmans Publishing Co. from *Evangelicalism and Modern America,* edited by George Marsden, 1984.

tions of eighteenth-century Pietism. The spiritual descendants of Alexander Campbell, especially in the Churches of Christ, continue to proclaim the nineteenth-century American ideal of restoring the practices of the New Testament church. Holiness and Pentecostal groups of many varieties stress similar emphases that developed slightly later and in somewhat differing contexts. Black Christians, responding to a cultural experience characterized by oppression, have developed their own varieties of most of the major American traditions, especially the Baptist, Methodist, and Pentecostal. Not only do these and other Evangelical denominations vary widely, but almost every one has carefully guarded its distinctiveness and usually avoid deep contact with many other groups.[2] Viewed in this light, Evangelicalism appears as disorganized as a kaleidoscope. One might wonder why Evangelicalism is ever regarded as a unified entity at all.

Nonetheless, once we recognize the wide diversity within Evangelicalism, we can properly speak of Evangelicalism as a single phenomenon. The meaningfulness of Evangelicalism as such a "denomination" is suggested by the fact that among Protestants the lines between Evangelical and nonevangelical often seem more significant than do traditional denominational distinctions.

Unity Despite Diversity

We can avoid many of the pitfalls in speaking about this single "Evangelicalism" if we simply distinguish among three distinct, though overlapping, senses in which Evangelicalism may be thought of as a unity. The first two are broad and inclusive, the third more narrow and specific.

First, Evangelicalism is a conceptual unity that designates a grouping of Christians who fit a certain definition. Second, Evangelicalism can designate a more organic movement. Religious groups with some common traditions and experiences, despite wide diversities and only meager institutional interconnections, can constitute a movement in the sense of moving or tending in some common directions. Third, within Evangelicalism in these broader senses is a more narrow, consciously "Evangelical" transdenominational community with complicated infrastructures of institutions and persons who identify with "Evangelicalism."

Since these three senses of "Evangelicalism" are not usually clearly distinguished, the word is surrounded by confusion. In part, this confusion is an inescapable characteristic of a loosely organized and diverse phenomenon. Much of the confusion, however, arises from the widespread tendency to confuse Evangelicalism in one of the first two broad senses with the more self-conscious community of the third sense.

In its broad usage, "Evangelicalism" designates simply a conceptual unity. Evangelicals in this sense are Christians who typically emphasize (1) the Reformation doctrine of the final authority of Scripture; (2) the real, historical character of God's saving work recorded in Scripture; (3) eternal salvation only through personal trust in Christ; (4) the importance of evangelism and missions; and (5) the importance of a spiritually transformed life.[3] Evangelicals will differ—sometimes sharply—over the details of these doctrines and some persons or groups may emphasize one or more of these points at the expense of others. But a definition such as this can identify a distinct religious grouping. Because Evangelicalism in this sense is basically an abstract concept, the diversities of the grouping may be more apparent than the organic unity.

One way of looking at Evangelicalism that has depended heavily on this definitional approach is the opinion survey. Pollsters deal best with abstractions and must reduce their topic to operational definitions. Whether or not one is an Evangelical is thus tested by whether one professes a combination of beliefs and practices that fit a certain definition. Evangelicalism delineated in this way will, of course, be somewhat different than if it is considered a movement—either in the broad or narrow sense. For instance, a 1978–79 *Christianity Today*-Gallup survey classified between forty and fifty million Americans as "Evangelicals," a number that accords with other estimates. However, even if the definition used to make such a determination is cleverly formulated and qualified, it will inevitably be inflexible, excluding some who would be "Evangelicals" by more intuitive standards, and including some whose Evangelicalism is marginal. For example, such surveys have no very adequate way of dealing with American folk piety. Also, a fair number of Americans seem ready to profess traditional religious beliefs even though these beliefs for them have little substance.[4] Thus, though definitions of Evangelicalism are necessary and helpful, they provide only limited ways of grasping the broad phenomenon.

A Dynamic Movement

The other major way to perceive Evangelicalism broadly is to view it not so much as a category but as a dynamic movement with common heritages, common tendencies, an identity, and an organic character. Though some Evangelical subgroups have few connections with other groups and support few common causes, they may still be part of the same historical movement. There may be an "evangelical mosaic" consisting of separate and strikingly diverse pieces, but it nonetheless displays an overall pattern. Thus, many American Evangelicals participate in a larger historical pattern, having substantial historical experiences in common. All reflect the sixteenth-century Reformation effort to get back to the Word of Scripture as the only ultimate authority and to confine salvation to a faith in Christ, unencumbered by presumptuous human authority. During the next centuries these emphases were renewed and modified in a variety of ways, often parallel or interconnected, by groups such as the Puritans, Pietists, Methodists, Baptists, nineteenth-century restorationists, revivalists, black Christians, holiness groups, Pentecostals, and others. Many Evangelical groups, now separate, have common roots and hence similar emphases. Widely common hymnody, techniques of evangelism, styles of prayer and Bible study, worship, and mores demonstrate these connected origins.

Moreover, common cultural experiences have moved this broad Evangelical movement in discernible directions. For instance, all American Evangelicals have been shaped to some extent by the experience of living in a democratic society that favors optimistic views of human nature, the importance of choosing for oneself, lay participation, and simple popular approaches. American materialism has also provided a common environment for most Evangelicals, and they have also been shaped by cultural and intellectual fashions. Nineteenth-century Evangelical hymnody of almost all denominations, for example, tended to be sentimental-romantic and individualistic, mirroring the larger culture. In addition, twentieth-century Evangelicals have often incorporated current cultural values into their messages.

On the other hand, the common or parallel experiences in the movement may involve resisting cultural trends. Most notably, twentieth-century Evangelicals have in common a belief that faithfulness to Scripture demands resistance to many prevalent intellectual and religious currents. While many in mainline American denominations and their educational institutions abandoned their Evangelical heritages during the first half of this century, all Evangelicals today hold firmly to traditional supernaturalist understandings of the Bible message. Simple love for the traditional gospel has no doubt been the chief force in this stance. But many secondary reasons also account for the resistance: because they were immigrants, because they were culturally or intellectually isolated, because they were strongly committed to evangelism and missions, because of traditions of biblical interpretation, or perhaps because of sheer cussedness. Nonetheless, the experiences were parallel, and the resulting willingness to assert the authority of the Bible against dominant cultural values was similar. So, alongside the striking diversities in heritages, emphases, and cultural experiences are extensive commonalities that make Evangelicalism discernible as a larger movement.

Evangelicalism as a Community

Evangelicalism is a single movement in a more narrow sense, too. Not only is it a grouping with some common heritages and tendencies, it is also for many a community. In this respect, Evangelicalism is most like a denomination. It is a religious fellowship or coalition of which people feel a part.

This sense of an informal Evangelical community or coalition goes back to the international Pietism of the eighteenth century. Common zeal for spreading the gospel transcended party lines. By the first half of the nineteenth century, this movement had assumed something like its present shape. Evangelicalism in this more specific sense is essentially a transdenominational assemblage of independent agencies and their supporters, plus some denominationally sponsored seminaries and colleges which support such parachurch institutions. During the first half of the nineteenth century, Evangelicals from Great Britain and America founded scores of "voluntary societies" for revivals, missions, Bible and tract publication, education, charity, and social and moral reforms. These voluntary agencies constituted an informal "Evangelical united front." In America, the expenditures of these independent agencies at times rivaled those of the federal government.[6] International revivalism, particularly that of Charles Finney in the first half of the century and Dwight L. Moody in the second, as well as efforts in world missions, helped foster a unity of purpose among Evangelicals from a variety of denominations.

Successful techniques developed in one revival group or mission quickly spread to others. The Evangelical Alliance, founded in 1846, was the most formal expression of this international Evangelical community. Evangelically oriented denominations often encouraged or directly supported some of the independent Evangelical agencies. For a few independents, such as Moody, Evangelicalism was, in effect, their denomination. For most Evangelical leaders, however, the relationship was a bit weaker. Evangelicalism was a fellowship with which they identified while they also participated in a body such as the Methodists, Baptists, Presbyterians, or Congregationalists. Many constituents at the grass-roots level, such as those who supported a Moody revival or an African mission, might be only dimly aware of their connection with a wider Evangelical coalition. They would know, however, that their Christian allegiance was wider than simply loyalty to their formal denomination.

'Winning the World for Christ'

During the nineteenth century this trans-Atlantic, trans-denominational Evangelical fellowship or coalition, though often strained by rivalries and controversies, was unified primarily by shared aspirations to win the world for Christ. In the early decades of the twentieth century, the basis for unity was modified, although never abandoned, in response to a deep crisis centered around conflicts between "Fundamentalists" and "Modernists" in formerly Evangelical bodies. Fundamentalists were militant Evangelicals who battled against the Modernists' accommodations of the gospel message to modern intellectual and cultural trends. Modernists, on the other hand, allowed little room for an authoritative Bible, traditional supernaturalism, or a gospel of faith in Christ's atoning work. In short, they had abandoned the essentials of Evangelicalism. To make matters worse, the leadership in the major Northern denominations tolerated or encouraged this revolution. In reaction, the new Fundamentalist coalition emerged at the forefront of the Evangelical fellowship. In the face of the modernist threat to undermine the fundamentals of evangelical faith—a threat magnified by the accompanying cultural revolution—much of surviving Evangelicalism took on a fundamentalist tone. The perennially upbeat mood of the nineteenth-century movement was now tempered by accents of fear and negativism.

The situation was complicated by the prominence of dispensationalist premillennialists in the leadership of interdenominational Fundamentalism. Dispensationalists, whose prophetic interpretations predicted the apostasy of old-line churches, made a virtue out of working independently of denominations. Accordingly, they had built a formidable network of evangelistic organizations, missions agencies, and Bible schools. Their transdenominational orientation and their evangelistic aggressiveness, together with a hard-line militance against any concessions to modernism, put them in a position to marshal, or at least to influence, many of the conservative Evangelical forces. During the 1920s, leaders of this movement presumed to speak for all Fundamentalists and did coordinate many Fundamentalist efforts. Thus they developed a disproportionate influence among conservatives in the old, interdenominational Evangelical movement, which during the next three decades was generally known as "Fundamentalist." Heirs of this Dispensationalist-Fundamentalist movement, especially after 1940, reorganized and revitalized the broader and more open branches of Fundamentalism. This "neo-evangelicalism," as it was known for a time, preserved many of the positive emphases of the old nineteenth-century coalition as well as some of the negativism of Fundamentalism.[7]

Close connections with Billy Graham gave this new leadership national impact and attention. For the two decades after 1950, the most prominent parts of this more narrowly self-conscious

Evangelicalism focused around Graham. Graham's prominence and the commanding position of former Fundamentalists in organizing this neo-evangelical effort, however, partially obscured for a time the fact that the movement, even as a conscious community, had many other foci and included many other traditions. Since the 1960s, and especially with the successes and growing self-awareness of "Evangelicalism" in the 1970s, the diversities that had always been present in the old Evangelical fellowship have become more apparent. In the 1980s, the movement faces a crisis of identity, evidenced by debates over "who is an Evangelical?"

With this background we can see more clearly how the third meaning of "Evangelical" refers to a consciously organized community or movement. Since mid-century there have been something like "card-carrying" Evangelicals. These people, like their nineteenth-century forebears, have some sense of belonging to a complicated fellowship and infrastructure of transdenominational organizations for evangelism, missions, social services, publications, and education. Typically, those who have the strongest sense of being "Evangelicals" are persons with directly Fundamentalist background, though persons from other traditions—Pentecostal, holiness, Reformed, Anabaptist, and others—often are deeply involved as well. Sometimes the people, groups, and organizations that make up "Evangelicalism" in this sense are rivals. Even in rivalry, however, they manifest the connectedness of a grouping that is quite concerned about its immediate relatives.

Fundamentalists As a Distinct Group

To look at Evangelicals this way requires some adjustment to account for those who still call themselves "Fundamentalists." By the end of the 1950s, the term "Fundamentalism" had come to be applied primarily to strict separatists, mostly dispensationalists, who were unhappy with the compromises of the new "Evangelical" coalition of Billy Graham. Fundamentalists were also adamant in condemning Pentecostal Evangelicalism, while the former Fundamentalist neo-evangelicals, despite some reservations, saw Pentecostals as allies in their preeminent task of leading people to Christ.

Since the 1970s, some Fundamentalists, centering around Jerry

Falwell and the Moral Majority, have begun to build broader coalitions, much like the neo-evangelicals of the 1940s and 1950s. Yet even the hard-line Fundamentalists, such as those at Bob Jones University, who condemn all such compromises, remain a part of the consciously Evangelical movement, at least in the sense of paying the closest attention to it and often addressing it. In another sense, however, hard-line Fundamentalists have formed a distinct submovement with its own exclusive network of organizations.

So, with the possible exception of one extreme position, Evangelicalism is a transdenominational movement in which many people feel at home. It is a movement as diverse as the politically radical Sojourners community in Washington, D. C. and the conservative Moral Majority. The leaders of these groups undoubtedly read many of the same periodicals and books and are familiar with the same set of evangelical organizations and names. Institutionally, this transdenominational Evangelicalism is built around networks of parachurch agencies. The structure is somewhat like that of the feudal system of the Middle Ages. It is made up of superficially friendly, somewhat competitive empires built up by Evangelical leaders competing for the same audience, but all professing allegiance to the same king. So we find empires surrounding Billy Graham, Jerry Falwell, Oral Roberts, Pat Robertson, Jim Bakker, Jimmy Swaggart, and other television ministers. Card-carrying Evangelicals are just as familiar with Campus Crusade for Christ, Youth for Christ, Young Life, Navigators, Inter-Varsity Christian Fellowship, L'Abri Fellowship, and other evangelistic organizations.

Other agencies for missions or social work have similarly broad interdenominational support. Educational institutions also long have provided institutional strength for Evangelicals, especially in hundreds of Bible institutes. Christian colleges, sometimes still under denominational control, help provide stability and continuity of leadership for the transdenominational movement. Wheaton College graduates, for instance, long have stood at the center of one of the most influential networks of organized Evangelical leadership. A similarly central role has been played by independent theological seminaries such as Gordon-Conwell, Fuller, Dallas, and Westminster. Some more clearly denominational schools, like

Trinity Evangelical, Covenant, Asbury, or Eastern Baptist, have also played direct roles in shaping the card-carrying Evangelical fellowship. Evangelical publishers also contribute importantly to the sense of community, both in major periodicals such as *Christianity Today, Eternity,* and *Moody Monthly,* and in the flood of books that keeps the community current with the same trends.

A Transdenominational Orientation

A decisive factor in distinguishing Evangelicals in the more narrow sense from Evangelicals in broader senses, then, is a degree of transdenominational orientation. So, for instance, many Missouri Synod Lutherans, Southern Baptists, Wesleyan Methodists, Church of the Brethren members, or Mennonites whose religious outlook is channeled almost exclusively by the programs and concerns of their own denomination, are hardly part of the card-carrying Evangelical fellowship, though they may certainly be Evangelicals in the broader senses. A few denominations, such as the Evangelical Free Church or the Evangelical Mennonites, have been so entirely shaped by twentieth-century contacts with organized transdenominational Evangelicalism as to be virtual products of that movement. Most ecclesiastical bodies, however, offer more distinctively denominational orientation, and "Evangelical" would not be a primary term which members would use to describe themselves. Yet still others in these same bodies are clearly Evangelicals in the narrow sense that they orient themselves substantially to the transdenominational movement. Thus Billy Graham and Harold Lindsell, for instance, are more "Evangelical" than they are Southern Baptist. Similarly, John Perkins and Tom Skinner are black Evangelicals because they identify in part with the general Evangelical community. The vast majority of black Bible-believers, however, though Evangelicals in the broader senses, are only distantly part of Evangelicalism as a narrower movement. Nor do they *think* of themselves as "Evangelicals."

Evangelicalism, then, despite its diversities, is properly spoken of as a single movement in at least two different ways. It is a broader movement somewhat unified by common heritages, influences, problems, and tendencies. It is also a conscious fellowship, coalition, community, family, or feudal system of friends and rivals who have some stronger sense of belonging together. These "Evangelicals" constitute something like a denomination, though an informal one. Some from the tradition of the original Fundamentalists and their neo-evangelical heirs, who have been the strongest party in this coalition, have attempted to speak or to set standards for Evangelicals generally. To perceive the difficulties in such artificial efforts to unify the diverse movement by fiat should not, however, obscure the actual unities of the movement, whether broadly or narrowly conceived.

Notes

1. Smith and his students have been working on a major collective historical study with the working title, "The Evangelical Mosaic."

2. See Cullen Murphy, "Protestantism and the Evangelicals," in *The Wilson Quarterly*, Vol. 4 (Autumn 1981), pp. 105–116, an essay written in consultation with Timothy Smith which presents an admirable summary of this approach. Murphy describes Evangelicalism as a "12-ring show" (p. 108). Robert E. Webber, *Common Roots: A Call to Evangelical Maturity* (Grand Rapids: Zondervan, 1978), p. 32, lists fourteen varieties of Evangelicalism based on distinctive emphases rather than just on denominational differences.

3. Among Lutherans, "Evangelical" has a more general meaning, roughly equivalent to "Protestant," and some neo-orthodox theologians have used it in its broad sense of "gospel-believer." The definition offered here, however, reflects the dominant Anglo-American usage.

4. For instance, of Americans who do not belong to, attend, or contribute to churches, 64 per cent say they believe that Jesus is God or the Son of God, 68 per cent believe in Jesus' resurrection, 40 per cent say they have made a personal commitment to Jesus, 27 per cent say the Bible is the actual Word of God and "is to be taken literally, word for word," and 25 per cent claim to have been "born again." See George Gallup, Jr., and David Poling, *The Search for America's Faith* (Nashville: Abingdon, 1980), pp. 90–92. Also, 84 per cent of Americans say the Ten Commandments are still valid for today, but only 42 per cent know at least five of them. For those classed as "Evangelicals," only 58 per cent could name five of the Ten Commandments, according to James W. Reapsome in "Religious Values: Reflections of Age and Education," in *Christianity Today*, May 7, 1980, pp. 23–25.

5. James Davison Hunter in *American Evangelicalism: Conservative Religion and the Quandary of Modernity* (Rutgers University Press, 1983) presents a valuable analysis of the polling data, but also illuminates the problem of conflating Evangelicalism in its broad definitional sense with its other senses. For discussion on this point, see George Marsden, "Evangelicalism in the Sociological Laboratory," in *The Reformed Journal* (June 1984).

6. Charles I. Foster, *An Errand of Mercy: The Evangelical United Front, 1790–1837* (Chapel Hill: University of North Carolina Press, 1960), p. 121.

7. Richard Lovelace aptly characterizes Jerry Falwell's activist Fundamentalism as "really a sort of Southern neo-Evangelical reform movement." See Lovelace's "Future Shock and Christian Hope," in *Christianity Today*, August 5, 1983, p. 16.

4. The Evangelical and Fundamentalist Revolt

By A. JAMES REICHLEY

Focus A. James Reichley calls the Evangelical resurgence in political affairs a "revolt of the Evangelicals" against what they perceive as an erosion of the moral foundations of American society. Reichley contrasts the Evangelical resurgence of the 1970s and 1980s with the Fundamentalists' and Evangelicals' retreat from public life after the "fiasco" of the Scopes Monkey Trial in 1925, and the repeal of Prohibition less than a decade later.

Reichley highlights the importance of the formation in 1942 of the National Association of Evangelicals (NAE), and the continuous popularity of Billy Graham. The activities of the NAE and the Graham organization regained for Evangelicals a sympathetic hearing in national affairs, in both religious and political communities. This was a necessary first step toward the dynamic re-emergence of Evangelical influence in the 1980s.

The NAE was established as an alternative to the American Council of Christian Churches (ACCC), a distinctly fundamentalist organization founded in 1941. "The NAE," Reichley writes, "aimed to combat modernism without resorting to 'dog-in-the-manger, reactionary, negative, or destructive type' tactics," and by eschewing "all forms of bigotry and intolerance." Building on this foundation, Billy Graham's nationwide crusades of the 1950s moved

Evangelicals back into the mainstream of American life—a feat that Reichley calls Graham's "great social achievement."

With their reputation for faith and tolerance restored, Evangelicals have been able to attack the changes in morality of the 1960s and 1970s without being dismissed, as were their counterparts, who fought Darwinism and supported Prohibition a generation earlier. The heartening thing about new Evangelical leaders, says Reichley, is that, "whether by a sense of social responsibility or political prudence," they are determined to reject intolerance even as they oppose what they believe to be a declining standard of public morality.

A. James Reichley has been a senior fellow in the Governmental Studies Program at the Brookings Institution since 1977. He is the author of *Religion in American Public Life* (Brookings, 1985).

AFTER THE SO-CALLED Scopes Monkey Trial in 1925, and the repeal of Prohibition in 1933, Evangelical Protestants largely withdrew from the public arena and even to a great extent from national public consciousness (except in novels and plays like *Elmer Gantry* and *Tobacco Road,* in which they were treated with contempt). Evangelical churches continued to hold their own, particularly in the rural South and Midwest, but evangelical preachers for the most part returned to the earlier view of John Leland and Dwight L. Moody that the churches should devote themselves to promoting individual salvation and had no business mixing religion with politics.

In 1941, a number of Fundamentalist churches, increasingly alarmed by the continuing advance of modernism, or modernity as it came to be called, joined to form the American Council of Christian Churches (ACCC). The ACCC promised to bear witness to "the historic faith of the church," which, it charged, was being abandoned by mainline denominations "in the darkening days of apostasy." Errors attributed to the mainline denominations included doubting the literal truth ("inerrancy") of the Bible, accommodating "impurity" in personal conduct (from divorce to going to the movies), and suggesting that salvation might be achieved through good works alone. The ACCC also had no truck with the Social Gospel, which it regarded as derived from the humanist heresy that man through his own resources can become master of his fate.[1]

The following year a somewhat larger body of Evangelicals, also disturbed over apostasy among the mainliners, but uncomfortable with the negative tone of the ACCC, formed the National Association of Evangelicals (NAE). The NAE aimed to combat modernism without resorting to "dog-in-the-manger, reactionary, negative, or destructive type" tactics. Mindful of the absolutist tendencies associated with Fundamentalism, the association prom-

---

Reprinted by permission of The Brookings Institution from *Religion in American Public Life,* by A. James Reichley, 1985.

ised to "shun all forms of bigotry, intolerance, misrepresentation, hate, jealousy, false judgment, and hypocrisy."[2]

The distinction between Evangelicalism and Fundamentalism was, and has remained, somewhat hazy. Evangelicalism is best defined as a branch of Christianity, descended from the pietist movement of the Reformation by way of the Great Awakening, that emphasizes direct experience by the individual of the Holy Spirit (being "born again") and that regards the Bible as an infallible source of religious and moral authority. Fundamentalism is an extreme form of Evangelicalism. All Fundamentalists are Evangelicals, but not all Evangelicals are Fundamentalists.

The Personalist Dimension of Faith

Evangelicalism's emphasis on individual spiritual experience places it on the personalist side of the religious spectrum. But its view of the Bible as infallibly authoritative partly offsets the socially centrifugal tendency of religious personalism. Fundamentalism carries insistence on biblical inerrancy to the point of absolutist reaction, not an uncommon tendency at the extremes of personalism. Fundamentalism fosters not only the spiritual enthusiasm bred by personalism, but also the dogmatism and social rigidity associated with absolutist idealism.

Evangelicals as a whole, including most Baptists and Disciples of Christ, many Methodists, Presbyterians, and Lutherans, and members of independent local Evangelical churches, now make up about one-fourth of the total population of the United States and about two-fifths of all Protestants. Demographic studies show that evangelicals tend to be more rural, more Southern, less affluent, and less well educated than the general population. Fundamentalists, concentrated in the independent churches, but found also among some of the organized denominations, particularly the Southern Baptists, Missouri Synod Lutherans, and Disciples of Christ, constitute about one-third of all Evangelicals. No part of the one-fifth of Evangelicals who are black are usually designated as Fundamentalists, though many of the independent black churches are theologically close to the doctrinal views of white Fundamentalists.[3]

In its early years, the National Association of Evangelicals steered clear of politics. But the American Council of Christian Churches, led by Carl McIntire, an eloquent preacher and skilled organizer, displayed a pronounced taste for political involvement. Drawing on the strand of Evangelical tradition, traceable to Jonathan Edwards and the Puritans, that holds that America has been specially chosen by God to launch the world's redemption, McIntire directed the ACCC into the anti-Communist crusade of the 1950s. Communism, seen as the principal adversary of God's chosen people, was identified with Satan.[4]

From the 1940s onward, conservative politicians recognized that Evangelicals battling modernism offered a potential source of electoral support. But the affinity of many Fundamentalists for anti-Catholicism, anti-Semitism, and racism caused most mainstream conservatives to play the evangelical card with caution. Robert Taft, Dwight Eisenhower, and Barry Goldwater were separated by substantial political and ideological differences, but all held in common the belief that the future health of the Republican Party depended on its ability to attract supporters from outside its Northern white Protestant base. Prudence as well as social responsibility therefore required that they keep their distance from right-wing preachers who could be depended upon to insult major groups from which recruits for the conservative coalition would have to be drawn.

Billy Graham's Influence

Billy Graham, representing the main body of less extreme Evangelicals, was another matter. Early in his career Graham could invoke the Red peril with the best of them. "Communism," he said in 1949, "is inspired, directed, and motivated by the Devil himself. America is at a crossroads. Will we turn to the left-wingers and atheists, or will we turn to the right and embrace the cross?"[5] He also confidently predicted the imminent arrival of the millennium. During the 1950s, however, it was Graham's great social achievement—apart from his more directly religious role—to move most evangelicals back into the mainstream of American life. Building on the platform established by the NAE, he shaped Evangelicalism as a positive force. In the process, he gradually came to terms with some aspects of modernity, for which he was eventually criticized by some purists on the Fundamentalist far right. But Graham's prestige among the mass of Evangelicals was such that efforts at detraction never had much effect.

Association with Graham was avidly sought by political leaders of both major parties, liberals as well as conservatives. He hob-nobbed with them all, particularly Eisenhower, Lyndon Johnson, and Richard Nixon. In 1960 he skirted the anti-Catholic enthusiasm that galvanized most Evangelicals against John Kennedy. Graham's closest political association was with Nixon. (On the morning after Nixon's election in 1968, he arrived at the successful candidate's hotel suite and announced, "We did it!" leaving unclear exactly what he meant by "we.")[6] After Nixon's fall he was more wary in his contacts with politicians. In the 1980s, once again proving his capacity to surprise, Graham spoke out forcefully against the arms race (while avoiding close identification with the organized peace movement) and set out to evangelize the Devil's own bailiwick, the Soviet Union.

The Electronic Church

Neither Graham nor the right-wing preachers had much success during the 1950s or 1960s in stirring the Evangelicals to political action. Several studies during the period showed "without exception . . . that evangelicals were less inclined toward political participation than were their less evangelical counterparts." One scholar concluded in 1971 that, "Evangelicals concentrate on conversion, and except for occasional efforts to outlaw what they deem to be personal vices, evangelical Protestant groups largely ignore social and political efforts for reform."[7]

Yet studies in the late 1970s and early 1980s just as uniformly have shown Evangelicals to be the religious group *most* favorable to political action by the churches. A Gallup survey in 1980 discovered that they were more likely to be registered to vote than nonevangelicals, despite being overrepresented in demographic groups that historically have been relatively low in political participation.[8]

What happened? The Evangelicals in part were responding to the urgings of a few highly visible television preachers, proprietors of the so-called electronic church. The Federal Communications

Commission (FCC) has always required television stations to devote a fixed amount of their airtime to religious programming. In the early years of television, most stations met this requirement by making time available free to local churches or to well-known evangelists with national followings, like Graham, Oral Roberts, and Rex Humbard. But in the early 1970s, many stations, with FCC approval, began charging for the time they set aside for religion. Most mainline churches declined to enter this market. Religious time therefore became available, usually at bargain rates, to enterprising preachers—almost all of them Fundamentalists or Evangelicals—who financed their programs through fund-raising appeals made in the course of their broadcasts. Some of these programs were linked to elaborate feedback systems, utilizing telephone banks and computerized files, through which individual viewers could obtain personalized counseling.[9]

Under this new arrangement, the audience for religious programs greatly expanded. A study in 1963 showed that only 12 per cent of all Protestants regularly watched or listened to religious broadcasts. Gallup polls taken in the late 1970s showed that this figure had more than doubled, and a poll in 1981 found that 27 per cent of the national public claimed to have watched more than one religious program in the preceding month. A study in 1984 by Gallup and the Annenberg School of Communications placed the regular audience for religious broadcasts at about 13.3 million.[10]

The older evangelists who maintained regularly scheduled broadcasts, like Oral Roberts and Rex Humbard, for the most part remained apolitical. But some of the younger preachers who were buying time on stations wherever they could attract an audience, including Jerry Falwell, James Robison, Pat Robertson, and Jim Bakker, began offering comments on political and social issues as part of their broadcasts.

In the 1960s, Falwell, an independent Baptist and pastor of Thomas Road Baptist Church in Lynchburg, Virginia, had been resolute in his commitment to the tradition of political noninvolvement. "We have few ties to this earth," he said in 1965. "We pay our taxes, cast our votes as a responsibility of citizenship, obey the laws of the land, and other things demanded of us by the society in which we live. But, at the same time, we are cognizant that our only purpose on the earth is to know Christ and to make Him known."[11]

Impact of Supreme Court Decisions

Events of the late 1960s and early 1970s led Falwell and many other Fundamentalists and Evangelicals to change their minds. The Supreme Court's 1961 decision prohibiting organized prayer in the public schools caused outrage in the Evangelical community (though many Evangelicals in the Baptist tradition had previously been critical of state-sponsored prayer). The 1973 abortion decision intensified the impression that the court had set out to achieve a completely secularized society. Partly in response to the prayer decision and other perceived challenges to traditional morality in public education—though also in part to evade the court's 1954 decision requiring racial desegregation of the public schools—many evangelical churches, mainly in the South, began establishing "Christian academies" in which the children of believers could be educated in "creationist" science and traditional values. Though the federal Internal Revenue Service at first routinely granted tax-exempt status to most of these schools, the schools' existence gave the churches a concrete interest in protecting themselves against governmental intrusion or regulation. The financial needs of the schools also weakened the Evangelicals' longstanding opposition to government aid for church-sponsored education.

More important than specific court decisions or concrete institutional interests was a general sense among Evangelicals in the 1970s that the moral foundations of American society were crumbling. Earlier many Evangelicals and even Fundamentalists seem to have begun to believe that modernism, much as it jarred their sensibilities, must after all represent the wave of the future. Modernism was associated with rising national prosperity, with burgeoning government programs to help the sick, elderly and the poor, increased personal freedom, and opportunities for travel and awareness of a wider world. Were not most of these developments, despite their disruptive effects on traditional ways, on the whole good things? But the Vietnam War, Watergate, and the violent social disorders of the late 1960s shook the aura of moral prestige that modernism had begun to acquire for some evangelicals—somewhat as these phenomena startled those at the other end of the ideological spectrum who were drawn to liberation theology. Even more damaging was the growth of what appeared to be pervasive social sickness. During the 1970s, divorce increased 67 per cent. Families headed by unwed mothers rose 356 per cent. By the end of the decade, 21 per cent of families with children under eighteen were headed by single parents. In 1979, 17 per cent of all children and 55 per cent of black children were born out of wedlock. Recreational drugs and pornography were readily available. Violent crime rose to an all-time high in 1980. A Gallup poll found one-third of Americans reporting a problem with alcoholism in their own families. If this be modernity, how much more could the nation take and survive?[12]

Most people agreed that these were alarming trends. But many secular social scientists, and many leaders of mainline Protestant and Jewish denominations and even of the Catholic church, argued either that their main concern was economic injustice—correctible through redistribution of wealth—or that the trends were so intertwined with progressive developments (like increased autonomy for women and youth) that the only fair way to deal with most of them was through expansion of welfare programs that would make their effects less painful or destructive. Most Evangelicals and Fundamentalists, as well as many Americans of other religious persuasions, were convinced that these social afflictions had best be met, at least in part, by some restoration of traditional morality.[13]

'Secular Humanism' As the Problem

Fundamentalists believed they had identified the prime source of moral decline: "secular humanism," a philosophy which Tim LaHaye, a leading Fundamentalist publicist, characterized as based on "amorality, evolution, and atheism." Francis Schaeffer, the best-known Fundamentalist theologian, charged that secular humanism is itself a religion "which the government and courts in the United States favor over all others!" Because it was being imposed by government, the only way to overcome its pernicious effects was to get control of government into different hands. To do this evangelicals would have to set aside their inhibitions against involvement in politics.[14]

By 1976 Jerry Falwell had moved so far from his earlier aversion for politics that he organized a series of "I Love America" rallies on the steps of state capitols all across the United States. But the spotlight of media attention that year was moving toward another evangelical who applied the values of "born-again" Christianity to national problems: Jimmy Carter. In my own observation along the campaign trail in 1975 and 1976, Carter was not retiring about stating his religious beliefs, but he did not exploit them. Everywhere he went, reporters asked him about his religion. In reply he would describe his conversion, and explain why he believed religious faith is a valuable moral asset for a political leader, but Carter would also state his adherence to the Baptist tradition of separation between church and state. Many reporters then went to their typewriters and wrote stories that Jimmy Carter insisted on parading his religion.

Without making much public effort, Carter attracted widespread support from Evangelicals and Fundamentalists, who regarded him somewhat as Catholics had regarded John Kennedy in 1960. Pat Robertson, one of the most popular of the television preachers, gave him an outright endorsement. In November, Carter outpolled Ford among white Baptists by 56 per cent to 43 per cent. Evangelicals gave him his margin of victory not only in the South (where he also was helped by regional pride), but also in such key northern states as Pennsylvania and Ohio with large rural populations that usually voted Republican. Because his national advantage in the popular vote was only two per cent, Carter may fairly be said to have owed his election to the Evangelicals (though also, of course, to blacks, Jews, and other groups that favored him by wide margins).

Disappointment and Jimmy Carter

Once in office, Carter was perceived by Evangelicals to have turned his back on them. The Carter administration made no effort to press for action on social issues like school prayer and abortion that had high priorities for evangelicals. "It was a tremendous letdown," said one Evangelical activist, "if not a betrayal, to have

Carter stumping for [the Equal Rights Amendment], for not stopping federally funded abortions, for advocating homosexual rights." Not incidentally, evangelical activists were not given federal jobs. "Carter promised in 1976 that if he were elected, he would appoint qualified Evangelical Christians to positions in the federal government," an Evangelical spokesman said in 1980. "He did not follow through."[15]

Despite their disappointment with Carter, many Evangelicals had found their experience with national politics exhilarating. "Evangelicals entered politics in the first place to defend their way of life," one said, "but before long they found that politics can be fun." A more faithful champion was soon available.[16]

Fundamentalists for Reagan

Some political conservatives had tried in 1976 to organize religious Fundamentalists behind the presidential candidacy of Ronald Reagan on the ground that his social views were congruent with Fundamentalist principles. Fundamentalist support apparently contributed to Reagan's breakthrough victory in the North Carolina primary, when his campaign seemed about to expire, and to his later successes in the South. After Reagan narrowly lost the Republican nomination to Ford, most of his Fundamentalist backers either switched to Carter or sat out the election.

Organizers of what was at that time coming to be known as the new right had, however, spotted a political potential. "The New Right is looking for issues that people care about," observed Paul Weyrich, director of the right-wing Committee for the Survival of a Free Congress. "Social issues, at least for the present, fill the bill." Weyrich's view was shared by the other two principal new right strategists, Richard Viguerie, who had practically invented mass direct-mail fund-raising for conservative candidates, and Howard Phillips, founder of the Conservative Caucus, a national organization of grassroots activists. Concentration on social issues was said to be a major difference between the new right and the old (identified with leaders like Goldwater and Reagan). The old right, according to *Conservative Digest,* published by Viguerie, had "stressed almost exclusively economic and foreign policy" issues. The new right, while not abandoning these issues, would emphasize concerns like "busing, abortion, pornography, education, traditional biblical moral values, and quotas," which specially motivated "ethnic and blue-collar Americans, born-again Christians, pro-life Catholics, and Jews."[17]

Because none of the triumvirate of new right strategists had roots in Evangelicalism (Weyrich and Viguerie are Catholics, and Phillips is a Jew), they needed outside help to make contact with the Fundamentalist part of their projected coalition. Weyrich cultivated the friendship of Robert Billings, a Fundamentalist educator whom he had met when Billings ran unsuccessfully for Congress in Indiana in 1976. Phillips recruited Edward E. McAteer, a former sales promoter for Colgate Palmolive with wide contacts among Evangelical preachers and their financial backers, as a field director for the Conservative Caucus.[18]

In 1978 the Carter administration tightened standards for tax-exempt status for church-operated schools, requiring that the percentage of their student bodies drawn from racial minorities be at least one-fifth of the percentage in the local community. The new right strategists saw the opening for which they had been waiting. With Weyrich's encouragement and counsel, Billings formed a national organization to represent the political interests of the Christian academies. Through Billings, Weyrich got to know Jerry Falwell.

The 'New Right' Takes Shape

The 1978 election turned out to be a trial run for the planned alliance bringing together the political new right, Protestant Fundamentalists, and Catholic right-to-lifers. Opposition to abortion (which formerly had not been much of an issue among Fundamentalists) became the unifying cause. Conservatives made gains in the congressional elections. Fundamentalist leaders began speaking of a religious new right that would be the dominant partner in a new conservative coalition. Pat Robertson, conductor of "The 700 Club," a religious talk show emanating from Virginia Beach, Virginia, said bluntly, "We have enough votes to run the country." Jim Bakker, a former protegé of Robertson's who founded his own talk show, "The PTL Club," in North Carolina, agreed: "Our goal is to influence all viable candidates on issues important to the church. We want answers. We want appointments in government." New right leaders decided that Billings's lobby for the Christian academies should be broadened to become a comprehensive organization that would work for the entire conservative agenda.[19]

The Moral Majority

Members of the new right's inner circle firmly believe that their moral attitudes are shared by the great majority of Americans, but that the preferences of this majority are being systematically thwarted by a liberal elite (the secular humanists) that controls the federal government, the national media, and the great universities (and probably also most of Wall Street). During a strategy session of new right leaders in the spring of 1979, Weyrich, making this point, used the expression "moral majority." Falwell, it is said, instantly recognized the phrase as summing up the theme of the new national political organization they were about to launch. The Moral Majority, Inc., with Falwell as its president and Billings as its executive director, came into existence in June 1979.[20]

Falwell sought to maintain the Moral Majority as an ecumenical body of political activists composed of "Catholics, Jews, Protestants, Mormons, Fundamentalists" united by the common goal of returning the United States to "moral sanity." In practice, most of the chairmen of the state chapters, all appointed by Falwell, were Fundamentalists. At least twenty-five of the state chairmen were affiliated with churches that sponsored Christian academies.[21]

Using the mailing list of 250,000 prime donors to Falwell's "Old Time Gospel Hour," the Moral Majority raised one-third of its projected $3 million first-year budget in one month. By the middle of 1980, the organization claimed a membership of 300,000, including 70,000 ministers.[22]

During its first year, the Moral Majority concentrated on getting its name well known and on registering voters for the 1980 election. At the first of these objectives it was spectacularly successful. A Gallup poll in December 1980 found that 40 per cent of a national sample had heard of the Moral Majority. Surveys taken in the South and Southwest found levels of recognition almost twice the national figure. Part of the Moral Majority's fame stemmed from the use of its name by national media and liberal publicists to designate the entire religious new right. Many of the people who had heard of the Moral Majority did not like it.[23]

The results of the Moral Majority's drive have been much debated. In his own church in Lynchburg, Falwell instituted an effective Sunday morning exercise. Following the regular worship service, he asked the entire congregation to stand. After telling the registered voters to sit down, he lectured those who remained standing on their duty to get on the election rolls and warned that he would repeat the same procedure every Sunday until election day. This routine was copied in other Fundamentalist churches. In some churches, voter registration booths were set up after services. At the end of the campaign the Moral Majority claimed to have registered from four million to eight million new voters (the kind of spread that automatically induces skepticism). Outside observers estimated that the entire religious right had registered about two million—still impressive. Voter turnout rose in the South—the evangelical stronghold—in 1980, while it declined on all other regions.[24]

Other organizations claiming to represent Evangelicals in politics took the field. Christian Voice, gathering most of its support from the West and Southwest, sponsored its own political action committee, which raised about $500,000 for conservative candidates in 1980. Religious Roundtable, founded by Ed McAteer and Jim Robison, a Texas evangelist, set out to attract evangelicals in the mainline denominations put off by the Moral Majority. Christian Voice achieved notoriety by issuing report cards, on which congressmen were given "moral ratings" on the basis of their votes not only on such issues as school prayer and abortion, but also on economic sanctions against Rhodesia, the American defense treaty with Taiwan, and the creation of the federal Department of Education. The media gleefully pointed out that, while a number of liberal congressmen who were active church members received zero ratings, a conservative Florida congressman convicted of accepting a bribe in the Abscam investigation was given a moral rating of one hundred percent.[25]

The 1980 Election

Ronald Reagan, still identified with the old right, was not the first choice for President of most religious right leaders in 1980. Some followed Richard Viguerie in supporting Congressman Phillip Crane, a full-blooded new rightist. Others preferred John Connally, the former governor of Texas. But Reagan seems from the start to have been the favorite among rank-and-file Fundamentalists. When the campaigns for Crane and Connally fizzled, religious right leaders rushed to get behind Reagan's candidacy. Christian Voice was the first to move. Falwell soon followed, promising that the Moral Majority would mobilize voters for Reagan "even if he has the devil running with him."[26]

After the Republican convention, the religious right's political operations were closely meshed with the Reagan campaign. Robert Billings left the Moral Majority to become coordinator of church groups supporting Reagan. Evangelical leaders were urged to submerge their theological differences in the common effort to restore conservative moral principles. "Knowing pastors as we did," Tim LaHaye said, "we all recognized that the only way to organize them was to make it clear that our basis of cooperation was moral, not theological. . . ." At a conclave of Evangelicals in Dallas organized by McAteer and Robison, Reagan announced, "Religious America is awakening, perhaps just in time for our country's sake. . . . If *you* do not speak your mind and cast your ballots, then who will speak and work for the ideals we cherish?" A bemused Evangelical observing the scene reported, "Thousands of people were cheering for all they were worth—cheering away the eschatalogical doctrines of a lifetime, cheering away the theological pessimism of a lifetime."[27]

Midway through the campaign, the news media discovered—and at first wildly exaggerated—the impact of the religious right. The *Washington Star* placed Falwell's weekly television audience at twenty-five million, making him the "second most watched TV personality in the country, surpassed only by Johnny Carson." *Newsweek* guessed that Falwell's televised appeals were reaching eighteen million every week. (The actual figure, according to Nielson and Arbitron ratings, was about 1.4 million.) The *New York Times* surmised that Falwell had "created something very similar to a political party." *U.S. News and World Report* found "a political holy war without precedent . . . in full swing in this country."[28]

Some leading evangelists apparently developed misgivings about the extent of their political involvements. Pat Robertson and Jim Bakker, who had earlier gone even further than Falwell in taking political positions, distanced themselves from the Reagan campaign. To a remarkable degree, however, most of the Fundamentalist leaders, normally a highly individualistic lot, held together in Reagan's support.

In the immediate aftermath of the 1980 election, the media attributed a large share of the cause for Reagan's victory and the Republicans' surprise capture of control of the Senate to the religious right. *Time* speculated that as much as two-thirds of Reagan's margin had come from a shift in political attitudes among white Fundamentalists. Some liberals drew the conclusion that a wave of religious repression was about the sweep the country. "I am beginning to fear," said Patricia Harris, secretary of health and human services under Carter, "that we could have an Ayatollah Khomeini in this country, but he will not have a beard . . . he will have a television program."[29]

A second round of analysis produced indications that the initial appraisals had greatly exaggerated the impact of the religious right. In a widely read article in *Commentary,* Seymour Martin Lipset and Earl Raab pointed out that, while Reagan had won the votes of 61 per cent of born-again white Protestants, he had also been supported by an even larger share—63 per cent—of other white Protestants. (This finding, however, was not necessarily inconsistent with the view that the religious right had played an important part in the election: mainline Protestants outside the South have always constituted the most important element in the Republican base, but votes won by Reagan among Evangelicals often came from persons who formerly either had voted Democratic or had not been politically active.) Case studies by political scientists on individual state chapters of the Moral Majority showed that many were little more than letterhead organizations composed of a few right-wing preachers and a mailing list. Polls revealed that even in states like Virginia and Texas, where the religious right was presumably strong, voters with unfavorable impressions of the Moral Majority greatly outnumbered those with favorable impressions. (Such polls, however, did not measure how much favorable or unfavorable impressions had actually influenced voting behavior.)

An NBC/Associated Press poll found that only 3 per cent of the public said they would be "more likely to vote for a candidate if asked by a member of the clergy." (But the effects of less direct political recommendations by the clergy were not measured.) Recovering from their earlier fright, some sophisticated liberals decided that the new religious right was little more than a phantasm. The Moral Majority, Andrew Greeley commented, was "a ghost, a spook, a bogey man . . . a fiction of the paranoia of some segments of the liberal media elite. . . ."[30]

A third round of analysis, carried out over an extended period, again shifted the balance of interpretation. Analyzing data gathered by the University of Michigan's 1980 National Election Survey, Arthur Miller and Martin Wattenburg found that, while only 6 per cent of the public indicated they felt "close to evangelical groups active in politics such as the Moral Majority," members of this core group had voted as a cohesive electoral block in 1980. Moreover, 26 per cent regarded themselves as born-again Christians, and 27 per cent said they felt general sympathy for "evangelical groups such as the Moral Majority," suggesting a pool of voters among whom the religious right might grow. "The conservative Christians," the analysis concluded, "represent an emerging political force in U.S. electoral politics. . . . The cohesiveness evident in their political attitudes and voter behavior suggests a unique impact attributable to shared religious interests and the mobilizing influence of the new Christian right leadership."[31]

Reagan and the New Right

As president, Ronald Reagan did not copy Jimmy Carter's performance in dealing with supporters among the religious right. He spoke out frequently in favor of constitutional amendments to restore school prayer and prohibit abortion. Though he clearly did not give so-called social issues the same amount of attention or political muscle he devoted to major economic or defense policies, he appeared to make good-faith efforts when bills embodying such issues were before Congress. The Reagan administration at first moved to drop the Internal Revenue Service ban against tax-exempt status for church schools that appear to discriminate against racial minorities (the issue that had been the immediate grievance triggering formation of the religious new right in 1978). Following an uproar among civil rights groups, however, the administration restored the ban, but then supported the appeal of Bob Jones University against it before the Supreme Court. The court upheld the ban.[32]

Some leaders of the religious right complained that Reagan did not do enough to promote their causes, and that powerful members of the White House staff were indifferent if not hostile to their interests. But rank-and-file Fundamentalists appeared satisfied that the President was on their side. Reagan spoke often before gatherings of evangelicals and expressed solidarity with their religious beliefs (the Bible, he said, contains "all the answers to all the problems that face us today"). His administration, moreover, awarded federal appointments to a few key individuals in the leadership of the religious right. Robert Billings, who had helped get the religious right started in 1978, was named director of regional offices in the Department of Education. Morton Blackwell, who had performed liaison duties between Evangelicals and the Reagan campaign, became a coordinator of political strategy on the White House staff.[33]

For its part, the religious right supported not only the administration's initiatives on moral and social issues, but also many of Reagan's positions on economic and foreign policy. While mainline Protestant denominations, Jewish welfare agencies, and the Catholic church protested against the administration's proposed cuts in domestic social programs, the religious right praised the President's efforts to give freer rein to the private sector. Falwell found the free-enterprise system "clearly outlined in the Book of Proverbs in the Bible." Other evangelicals quoted the advice of the apostle Paul to the Thessalonians: "If any would not work, neither should he eat." (When Falwell was asked why he had not included "helping the poor" among the objectives of the Moral Majority, he replied: "We could never bring the issue of the poor into Moral Majority because the argument would be, Who is going to decide what will reach those people? Mormons, Catholics? No, we won't get into that.")[34]

The religious right supported the administration's drive to strengthen national defense by arguing that only a strong America will be able to play its assigned role in the drama preceding the prophesied final days of history. The Moral Majority took full-page ads in major newspapers warning, "We cannot afford to be number two in defense! But, sadly enough, that's where we are today. Number two. And fading!" Falwell declared it a "sad fact" that in an all-out nuclear exchange the Soviet Union "would kill 135 million to 160 million Americans, and the United States would kill only 3 to 5 per cent of the Soviets. . . ." Yet with no apparent sense of inconsistency, Falwell sometimes returned to the optimistic fatalism characteristic of some forms of religious idealism: "If God is on our side, no matter how militarily superior the Soviet Union is, they could never touch us. God would miraculously protect America," a statement that, if interpreted literally, would seem to require no military defense at all and would place Falwell in agreement with Christian pacifists.[35]

An Uncertain Future

The future political durability of the religious new right remains uncertain. Economic recession in 1982 drew many evangelicals with Democratic roots who had voted for Reagan in 1980 back to their former attachments. Some commentators suggested that the new religious right as a political force had passed its peak and probably would have little impact on future elections.

In 1984, however, the religious right was more active and apparently more effective than ever. Through much of the South, white evangelical churches conducted drives to get more of their members registered as voters. In the competition between conservative white evangelical church groups seeking to increase registration among their constituents, and black churches working to register supporters of first Jesse Jackson and then Walter Mondale, the white evangelicals were the clear winners in terms of total voters registered, partly because white evangelicals greatly outnumber blacks. In North Carolina, for example, black registration increased by 179,373, but this impressive gain was more than offset by the huge increase of 307,852 among whites, many of them evangelicals. Registration drives by evangelical churches apparently contributed to sharp rises in Republican strength in Florida and Texas.

On election day, 81 per cent of white evangelicals voted for Reagan, an increase of almost one-third over 1980. Perhaps even more important, 77 per cent of white Evangelicals voting in congressional elections supported Republican candidates for the House of Representatives. If anything approaching this level of support is maintained in future elections, and if it eventually is translated into voting for Republicans for state and local offices without offsetting losses among economic conservatives with more liberal social views, the Republican party would be well on its way to regaining the majority party status it lost in the 1930s.[36]

The Conservative Coalition

One reason Evangelicalism declined as a social force during the first half of the twentieth century was that it allowed itself to become isolated from social conservatives in other religious groups. Jerry Falwell, in particular, has been determined that this shall not happen to the religious new right. He has, for instance, emphasized the tie of Fundamentalists to Jews as the chosen nation of the Old Testament: "Every nation that has ever stood with the Jews has felt the hand of God's blessing on them. I firmly believe that God has blessed America because America has blessed the Jew." There is no reason to question the sincerity of such statements. But it cannot have escaped the attention of leaders of the religious right that a positive relationship with the Jewish community is politically and socially advantageous.[37]

Much more sensational is the friendly relationship that has developed between Falwell's camp and conservative Catholics, Catholicism having traditionally been viewed among right-wing Protestants as at least as reprehensible as secular humanism. This change represents a broad conclusion among most conservative religious groups (also including Mormons, another historical antagonist of both evangelicals and Catholics) that the forces of secular humanism have grown so strong that all forms of theistic religion must band together if they are to have any hope of standing off the common foe. The issue immediately uniting them is the drive to overthrow the Supreme Court's decision establishing a constitutional right to abortion.

Although it has become a major concern among Fundamentalists only recently (partly because it did not enter public debate until the 1960s), the abortion issue has acquired extraordinary emotional intensity for the religious right. Francis Schaeffer suggested that if the federal government should resume financing abortions, Christians at some point must consider refusing "to pay some portion of their tax money." Cal Thomas, director of public relations for the Moral Majority, said in 1982 that "if the abortion problem is not solved through legal means, it will be necessary to take some form of radical action."[38]

The possibility of martyrdom in the struggle to stop abortion seems to fire the imaginations of some Fundamentalists—in part, it appears, because on this issue they are certain they are on the side of the angels. Many Fundamentalists, including Falwell, at one time supported racial segregation and most have never given strong backing to civil rights. At least some Fundamentalists recognize that the conservative defense and economic policies that they endorse involve moral ambiguities. But on the issue of abortion, they believe it is the liberals who are countenancing mass destruction of potential life, while Fundamentalists, in alliance with Catholics, stand up for the rights of the most vulnerable of all forms of human life, the unborn. "The strength of Martin Luther King," Cal Thomas has said, "came through his willingness to go to jail. By dramatizing his belief in black equality, he went to work on the conscience of the nation. Those who regard abortion as infanticide have got to show that this is not just a bunch of philosophic beliefs they are holding—that they are prepared to suffer in order to stop the killing."[39]

There Still Are Separatists

Not all Evangealicals have been swept up by the religious new right. Many Fundamentalist preachers in the separatist tradition continue to rail against the blasphemy of mingling religion with politics. During the 1980 campaign Bob Jones II described Falwell as "the most dangerous man in America so far as Biblical Christianity is concerned." (Falwell replied that he was "dangerous to liberals, feminists, abortionists, and homosexuals, but certainly not to Bible-believing Christians.")[40]

More moderate Evangelicals, while not faulting the religious right for entering politics, have criticized the stridency of expression sometimes employed by groups like the Moral Majority and the willingness of the political preachers to take positions on all kinds of economic and foreign policy issues (following the example of some of the mainline denominations). Carl F. H. Henry, the most respected Evangelical theologian, has spoken out against efforts to impose "goose step morality." Billy Graham told an interviewer, "It would disturb me if there were a wedding between the religious Fundamentalists and the political right. The hard right has no interest in religion except to manipulate it." Senator Mark Hatfield of Oregon, an active Baptist layman and moderate Republican, questioned the religious right's choice of issues: "Many Evangelicals share my concern that the grievous sins of our society are militarism and materialism, rather than the Taiwan treaty, the Equal Rights Amendment, or the Panama Canal." In the early 1980s the National Association of Evangelicals, following the course set by its Washington director, Robert Dugan, edged cautiously toward the political arena, while avoiding identification with what Graham called the "hard right."[41]

On the left, a small segment of Evangelicals, centered on the Sojourners community in Washington, D.C., has been in the vanguard of the movement to stop American participation in the nuclear arms race, through civil disobedience if necessary. The Sojourners group, however, has maintained solidarity with more conservative Evangelicals on social issues like abortion.[42]

Concerned About Moral Decline

Social scientists have described the rise of the religious right as an example of "status politics," the struggle of a declining social group to recapture some of its lost prestige and power. Status anxieties have no doubt helped motivate Fundamentalists and Evangelicals to participate in politics—as they also have entered, though less remarked, the bundle of motives carrying mainline Protestant, Catholic, and Jewish establishments into political involvements. But as with mainline Protestants, Catholics, and Jews, evangelicals have also been propelled by substantive concerns over objective conditions in social reality. The central concern that has motivated most of those drawn to politics is the decline of moral standards, particularly those relating to the family.

It may be that the remedies proposed by the Evangelicals to reverse this decline would not work, or that the measures they propose would cause inequities outweighing whatever good they might do, or that, in any case, current social and political limits ensure that such remedies will never be tried. ("Everyone can 'affirm' family values, of course," Phillip Hammond has noted, "but divorce rates are not likely to decrease, birth rates are not likely to increase, women's participation in more and more arenas outside of the house is not likely to be reversed, and children are not likely to find home an adequate substitute for the technical training required to live in this modern world. Traditional family values can be affirmed, therefore, but they are doomed to be elusive in reality.")[43]

Survey evidence indicates, nevertheless, that the moral concerns expressed by Evangelicals are shared far beyond the ranks of the organized religious right. A nationwide survey by the National Opinion Research Center in the late 1970s that included a series of questions on such social issues as homosexuality, school prayer, the role of women, and abortion, found that predominantly conservative answers were given by 82 per cent of Baptists, 77 per cent of Methodists, 75 per cent Lutherans, 72 per cent of Presbyterians, and 70 per cent of Catholics—though only 48 per cent of Episcopalians and 37 per cent of Jews.[44]

Even some dedicated political opponents of the religious right have welcomed its appearance as a counterforce to the atomizing effects of egoism and materialism. Dean Kelley, far from a right-wing Fundamentalist, has asserted, "I disagree strenuously with many of the objectives of the 'moral majority' and will do my best to oppose them on those objectives. But I think their influence can be salutary for the nation as a whole. . . . A period of regularizing rigor may be distressing and even destructive to some persons and groups, but the continued atomization and deterioration of this culture is the way of social destruction and death, not for one or a few, but for all."[45]

Evangelicals, Fundamentalists, and Pluralism

Why, then, do national polls consistently show that a majority of the public regards the religious New Right as threatening? The cause of this concern does not appear to lie primarily in objection to the moral attitudes that the right claims to represent, but rather in the widely held impression that conservative religious groups aim to impose narrowly conceived formulations of these attitudes through official coercion. The public suspects, in short, that the religious right is not fully committed to democratic pluralism.

The shrewder or perhaps more enlightened among the managers of the religious right have tried to dispel this impression. The first item in the platform of the Moral Majority reads, "We believe in the separation of church and state." When Ronald Godwin, vice president of the Moral Majority and director of its Washington office, was asked if the group aims to make the United States a Christian nation, he replied, "No, no, no, that is the furthest thing from our minds. . . . If America were Christian today, it could be Moslem tomorrow. What we need is a pluralist society. The Moral Majority is not trying to impose its values on others. The last thing we want is a theocracy."[46]

Yet many pronouncements by leaders of the religious right do have an absolutist ring. "People want leadership," Robert Billings has said. "They don't know what to think for themselves. They want to be told what to think by some of us here close to the front." Tim LaHaye looks forward to the time when "the real American people will regain their country and culture." LaHaye has also expressed the view that "no humanist is qualified to hold any governmental office in America—United States senator, congressman, cabinet member, State Department employee, or any other position that requires him to think in the best interest of America" (an opinion that would appear to run counter to the constitutional provision that "no religious test shall ever be required as a qualification to any office of public trust under the United States"). In 1981, Ed McAteer said with regard to the controversy over the teaching of evolution that he would, if it were possible, "go to the extreme and prohibit the teaching of evolution altogether, since it is contrary to the Word of God, but since that is not now practical, all we are asking is that creationism and evolution be presented as alternatives." Falwell has likened the church to "a disciplined, charging army. . . . Christians, like slaves and soldiers, ask no question." Paul Weyrich has said flatly: "We're radicals working to overturn the present structure in this country—we're talking about Christianizing America."[47]

There has always been a strain of absolutist idealism in American Fundamentalism and in the Puritan tradition from which it is partly descended. This tendency clearly influences the religious New Right. The heartening thing from the standpoint of democratic pluralism, however, is that some of the ablest leaders of the religious right feel obliged, whether by a sense of social responsibility or political prudence, to struggle to prevent this absolutist tendency from becoming dominant.

Notes

1. James Davison Hunter, *American Evangelicalism: Conservative Religion and the Quandary of Modernity* (New Brunswick, N.J.: Rutgers, 1983), p. 41.
2. Ibid.
3. Ibid., pp. 50–54.
4. Ibid., pp. 43–44.
5. Ibid., pp. 44–45.
6. Ibid., pp. 46, and Joe McGinniss, *The Selling of the President, 1968* (Trident, 1969), p. 163.
7. Robert Wuthnow, "Political Rebirth of American Evangelicalism," in Wuthnow and Robert C. Liebman, editors, *The New Christian Right*, (Hawthorne, New York: Aldine Books, 1983), p. 168.
8. Ibid., p. 169.
9. Frances Fitzgerald, "A Disciplined, Charging Army," in *The New Yorker* (May 18, 1981), pp. 54–59.
10. Wuthnow, "Political Rebirth," p. 173, and George Gerbner and others, *Religion and Television* (Annenberg School of Communications, 1984), p. 3.
11. Fitzgerald, "Disciplined, Charging Army." p. 63.
12. "Homes Headed by Unwed Mothers Up 356%," *Washington Post*, June 18, 1982; Victor R. Fuchs, "The Soaring Rate of Unwed Mothers," *Wall Street Journal*, January 29, 1982; Bruce Chapman, "Seduced and Abandoned: American's New Poor," *Wall Street Journal*, October 5, 1982; and Philip J. Hilts, "Drinking Found to Trouble One in Three Families," *Washington Post*, November 16, 1982.
13. Pamela Johnston Conover, "The Mobilization of the New Right: A Test of Various Explanations," in *Western Political Quarterly*, Vol. 36 (December 1983), pp. 632–46.
14. Tim LaHaye, *The Battle for the Mind*, (Old Tappan, New Jersey: Revell,

1980), p. 59; and Francis A. Schaeffer, *A Christian Manifesto* (Westchester, Illinois: Crossway, 1981), p. 54.

15. Michael Johnson, "The New Christian Right in American Politics," in *The Political Science Quarterly*, Vol. 53 (April–June 1982), p. 184; and interviews with William Billings, president of the National Christian Action Coalition, October 22, 1980, and Gary Jarmin, legislative director, Christian Voice, November 13, 1980.

16. Interview with Ronald Godwin, October 27, 1981.

17. George G. Higgins, "The Prolife Movement and the New Right," in *America* (September 1980), p. 227.

18. For ties between the secular new right and its religious counterpart, see Gillian Peele, *Revival and Reaction*, (New York: Oxford, 1986), pp. 101–116.

19. Frances Fitzgerald, "Disciplined, Charging Army," p. 60.

20. Interviews with Ronald Godwin; Paul Weyrich, December 9, 1980; Richard Viguerie, November 12, 1980; Robert Billings, September 30, 1981; and Howard Philips, December 18, 1984.

21. Robert C. Liebman, "Mobilizing the Moral Majority," in *New Christian Right*, p. 67.

22. James L. Guth, "The New Christian Right," in *New Christian Right*, p. 32.

23. Joseph B. Tanney and Stephen D. Johnson, "The Moral Majority in Middletown," in the *Journal for the Scientific Study of Religion*, Vol. 22 (June 1983), p. 150.

24. Interview with Morton Blackwell, December 3, 1981; and Guth, "The Christian Right," pp. 37–38.

25. Margaret Ann Latus, "Mobilizing Christians for Political Action: Campaigning with God on Your Side," a paper delivered at the 1982 meeting of the Society for the Scientific Study of Religion, Providence, R.I., pp. 2–5; and interviews with Jarmin and E. E. McAteer, December 17, 1981.

26. Guth, "New Christian Right," p. 36.

27. Wuthnow, "Political Rebirth," p. 182; and Donald Heinz, "The Struggle to Define America," in *New Christian Right*, p. 136.

28. Tina Rosenberg, "How the Media Made the Moral Majority," *Washington Monthly* (May 1982), pp. 26–32.

29. Samuel S. Hill and Dennis E. Owen, *The New Religious Right in America* (Nashville: Abingdon, 1982), p. 78.

30. Seymour Martin Lipset and Earl Raab, "The Election and the Evangelicals," in *Commentary* (March 1981), pp. 25–31; Robert Zwier, "The Moral Majority in the 1980 Elections: The Cases of Iowa and South Dakota," a paper delivered at the 1981 meeting of the American Political Science Association, New York City; Tanney and Johnson, "Moral Majority in Middletown"; James L. Guth, "The Politics of Preachers: Southern Baptist Ministers and the Christian Right," a paper delivered at the 1982 Citadel Symposium on Southern Politics, Charlestown, S. C.; Richard V. Pierard, "No Hoosier Hospitality for Humanism: The Moral Majority in Indiana," a paper delivered at the 1982 meeting of the Society for the Scientific Study of Religion, Providence, R. I.; Anthony Obserschall and Steve Howell, "The Old and New Christian Right in North Carolina," a paper delivered at the 1982 meeting of the Society for the Scientific Study of Religion, Providence, R. I.; and Greeley, quoted by Arthur H. Miller and Martin D. Wattenberg, "Religious Orientations and the 1980 Elections," a paper dated June 1982, p. 18.

31. Miller and Wattenberg, "Religious Orientations."

32. Fred Barbash, "Court Bars Two Schools' Tax Break," *Washington Post*, May 25, 1983.

33. Interviews with R. Billings and Blackwell.

34. Jerry Falwell, *Listen America*! (New York: Doubleday, 1980), p. 13; interview with Godwin; and "Interview with Jerry Falwell," in *Christianity Today* (September 4, 1981), p. 27.

35. Haynes Johnson, "A Preacher for 'Peace Through Strength' " in the *Washington Post*, April 3, 1983; and Falwell, *Listen, America*! p. 106.

36. Curtis B. Gans, *Non-Voter Study* of 1984–1985; Ann Cooper, "Voter Turnover May be Higher on Nov. 6," in *National Journal*, November 3, 1984; and Adam Clymer, "Religion and Politics Mix Poorly for Democrats," *New York Times*, November 25, 1984.

37. Falwell, *Listen, America*!, p. 113.

38. Schaeffer, *Christian Manifesto*, p. 108; and interview with Cal Thomas, May 10, 1982.

39. Interview with Cal Thomas.

40. Dinesh D'Souza, "Jerry Falwell's Renaissance," in *Policy Review* (Winter 1984), p. 39.

41. Hill and Owen, *The New Religious Political Right in America*, p. 17; Peggy L. Shriver, *The Bible Vote* (New York: Pilgrim Press, 1981), p. 54; and interview with Robert Dugan, October 21, 1981.

42. Interview with Jim Wallis, editor of *Sojourners*, January 13, 1982.

43. Phillip E. Hammond, "Another Great Awakening," in *New Christian Right* p. 219.

44. John H. Simpson, "Moral Issues," pp. 193–94. The survey tested attitudes on homosexual relations between adults, the Supreme Court rulings on prayer and Bible reading in the public school, the statement, "It is much better for everyone involved if the man is the achiever outside the home and the woman takes care of the home and the family," and abortion for any reason.

45. Dean M. Kelley, "How Much Freedom of Speech Is Allowed to the Churches?" in *Christianity and Crisis*, Vol. 41 (October 5, 1981), p. 264.

46. Interview with Ronald Godwin.

47. James L. Guth, "New Christian Right," p. 37; Hill and Owen, "*New Religious Political Right*," p. 109; LaHaye, *Battle for the Mind*, p. 78; interview with McAteer; Fitzgerald, "Disciplined, Charging Army," p. 107; and James David Fairbanks, "The Evangelical Right: Beginning of Another Symbolic Crusade," a paper delivered at the 1981 American Political Science Association meeting, p. 16.

Part Two

Speaking for Themselves

5. *Making Political Decisions: An Evangelical Perspective*

By CARL F. H. HENRY

Focus

Carl F. H. Henry believes that many Evangelicals have come to doubt whether the U.S. political system can "cope with the debilitating forces in American society." Evangelicals are concerned that "the burgeoning secular mindset" has repudiated the biblical principles inherent in the Constitution and dominant in public life for most of the past two centuries. Ironically, these doubts have deepened Evangelicals' "sense of political alienation" during the very decade in which millions of Evangelicals have become politically engaged.

Henry affirms the relative justness of the American political system. But he notes that "the values traditionally considered normative in American society are now flouted with impunity" by many public schools, by the mass media, and even by national political leaders. Government is established by God, and human beings receive their "rights" from God; all human activity, therefore, is essentially religious. Every political act, Henry insists, reflects underlying religious assumptions. Thus politics cannot be religiously neutral.

Henry attributes the "lack of spiritual sensitivity and moral consensus in American life" in recent years to three factors: the spiritual and moral ambiguity of public education, trends in mass communications, and confusion in the American home. In the "Evangelical perspective," these problems can be addressed only by the principled politician—who "serves his country and his God best, and his own constituency as well, if he risks all other claims in the promotion of what he believes to be right and just."

Carl F. H. Henry is lecturer-at-large for World Vision International and the founding editor of *Christianity Today*. He is the author of the six-volume *God, Revelation, and Authority,* and of *Christian Countermoves in a Decadent Culture* (Multnomah, 1986).

THE EVANGELICAL CHRISTIAN challenges the current normative mode of American politics. He does so in a manner different from the radical Anabaptist tradition, which rejects direct political participation and encourages negative criticism. While Evangelicals emphasize the church's distinctive community witness within society, they also advocate direct political participation. They do not view political pursuit of the public good as mere rhetoric that cloaks private interest, nor do they believe that the American political system suppresses Christian public concerns.

But despite their sense that American political processes can adequately reflect the common good, the evangelical community is increasingly apprehensive that the two major political parties, despite their differences, may through their presently shared policy perspectives signal the need for a fundamental counterthrust. This Evangelical dissatisfaction is not focused on the American Constitution, nor on the established American political tradition, but instead questions the sanctity of the two-party system, the growing power of vocal minorities, and the final political authority even of majorities.

Despite the personal religious faith of many of the nation's political leaders, despite the public virtues still cherished by the grassroots citizenry, and despite the emphasis on representative pluralism which is declared to comprehensively reflect national concerns, the values traditionally considered normative in American society are now flouted with impunity in many of the nation's influential and prestigious educational institutions, in the mass media, and even by some political leaders. Since the public good is unapologetically linked in Evangelical political perception with ethical priorities, this trend raises doubts among Evangelicals about the ability of traditional political processes to cope with debilitating forces in American society. Every society postulates common convictions or values, and in their absence no political

---

association remains stable or endures. The decreasing affirmation in American public life of inherited biblical values has engendered an increasingly pragmatic, often unintegrated, and sometimes relativistic policy toward national values.

Many Evangelicals have come to doubt whether obedience to God can be effectively expressed in the context of the burgeoning secular mindset in American society. Evangelicals doubt, for example, whether the American political framework still constitutes a relatively just system within which Christian political expression is possible. These doubts have deepened Evangelicals' sense of political alienation in the very decade in which political involvement is understood to be a Christian duty.

Human Rights Endowed by God

Evangelical Christianity acknowledges God as Lord of the cosmos, of history, and of human life, and hence as the transcendent source, stipulator, and sanction of human responsibilities and rights. The emphasis is prominently reflected in the U.S. Declaration of Independence, which affirms that the human person is "endowed by [the] Creator with certain unalienable rights." Civil government must preserve and protect these rights or forfeit its legitimacy, and the citizen must live in responsible awareness that his or her rights end where those of a fellow citizen begin, and that citizens have responsibilities to the government which maintains liberty.

Civil Government Established by God

The revealed will of God, published in the Judeo-Christian Scriptures, sanctions the role of civil government as the preserver of justice and promoter of social order and peace (Romans 13). This divine requirement will be enforced upon all nations when the returning Messiah, Jesus Christ, reigns in power and glory. Its content is set forth in God's New Covenant, which embraces not only universal justice and harmony among the nations, but the etching of the purposes of God upon the hearts of human beings. Individuals and institutions thus fall under the searching scrutiny of God's holy will for man in society. The church as the New Society—a spiritually obedient vanguard of morally regenerate persons—is to mirror to the larger family of mankind the standards by which the returning Christ will judge individual human beings and entire nations. Yet the Christian shares in the present tragedy of rebellious human existence, and therefore is called to active participation in approving and advancing the divinely willed function of government.

All Human Activity Religious

The Christian concept of redemption anticipates the rescue of the penitent human person from the guilt, penalty, power, and presence of sin in all relationships, both personal and social. It anticipates that all rulers and nations will ultimately acknowledge Jesus Christ as King.

All human activity, including political activity, is religious and involves the human service of either the true God or false gods. Every political proposal, decision, and act reflects underlying assumptions, however obscure. Every formulation presupposes a personal faith and public objectives. Politics is so far from being religiously neutral that Jacques Ellul has called it the modern man's god, the hopeful miracle worker trusted by the underprivileged for economic salvation.

The living God seeks in history to advance certain purposes through the church as a channel of redemptive grace, and directs other purposes through civil government as the instrumentality of justice. There is, therefore, a sense in which the church is not to impose sectarian religious objectives upon the the nation, nor is civil government to coerce personal faith or to require or disallow what God requires or disallows. Yet the church is rightly concerned about public conscience, virtue, and justice, and has a necessary interest in the common good, while civil government is properly obliged to hold even voluntary religious associations answerable to just laws that are binding upon the body politic.

Public Policy Norms Provided by Scripture

God's New Covenant and principles of social ethics, both divinely revealed, supply for Evangelicals the norms and criteria of public policy. The apostle Paul indicates that Christian and non-Christian alike stand in a relationship of conscientious submission to civil government in respect to public duties. The classic New Testament passage on civil responsibility (Romans 13) affirms that civil government has a divine sanction to preserve public order for the social good—the good of Christians as well as others. The New Testament condemns anarchy, and affirms civil government as a necessary institution even while acknowledging that particular governments may be tyrannical and even anti-God, for example, the beast-state of Revelation 13.

The New Testament recognizes the right of conscientious personal protest and disobedience, but insists that the resister should be prepared to pay the legal penalties of civil disobedience. The fact that Paul calls the believer to submission (Romans 13:1,5), rather than to unqualified civil obedience, reflects the emphasis of Acts 5:29 that, when civil government requires what is contrary to God's revealed will, it is God rather than men whom the Christian must obey.

Determining Political Loyalties

How, then, does the Christian decide whether to disobey or obey the governing authority? Since the Christian political statesmen seeks to sponsor and support just laws and to avoid impositions that might require citizens to act contrary to the will of God, this question also reflects a larger concern: How among the wide range of public policy options does the Evangelical discern the concrete proposals he or she should support?

Maintaining a Biblical Perspective

The New Testament is not a book of ethical rules, although it does contain some rules ("pay your taxes," "pay just wages," "earn your pay"), nor is it a book of political models. It does not approve any one form of government—whether monarchy, republic, or democracy—as ideal, although it does condemn tyranny. The New Testament assumes the legitimate existence of different nations. There is no single theological motif—whether the doctrine of creation, the Hebrew exodus, the Mosaic law (prophetic convenant and theocracy), the kingdom of God, Jesus' teaching and example, or the teaching and example of the apostles—from which answers to all questions about public policy issues can be directly drawn from the Scriptures.

What the Bible does supply are a theistic perspective, norms, principles, some examples, and a few rules. In view of these, man in society is obliged everywhere to obey God and to love and serve God and man. The Christian knows that he is redeemed by the mercy of God in Christ and cannot earn God's love. He seeks nevertheless, through the enabling grace of the Holy Spirit, to serve God in gratitude for grace. The mandate of God's law and of universal justice and love transcends obedience to all earthly authority. The claim that rulers make upon human beings must not annul the social commandments of the Ten Commandments ideally fulfilled in a spirit of love of neighbor, irrespective of race, color, belief, or class. The very chapter in which the apostle Paul defines a citizen's obligation to civil government also insists that no claim must frustrate the love that fulfills the commandments of God:

> He who loves his fellow man has fulfilled the law. The commandments, "Do not commit adultery," "Do not murder," "Do not steal," "Do not covet," and whatever other commandment there may be, are summed up in this one rule: "Love your neighbor as yourself." Love does no harm to its neighbor. Therefore love is the fulfillment of the law (Romans 13:8-10).

Each nation is therefore to be conceived first and foremost not as a world power, but as the servant of God in the righteous service of mankind at home and abroad. It places itself in the service of injustice when it accommodates or winks at adultery, murder, theft, and even covetousness, which arises from a confusion of human rights with human wants. The classic American political documents champion "the pursuit of happiness"; they do not guarantee happiness or envision a utopia.

Legislation that professes to be humanitarian while it lightens the seriousness of criminal offenses is a service neither to God nor to man. The primary purpose of punishment is not the reform of the offender, but the vindication of the right and the peace and safety of society. A society that finds no basis for capital punishment (other than for acts of terror made possible by twentieth century technology) retains only a shadow of biblical sensitivity to the worth of human life, and elevates the value of the survival of criminals above that of their victims. Yet a compassionate interest in the prisoner (Matthew 25:36, 43), and a spirited concern for prison conditions, belongs equally to the Christian social ethic and is specially imperative in view of the corrupting environment of many penal institutions.

Politics in Need of Clarity

Contemporary politics stands in dire need of clarity in respect to philosophy of law itself and the definition of justice. In a day when predatory totalitarian states violate human rights, treaty signatories must be condemned for renouncing their United Nations Charter commitments.

While U.S. foreign policy must strive for international security and peace, the protection of human rights must be emphasized. The arrest and imprisonment of citizens without public disclosure of charges, the use of torture to gain confessions, and the denial of prisoner contact with families and loved ones are repressive practices of many governments that the United States must deplore.

A discussion of the United States' role as the servant of justice raises inevitably the problem of duties and treaty commitments to smaller powers. The temptation is to deem some governments moral only while they serve our national interest and to abandon them amid the fluctuations of power politics. In relation to Taiwan, for example, is it just of the United States to forsake that nation's right to independent sovereignty because we seek improved relations with mainland Communist China, even if we no longer consider the Taiwanese government to be the legitimate voice of the Chinese people?

The principle of national servanthood requires something other than a permanent commitment to the notion of international power blocs that involve an escalating and unending arms race. To be sure, the presence of predator powers, whose historical record leaves little doubt of their readiness to conquer weaker countries, renders unwise a policy of unilateral disarmament. But any nation disturbed about the perpetuation of nuclear rivalry will warn all human beings—those of predator powers as well as our own—of what present nuclear arms policy is doing to mankind.

Whatever are the requirements of a sound defense policy, the Christian's duty is to strive for world peace. Only with deep indignation over international policies can Christians condone vast military expenditures. In a time of widespread poverty, these same moneys could provide for millions.

Hostility to Communism is not the surest sign of competent foreign policy, despite all the Communists' unconscionable repression of human liberty. The only adequate program consists in the sound promotion of freedom, peace, justice, and human worth. In this cause we need to ally ourselves with voices for freedom and democracy that rise now and again within the Communist sphere, reminding the masses that even Lenin held that a true socialist victory requires a context of political democracy.[1]

The Free World yields too easily to the notion that Marxism champions human rights over property rights. At the same time, while acknowledging valid Marxist criticism of economic wrongs, one need not uncritically espouse either secular capitalism or secular socialist alternatives. The failure of non-Marxist societies to engage in penetrating self-criticism should not cause us to acquiesce in supposedly ideal Marxist alternatives.

If such broad emphases should commend themselves to all Christian statesmen, the fact remains that deep-seated differences or priorities in policy often vex political leaders of devout evangelical commitment. One major party may consider inflation a higher priority than employment, while the other party may consider employment a higher priority than inflation. There can be little doubt that ongoing inflation is a serious moral problem: it dissolves the worth of savings, discourages thrift, and erodes purchasing power. At the same time, to provide benefits to those who will not work is harmful to the individual and to the nation. A political situation in which both concerns are held in tension can be creatively served by leaders of either major political party.

Political Process as the Service of God

The lack of spiritual sensitivity and of moral consensus in American life has in recent decades largely been a reflection of three factors: the spiritual and moral ambiguity of the public schools and universities, the trend of the mass media, and the confusion in the American home (which in many respects reflects these influences). Insofar as American community life resists this tide of ethical relativism, the churches and spiritually conscientious families remain the major constructive influence.

But the Founding Fathers acknowledged religion and morality to be the twin supports of a worthy republic. (That by "religion" many if not most meant revealed religion is clear from the obvious fact that many other ancient religions accommodated ferocious totalitarian government.) The American political process necessarily involves compromises among competing claims. Statesmen who seek the ideal know that they must vote for the best approximation of an ideal among the surviving options. They do so in humility born of an awareness that they, too, exist as members of a finite and fallen society, and in the confidence that, despite limited insights, they can rely on the providence of God. The laws that the Christian statesman sponsors are those that he conscientiously considers better than rival options, yet he does not deem them perfect; the passing of years, sometimes only of months, may suggest a preferable alternative.

Politics is the obedient service of God in the midst of changing history. The norms and principles are fixed, and Christ at his return will demonstrate the superiority and durability of their uncompromised translation into history. In a society in which human beings remain free to mold their immediate political destiny, the principled politician will stimulate the conscience and will of his generation to reach for the lasting good. The political leader serves his country and his God best—and his own constituency as well—if he risks all other claims to promote what he confidently believes to be right and just. The scriptural norms and principles will identify the worthiest alternatives.

Notes

1. Lenin, *On Socialist Democracy*.

6. *An Agenda for the 1980s*

By JERRY FALWELL

Focus

Restoring America to "moral sanity" is crucial in this "decade of destiny," according to Jerry Falwell. As founder of the Moral Majority, Falwell has been the leader most often credited—or criticized—for the conservative religious resurgence in national political affairs.

An independent Baptist minister in Lynchburg, Virginia, Falwell insists that political liberalism has eroded America's traditional values and, therefore, has lost its intellectual and moral credibility. He argues that Fundamentalists and Evangelicals can return America to its spiritual and moral foundations, and explains the positions of the Moral Majority on major issues. In response to critics who label him "arrogant, irresponsible, and simplistic," Falwell also explains "what the Moral Majority is not." He lists six ways in which the Moral Majority is helping to restore moral sanity to American life.

"We must continue to exert a strong moral influence if our children and grandchildren are to enjoy the same freedoms that we have known," Falwell writes. His central point throughout is that the individual liberties that Americans prize cannot be maintained without this influence.

Falwell is quick to define himself as a Fundamentalist—"with a big F!" He traces the origins and nature of Fundamentalism in America, and admits that Fundamentalists have sometimes been "irresponsible as Christian citizens" because of an undue pessimism about politics. At the same time, he criticizes many Evangelicals for hesitating to take firm stands on national issues, and says that Evangelicals are often too concerned about their reputation with the secular "world."

If Fundamentalists and Evangelicals would take advantage of their common theological and cultural roots, Falwell believes, they could help bring about "a great revival of true Christianity in America and the world in our lifetime." Falwell's views may be usefully compared with those of Richard John Neuhaus (selection 1) and Grant Wacker (selection 22).

Jerry Falwell is pastor of Thomas Road Baptist Church and chancellor of Liberty University, both in Lynchburg, Virginia. He is the founder of the Moral Majority (which in 1986 came under the umbrella of a new organization, the Liberty Federation) and producer of the nationally broadcast TV program, "Old-Time Gospel Hour."

THESE ARE THE GREATEST days of the twentieth century. We have the opportunity to formulate a new beginning for America. For the first time in my lifetime, we have the opportunity to see spiritual revival and political renewal in the United States. We now have a platform to express the concerns of the majority of moral Americans who still love those things for which this country stands. We have the opportunity to rebuild America to the greatness it once had as a leader among leaders in the world.

The 1980s are certainly a decade of destiny for America. The rising tide of secularism threatens to obliterate the Judeo-Christian influence on American society. In the realm of religion, liberal clergy have seduced the average American away from the Bible and the kind of simple faith on which this country was built. We need to call America back to God, back to the Bible, and back to moral sanity.

Christianity recognizes that reformation of the institutional structure of the church is futile without the spiritual revitalization of people's lives. It is the people whose lives have been dynamically changed by their personal relationship to Jesus Christ who are the real strength of the church. It is no "mere pietism" that will dynamically energize the evangelical church into social action. In our attempt to rally a diversity of morally conservative Americans together in the Moral Majority, we were convinced that millions of people were fed up with the fruits of liberalism, both in politics and in religion. I am well aware that it is unpopular in some circles to equate the two, but I say that they must be viewed as cousins of the same family because both rest upon the same foundational presupposition of the inherent goodness of mankind. The ultimate product of theological liberalism is a vague kind of religious humanism that is devoid of any true gospel content.

In 1969, Harold O. J. Brown observed that there was still a "moral majority" left in America when he said: "The United

---

States may have a great deal of Christianity deep down. There is evidence of this. There is much to indicate that something basic in America is still healthy, both in a spiritual and in a moral sense. But wherever it is and whatever it is doing, it is not setting the tone, it is not giving direction to twentieth century America. It is not immune to disease. There is plenty of reason to think that America has a large reservoir of Christian faith, sound morality, and of idealism. But there is also a great deal of reason to fear that this reservoir is in danger of being polluted."[1]

Dr. Brown further observed that it was the influence of the liberal impulse in American theology that had produced a climate that spawned celebrated "theologians" who openly taught atheism and left the average person in search of God as a "prisoner of the total culture."[2] During the 1960s and 1970s, people felt confused and began to turn away from the liberalized institutional church that was not meeting their spiritual needs. As attendance drastically declined in the mainline denominations, it dramatically increased in conservative denominations. Liberalism is obviously losing its influence on America. The time has come for Fundamentalists and Evangelicals to return our nation to its spiritual and moral roots.

The Imperative of Morality

As a pastor, I kept waiting for someone to come to the forefront of the American religious scene to lead the way out of the wilderness. Like thousands of other preachers, I kept waiting, but no leader appeared. Finally, I realized that we had to act ourselves. Something had to be done. The federal government was encroaching upon the sovereignty of both the church and the family. The U.S. Supreme Court had legalized abortion-on-demand. The Equal Rights Amendment, with its vague language, threatened to do further damage to the traditional family, as did the rising sentiment toward so-called homosexual rights. Most Americans were shocked, but kept hoping someone would do something about all this moral chaos.

Facing the desperate need in the impending crisis of the hour, several concerned pastors urged me to put together a political organization that could provide a vehicle to address these crucial issues. Men like James Kennedy of Fort Lauderdale, Florida, Charles Stanley of Atlanta, Georgia, Tim LaHaye of San Diego, California, and Greg Dixon of Indianapolis, Indiana, shared with me a common concern. They urged that we formulate a nonpartisan political organization to promote morality in public life and combat legislation that favored the legalization of immorality. Together we formulated the Moral Majority, Inc. Today Moral Majority, Inc., is made up of millions of Americans, including 72,000 ministers, priests, and rabbis, who are deeply concerned about the moral decline of our nation, the traditional family, and the moral values on which our nation was built. We are Catholics, Jews, Protestants, Mormons, Fundamentalists—blacks and whites—farmers, housewives, businessmen, and businesswomen. We are Americans from all walks of life united by one central concern: to serve as a special-interest group providing a voice for a return to moral sanity in these United States of America.

Moral Majority is a political organization and is not based on theological considerations. We are Americans who share similar moral convictions. We are opposed to abortion, pornography, the drug epidemic, the breakdown of the traditional family, the establishment of homosexuality as an accepted alternate lifestyle, and other moral cancers that are causing our society to rot from within. Moral Majority strongly supports a pluralistic America. While we believe that this nation was founded upon the Judeo-Christian ethic by men and women who were strongly influenced by biblical moral principles, we are committed to the separation of Church and State.

Here is how Moral Majority stands on today's vital issues:

1. *We believe in the separation of Church and State.* Moral Majority, Inc., is a political organization that provides a platform for religious and nonreligious Americans who share moral values to address their concerns. Members of Moral Majority, Inc., have no common theological premise. We are Americans who are proud to be conservative in our approach to moral, social, and political concerns.

2. *We are pro-life.* We believe that life begins at fertilization. We strongly oppose the massive "biological holocaust" that is resulting in the abortion of one-and-a-half-million babies each year in

America. We believe that unborn babies have the right to life as much as babies who have been born. We are providing a voice and a defense for the human and civil rights of millions of unborn babies.

3. *We are pro-traditional family.* We believe that the only acceptable family form begins with a legal marriage of a man and woman. We feel that homosexual relationships and common-law relationships should not be accepted as traditional families. We oppose legislation that favors these kinds of "diverse family form," thereby penalizing the traditional family. We do not oppose civil rights for homosexuals. We do oppose "special rights" for homosexuals who have chosen a perverted lifestyle rather than a traditional way-of-life.

4. *We oppose the illegal drug traffic in America.* The youth of America are in the midst of a drug epidemic. Through education, legislation, and other means, we want to do our part to save our young people from death on the installment plan through illegal drug addiction.

5. *We oppose pornography.* While we do not advocate censorship, we do believe that education and legislation can help stem the tide of pornography and obscenity that is poisoning the American spirit today. Economic boycotts are a proper way in America's free enterprise system to help persaude the media to move back to a sensible and reasonable moral stand. We most certainly believe in the First Amendment for everyone. We are not willing to sit back, however, while many television programs create cesspools of obscenity and vulgarity in our nation's living rooms.

6. *We support the state of Israel and Jewish people everywhere.* It is impossible to separate the state of Israel from the Jewish family internationally. Many Moral Majority members, because of their theological convictions, are committed to the Jewish people. Others stand upon the human and civil rights of all persons as a premise for support of the state of Israel. Support of Israel is one of the essential commitments of Moral Majority. No anti-Semitic influence is allowed in Moral Majority, Inc.

7. *We believe that a strong national defense is the best deterrent to war.* We believe that liberty is the basic moral issue of all moral issues. The only way America can remain free is to remain strong.

Therefore we support Reagan administration efforts to regain our position of military preparedness—with a sincere hope that we will never need to use any of our weapons against any people anywhere.

8. *We support equal rights for women.* We agree with President Reagan's commitment to help every governor and every state legislature to move quickly to ensure that, during the 1980s, every American woman will earn as much money and enjoy the same opportunities for advancement as her male counterpart in the same vocation.

9. *We believe ERA is the wrong vehicle to obtain equal rights for women.* We feel that the ambiguous and simplistic language of the proposed amendment could lead to court interpretations that might put women in combat, sanction homosexual relationships, and financially penalize widows and deserted wives.

10. *We encourage our Moral Majority state organizations to be autonomous and indigenous.* Moral Majority state organizations may, from time to time, hold positions that are not held by the Moral Majority, Inc., national organization.

We have been labeled by our critics as arrogant, irresponsible, and simplistic. They accuse us of violating the separation of church and state. However, the National Council of Churches (NCC) has been heavily involved in politics for years, and virtually no one has complained. Since many moral problems, such as abortion, require solutions that are both legal and political, it is necessary for religious leaders to speak on these matters in order to be heard.

What Moral Majority Is Not

1. *We are not a political party.* We are committed to working within the multiple-party system in this nation. We are not a political party and do not intend to become one.

2. *We do not endorse political candidates.* Moral Majority informs American citizens regarding the vital moral issues facing our nation. We have no "hit lists." While we fully support the constitutional rights of any special-interest group to target candidates with whom they disagree, Moral Majority, Inc., has chosen not to take this course. We are committed to principles and issues, not candidates and parties.

3. *We are not attempting to elect "born-again" candidates.* We are committed to pluralism. The membership of Moral Majority, Inc., is so totally pluralistic that the acceptability of any candidate could never be based upon one's religious affiliation. Our support of candidates is based upon two criteria: (1) the commitment of the candidate to the principles that we espouse; (2) the competency of the candidate to fill that office.

4. *Moral Majority, Inc., is not a religious organization attempting to control the government.* Moral Majority is a special-interest group of millions of Americans who share the same moral values. We simply desire to influence government—not control government. This, of course, is the right of every American, and Moral Majority, Inc., would vigorously oppose any tyrannical person's pursuit of power in this country.

5. *We are not a censorship organization.* We believe in freedom of speech, freedom of the press, and freedom of religion. Therefore, while we do not agree that the Equal Rights Amendment would ultimately benefit the cause of women in America, we do agree with the right of its supporters to boycott those states that have not ratified the amendment. Likewise, we believe that all Americans have the right to refuse to purchase products from manufacturers whose advertising dollars support publications and television programming that violate their own moral code.

6. *Moral Majority, Inc., is not an organization committed to depriving homosexuals of their civil rights as Americans.* While we believe that homosexuality is a moral perversion, we are committed to guaranteeing the civil rights of homosexuals. We do oppose the efforts of homosexuals to obtain special privileges as a bona fide minority, and we oppose efforts by homosexuals to flaunt their perversion as an acceptable lifestyle. We view heterosexual promiscuity with the same distaste which we express toward homosexuality.

7. *We do not believe that individuals or organizations that disagree with Moral Majority, Inc., belong to an immoral minority.* We do believe, however, that our position represents a consensus of the majority of Americans. This belief in no way reflects on the morality of those who disagree with us or who are not involved in our organizational structures. We are committed to the total freedom of all Americans regardless of race, creed, or color.

From Pew to Precinct

Many Christians are raising the question of whether or not they should be involved in politics at all. Some raise the question of the separation of church and state; others think that politics is the devil's arena and Christians should stay out; and others say that politics requires compromising and Christians should not compromise. Many liberal church people claim that Evangelicals and Fundamentalists are violating the separation of church and state. Recently Richard Dingman said: "As one who has held local public office for ten years and worked in congress for eleven years, it is my opinion that it is not only proper for Christians to become involved, but it is absolutely biblical and absolutely necessary."[3]

The recent emergence of Fundamentalists and Evangelicals in politics in no way violates the historical principles of this nation. The incorporation of Christian principles into both the structure and the basic documents of our nation is a matter of historical fact. The doctrine of the separation of church and state simply means that the state shall not control religion and religion shall not control the state. It does not mean that the two may never work together.

Here is how Moral Majority, Inc., is contributing to bringing America back to moral sanity:

1. *By educating millions of Americans concerning the vital moral issues of our day.* This is accomplished through such avenues as our newspaper, called the *Moral Majority Report*, a radio commentary by the same name, seminars, and other training programs conducted daily throughout the nation.

2. *By mobilizing millions of previously "inactive" Americans.* We have registered millions of voters and reactivated more millions of frustrated citizens into a special-interest group who are effectively making themselves heard in the halls of Congress, in the White House, and in every state legislature.

3. *By lobbying intensively in Congress to defeat any legislation that would further erode our constitutionally guaranteed freedom,* and by introducing and/or supporting legislation that promotes traditional family and moral values, followed by the goal of passage of a Human Life Amendment, which is a top priority of the Moral Majority agenda. We support the return of voluntary prayer to public schools, though we oppose mandated or written prayers. We promote legislation to keep America morally balanced.

4. *By informing all Americans about the voting records of their representatives so that every American, with full information available, can vote intelligently following his or her own convictions*. We are nonpartisan. We are not committed to politicians or political parties; we are committed to principles and issues that we believe are essential to America's survival at this crucial hour. It is our desire to represent these concerns to the American public and allow it to make its own decisions on these matters.

5. *By organizing and training millions of Americans who can become moral activists*. This heretofore silent majority in America can then help develop a responsive government which is truly "of the people, by the people, for the people," instead of "in spite of the people," which we have had too many years.

6. *By encouraging and promoting private schools in their attempt to excel in academics while simultaneously teaching traditional family and moral values*. There are thousands of private schools in America that accept no tax moneys. Some of these schools are Catholic, Fundamentalist, Jewish, Adventist, or of other faiths. Some are not religious. But Moral Majority, Inc., supports the right of these schools to teach young people not only how to make a living, but how to live.

Moral Majority, Inc., does not advocate the abolition of public schools. Public schools will always be needed in our pluralistic society. We are committed to helping public schools regain excellence. That is why we support the return of voluntary prayer to public schools and strongly oppose the teaching of the "religion" of secular humanism in the public classroom.

The First Amendment declares: "Congress shall make no law respecting an establishment of religion, or prohibiting the free exercise thereof." This does not rule out church influence in government. Presbyterian theologian John Gerstner has said: "Establishment of religion is not the same thing as no influence of religion. I think Moral Majority is right in stating that the church should seek to have influence in political matters."[4]

California pastor Tim La Haye believes that the pulpit must be active in resisting an encroaching federal bureaucracy that threatens both the church and the traditional family. He has stated: "God founded the government to protect the home against external enemies. The prophet of God is derelict if he does not, in God's name, rebuke government when it fails to protect the family."[5]

Catholic theologian and journalist Father Robert Burns, C. S. P., stated in the national Catholic weekly *The Wanderer:* "If our great nation collapses, it will not be because of the efforts of some foreign power, Soviet or otherwise, but, rather, for the same reason that ancient Rome collapsed—because it was morally rotten to the core." He further commented: "The members of Moral Majority believe in fighting for the basic moral values on which this nation was built and upon which its strength rests. They are determined to prevent materialists, secular-humanists, and non-believers from destroying these values by replacing them with a valueless, amoral society."[6]

Christians are now realizing again that governmental actions directly affect their lives. They are questioning the government's right to carry out such programs. They are beginning to realize again that the only way to change the actions of government is to change those elected to govern. We are now beginning to do just that. We must continue to exert a strong moral influence upon America if our children and grandchildren are to enjoy the same freedoms that we have known.

An Appeal to Fundamentalists

I have always made it clear that I am a Fundamentalist—big F! A Fundamentalist believes the Bible to be verbally inspired by the Holy Spirit and therefore inerrant and absolutely infallible. Fundamentalists believe in the deity of Jesus Christ. They readily accept His virgin birth, sinless life, and vicarious death. They believe in His literal resurrection, His ascension into heaven, and His second coming. A Fundamentalist believes in evangelism and discipleship through the local church as the proper fulfillment of the Great Commission of our Lord.

I am also a separatist. We Fundamentalists practice separatism from the world and all of its entanglements. We refuse to conform to the standards of a sinful society. We practice personal separation as well as ecclesiastical separation. Most of us are "independents" in our associations. We are at our best when we are free from hierarchical structures that would tie us down to denominational mediocrity. We are our own people. We are not intimidated by academic degrees or ecclesiastical positions. We do our own thinking, and we do not care what liberals think about anything!

We are not, however, without our weaknesses. We can tend to be negative and pessimistic. For too many years now, we have been sitting back waiting for apostasy to take over at any moment, and have nearly let the country go down the drain. We have been irresponsible as Christian citizens. We have almost totally avoided the political process and the social life of our country. We have neglected reaching the whole person for the cause of Christ. We have blasted the Liberals and derided the Evangelicals for their feeble attempts at the social application of the Gospel, while doing almost nothing ourselves.

We love to extol the virtues of fidelity to the historic Christian faith. We pride ourselves that we are not as others who have compromised. Yet our lack of capacity for honest self-criticism has often left us hiding behind our honorary degrees while attacking the value of education. Our emphasis on belonging to the right group has caused us at times to overlook our own sins. We have just as many failures in our ranks as do the Evangelicals—maybe more. We cannot be blinded by our tendency to use our people to build our churches, instead of using our churches to build our people.

In spite of our weaknesses, we Fundamentalists have much to offer our Evangelical brethren that they need. We preach the Bible with authority and conviction. Where they hesitate and equivocate, we loudly thunder, "Thus saith the Lord!" Where they are overly theoretical and impractically idealistic, we have become practical evangelists and experts at church growth. While the Evangelicals are always defining and redefining, we are out building great churches to the glory of God. We preach the gospel to the lost. We have the highest percentage of converts and the fastest-growing churches in America.

In a similar "Agenda for the 1980s," Evangelical spokesman Billy Graham appealed to pastors for three things that we Fundamentalists need:[7]

1. Integrity of Life.
2. Compassion.

3. Vision.

If we are going to reach millions of Americans with the gospel, we must live the message we proclaim. Personal integrity is a must in our own lives, in our families, in our churches, and in our communities. As we stand for the truth, we must also show compassion for a lost world in need of our Savior. Our mission is to see, not how many people we can hate, but how many we can love for Christ's sake. Further, we must extend our vision to evangelize the world. We must stop being so negative and critical of everyone who is trying to reach people with the gospel but does not wear our label. We must realize that it is going to take our full commitment to the task of evangelism, discipleship, and church-planting to do the job. The Lord has set before us an open door of opportunity, and we must use it to His glory.

An Appeal to Evangelicals

The Evangelical movement has been a vital part of this country for two centuries. Evangelical pastors have provided mature and stable leadership for the churches of America. They have demonstrated the love of Christ to their congregations, and have been expositors and defenders of the Christian faith. When others have been extreme, they have remained balanced. They have attempted to apply the truth of the gospel to the needs of society. In general, the Evangelical movement has been faithful to the fundamental doctrines of the Christian faith.

In reality, there is little difference theologically between Fundamentalists and Evangelicals. We both hold to a strong belief in the inspiration and inerrancy of the Bible. We hold to the deity of Christ, and to the necessity of personal salvation. Though Evangelicalism tends to be tolerant of varying viewpoints, the vast majority of Evangelical pastors tell me that they are concerned about the drift to the Left of so-called "Young Evangelicals." They do not like the current trend within the movement, which is getting dangerously close to liberalism.

The lines are not clearly drawn today among Evangelicals. The movement is so broad at times that it encompasses everything from Bible churches to charismatic Catholics. Theologically it extends from Josh McDowell to Helmut Thielicke. Philosophically, it includes strong inerrancy defenders such as Norman Geisler and John W. Montgomery. It has provided the conservative movement in general with such able social critics as Harold O. J. Brown. But at the same time, Evangelicalism unfortunately includes some who are ready to deny their Fundamentalist heritage and exchange their theological birthright for a mess of socio-academic pottage!

We Fundamentalists appeal to our Evangelical brethren to stand with us for the truth of the gospel in this hour when America needs us most. Stop looking down your theological and ecclesiastical noses at your Fundamentalist brethren. As the English theologian James Barr has already pointed out, non-Evangelicals already view Evangelicals and Fundamentalists alike. We have so much in common. Only the radicals among us (to the Left and to the Right) divide us. I say it is time we denied the "lunatic fringe" of our movements and worked for a great conservative crusade to turn America back to God. We do not need an organic unity; such is not necessary in order to achieve mutual appreciation and respect.

We Fundamentalists appeal to you to reacknowledge your Fundamentalist roots. Stop being intimidated by what others think. Stop worrying about academic credibility and social acceptability. If Evangelicals have one glaring weakness, it is that they are too concerned about what the world thinks. Evangelicals are hesitant to speak up on vital issues for fear of what the intellectual elite may think. Let them think what they wish. They have been wrong before, and they will be wrong again!

In his monumental book, *Earnestly Contending for the Faith,* the late John R. Rice wrote:

> The greatest preachers, the greatest soul winners through the ages, have earnestly contended for the faith. So did Luther and Calvin and Zwingli and Savonarola and Huss. The persecution, the slander, and the blood of martyrs is their witness. Whitefield in England and America, T. DeWitt Talmage in Brooklyn, I. M. Haldeman and John Roach Straton in New York City, W. B. Riley in Minneapolis, Mark Matthews in Seattle, Bob Shuler in Los Angeles, Dr. R. G. Lee in Memphis, W. R. Criswell in Dallas, and many other faithful leaders in Christendom, have earnestly contended for the faith as the Scripture commands a Christian to do.[8]

Evangelicals need to reaffirm the foundation. Come back to the fundamentals of the Christian faith, and stand firm on that which is essential. Throw down the anchor of truth and stop drifting with every new wave of religious fad. Stop trying to accommodate the gospel to the pitiful philosophies of unregenerate humankind. You have the truth, and the truth shall set you free.

Evangelicals talk much of love, but often have only words of bitter contempt for those of us who call ourselves Fundamentalists. Evangelicals should not be embarrassed because we believe the same things they do. They should acknowledge us, accept us as Bible-believing brethren who love the same Christ, and let us work to reach the world for Christ.

Conservative Fundamentalists and Evangelicals can be used of God to bring about a great revival of true Christianity in America and the world in our lifetime.

Notes

1. H. O. J. Brown, *Protest of a Troubled Protestant* (New York: Arlington House, 1969), p. 72. See also the excellent study on the relationship of true revival to social action by R. F. Lovelace, *Dynamics of Spiritual Life: An Evangelical Theology of Renewal* (Downers Grove, Ill.: Inter-Varsity Press, 1979), and his more recent article, "Completing an Awakening," *The Christian Century* (March 18, 1981), pp. 296–300.
2. Brown, *Protest of a Troubled Protestant*, p. 205.
3. R. Dingman, in *Moral Majority Report* (June 6, 1980), p. 4.
4. J. Gerstner, quoted in an article in the *Birmingham News,* Sept. 26, 1980.
5. T. La Haye, in *Moral Majority Report* (June 6, 1980). See also his incisive study on the influence of secular humanism in *The Battle for the Mind* (Old Tappan, N. J.: Revell, 1980). For a more technical study, see R. J. Rushdoony, *The Messianic Character of American Education* (Nutley, N. J.: Craig Press, 1979).
6. R. Burns, in *The Wanderer,* Oct. 2, 1980.
7. Billy Graham, "An Agenda for the 1980s," *Christianity Today* (January 4, 1980), pp. 23–27.
8. J. R. Rice, *Earnestly Contending for the Faith* (Murfreesboro, Tenn: Sword of the Lord, 1965), p. 13.

7. *The Two Faces of Evangelical Social Concern*

By RONALD NASH

Focus Evangelical liberals, and especially Evangelical radicals, cling, in Ronald Nash's view, to a political and economic position that is "long on heart and short on wisdom." Secular thinkers across the political spectrum, for example, have been reassessing Federal anti-poverty programs. But many Evangelicals suffer from both uncritical acceptance of such programs and "an inadequate grasp of economics." Liberal Evangelical leaders, Nash says, show good intentions that "cannot be successful because they are not based on sound economic theory and practice."

Nash declares: "It is not enough to feel compassion for the poor and oppressed. Compassion and love must be coupled with a careful grounding in the relevant philosophical, economic, political, and social issues." Many of the governmental programs championed by liberal Evangelicals could deepen dependency on welfare and lead to an increasingly coercive state system. Conservative Evangelicals oppose such government programs, Nash suggests, not because they lack compassion, but because they believe the programs do more harm than good.

Nash also challenges liberal Evangelicals' interpretation of justice in the Bible: "Because Evangelical social liberals are inattentive to important distinctions within the notion of justice, many of their appeals to the biblical uses of 'justice' are compromised since they simply assume that biblical endorsements of justice are divine commands to support economic redistribution." In addition, because Evangelical social liberals confuse love and justice, they unwisely call on government to "force people to fulfill the demands of love." A different view of radical Evangelical social concern is offered by Ronald Sider (selection 8).

Ronald Nash is the chairman of the department of philosophy and religion at Western Kentucky University. He is the author of *Poverty and Wealth* (Crossway, 1986) and many other books.

THIRTY YEARS AGO or so, one often heard the claim that Evangelicals had abandoned social action to theological liberals. Evidence offered in support of this doubtful claim was the Social Gospel. Whether the assertion was ever really true, it is certainly not true today. Evangelicals have become increasingly involved in social action. They have come to recognize that as Christians they have an obligation to be concerned about more than the condition of their neighbor's soul. They understand their duty to be concerned about the plight of the poor, about social injustice, about urban blight, and about other issues of social significance.

As important as the social concern of the contemporary Evangelical may be, however, it is only one side of the story. One of the two sides of Christian social concern is the Christian's clear obligation to care and to be concerned about the poor and oppressed, and to do what he can on their behalf. But the other dimension of Christian social concern is the stipulation that, if a Christian wishes to make pronouncements on complex social, economic, and political issues, he has a duty to become informed about those issues. That duty requires a careful study of economics and other social sciences. In reality, many writings and speeches of Christian social activists evidence an inadequate grasp of economics. The late Benjamin Rogge, a professor of economics and Lutheran layman, lamented that

> . . . the typical American who calls himself a Christian and who makes pronouncements . . . on economic policies or institutions, does so out of an almost complete ignorance of the simplest and most widely accepted tools of economic analysis. If something arouses his Christian concern, he asks not whether it is water or gasoline he is tossing on the economic fire—he asks only whether it is a well-intended act. As I understand it, the Christian is required to use his God-given reason as well.[1]

Few Evangelicals, whatever their political persuasion, have made the effort to study the foundational issues that underlie social

---

justice problems. It is not enough, for example, to feel compassion for the poor and oppressed. Compassion and love must be coupled with a careful grounding in the relevant philosophical, economic, political, and social issues.

If the Evangelical social activist proceeds in ignorance of the accepted tools of economic analysis, he risks turning bad situations into something far worse. Witness for example, Ronald Sider's book, *Rich Christians in an Age of Hunger,* that gained wide acceptance among Evangelical readers.[2] Many people learned by that book of the terrible plight of many of the world's poor. Sider had one side of the equation right: the Christian needs to care. Unfortunately, his book contained many proposals which, if put into effect, would subject the poor he was attempting to aid to even more serious economic devastation. Sider suggested that Americans should unilaterally begin to pay more than a market price for certain commodities from poor countries. He seemed blissfully unaware of the long-range consequences such policies would have on the economy of poorer nations. But such economic short-sightedness did not escape the attention of George Mavrodes, a University of Michigan philosopher:

> Sider usually seems unaware that his policies may have different results than he intends. Suppose that we [Americans] voluntarily increased the price that we pay for crude rubber (a recurrent suggestion of Sider's), then, Sider says, rubber workers would get higher wages. Fine. But wouldn't rubber producers scramble to increase production? And wouldn't land and labor be diverted from other enterprises, such as food production, to cash in on higher rubber prices? Since we don't need more rubber, the increased production would represent a waste of resources. Sider seems not to notice such consequences.[3]

Robert Frykenberg, a professor of history at the University of Wisconsin, is another Evangelical critic of Sider. Writing in *Christianity Today,* Frykenberg points out that it is easy for writers like Sider to announce that the world's poor need food and help. Sider stops short, however, of the much more difficult task of describing some effective and realistic way of meeting those needs:

> But without showing us exactly how the world's hungry are to be fed, nothing results except the mouthing of pious platitudes and highly emotional exhortations to act. Such well-meaning efforts

to help are at best inefficient and wasteful, and, at worst, utterly self-defeating and demoralizing. Often, like the children's crusades, they end up doing more harm than good.[4]

Good Intentions, Bad Solutions

Sider's book typifies the approach that many contemporary Evangelicals take toward social problems. There is no question about the fact that they care. But their compassion is often wedded to a political and economic ideology that is long on heart and short on wisdom. The emotional side of Evangelical social concern—loving and caring—is only half the story. The best intentions cannot aid the poor unless they are channeled into actions that are informed by sound economic theory and practice. When "aid" is grounded on bad economics, it will usually make any bad situation worse.

All of this obviously leads to a question: What exactly constitutes sound economic and social theory? It should come as no revelation that this question is the basis of a dispute that divides Evangelicals and millions of Christians into several camps. It should also come as no surprise that these divisions parallel ideologies that separate non-Christian thinkers. There was a day—not too long ago actually—when the options espoused by Evangelicals were few and fairly simple to identify. Some Evangelicals were political conservatives, while others were liberals. Hardly anyone knew for sure what these labels meant, but conservatives and liberals had little difficulty applying the labels to people.

Suddenly the world has become a far more complex place. One can now hear Evangelicals identifying themselves as socialists, and even, in the case of a few radicals, as Marxists. As Klaus Bockmuehl explains:

> Marxism in the West today has become a potent temptation for gifted, forward-looking young Christians, Evangelicals among them. They are fascinated not so much by its radical secular humanism as by its socialism. Because Evangelicals have little knowledge of Marxism, they identify Marxism with social reform and regard it as an energetic attempt to realize liberty, equality and fraternity, or simply claim that Marxists are 'for the poor.'[5]

The current debate on social issues among Evangelicals is

characterized by a noticeable swing to the Left on the part of many Evangelical intellectuals. Almost without exception, the major Evangelical books about social justice since 1960 have been authored by writers who condemn political conservatism as a cruel, heartless, and uncaring philosophy out of step with the Bible. Most recent Evangelical publications on the subject insist that the Christian's undisputed obligation to demonstrate love for the needy obliges him to adopt liberal statist means to aid the poor. This assertion is supplemented by allegations that, because political conservativism lacks compassion for the poor, and allegedly fails to support programs to alleviate poverty, hunger, and need, conservatism is unacceptable to the Evangelical.[6]

The Meaning of Justice

Basic to the Evangelical theory that finds liberalism, socialism, or even Marxism attractive is an appeal to social justice. Lewis Smedes, for example, justifies his political liberalism "not on the basis of compassion, but on the basis of justice."[7] Vernon Grounds criticizes politically conservative Christians for what he describes as their casual indifference to social injustice.[8] Grounding one's own position on an appeal to social justice as these Evangelical leaders do carries a built-in advantage. As Antonio Martino points out, the expression "social justice"

> . . . owes its immense popularity precisely to its ambiguity and meaninglessness. It can be used by different people, holding quite different views, to designate a wide variety of different things. Its obvious appeal stems from its persuasive strength, from its positive connotation, which allows the user to praise his own ideas and simultaneously express contempt for the ideas of those who don't agree with him.[9]

After all, when a political liberal praises social justice, it seems to follow that anyone who disagrees with him must favor injustice. Once this notion is established, it is but a short step to the conclusion that anyone who disagrees with the liberal's noble goals must be dishonorable. Martino does not question the sincerity of those who appeal so fervently to social justice:

> It cannot be denied that advocates of 'social justice' are quite often motivated by lofty ideals. Such is the case, for example, of

> those who are genuinely concerned about poverty and the need to do something about it. Their sincere compassion for the poor is undoubtedly a noble sentiment, and it deserves respect and admiration. However, their belief that the way to help the poor is by remodelling the whole of society (according to their preferred general plan) is more likely to hurt everybody than to achieve their aim.[10]

Martino warns about the ease with which the phrase "social justice" can be used in support of political measures harmful to individual liberty:

> The expression 'social justice' is more popular among advocates of statism than it is among individualists, since it is often used to justify (and praise) faith in the omnipotence of government. In this respect, it is intended to provide the 'moral' justification for what Sir Karl Popper calls 'holistic social engineering.'[11]

Serious questions can be raised about the liberal Evangelical's grasp of the complex social, political, and economic foundations of justice. The liberal Evangelical is often inattentive to important distinctions in the notion of justice: he fails to see how his claims draw him into an unavoidable and dangerous dependence upon a coercive state; he is blind to the fact that many of his preferred programs to help the poor end up being self-defeating; and he is unaware of the confusion that pervades his interpretation of the biblical teaching about justice. It is therefore important to challenge the liberal assumption that social, political, and economic conservatism is necessarily tied to a lack of compassion for the poor. Many Evangelicals who are politically conservative oppose liberalism precisely because they believe that liberal programs end up by doing far more harm than good to the poor.

A 'Social' Religion

One interesting feature of the liberal Evangelical's infatuation with statism is the affection with which it is held by many clergymen. Friedrich Hayek is struck by the fact that much of the current interest in so-called social justice occurs in clergy "who, while increasingly losing their faith in a supernatural revelation, appear to have sought a refuge and consolation in a new 'social' religion which substitutes a temporal for a celestial promise of justice, and who hope that they can thus continue their striving to do good."[12]

Several theologically liberal Christian organizations have, for example, made large donations in the name of "social justice" to terrorists groups in Africa and Latin America. Liberal Evangelical social activists who are theologically conservative have not yet done anything this extreme, but they nonetheless believe that the Christian's social responsibility requires liberal and statist means of aiding the poor. Some even cast aspersions about the genuineness of a religious commitment that does not openly embrace a statist approach to social justice.

The notion of justice appears frequently in the Scriptures. But the biblical word "justice" has a variety of meanings. It is therefore disconcerting to hear liberal Evangelicals quote a biblical text containing the word "justice," but ignore all questions about the particular meaning of the term in its context. The liberal Evangelical simply presumes that the verse functions as a proof-text for his position. For example, many Bible passages refer not to distributive justice but to remedial justice. This is clearly true in the case of Exodus 23:6, which warns against depriving the poor man of justice, but emphasizes that the justice in view is that found in a court of law. The same chapter (Exodus 23:3) also warns against showing partiality toward the poor in a court of law.

Interpretation and Application of Scripture

One recurring error in many attempts to support a particular ideology with biblical texts that mention justice is the failure to distinguish between the *interpretation* of a verse and its *application*. For this reason, the writings of liberation theologians and Evangelical social activists should be carefully studied. Anxious to make their point, such writers often quote a particular passage and jump immediately to what they regard as its self-evident application. In doing so, they skip important questions about the interpretation of the text. A good example of this is an article by Eric Beversluis in *Christian Scholar's Review*.[13] Beversluis quotes Exodus 22:26–27, which states that, if a neighbor has turned over his cloak as collateral for a loan, and if that neighbor has no other way to protect himself from the cold, then the person holding the cloak should make it available during times when it is needed. The interpretation of the passage poses no special problems, but Beversluis leaps at once to his application: "A person has a right to the material goods she or he needs for a decent existence. Thus the Bible teaches that there are rights to specific kinds of economic goods, and that these rights bind governments as well as individuals."[14] Most readers of Beversluis's article would be surprised at the ease with which he gets all this from those two simple verses. Many will conclude, with justification, that he simply reads his position into the texts. Obviously, whatever he is doing, it is not exegesis.

The most obvious application of Exodus 22:26–27 suggests that, if a persons loans money and the borrower assigns as collateral for the loan something that he subsequently needs to meet some temporary emergency, then the lender has an obligation not to withhold that which the borrower needs. But what does Beversluis extract from the text? He has used the passage to support a theory of state-enforced economic redistribution. Though it may be true that people have economic rights that bind governments, such an idea cannot be found in Exodus 22:26–27.

So, one important hermeneutical principle commonly ignored by Evangelical social activists is the distinction between interpretation and application. Another principle that gets short-changed in their treatment of Scripture is the importance of reading a passage in the light of its context. Beversluis does not say anything in his article about other related verses in Exodus 22; his silence is understandable. Since the entire chapter contains a large number of other injunctions, it is interesting to speculate how many of them should also be sanctioned by Beversluis's notion of government. Exodus 22:18–20 is a good example. If Beversluis handled these three verses in the same way he treats verses 26–27, his contemporary state would be obliged to execute witches, sexual perverts, and idolaters. As Jacob Petuchowski of Hebrew-Union College pointed out several years ago:

> It becomes a matter of biblical exegesis and hermeneutics to determine whether or not the biblical texts, originally addressed to a primitive agrarian society, really commit the latter-day believer to an espousal of socialism in the modern world. . . . Still it is quite possible to produce one-sided and partisan collections of biblical and rabbinic proof-texts which would

> clearly demonstrate that religion commits us to this or that political program or social action platform.[15]

Universal and Particular Justice

Much of the confusion in liberal Evangelicals' attempt to locate a simple theory of distributive justice in the Bible results from their inattention to the classical distinction between a universal and particular sense of justice. Because of this inattention, many Evangelical appeals to biblical uses of "justice" are compromised since they simply assume that biblical endorsements of justice are divine commands to support economic redistribution. This kind of error is illustrated in Robert Johnston's book, *Evangelicals at an Impasse*. Johnston writes:

> Although it is not the Bible's purpose to give a careful scientific definition of what our 'needs' are, Scripture does repeatedly identify justice with assistance for the poor, the sick, and the powerless.[16]

Johnston emphasizes Job 29:14–17, and then cites several other texts where the notion of justice is conjoined with helping the poor (Jeremiah 22:15–16; Deuteronomy 10:12–22; Psalms 103:6; Psalms 146:7–9). Such verses prove, in Johnston's judgment, that biblical justice is closely related to an economic redistribution that will meet the needs of the poor and the helpless.

It is certainly not my intent to challenge the belief that God cares for the poor and helpless. The question is whether Johnston and other Evangelical liberals correctly interpret Scripture. In this case, it seems that they do not. Is Job 29:14–17 an endorsement of the kind of coercive redistribution of people's holdings that is essential to liberal statism? The obvious point to the text flows from the distinction between universal and particular senses of justice. "Justice" is frequently used in classical times as a synonym for personal righteousness. In that universal sense, justice did indeed entail a possession of all the other major virtues *including* helping the poor. It is not surprising, therefore, that Scripture repeatedly mentions justice in contexts that also refer to love, to helping the poor, and to giving food to the hungry. But are these biblical appeals to the kind of universal "justice" that is synonymous with personal righteousness, or are they references to a particular theory of distributive justice? Obviously, they are the former. What the text in Job teaches is that God expects every truly righteous person to care about the poor and to help them. But it begs the question to maintain that this concern can be expressed only by endorsing the coercive and redistributory statism of contemporary collectivist approaches to justice. Evangelical liberals therefore ignore the several different senses of "justice" because they simply assume that the kind of justice mentioned in their proof-texts is distributive justice.

The line of argument against Robert Johnston's proof-texts has been criticized by Eric Beversluis.[17] Beversluis thinks he discovers a fatal flaw in the argument by suggesting that "particular justice" is actually only a species of "universal justice." It deserves careful consideration. To do so, Aristotle's discussion of justice is a good starting point because it distinguishes among the types of justice:

UNIVERSAL JUSTICE

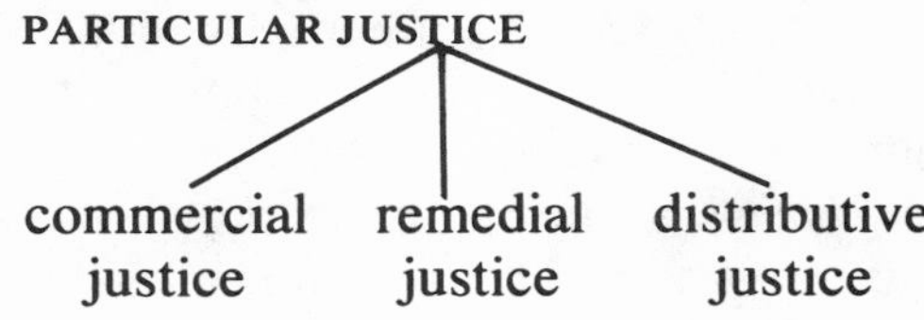

While the word "justice" is now seldom used in Aristotle's universal sense, his usage was very common in the ancient world. Plato said much about it in his *Republic* and, of course, it appears prominently in the Bible. "Universal justice" is synonymous with "personal righteousness" and might be called *justice as virtue*. When the Bible says that Noah was a just man, it doesn't mean he voted the straight Democratic ticket: it simply means he was a virtuous man. "Particular justice" is especially concerned with "fairness." The man or woman who is "just" in Aristotle's particular sense is one who does not seek more than a fair share. Particular justice is, therefore, *justice as fairness*. Fairness comes into play in many areas of life. Identifying three contexts in which particular justice is especially important, Aristotle referred to "commercial, remedial, and distributive" justice—namely, justice in economic exchanges, in courts of law, and in situations in which some good or burden is to be distributed between two or more people.

'Treating People Fairly'

Two questions must now be asked: First, what is the relationship between "particular justice" on the one hand and, on the other, "commercial, remedial, and distributive justice"? The answer is that all three are species of "particular justice." Particular justice means treating people fairly. Commercial, remedial, and distributive justice are three different settings in which the question of fair treatment arises. Second, what is the relationship between "universal" and "particular" justice? Beversluis simply assumes that particular justice is a species of universal justice. This leads him to write: "Clearly the particular virtue of justice . . . is *part of* universal justice. . . . But then if the Bible mandates universal justice, it thereby mandates its parts, including distributive (economic) justice."[18] Perhaps Beversluis got confused by Aristotle's labels. It might be easy to suppose that Aristotle called one kind of justice "particular justice" because he viewed it as a part of universal justice. But the supposition is mistaken. Universal justice is universal because it is a kind of justice that can be practiced by all human beings: it is not necessary for a person to occupy a particular role, or be in a particular situation, in order to be personally righteous. One can therefore be just in Aristotle's universal sense whether or not he is a businessman, a judge, or someone charged with the responsibility of distributing some good. Universal justice is universal because it is the standard of conduct for every human being, that is, it is supposed to be universal in scope.

Being virtuous should not depend upon one's being in a particular type of situation. But particular justice is situational in the sense that people can practice these kinds of justice if—and only if—they are in a particular type of situation. A person can practice commercial justice if—and only if—he is involved in an economic exchange. A person can practice remedial justice if—and only if—he occupies one of several possible roles with regard to criminal or civil law. And a person can practice distributive justice if—and only if—he is in a situation in which he is involved in the distribution of some good or some burden. The reason why commercial, remedial, and distributive justice are types of particular justice, then, is that they are possible only for people in particular situations. Beversluis's claim that particular justice is a species of universal justice is therefore mistaken.

It may help to point out, with regard to the forms of particular justice, that a distinction can be drawn between *practicing justice* and *promoting justice*. The various kinds of particular justice can be *practiced* only by people who occupy certain positions or fill certain roles. But all of us can do things that will *promote* the various kinds of particular justice. We can, for example, promote remedial justice by working for the election of honest and competent judges.

The Influence of Love

A consideration of the Bible's teaching about justice eventually turns to a consideration of the relationship between justice and love. In some senses, obviously, love and justice are closely related. But serious questions about the relationship of love and justice can arise in cases in which justice is viewed as a necessary trait of governmental action—for example, criminal justice or governmental control over the distribution of some good or burden. It often seems in such cases that Evangelical liberals are prone to a confusion of justice and love. They forget that, by its very nature, the state is an institution of coercion that operates by the use of force. Furthermore, if the state is to appear just, it must operate impersonally. Not to act impersonally would be to discriminate among persons. To the extent that governmental regulation and action is relevant to the particular senses of justice, that justice can be effected only through a state which uses force that is dispensed impersonally in accordance with law. But this analysis of justice conflicts with the nature of love.

Love, by definition, must be given voluntarily: no one can be forced to love, whereas the state always must resort to coercion. Moreover, love is always personal in the sense that it is directed to specific individuals. Such discrimination on the part of the state, however, would be an injustice. Finally, love should be willing to sacrifice, to go beyond the ordinary moral and legal requirements of a situation. A necessarily coercive state cannot serve as an instrument of love. The state's required use of force is incompatible with the nature and demands of love. As soon as the coercive state enters the picture, love must leave.

When the Evangelical statist confuses love with justice, he is doing more than simply urging others in society to manifest a compassionate love for the needy. He is in effect demanding that the state force people to fulfill the demands of love. Christians have often made the mistake of encouraging the state to use its vast powers of coercion to help attain their ends. The specter of the Inquisition is the most familiar example. No Christian should favor compulsion in bringing people to theological commitment. But is voluntarism any less essential to social virtue? The political liberal's statist approach ignores *giving,* and places all its emphasis on *receiving*—on who gets what. Given the nature of statism, *giving* is of course supplanted by *taking*—a taking effected by the state through its powers of taxation.

The Year of Jubilee

Almost every Christian liberal or socialist who writes about social justice refers, sooner or later, explicitly or implicitly, to the Old Testament notion of the Year of Jubilee in Leviticus 25:

> Count off seven sabbaths of years—seven times seven years—so that the seven sabbaths of years amount to a period of forty-nine years. Then have the trumpet sounded everywhere on the tenth day of the seventh month; on the Day of Atonement sound the trumpet throughout your land. Consecrate the fiftieth year and proclaim liberty throughout the land to all its inhabitants. It shall be a jubilee for you; each one of you is to return to his family property and each to his own clan. The fiftieth year shall be a jubilee for you; do not sow and do not reap what grows of itself or harvest the untended vines. For it is a jubilee and is to be holy for you; eat only what is taken directly from the fields. (Leviticus 25:8-12).

Stephen Charles Mott sees the Jubilee Year as a divine endorsement of egalitarianism.[19] The fact that, under certain conditions, land would revert to the family of the original owners every fifty years could appear to support the kind of egalitarian redistribution favored by many liberals. Before that conclusion is asserted dogmatically, however, the entire chapter should be carefully studied in the light of accepted hermeneutical procedures. For example, care should be exercised to distinguish between the interpretation of the text and its possible applications to cultural settings that differ in important respects. Moreover, the *entire* chapter should be studied: one should not simply extract from the passage those verses that appear to support an egalitarian redistribution of holdings, but ignore other verses that suggest something quite different. Finally, serious attention should be given to such questions as these: did Israel ever institute the Jubilee Year? If not, why not? How relevant are principles originally given to a largely agrarian people to the totally different economic and cultural situations of contemporary nations?

A careful examination of Leviticus 25 suggests that many liberation theologians and Christian liberals who appeal to the passage give the chapter a highly selective reading. For one thing, the intended redistribution every fifty years did not affect every form of wealth. The only forms of wealth that were affected were slaves and land outside walled cities.[20] It is important to note that some land was unaffected by the principles of the Jubilee Year. Sold property within walled cities could be redeemed within a year. After the passage of a year, the exchange was regarded as permanent and immune to the changes otherwise affected by the Jubilee (Lev. 25:29–30). Other forms of income, such as fishing boats, also were excluded from the Jubilee practice. Though it may be true that land was the most prevalent and important basis of wealth in ancient Israel, the fact that several forms of wealth were excluded from redistribution in the Jubilee is usually slighted in the writings of liberation and liberal Evangelical theologians.

It is also true that the Jubilee did not benefit all the poor. It did not, for example, help immigrants who had no original inheritance. Moreover, given the relatively short life span of people in those days, the fifty-year interval between Jubilees made it inevitable that many people (those born after one Jubilee who died before the next) were never helped at all. Many theologians who are enthusiastic about the Jubilee concept also forget an important fact about a vital effect the Jubilee would have had on such economic activity as the buying and selling of land: Had the Jubilee ever been observed, it would have terminated the buying and selling of land as we know it in favor of leases made more or less valuable by the number of years remaining until the next Jubilee. Under such conditions, anyone contemplating the acquisition of land would know that he was buying the use of the land only for a certain number of years. Land would thus be most valuable in the first years immediately following a Jubilee, but would be worth relatively little in the years just before a Jubilee.

Many liberal claims about the Jubilee are therefore exaggerated. If the Jubilee's purpose was to encourage and endorse an egalitarian redistribution of wealth, why were some important forms of wealth unaffected? Why were some of the poor not included? Why was the distribution scheduled at such distant intervals as to leave unhelped many people who were born and died between Jubilees? Is it important that the Jubilee could not have been instituted outside Palestine?[21] Is it important that, for all that anyone knows, the Jubilee was never instituted within Palestine? Is it relevant that the principles of the Jubilee could not possibly be instituted today—even within Palestine?

One of the most surprising things about the current interest in finding biblical passages that support a collectivist ideology is this: while many liberal theologians exhibit great ingenuity in discovering hitherto unrecognized implications in ambiguous Old Testament passages, hardly any of them bother to look at several clear texts in the New Testament. Consider just one:

> Now we command you, brethren, in the name of our Lord Jesus Christ, that you keep away from any brother who is living in idleness and not in accord with the tradition that you received from us. For you yourselves know how you ought to imitate us; we were not idle when we were with you, we did not eat any one's bread without paying, but with toil and labor, we worked night and day, that we might not burden any of you. . . . For even when we were with you, we gave you this command: if any one will not work, let him not eat. For we hear that some of you are living in idleness, mere busybodies, not doing any work. Now such persons we command and exhort in the Lord Jesus Christ to do their work in quietness and to earn their own living.[22]

One final observation: some Evangelical social liberals attempt to use the doctrine of Christian stewardship in the service of their ideology. No believer should deny that God is the ultimate owner of all we possess; we are simply stewards or trustees of what He has blessed us with. But some Evangelical liberals twist the doctrine of stewardship into the view that the believer must surrender his will and judgment in regard to his holdings to God's surrogate on earth, that is, the state. Once again, the liberal Evangelical seems incapable of discovering any alternative means to his otherwise worthy ends than giving the state more power and control over the lives of its citizens.

Liberal Evangelicals' attempts to ground a statist approach to justice on the Bible leave much to be desired. Their efforts often exhibit questionable hermeneutical principles and are often inattentive to the classical distinction between a universal and particular sense of justice. Because of the nature of universal justice, it is a simple matter to find justice conjoined in Scripture with love, charity, kindness to the poor, and help for the hungry. But it is irresponsible to infer from these statements that God endorses any contemporary theory of distributive justice.

NOTES

1. Benjamin Rogge, "Christian Economics: Myth or Reality?" in *The Freeman,* December 1965.

2. Ronald Sider, *Rich Christians in an Age of Hunger* (Downers Grove, Illinois: Intervarsity Press, 1977).

3. George Mavrodes, "On Helping the Hungry," in *Christianity Today,* December 30, 1977, p. 46.

4. Robert Frykenberg, "World Hunger: Food is Not the Answer," in *Christianity Today,* December 11, 1981, p. 36.

5. Taken from Klaus Bockmuehl, *The Challenge of Marxism* (Downers Grove, Illinois: Intervarsity Press, 1980), and used with permission.

6. Books that illustrate how easily Christian sentiments can be used to support collectivist policies include J. Philip Wogaman, *The Great Economic Debate: An Ethical Analysis* (Philadelphia: Westminster Press, 1977); Larry L. Rasmussen, *Economic Anxiety and Christian Faith* (Minneapolis: Augsburg Press, 1981); David M. Beckmann, *Where Faith and Economics Meet* (Minneapolis: Augsburg, 1981); and Stephen Charles Mott, *Biblical Ethics and Social Change* (New York: Oxford, 1982). Of these, perhaps only Mott would insist on being called an Evangelical. While earlier Evangelical criticisms of political conservatism seldom

demonstrated competence in economics, they repeated charges that political conservatives lacked compassion. See Robert G. Clouse, *The Cross and the Flag* (Carol Stream, Illinois: Creation House, 1972); Richard V. Pierard, *The Unequal Yoke* (Philadelphia: J. B. Lippincott, 1970); Vernon Grounds, *Evangelicalism and Social Responsibility* (Scottsdale, Pennsylvania: Herald Press, 1969); and Donald Dayton, *Discovering an Evangelical Heritage* (New York: Harper and Row, 1976). They contain repeated warnings about the dangers present in any alliance between Christianity and political conservatism, but it is clear that what they call political conservatism is some kind of radical extremism of the right that bears little resemblance to responsible conservatism.

7. Lewis B. Smedes, "Where Do We Differ?" in *Reformed Journal,* May-June, 1966, p. 10.

8. Vernon Grounds, *Evangelicalism and Social Responsibility,* p. 4.

9. Antonio Martino, "The Myth of Social Justice," in Arnold Beichman, Antonio Martino, and Kenneth Minogue, *Three Myths* (Washington, D.C.: Heritage Foundation, 1982), p. 23.

10. Ibid., p. 24.

11. Ibid., p. 23.

12. Friedrich Hayek, *Law, Legislation, and Liberty,* Vol. II (Chicago: University of Chicago Press, 1976) p. 66.

13. Eric Beversluis, "Christianity, Economic Justice, and the State," in *Christian Scholar's Review,* Fall 1982.

14. Ibid.

15. Jacob J. Petuchowski, "The Altar-Throne Clash Updated," in *Christianity Today,* September 23, 1977, p. 20.

16. Robert K. Johnston, *Evangelicals at an Impasse* (Atlanta: John Knox Press, 1979), p. 99.

17. Johnston's procedure is similar to that of several liberation theology proponents, and also to that by Stephen Charles Mott in his paper, "Egalitarian Aspects of the Biblical Theory of Justice," in *Selected Papers of the American Society of Christian Ethics,* 1978.

18. Eric Beversluis, "Christianity, Economic Justice, and the State," errs in equating distributive and economic justice. Many instances of distributive justice such as the distribution of grades in a philosophy class have nothing to do with economics.

19. Stephen Charles Mott, *Biblical Ethics and Social Change* (New York: Oxford), 1982, Chapter 4.

20. Israelites who had been sold into slavery would not be freed in the Jubilee. Slaves who were not Israelites would not be freed.

21. This is the case because of the original allotment of the land to the tribes of Israel.

22. II Thessalonians 3:6. See also I Thessalonians 4:10–11, and Ephesians 4:28.

8. *An Evangelical Theology of Liberation*

By RONALD J. SIDER

Focus

Arguing that Evangelical theologians have ignored the radical imperatives of the Bible, Ronald Sider suggests that the central teaching of the Scriptures is that "God is on the side of the poor and oppressed." Sider declares that, by largely ignoring this teaching, "Evangelical theology has been profoundly unorthodox."

Sider contrasts the emerging movement known as "liberation theology" with what he calls a genuinely Evangelical theology of liberation. He stresses three points: "First, at the central points of revelation history, God acted to liberate the poor and oppressed. Second, God acts in history to exalt the poor and oppressed and to cast down the rich and oppressive. Third, God's people, if they are truly God's people, are also on the side of the poor and oppressed."

To support his position, Sider offers interpretations of three episodes in biblical history. In leading Israel on its Exodus from captivity in Egypt, God revealed both His opposition to oppression and His liberation of the poor. In subjecting Israel to subsequent enslavement in Babylon, God punished His people for their economic exploitation and mistreatment of the poor. Finally, in the Incarnation, Jesus Christ further demonstrated God's concern for the poor by preaching "good news to the poor" and "release to the captives."

Sider chides Evangelicals for abandoning the examples set by John Wesley, Charles Finney, and William Wilberforce in the eighteenth and nineteenth centuries. All three, he points out, focused on "justice for the poor." Evangelicals today have largely sided with the "rich oppressors" against the "oppressed poor," and are therefore unbiblical. Current Evangelical theology, Sider argues, is determined by the "economic preferences of our materialistic contemporaries rather than by Scripture. We have allowed the values of our affluent materialistic society to shape our thinking."

This selection should be compared with Ronald Nash's perspective (selection 7) on biblical responsibilities and economic justice.

Ronald J. Sider is an associate professor of theology at Eastern Baptist Theological Seminary, chairman of Evangelicals for Social Action, and the author of *Rich Christians in an Age of Hunger* (Inter-Varsity, 1984).

THE EMERGENCE OF theologies of liberation—whether black, feminist, or Latin American—is probably the most significant theological development of our time. At the heart of liberation theology is the attempt to rethink theology from the standpoint of the poor and oppressed. The central theological foundation of this approach is the thesis that God is on the side of the poor and oppressed.

It is that basic thesis that I want to probe. In doing so, I want to answer two questions: How biblical is the view that God is on the side of the poor and the oppressed? and, in light of the answer to this first question, how biblical is evangelical theology?

One of the central biblical doctrines is that God is on the side of the poor and the oppressed. Tragically, evangelical theology has largely ignored this central biblical doctrine and thus our theology has been unbiblical—indeed even heretical. I do not mean that material poverty is a biblical ideal. This glorious creation is a wonderful gift from our Creator. He wants us to revel in its glory and splendor. I also do not mean that the poor and oppressed are, because they are poor and oppressed, to be idealized or automatically included in the church. The poor sinfully disobey God in the same way that wretched middle-class sinners do, and they therefore need to enter into a living personal relationship with Jesus Christ. Only then do they become a part of the church.

One of the serious weaknesses in much of liberation theology is an inadequate ecclesiology, especially the tendency to blur the distinction between the church and the world. And one can understand why. It is understandable that black and Latin American theologians would be impressed by the double fact that, whereas most of the organized church regularly ignores the injustice that causes poverty and oppression, those who do care enough to risk their lives for improved conditions are often people who explicitly reject Christianity. Hence one can understand why someone like Hugo Assmann would conclude that:

Reprinted by permission of Baker Book House from *Perspectives on Evangelical Theology,* edited by Kenneth S. Kantzer and Stanley Gundry, 1981.

> the true Church is "the conscious emergence and the more explicit enacting of the one meaning of the one history," in other words, a revolutionary consciousness and commitment. The explicit reference to Jesus Christ becomes in this view gratuitous in the original sense of the word—something which is not demanded by or needed for the struggle [of socio-economic liberation]. . . . The reference to Jesus Christ does not add an "extra" to the historical struggle but is totally and without rest identified with it.[1]

In spite of deep appreciation for the factors that lead the church to identify with the poor and oppressed, or with the revolutionary minority that seeks liberation for them, one must insist that such a view is fundamentally unbiblical.

When I say that God is on the side of the poor and oppressed, then, I do not mean that God cares more about the salvation of the poor than the salvation of the rich, or that the poor have a special claim to the gospel. It is sheer nonsense to say with Enzo Gatti:

> The human areas that are poorest in every way are the most qualified for receiving the Saving Word. They are the ones that have the best right to that Word; they are the privileged recipients of the Gospel.[2]

God cares equally about the salvation of the rich and the poor. To be sure, at the psychological level, Gatti is partly correct. Church growth theorists have discovered what Jesus alluded to long ago in his comment on the camel and the eye of a needle. It *is* extremely difficult for rich persons to enter the kingdom. The poor *are* generally more ready to accept the gospel than the rich.[3] But that does not mean that God desires the salvation of the poor more than the salvation of the rich.

Justice for the Poor

To say that God is on the side of the poor is also not to say that knowing God is nothing more than seeking justice for the poor and oppressed. Some—although certainly not most—liberation theologians do jump to this radical conclusion. José Miranda, for example, says bluntly: "To know Jaweh is to achieve justice for the poor."[4] "The God who does not allow himself to be objectified, because only in the immediate command of conscience is he God, clearly specifies that he is knowable *exclusively* in the cry of the poor and the weak who seek justice."[5] Tragically, Miranda's one-sided, reductionist approach offers comfortable North Americans a plausible excuse for ignoring the radical biblical Word that seeking justice for the poor is inseparable from—even though it is not identical with—knowing Yahweh.

Finally, when I say that God is on the side of the poor, I do not mean that hermeneutically we must start with some ideologically interpreted context of oppression (for instance, a Marxist definition of the poor and their oppressed situation), and then reinterpret Scripture from that ideological perspective. Black theologian James H. Cone's developing thought is interesting at this point. In 1969, in *Black Theology and Black Power,* he wrote:

> "The fact that I am Black is my ultimate reality." My identity with *blackness,* and what it means for millions living in a white world, controls the investigation. It is impossible for me to surrender this basic reality for a "higher more universal reality."[6]

By the time Cone wrote *God of the Oppressed,* however, he realized that such a view would relativize all theological claims including his own critique of white racist theology:

> How do we distinguish our words about God from God's Word. . . ? Unless this question is answered satisfactorily, black theologians' distinction between white theology and Black Theology is vulnerable to the white contention that the latter is merely the ideological justification of radical black polities.[7]

To be sure, Cone believes as strongly as other liberation theologians that the hermeneutical key to Scripture is God's saving action to liberate the oppressed. But how does he know that?

> In God's revelation in Scripture we come to the recognition that the divine liberation of the oppressed is not determined by our perceptions but by the God of the Exodus, the prophets, and Jesus Christ who calls the oppressed into a liberated existence. Divine revelation *alone* is the test of the validity of this starting point. And if it can be shown that God as witnessed in the Scriptures is not the liberator of the oppressed, then Black Theology would have either to drop the "Christian" designation or to choose another starting point.[8]

One can only wish that all liberation theologians agreed with Cone!

When then I say that God is on the side of the poor, I do not mean that poverty is the ideal; that the poor and oppressed are the church or have a special right to hear the gospel; nor that seeking justice for the oppressed is identical with knowing Yahweh; nor that one should begin with some ideologically interpreted context of oppression and then reinterpret Scripture from that perspective.

In what sense then *is* God on the side of the poor and oppressed? I want to develop three points:[9] first, that at the central points of revelation history, God also acted to liberate the poor and oppressed; second, that God acts in history to exalt the poor and oppressed and to cast down the rich and oppressive; third, that God's people are also on the side of the poor and oppressed.

To support these points, I refer to the exodus, the destruction of Israel and Judah, and the Incarnation. At each of these central moments when God displayed his mighty acts in history to reveal his nature and will, God also intervened to liberate the poor and oppressed.

God displayed his power at the exodus in order to free oppressed slaves. When God called Moses at the burning bush, he informed Moses of his intention to end suffering and injustice: "I have seen the affliction of my people who are in Egypt, and have heard their cry because of their taskmasters; I know their sufferings, and I have come down to deliver them out of the hand of the Egyptians" (Exod. 3:7–8). Each year at the harvest festival, the Israelites repeated a liturgical confession celebrating the way God had acted to free a poor, oppressed people:

> A wandering Aramean was my father; and he went down into Egypt and sojourned there. . . . And the Egyptians treated us harshly and afflicted us, and laid upon us hard bondage. Then we cried to the Lord, the God of our fathers, and the Lord heard our voice, and saw our affliction, our toil, and our oppression; and the Lord brought us out of Egypt with a mighty hand . . . (Deut. 26:5ff).

Lessons of the Exodus

Unfortunately, some liberation theologians see in the exodus only God's liberation of an oppressed people and miss the fact that God also acted to fulfill his promises to Abraham, to reveal his will, and to call out a special people. Certainly God acted at the exodus to call a special people so that through them he could reveal his will and bring salvation to all people. But his will included the fact—as he revealed ever more clearly to his covenant people—that his people should follow him and side with the poor and oppressed. The fact that Yahweh did not liberate all poor Egyptians at the exodus does not mean that he was not concerned for the poor everywhere, just as the fact that he did not give the Ten Commandments to everyone in the Near East does not mean that he did not intend them to have universal significance. Because God chose to reveal himself in history, he disclosed to a particular people at a particular time what he willed for all people.

At the exodus, God acted to demonstrate that he is opposed to oppression. We distort the biblical interpretation of the momentous event of the exodus unless we see that the Lord of the universe was at work correcting oppression and liberating the poor.

The prophets' explanation for the later destruction of Israel and Judah underlines the same point. The explosive message of the prophets is that God destroyed Israel, not just because of Israel's idolatry (although certainly because of that), but also because of economic exploitation and mistreatment of the poor!

The middle of the eighth century B.C. was a time of political success and economic prosperity unknown since the days of Solomon. But it was precisely at this moment that God sent his prophet Amos to announce the unwelcome news that the northern kingdom of Israel would be destroyed. Why? Penetrating beneath the facade of current prosperity and fantastic economic growth, Amos saw terrible oppression of the poor. He saw the rich "trample the head of the poor into the dust of the earth" (Amos 2:7). He saw that the affluent lifestyle of the rich was built on oppression of the poor (Amos 6:1–7). Even in the courts the poor had no hope because the rich bribed the judges (Amos 5:10–15).

God's word through Amos was that the northern kingdom would be destroyed and the people taken into exile (Amos 7:11, 17). Only a very few years after Amos spoke, this happened just as God had prophesied. God destroyed the northern kingdom because of its mistreatment of the poor. The cataclysmic catastrophe of national destruction and captivity reveals the God of the exodus still at work correcting the oppression of the poor.

Jesus and the Poor

When God acted to reveal himself most completely in the Incarnation of God the Son, he continued to demonstrate his special concern for the poor and oppressed. St. Luke used the programmatic account of Jesus in the synagogue at Nazareth to define Jesus' mission. The words which Jesus read from the prophet Isaiah are familiar to us all:

> The Spirit of the Lord is upon me,
> because he has anointed me to preach good news to the poor.
> He has sent me to proclaim release to the captives
> and recovery of sight to the blind,
> to set at liberty those who are oppressed,
> to proclaim the acceptable year of the Lord (Luke 4:18–19).

After reading these words, Jesus informed the audience that this Scripture was now fulfilled in himself. The mission of the Incarnate One was to preach the good news to the poor and free the oppressed.

Many people spiritualize these words either by assuming that Jesus was talking about healing blinded hearts in captivity to sin, or by appealing to the Old Testament idea of "the poor of Yahweh." It is true that the Psalms and intertestamental literature use the terms for the poor to refer to pious, humble, and devout Israelites who place all their trust in Yahweh.[10] But that does not mean that Jesus' usage had no connection with socio-economic poverty. Indeed, it was precisely the fact that the economically poor and oppressed were the faithful remnant that trusted in Yahweh that led to the new usage by which the poor were the pious faithful.

The Hebrew words for the poor were *'ani, 'anaw, 'ebyon, dal,* and *raš*. *'Ani* (and *'anaw,* which originally had approximately the same basic meaning) denotes one who is "wrongfully impoverished or dispossessed."[11] *'Ebyon* refers to a beggar imploring charity. *Dal* connotes a thin, weakly person, e.g., an impoverished, deprived peasant.[12] Unlike the others, *raš* is an essentially neutral term. In their persistent polemic against the oppression of the poor, the prophets used the terms *'ebyon, 'ani,* and *dal.*

Later these same words were used to designate the faithful remnant, or the "pious poor" who trust solely in Yahweh.[13] But that does not mean that the older socio-economic connotations were lost. Richard Batey puts it this way:

> Beginning with the experience that the poor were often oppressed by the wicked rich, the poor were considered to be the special objects of Yahweh's protection and deliverance (Pss. 9:18, 19:1–8 . . .). Therefore the poor looked to Yahweh as the source of deliverance from their enemies and oppressors. This attitude of trust and dependence exemplified that piety that should have characterized every Israelite. In this way the concept of the "pious poor" developed.[14]

Zondervan's *New International Dictionary of the New Testament* makes the same point:

> Only in the setting of this historical situation can we understand the meaning in the Psalm of "poor" and "needy." The poor man is the one who suffers injustice; he is poor because others have despised God's law. He therefore turns, helpless and humble, to God in prayer. . . . Through the self-identification, generation after generation, of those who prayed with the poor in psalms of individual lamentation and thanksgiving . . . there gradually developed the specific connotation of "poor" as meaning all those who turn to God in great need and seek his help. God is praised as the protector of the poor (eg. Pss. 72:2, 4, 121; 132:15), who procures justice for them against their oppressors.[15]

This same usage is common in inter-testamental literature. When Greece and then Rome conquered Palestine, Hellenistic culture and values were imposed upon the Jews. Those who remained faithful to Yahweh often suffered financially. Thus the term "poor" was, as J. A. Ziesler says, "virtually equivalent to 'pious,' 'God-fearing,' and 'godly,' and reflects a situation where the rich were mainly those who had sold out to the incoming culture and had allowed their religious devotion to become corrupted by the new ways. If the poor were the pious, the faithful, and oppressed, the rich were the powerful, ungodly, worldly, even apostate."[16] Thus the faithful remnant at Qumran called themselves "the poor" (*'ebyon*).[17] And they and other first century Jews yearned eagerly for the new age when the Messiah would come to fulfill the messianic promises, for example, Isaiah 11:4, and bring justice to the poor.[18]

When Jesus read from Isaiah 61 in the synagogue at Nazareth and proclaimed good news to the poor, he was announcing to the faithful remnant who trusted in Yahweh, and therefore were also poor socio-economically, that the messianic age of justice for the poor had arrived.

Other aspects of Jesus' teaching support this interpretation. In the Gospel of Luke, the Beatitudes promise blessing to the poor and hungry. The messianic kingdom in which the pious, but therefore also socio-economically poor, will receive justice is now coming in the person of Jesus. Nor does Matthew represent a spiritualized version of the Beatitudes.[20] The poor "in spirit" are the pious poor who are also socio-economically deprived. They hunger and thirst for righteousness—i.e., justice! As Herman Ridderbos rightly insists, the word "righteousness" here "must not be understood in the Pauline forensic sense of imputed forensic righteousness, but as the kingly justice that will be brought to light one day for the salvation of the oppressed and the outcasts, and that will be executed especially by the Messiah. . . . It is this justice to which the 'poor in spirit' and 'the meek' look forward in the Sermon on the Mount."[21]

This is not to imply that Jesus' mission focused exclusively on socio-economic concerns. His message included a central concern for forgiving sinners and he came to die on the cross for the sins of the world. But to spiritualize Jesus' message is to overlook the fact that the mission of the Incarnate One was to bring justice to the poor and oppressed. Jesus' warning that those who do not feed the hungry, clothe the naked, and visit prisoners will experience eternal damnation (Matt. 25:31ff) does not represent a peripheral concern. It represents a central focus of his messianic mission.

At the supreme moment of history when God himself took on human flesh, we see the God of Israel liberating the poor and oppressed, and summoning his people to do the same.

Casting Down the Rich

The second aspect of the biblical teaching that God is on the side of the poor and oppressed is that God works in history to cast down the rich and to exalt the poor.

Mary's Magnificat puts it simply and bluntly:

> My soul magnifies the Lord. . . .
> He has put down the mighty from their thrones
> and exalted those of low degree;
> he has filled the hungry with good things,
> and the rich he has sent empty away (Luke 1:46–53).

In James 5:1 we read: "Come now, you rich, weep and howl for the miseries that are coming upon you." This is a constant theme of biblical revelation.

Why does Scripture declare that God regularly reverses the good fortunes of the rich? Is God engaged in class warfare? The texts never say that God loves the poor more than the rich. But they assert that God lifts up the poor and disadvantaged. The texts also insist that God casts down the wealthy and powerful. Why? Because, according to Scripture, the rich often become wealthy by oppressing the poor, and because the rich fail to feed the hungry.

Why did James warn the rich to weep and howl because of impending misery? Because they had cheated their workers: "You have laid up treasures for the last days. Behold, the wages of the laborers who mowed your fields, which you kept back by fraud, cry out; and the cries of the harvesters have reached the ears of the Lord of hosts. You have lived on the earth in luxury and in pleasure; you have fattened your hearts in a day of slaughter" (James 5:35). God does not have class enemies, but he hates and punishes injustice and neglect of the poor. The rich, if we accept the repeated warnings of Scripture, are frequently guilty of both.

Long before the days of James, Jeremiah also declared that the rich were often rich because of oppression (Jer. 5:26-29). Hosea and Micah made similar charges (Hosea 12:7-8; Micah 6:9-12).

One more example from Isaiah is important. Through his prophet Isaiah, God declared that the rulers of Judah were rich because they had cheated the poor. Surfeited with affluence, the wealthy women were wantonly oblivious to the suffering of the oppressed. The result, God said, would be devastating destruction (Isaiah 3:14). Because the rich oppress the poor and weak, the Lord of history is at work pulling down their houses and kingdoms.

The Sin of Sodom

Sometimes Scripture does not charge the rich with direct oppression of the poor, but accuses them of failure to share with the needy. But the condemnation is the same. The biblical explanation of Sodom's destruction provides one illustration of this terrible truth. When asked why Sodom was destroyed, virtually all Christians point to the city's gross sexual perversity. But that is a one-sided recollection of what Scripture actually teaches. Ezekiel shows that one important reason God destroyed Sodom was because she stubbornly refused to share with the poor! (Ezekiel 16:49-50). The text does not say that the people of Sodom oppressed the poor (although they probably did). It simply accuses them of failing to assist the needy.

The third aspect of the biblical teaching that God is on the side of the poor and oppressed is that the people of God, if they are really the people of God, are also on the side of the poor and oppressed. Those who neglect the poor and the oppressed are not really God's people—no matter how frequent their religious rituals or how orthodox their creeds. The prophets sometimes made this point by insisting that the knowledge of God and the service of justice for the oppressed are inseparable. At other times, the prophets condemned the religious rituals of oppressors who tried to worship God while continuing to oppress the poor, as in Jeremiah 22:13-16.

The same correlation between seeking justice for the poor and knowledge of God is clear in the messianic passage of Isaiah 11:1-9. Of the shoot of the stump of Jesse, the prophet says: "With righteousness he shall judge the poor and decide with equity for the meek of the earth." In this ultimate messianic shalom, "the earth shall be full of the knowledge of the Lord as the waters cover the sea" (Isaiah 11:9).

The prophets also announced God's outrage against worship in the context of mistreatment of the poor and disadvantaged. Isaiah denounced Israel (he called her Sodom and Gomorrah!) because she tried to worship Yahweh and oppress the weak at the same time (Isaiah 10–17).

God's words through the prophet Amos are also harsh. See, for example, Amos 5:21-24. Earlier in the same chapter, Amos condemned the rich and powerful for oppressing the poor. The rich bribed judges to prevent redress in the courts. God wants justice, not mere religious rituals, from such people. Otherwise their worship is a mockery and abomination.

God Has Not Changed

God has not changed. Jesus repeated the same theme. He warned about scribes who secretly oppress widows while making a public display of their piety. The scribes' pious-looking garments and frequent visits to the synagogue are a sham. Woe to religious hypocrites "who devour widows' houses and for a pretense make long prayers" (Mark 12:38–40). Like Amos and Isaiah, Jesus announced God's outrage against those who try to mix pious practices and mistreatment of the poor.

The prophetic word against religious hypocrites raises difficult questions: Are the people of God truly God's people if they oppress the poor? Is the church really the church if it does not work to free the oppressed?

God declared through Isaiah that the people of Israel were really Sodom and Gomorrah rather than the people of God. God simply could not tolerate their idolatry and their exploitation of the poor and disadvantaged any longer. Jesus was even more blunt and sharp. To those who do not feed the hungry, clothe the naked, and visit the prisoners, he will speak a terrifying word at the final judgment: "Depart from me, you cursed, into the eternal fire prepared for the devil and his angels" (Matt. 25:41). The meaning is clear and unambiguous: Jesus intends his disciples to imitate his concern for the poor and needy; those who disobey will receive eternal damnation.

But perhaps we have misinterpreted Matthew 25. Some people think that "the least of these" (verse 45) and "the least of these my brethren" (verse 40) refer only to Christians. This exegesis is not certain. But even if the primary reference of these words is to poor believers, other aspects of Jesus' teaching not only permit but require us to extend the meaning of Matthew 25 to both believers and unbelievers who are poor and oppressed. The story of the good Samaritan (Luke 10:29) teaches that anybody in need is our neighbor. Matthew 5:43 is even more explicit. Even in the Old Testament, Israelites were commanded to love the neighbor who was the son of their own people and ordered not to seek the prosperity of Ammonites and Moabites (Leviticus 19:17–18; Deuteronomy 23:3–6). Jesus explicitly forbids his followers to limit their loving concern to the neighbor who is a member of their own ethnic or religious group. He explicitly commands his followers to imitate God who does good for all people everywhere.

As George Ladd has said, "Jesus redefines the meaning of love for neighbor; it means love for any man in need."[21] In light of the parable of the Good Samaritan and the clear teaching of Matthew 5:43, it is clear that part of the full teaching of Matthew 25 is that those who fail to aid the poor and oppressed (whether they are believers or not) are simply not the people of God.

Lest we forget the warning, God repeats it in 1 John: "But if any one has the world's goods and sees his brother in need, yet closes his heart against him, how does God's love abide in him? Little children, let us not love in word or speech but in deed and truth" (I John 3:17–18). Again, the words are plain. What do they mean for Western Christians who demand increasing affluence each year while people in the Third World suffer malnutrition, deformed bodies and brains, even starvation? The text clearly says that if we fail to aid the needy, we do not have God's love—no matter what we may say.

Punishment for the Disobedient

But still the question persists: Are professing believers no longer Christians because of continuing sin? Obviously not. The Christian knows that sinful selfishness continues to plague even the most saintly. Christians are the people of God not because of their own righteousness, but solely because of Christ's atoning death.

That response is extremely important and very true. But all the texts from both testaments previously examined mean more than that the people of God are disobedient (but still justified all the same) when they neglect the poor. These verses pointedly assert that some people so disobey God that they are not his people at all—in spite of their pious profession. Neglect of the poor is one of the oft-repeated biblical signs of disobedience. There comes a point—and, thank God, He alone knows where!—when neglect of the poor is no longer forgiven. It is punished. Eternally.

God is on the side of the poor and oppressed. But that does not mean God is biased. More than once the Scriptures explicitly condemn bias toward the poor (Leviticus 19:15; Deuteronomy

1:17). God cares equally about all. Unlike God, however, many rich and powerful people care more about themselves than about the poor. By contrast with their partiality, God's impartiality looks like a bias, but it is not. It is simply a concern for justice for all. But this does not mean God is neutral. He is opposed to laziness, injustice, and neglect of the poor. Therefore God acts in history to pull down the rich and powerful who neglect the poor or become rich by oppression. It is in this sense that God is on the side of the poor and oppressed, seeking to empower them to have dignity, self-sufficiency, and the ability to share their lives.[22]

In light of this clear biblical teaching, how biblical is evangelical theology? Certainly there have been some great moments of faithfulness. John Wesley, William Wilberforce, and Charles Finney's evangelical abolitionists stood solidly in the biblical tradition in their search for justice for the poor and oppressed of their time. But the twentieth-century evangelical community is largely on the side of the rich oppressors rather than the oppressed poor. Imagine what would happen if evangelical institutions—youth organizations, publications, colleges, seminaries, congregations, and denominational headquarters—dared to undertake a comprehensive two-year examination of their total program and to answer this question: Is there the same balance and emphasis on justice for the poor and oppressed in Evangelical programs as there is in Scripture? If that were done with an unconditional readiness to change whatever did not correspond with the scriptural revelation of God's special concern for the poor and oppressed, evangelicals would unleash a new movement of biblical social concern that would change the course of modern history.

The Evangelicals' problem is not primarily one of ethics; it is not that Evangelicals fail to live as their teachers have taught. Evangelical theology has been unbiblical, and therefore heretical. James Cone is right when he says:

> When church theologians, from the time of Constantine to the present, failed to see the ethical impact of the biblical God for the liberation of the oppressed, that failure occurred because of defective theology. To understand correctly the church's ethical mistake, we must see it in connection with a prior theological mistake. . . . *Theologians of the Christian Church have not*

interpreted Christian ethics as an act for the liberation of the oppressed because their views of divine revelation were defined by philosophy and other cultural values rather than by the biblical theme of God as the liberator of the oppressed. . . . We cannot say that Luther, Calvin, Wesley, and other prominent representatives of the church's traditions were limited by their time, as if their ethical judgments on oppression did not affect the essential truth of their theologies. They were wrong ethically because they were wrong theologically. They were wrong theologically because they failed to listen to the Bible.[23]

Theological Error the Problem

By largely ignoring the central biblical teaching that God is on the side of the poor, Evangelical theology has been profoundly unorthodox. The Bible has just as much to say about this doctrine as it does about Jesus' resurrection, and yet Evangelicals insist on the resurrection as a criterion of orthodoxy, but largely ignore the equally prominent biblical teaching that God is on the side of the poor and the oppressed.

Evangelicals have fallen into theological liberalism. Of course they usually think of theological liberalism in terms of nineteenth-century liberalism that denied the deity, atoning death, and bodily resurrection of Jesus the Lord. People who abandon those central biblical doctrines have fallen into terrible heresy, but the essence of theological liberalism is in allowing Christian thinking and living to be shaped by society's views and values, rather than by biblical revelation. Liberal theologians believe that the doctrines of the deity of Jesus Christ and his bodily resurrection are incompatible with the modern scientific world view. In so believing, they have followed scientific society rather than Scripture.

Evangelicals have rightly called attention to this heresy—and then tragically made exactly the same mistake in another way, by allowing the values of affluent materialistic society to shape their thinking about the poor. It is much easier in evangelical circles today to insist on an orthodox Christology than to insist on the biblical teaching that God is on the side of the poor. Evangelicals have allowed their theology to be shaped by the economic preferences of materialistic contemporaries rather than by Scripture. To do so is to fall into theological liberalism. Evangelicals have not been nearly as orthodox as they have claimed.

Past failure, however, is no reason for despair. Evangelicals are sincere when they affirm doctrinal statements that boldly declare they will not only believe, but also live, whatever Scripture teaches. But unless Evangelicals drastically reshape both their theology and entire institutional church life, so that the fact that God is on the side of the poor and oppressed becomes as central to evangelical theology and institutional programs as it is in Scripture, they will demonstrate to the world that the verbal commitment to "sola scriptura" is a dishonest ideological support for an unjust, materialistic status quo. But if evangelicals will allow the biblical teaching that God is on the side of the poor and oppressed to fundamentally reshape their culturally conditioned theology and unbiblically one-sided programs and institutions, they will forge a new, truly evangelical theology of liberation that will change the course of modern history.

NOTES

1. J. M. Bonino, *Doing Theology in a Revolutionary Situation* (Philadelphia: Fortress, 1975), pp. 161–162.
2. E. Gatti, *Rich Church-Poor Church* (Maryknoll: Orbis, 1974), p. 43.
3. See Samuel Escobar's summary of Donald McGavran in S. Escobar and J. Driver, *Christian Mission and Social Justice* (Scottsdale: Herald, 1978) pp. 45–47.
4. J. Miranda, *Marx and the Bible* (Maryknoll: Orbis, 1974), p. 44.
5. Ibid., 48.
6. J. H. Cone, *Black Theology and Black Power* (New York: Seabury, 1969), pp. 32–33. But see a conflicting, more biblical emphasis on pp. 34, 51.
7. J. H. Cone, *God of the Oppressed* (New York: Seabury, 1975), p. 84.
8. Ibid., p. 82. Cone's italics.
9. The following section relies heavily on chapter three of my *Rich Christians in an Age of Hunger* (Downers Grove: InterVarsity, 1977, revised, 1984).
10. See. R. Batey, *Jesus and the Poor: The Poverty Program of the First Christians* (New York: Harper, 1972), pp. 83–87; A. Gelin, *The Poor of Yahweh* (Collegeville, Minnesota: Liturgical Press, 1964). See also C. Schultz, " 'Ani and 'Anaw in Psalms" (Unpublished Ph.D. Dissertation, Brandeis University, 1973); P. D. Miscall, "The Concept of the Poor in the Old Testament" (Unpublished Ph.D. Dissertation, Harvard University, 1972).
11. Gerhard Kittel and Gerhard Freidrich, editors, *Theological Dictionary of*

the New Testament Vol. 6, (Grand Rapids: Eerdmans, 1964), p. 888 (hereafter cited as *TDNT*).

12. Gelin, *The Poor of Yahweh,* pp. 19–20.

13. Ibid., p. 50.

14. R. Batey, *Jesus and the Poor,* p. 92.

15. Colin, Brown, editor, *The New International Dictionary of New Testament Theology,* Vol. 2 (Grand Rapids: Zondervan, 1976) pp. 822–823.

16. J. A. Ziesler, *Christian Asceticism* (Grand Rapids: Eerdmans, 1973), p. 52.

17. Kittel and Friedrich, Vol. 6, *TDNT,* pp. 896–899.

18. Batey, *Jesus and the Poor,* p. 93; *TDNT,* Vol. 6, p. 895.

19. See *TDNT,* Vol. 6, p. 904, n. 175.

20. H. Ridderbos, *The Coming of the Kingdom* (Philadelphia: Presbyterian and Reformed, 1962), p. 190.

21. G. E. Ladd, *A Theology of the New Testament* (Grand Rapids: Eerdmans, 1974), p. 133.

22. It should be obvious that nothing in this essay advocates socialism or denies the importance of work and personal responsibility. I am opposed to state ownership of the bulk of the means of production. And I think personal responsibility and work are central to what it means to be human. For further discussion of these issues, see chapter four of my forthcoming book *What Does It Mean to be Pro-Life?* (Downers Grove: InterVarsity, 1987) and the revised edition of my *Rich Christians in an Age of Hunger* (Downers Grove: InterVarsity, 1984), especially pp. 80–82, 101–116.

23. Cone, *God of the Oppressed,* pp. 199–200; Cone's italics.

9. *Public Justice and True Tolerance*

By James Skillen

Focus

For James Skillen, Jesus' parable of the wheat and the tares succinctly expresses the proper Christian understanding of the relationship of religion and politics. "The entire New Testament," he writes, "suggests that Christians must not try to establish an earthly state or political community that would be for Christians only, or that would be fully open only to those who confess Christian faith."

Instead, public life is best served when Christians and all citizens are truly tolerant of divergent views. "The biblical view of justice [means] that Christians work politically for the achievement of governmental policies that protect, encourage, and open up life for every person and community, whatever their religious confession and view of life." The government, or state, Skillen adds, "is not a community of Christian faith; it is a community of public legal care for all people which must not favor or persecute any particular group of society."

Still, politics cannot be devoid of religious influence. "Politics is always God's business," Skillen argues. The United States, through its "supposedly neutral, secular" political tradition, has produced a "democratic nationalism [that] has developed into one of the most powerful 'civil religions' in the modern world." He classifies American civil religion with nationalism and Marxism as "a religion of secularized Christianity."

Christians have an obligation, Skillen concludes, to be politically informed and active. "We must grow up into Christ so that we can gain a common Christian political mind." Christians have a particular obligation to devise and support public policies "in the light of the Christian norm of patient, gracious, loving justice."

James W. Skillen is executive director of the Association for Public Justice in Washington, D. C. He formerly taught political science at Dordt and Gordon colleges.

POLITICS USUALLY BEGINS and ends with "The People," perhaps in the form of "We the people of the United States. . . ," or "The People's Republic of China," or "the will of the people. . . ," or "return power to the people." Christian politics begins and ends with "The King of kings and the Lord of lords." (cf. Rev. 15:3–4).

Jesus acknowledged that *people* have political responsibilities and belong in certain political offices (cf. Matt. 22:15–22; Mk. 12:13–17; Lk. 20:19–26; Jn. 19:11). But in the biblical view of life, human responsibility in earthly politics is never a self-contained and self-sufficient affair of "The People": politics is always God's business.

The biblical perspective places political responsibility in the context of God's sovereignty and Christ's lordship. The Old Testament places politics in the context of the anticipation of One who would come as the Prince of Peace, the Just King, the Righteous Lord, the Perfect Judge, the Mighty God (Is. 9:6–7; 40:9–11; Jer. 23:6; Ps. 82:8; 98:4–9). When Christ did appear, He announced boldly that "All things have been delivered to me by my Father" (Matt. 11:27, *RSV*). All authority in heaven and on earth, He said, "has been given to Me" (Matt. 28:18). Christ has come to establish the rule of His Father over the whole earth (Lk. 4:1–21; I Cor. 15:20–28; Phil. 2:5–11; Col. 1:15–20; Rev. 10:1–16).

The Politics of Grace

The biblical revelation also declares that the time between Christ's first appearance and His second coming is a time of great patience, long-suffering, and grace on God's part. He is not willing that anyone should perish, and so the call goes out for people to repent and to believe the gospel of His kingdom (Mk. 1:15; II Pet. 3:9). God's gracious patience has significance for politics because Christ does not ask His people to administer any kind of forceful, political separation of non-Christians from Christians. In fact Christ gives the opposite responsibility to Christians: we are to

---

Reprinted by permission of the author from *Confessing Christ and Doing Politics*, (c) Association for Public Justice Education Fund, 1982.

love our enemies (Matt. 5:43–48); we are to look after the welfare of those who might do evil to us (Matt. 5:38–42; Rom. 12:20); we are to pray for God's will to be done on earth as it is done in heaven (Matt. 6:10). In all of this, Christians are to leave the responsibility for separating the wheat from the chaff in the hands of the King Himself (Matt. 26:51–54; Lk. 3:15–17; Rev. 5:1–14).

A biblical parable which brings to focus the gracious character of this age is the one in Matthew 13:24–30. Jesus told the parable this way:

> The kingdom of heaven may be compared to a man who sowed good seed in his field; but while men were sleeping, his enemy came and sowed weeds among the wheat, and went away. So when the plants came up and bore grain, then the weeds appeared also. And the servants of the householder came and said to him, "Sir did you not sow good seed in your field? How then has it weeds?" He said to them, "An enemy has done this." The servants said to him, "Then do you want us to go and gather them?" But he said, "No; lest in gathering the weeds you root up the wheat along with them. Let both grow together until the harvest; and at harvest time I will tell the reapers, Gather the weeds first and bind them in bundles to be burned, but gather the wheat into my barn" (*RSV*).

The entire New Testament suggests that Christians must not try to establish an earthly state or political community that would be for Christians only, or that would be fully open only to those who confess Christian faith. It is not *Christian* justice for Christians to enjoy any political privilege at the expense of non-Christians. Non-Christians must be given every blessing in the political arena that Christians enjoy. Just as the wheat and the tares enjoy the same sun, rain, and cultivation, so Christians and non-Christians should enjoy equally the benefits of God's grace given to the field of this world in the present age.

The Christian view of political justice should be built directly on this understanding of God's gracious patience and love. If this is done, Christian politics will not manifest itself as the Church's selfish attempt to control the state, or as an interest-group effort to "get" benefits primarily for Christians, or as a campaign to flood political offices with Christians so that Christians can control the government for the enforcement of Christian doctrine on the populace. Instead, the biblical view of justice for every earthly creature will mean that Christians will work politically for the achievement of governmental policies that will protect, encourage, and open up life for every person and community, whatever their religious confession and view of life. Justice in political life cannot be based on the biblical teaching about church discipline because earthly states are not churches. The state is not a community of Christian faith; it is a community of public legal care for all people which must not favor or persecute any particular group of society.

The difficulty of this biblical perspective is quite understandable considering the history of politics in the West since the time of Christ. The Roman empire did not promote an evenhanded justice which comes from God's grace, but frequently persecuted Christians and Jews. Later, when Christianity was accepted by the Roman emperors and established as the religion of the empire, the emperors frequently persecuted or discriminated against non-Christians instead of Christians. This was no more just in a biblical sense than the former Roman practice. The Roman empire in both instances falsely identified itself with *God's* empire, and the emperors wrongly assumed responsibility for getting rid of heretics (rooting up the tares)—a responsibility which Christ gave to no human being.

Still later in history the church gained such strength and prominence that it became the chief power behind most of Europe's politics. "Christian politics" then came to mean "church-controlled politics" and the Roman church leaders assumed some of the same power, and held on to some of the same ideas, that the Roman emperors once had. Political justice reflecting biblical patience and grace was still not operative, for the most part.

There was so much political debate, warfare, persecution, and turmoil during and after the Reformation, when most Christians were still confusing the church's and the state's responsibilities, that many people came to believe that political life ought to be organized without reference to religion. Our American political roots go back to this period when people were trying to organize government and politics according to "neutral," non-religious principles. They believed that, if they could only keep religion in their private lives and in the churches, away from the political arena where all people participate in common, religious conflict would not interrupt political life and everyone would enjoy peace and prosperity.

But this was no more just than earlier systems of political organization because not everyone agreed that politics was neutral or that religion belonged only to private life. In the political arena, therefore, people were still discriminated against and frequently persecuted if they did not go along with this new idea of a common "religionless" politics.

New Political Religions

What we have seen in the last two centuries is that our supposedly neutral, secular political communities have given birth to the most passionate and unjust *religions* that now control most of these political communities. Nationalism, which is a religious faith in the nation itself, has become the dominant power in modern political life around the world. Various forms of Marxism, which is a religion of materialistic humanism, dominate many states, persecuting and discriminating against those who do not confess the party line. Many western democracies, including the United States, allow little or no room for minority participation in politics unless the minorities agree to play by the rules that supposedly keep religion out of politics (and out of the schools) and that keep the majority in charge of directing society. This means unjust discrimination against many people.

American democratic nationalism has developed into one of the most powerful "civil religions" in the modern world. It is not Marxist; it is not Roman Catholic; it is not Protestant; it is not styled after the old Roman empire's elevation of the emperor to the position of God. It is, rather, a religion of secularized Christianity whereby the American nation has come to be seen as God's specially chosen kingdom—the political community through which the world will be saved politically. In America, God's will is supposedly revealed through the will of a political majority, and all private religions have their primary place of honor as supporters of the nation's common, unified progress through history as God's nation.

The American civil religion not only leads to political injustice at home, but it promotes injustice abroad in so far as "American interests" dominate world politics and economics. "What is best for America is best for the world," is a slogan in the minds of many American citizens and public officials. On the world scene, this attitude operates in much the same way that the dominance of one group operates in the internal life of a nation. It means injustice and discrimination against the poor in favor of the rich, against one class in favor of another class, and against one religious group in favor of another religious group.

Politics does not exist as a neutral enterprise. Religion cannot be kept out of the life of states. If a Christian approach of patient, gracious justice does not rule human political life, then some other religious dynamic will control it. If all people are not cared for in an evenhanded way in the public legal domain, then another religious impulse will lead to injustice and discrimination. Christians must wake up to this fact today and recognize that, if they are not serving Christ in politics according to the norm of biblical justice, they are serving some false god that will lead to injustice. In America today, many believe that we are doing justice to all people by keeping religion out of politics and letting the majority rule. But in doing so, we are keeping a truly Christian work of justice out of politics only to have a democratic religion of the people dominate majorities and minorities in a way that oppresses and discriminates against certain people and communities. The only answer to the present difficulties facing democratic political systems (as well as non-democratic systems) is to recognize that, because people are basically religious creatures, religion cannot be kept out of politics. Political life must be opened up to the full diversity of religious impulses, and evenhanded justice must be the norm by which this diversity is affirmed in public life.

A Christian Political Response

In the contemporary world of both domestic and international injustice, Christian politics begins with the repentance of Christians who come to see that they have not always been ministers of God's gracious, patient justice to others. Christian politics will grow when Christians begin to take seriously Christ's command for us to love our neighbors. This will lead us to be dissatisfied with every type of organization of political life which discriminates against some to the advantage of others.

Christian politics will mature in America when Christians recover the biblical vision of the *communal* responsibility they have for others. When we begin to see that the body of Christ is not a "part time" or "private" organism unrelated to political realities, we will be able to break away from the *individualistic* conception of political responsibility which presently dominates our democratic political system. We will no longer be willing to have the major political parties practice all of our politics for us on their terms—terms which presuppose the individualistic character of political responsibility, the rule of the majority for determining what justice is all about, and the neutral secularity of the political dimension of life. Instead, we will be driven by the Spirit of Christ to begin working together as a *political community* and not just as an ecclesiastical community or as an educational community. We will see that politics is our business as a community with a distinct view of life unlike the views of other communities. We will begin to practice politics as unto the Lord.

Once we Christians begin to take political responsibilities seriously, we will be able to take up such complex issues as inflation, poverty, taxation, education, foreign policy, and racism, and examine present government policies and political processes in the light of the Christian norm of patient, gracious, and loving justice. Then, as the Lord guides us into a deeper understanding of modern political realities from the standpoint of His merciful justice, we will be able to make the necessary tactical decisions about how we should organize our talents and energies for the service of justice. We may find that the present political system will allow us little room for unique Christian service besides writing and speaking about alternative policies. Or we may find that after considerable labor some significant avenues will open up for our organized efforts to restructure the system and to enact policies and laws of greater justice.

To develop a Christian political option, therefore, we must begin by studying the Word of God together in order to see what it teaches about the kingdom of God in Christ. We must pray and talk together in order to grasp the principles of that kingdom as they hold for earthly politics. We must grow up into Christ so that we can gain a *common Christian political mind*. It is not enough for us to say that we have Christ in common if our lives manifest a confusion of divergent approaches to politics. It is not enough for us to say that we all believe that Christ's kingdom is coming if we live in a way that shows no communal unity in our service of the King. If we are children of the light, then our lives should manifest the communal bond that the light gives to us. Politics is a major part of the life we now live by faith. We need the mind of Christ in us. We need to be renewed in all our thought and life by Christ, including our thinking and living in politics.

With our communal growth as the body of Christ, we must also encourage individuals among us to lead us in working out the details of our Christian political option. What are the problems facing modern nations today? What can be done to reform our present systems and policies so that greater justice can be done? What is an equitable tax policy? What is justice in education, or in broadcasting? If we are to get answers to these and thousands of other questions, we will have to have economic, legal, historical, and political experts to guide us. They will need to work full time as part of a Christian team, developing the implications of the biblical view of God's rule in Christ over the whole earth.

We must work and pray together for the Lord's guidance in our lives as we seek communally to fulfill our political responsibilities before His face. But to do this we must be sure to recognize the talents and gifts that God has already given to certain individuals among us in the area of political understanding. If we do not seek to discover and encourage such men and women to do this special service, and if we do not organize for the support of them, it will not be enough for us to pray that God will help us in our political service. God is already richly blessing us with men and women who are able to give political leadership. Let us consider how we can be good stewards politically of what God has already given.

10. *The Lures and Limits of Political Power*

By CHARLES W. COLSON

Focus

Charles W. Colson believes that "civil religion is nothing but idolatry, while privatized faith is really no faith at all." He criticizes both those who suggest that religious faith may be "privately engaging, but [is] publicly irrelevant," and those Fundamentalists and Evangelicals who confuse patriotism and faith. "The debate over religion and politics has . . . seemed to pose two choices: one side arguing that faith in God and country are inseparable—a position known historically as civil religion; the other side asserting that one's religion is entirely a private matter."

As an Evangelical, Colson reminds Evangelicals that "The Kingdom of God will not arrive on Air Force One." Christians of all traditions must eschew the illusion that political power can be harnessed for religious ends.

In assessing the limits as well as the lures of political power, Colson advocates "courage and realism" for Evangelicals who seek to increase their influence on public issues. Participation in the national dialogue over crucial moral questions, rather than dominance of the debate, should be the Evangelicals' primary objective. "Seek justice, not power," Colson admonishes. Evangelicals can do this, he suggests, if they "reject the illusions, seductions, and false alternatives of the current political scene," and realize that "the problems of our society are moral and spiritual in nature—institutions and politicians are limited in what they can do."

Charles W. Colson was a special assistant to President Richard Nixon from 1969–1973. In 1976 he founded Prison Fellowship, Inc. He is the author of *Born Again, Life Sentence, Loving God,* and *Who Speaks for God?*

THE DEBATE OVER religion and politics has so far failed to clarify one very important issue for Christians. The debate has seemed to pose two choices: one side arguing that faith in God and country are inseparable—a position known historically as civil religion; the other side asserting that one's religion is entirely a private matter. The public, including many Christians, has been left believing that religion's proper role in American life has to fall into one of these two politically defined alternatives. But neither of these options has anything to do with historic Christianity—and there is the danger. For example, let us consider the generic civil religion advocated by one camp. "Religion plays a critical role in the political life of our nation," said one candidate. What kind of religion? "If you practice a religion, whether you are Catholic, Protestant, Jewish, or guided by some other faith, then your private life will be influenced by a sense of obligation and so, too, your public life."

Thus, in the civil religionists' view, America has a "tolerant" society, "open to and encouraging of all religions." This is because religion is the great prop of the duties of citizens. This prop is necessary because we can see that, whenever a great civilization has fallen, one of the significant forerunners of the fall was its turning away from God or its gods. As a former President once argued, the American government makes no sense "unless it is founded in a deeply felt religious faith—and I don't care what it is."

Countering this view is the notion that "faith [is] intensely personal"; there are many "faiths," all of which are "true" for those who hold them. To have religion enter political debates might require that a person defend his religious beliefs! What could be more uncivil?

Perhaps the best example of this kind of religion was found in New York Governor Mario Cuomo's much publicized speech at Notre Dame. There, with eloquence and sophistication, he argued

---

Reprinted with permission from the January 1986 issue of *Pastoral Renewal* (© Pastoral Renewal, Box 8617, Ann Arbor, MI 48107).

that an officeholder who professes to be a sincere Christian can advocate positions clearly contrary to his church's teaching.

Cuomo thus stated his view that, as a practicing Roman Catholic, he subscribes to his church's teachings on the question of abortion, but, he argued, as an officeholder in a secular society, he could not impose his views on anyone else. So far, so good.

But Governor Cuomo did not stop there. He went on to say that he is under no obligation to advocate the views of his church or to work to seek a public consensus based on those views (which views he confesses to be the truth of God) until there is what he calls a "prudential judgment" which could justify such a course. Another way of saying this is that you do not act on a sticky question until the majority of voters agree with you. That, of course, is how you get elected and stay in office. The judgment of prudence appears to be pretty good politics.

Yet, this kind of logic, however effective as a political ploy, gives sophistry a bad name. No more do we have the claim of the Christian religion that it declares the truth of God, which alone is able to make men and women "wise unto salvation." Rather, we have a religion that is a matter of personal taste. The ancients had counsel for us in this regard: *de gustibus non est disputandum,* translated as "There is no disputing about tastes." Thus we dare not bring faith into politics; such a course would reduce political debate to futility. How can one argue with the flavor of religion that I happen to favor?

Here generic faith is protected from public scrutiny: whatever concerns may grow out of such faith are not to be brought to the hard decisions of the political sphere. No one should attempt to transform policy debates into theological disputes. Held consistently, this view leads to the notion that it is morally possible to believe with your church that abortion is murder, while supporting the practice with your vote.

A Narrow Debate

In plain terms, what we have today is a debate between those who believe that generic religion is a crucial prop to public morality and civic duty—and is thus to be publicly encouraged and endorsed—and those who believe that generic faith is to be privately engaging, but publicly irrelevant.

Any who fear the specter of theocracy in response to this debate wildly overrate the power of such insipid religion. Neither civil religion nor privatized religion is likely to have a long-lasting impact on our governmental institutions, for in both cases there is virtually nothing to impose.

One commentator seemed to get this point. She wrote longingly of ancient Rome as a model of the place that generic religion might have in a "tolerant" society: "The people regarded all the modes of worship as equally true, the intellectuals regarded them as equally false, and the politicians regarded them as equally useful. What a well-blessed time."

Of course, we Christians should know that such emptiness and cynicism has nothing to do with blessing. Yet, in the heat of the [1984] presidential campaign, there was a great temptation to quietly opt for one of these false paths as a way to express bibilcal faith.

For example, ought a candidate to have received a Christian's enthusiastic support because he supports certain religious values? What about prayer in public schools? Prayer is surely a religious act, and religion is surely advanced by such acts. But is this Christian? The Bible teaches that the only persons who may call God Father are those *adopted* into his family through Jesus Christ; therefore, only those who are praying in the name of Christ have a right to pray to God as *Father*.

How then can a Christian be thrilled by an endorsement of general religiosity when that amounts to a denial of one of the choice benefits given only to those who are in Christ? How can we encourage a practice which leads people to believe that they may have access to the throne of God apart from Christ? Yet this appears to be exactly what we are doing in our political support for generic religion. We may find that it is the best course to support such a candidate for other reasons, but we must never allow people to be misled into confusing such religiosity with obedience to Christ.

On the other hand, if we find ourselves in disagreement with the extreme theocratic views held by some religionists—views which appear to erase the distinction between church and state—is the only option available that we retreat into the privatized irrelevance of a faith that remains quietly on the reservation and brings no prophetic word to culture? Should we let our duty to accept the rights of other religions *in the civil sphere* be translated into a timidity about declaring what the Bible teaches concerning the uniqueness of the Christian faith, for fear of being branded moral McCarthyites? Can we as Christians rejoice with a candidate's claim that the supposed "wall of separation between church and state . . . has made us the most religious people on earth," when mere religion is as hopeless a course as outright paganism so far as the gospel of Jesus Christ is concerned? I think not.

It is true that a political candidate must attempt to build a unified constituency out of diverse groups, and thus must try to lessen differences and emphasize his similarities to all. The great temptation is for Christians to actually adopt this false image as reality. We may find that, for other reasons it is the best course to support such a candidate, but, we must never allow people to be misled into confusing such religiosity with the gospel of God.

If I have correctly outlined the competing positions in the current debate, the real danger should be apparent to those who have eyes to see: If we Christians allow ourselves to be forced to choose between these unbiblical alternatives, the opportunity provided by the new place currently being given to religion in public discourse will be lost; if we fail to speak clearly and boldly for Christ, the cutting edge of historic Christianity in our culture will be dulled—replaced by a generic American religion used by both parties for political advantage.

'Civil Religion' is Idolatrous

It is at this point that the Christian must take his stand because biblical Christianity declares that civil religion is idolatry and privatized faith is no faith at all. Both of these false options deny the truth of the Christian gospel—its unique character and its demand for the unrivaled lordship of Christ.

The danger is real. Enamored by the new power we appear to have in public life, Christians may succumb to the belief that a particular political program will usher in the kingdom of God. We would thus mute the more impolitic truths of the Christian message and trade our precious birthright—the eternal and unique gospel of Jesus Christ—for a mess of temporal political porridge. May God forbid!

And yet, though there is great temptation here, we cannot retreat from the political realm in order to safeguard the truth of the Christian faith. Christ himself will not permit it, and love for our neighbor cannot condone it. Why? Because it is Christ's teaching concerning his kingdom that so exposes the illusion of power of political kingdoms, and therefore frees us from the idols which hold much of the world in bondage.

This is a part of our Christian heritage that we must reclaim. Saint Augustine understood the nature of Christ's kingdom with great insight. When, in 410, he was told that Rome had been sacked, he was deeply troubled, yet he did not despair, for as he counseled his people: "All earthly cities are vulnerable. Men build them and men destroy them. At the same time there is the city of God which men did not build and cannot destroy and which is everlasting."

Unsolvable Problems

This knowledge destroys the political illusion that so insidiously infects Western culture. And, for want of the inoculation that this knowledge provides, Christians are catching the same disease. Its carriers are all around us.

In an evening newscast before the 1984 elections, a parade of political candidates virtually promised to end the arms race, eliminate the deficit, settle the Middle East turmoil, and produce full employment. It was breathtaking to watch.

Then I tried to remember—and couldn't—a single instance in which a candidate for any office, from city councilman to President, had ever admitted any problem that he or she could not solve once elected. But in truth many problems cannot be cured—at least not the way politicians promise. Even officials in the most powerful offices sometimes discover that they are not so powerful after all.

I remember one Friday afternoon in 1970 when President Richard Nixon called me into his office. "I want an executive order creating a commission to study aid to nonpublic schools," he snapped. "Have it on my desk nine o'clock Monday morning." Mr. Nixon was frustrated that the creation of the commission—a campaign pledge—had been ignored for eighteen months by the Justice Department.

Simple enough, I thought. All I had to do was to find the right form, check it out with other staffers, and have it typed. Then bedlam broke loose. Another presidential assistant, John Erlichman, protested that I was "invading his area." The Attorney General was on the phone, as was the Commissioner of Education. Memos began flying back and forth as the bureaucracy suddenly came alive.

The battle that began that weekend went on for months. Eventually the order was issued, only to be soon forgotten.

This was no isolated instance. Career bureaucrats outlast presidents and are experts at stymieing orders they do not like. Many programs are deadlocked between Congress and the President; some agencies, after being launched with great fanfare, simply watch the problems they were created to solve steadily worsen.

Yet politicians of both parties continue to promise—and the electorate continues to expect—political solutions to all our ills. We go through the same cycle every election year. Why?

Two decades ago, Jacques Ellul, a French sociologist, addressed this question in a remarkably prophetic book, *The Political Illusion.* Ellul theorized that modern man increasingly turns to the state for answers to problems even though the state cannot solve them. Politicians perpetuate the myth that it can solve them because the illusion perpetuates their power; the media willingly collaborate because their coverage of government fuels their own power. The result, Ellul wrote, is a "boundless growth" of a state with an insatiable appetite for power. Independent groups which involve people in meeting society's needs are the only way to lessen dependence on government and its eventual totalitarian control.

The Spiritual Dimension

We Christians, of all people, should see through the political illusion. We should understand that the real problems of our society are, at their root, moral and spiritual. Institutions and politicians are limited in what they can do, and we dare not confuse this limited good with the infinite good of the gospel. The kingdom of God will not arrive on Air Force One.

Certainly that is so in the criminal justice field. Crime is the result of wrong moral choices. Laws are needed to restrain evil, but penal institutions cannot deal with the ultimate problem: the human heart. That is why the gospel of Christ is the only real answer.

Even in foreign policy, governments are not all-powerful, as we are accustomed to think. The Marine presence in Lebanon was no deterrent to the centuries-old civil strife there. The British have learned the same lesson in Ulster.

Or take the example of Poland. Against the "powerful" array of Soviet divisions, thousands of school children have marched with their crucifixes held high, successfully resisting the Communist government's edict to remove crosses from their classrooms. Where is the real power in Poland? Certainly not in the Politburo.

The Political Illusion

The political illusion poses three grave dangers:

First, as political solutions fail and problems worsen, people become cynical. In time, they become alienated from their own political process. We see this at both ends of the social spectrum. On the one hand, many of our poor disparage the political process, see no real hope for any change, and drop out of the system altogether. On the other hand, we see the growing indifference of the "yuppies"—former political utopians now concerned for political good only as it contributes to private gain and personal comfort.

Second, the political illusion fosters a false security. Because the government is promising to deal with our problems, we do not have to bother. The government becomes our "brother's keeper," so we feel we are let off the hook.

Many of the federal government programs of the 1960s offer cases in point. As social programs mushroomed, private welfare agencies declined. Because of the illusion that the government would take care of things, many individuals stopped caring for others.

As Alexander Solzhenitsyn charged at Harvard in 1978:

> We have placed too much hope in politics and social reforms, only to find out that we were being deprived of our most precious possession: our spiritual life. It is trampled by the party mob in the East, by the commercial one in the West. We are at a harsh spiritual crisis and a political impasse. All the celebrated technological achievements of progress . . . do not redeem the 20th century's moral poverty.

Political institutions provide no panaceas to the ills of our age, no matter how attractive they sound. They are surely no substitute for individual responsibility.

Third, and perhaps most dangerous, the political illusion suggests we must accumulate worldly power to advance the cause of Christ. But because that power can neither achieve utopia nor establish the ends of the gospel, another goal is soon substituted—power for its own sake.

I know about such things because I have seen the White House transform young political idealists into prideful "supermen," myself included. The same thing can happen to the prestige-conscious businessman, the bullying shop steward, or the domineering parent, because worldly power, though not inherently evil, is powerfully corrupting. We Christians are not exempt from its temptations.

When I worked in President Nixon's White House, one of my assignments was as a liaison with special-interest groups. For us, that included the religious.

From 1970 to 1972, I arranged special briefings in the Roosevelt Room for religious leaders, ushered wide-eyed denominational leaders into the Oval Office for private sessions with the President, and even arranged dinner cruises on the presidential yacht for key leaders who just happened to come from states we had targeted in the 1972 election.

From these meetings grew very agreeable alliances. Religious leaders were able to make their points with the President—though most were so in awe that they didn't. More important to us, we reaped handsome dividends on election day. The significance of Nixon's frequent photos with Evangelical and Fundamentalist leaders was not lost on Bible Belt voters, and, in the electoral-rich states of the Northeast, his open courting of the blue-collar Roman Catholic vote proved decisive.

I arm-twisted more than one religious leader into a partisan endorsement, and, on the whole, of all the groups I dealt with, I found religious leaders the most naive about politics. Maybe that is because so many come from sheltered backgrounds, or perhaps it is the result of a mistaken perception of the demands of Christian charity: though Christian leaders understand abstract theological concepts about the depravity of man—which indeed includes politicians—they often want, perhaps with undue optimism, to see the best in them. Or, most worrisome of all, they may simply like to be around power.

Popularity Has a Price

It is easy to become enthralled with access to power. In time, however, without even knowing it, well-intentioned attempts to influence public policy can be so entangled with the politics of power that the pastor's primary goal becomes maintaining political access. When that happens, the gospel of Jesus Christ is held hostage to a political agenda—and religious leaders are little able to speak out and criticize it.

I cannot blame the politician when this happens. It is only natural that he will seek votes and electoral influence—just as Nixon did—and as all politicians have done before and since. That is what politics is all about.

But the religious world must be on guard. Christians in particular must heed our Lord's words: he who would lead, let him serve. That admonition is radically opposed to the self-aggrandizing nature of American politics. For the Christian, the goal in politics is not power, but justice.

The Old Testament prophets could serve as worthy models for today's leaders. They were political activists who angrily denounced the abuse of privilege in places of power. But they were not taken with invitations to the palace. Indeed, they fiercely guarded their independence, and knew that they owed allegiance only to the King of all kings. This was true, too, of the early Christians, who because they refused to give Caesar equal billing with God were fed to the lions.

But I am not at all confident that this is true today. There are all too many examples of religious leaders from both ends of the political spectrum who are sacrificing their integrity to the demands of political popularity. Christianity has survived persecution through the centuries—thrived on it in fact, but its leaders have never handled power very well.

Christians must therefore make plain that the goal of our political involvement is neither a "religious establishment" nor an absolute wall of separation. These false options are dangerous both to the state and to the church. But at the same time we must boldly bear witness to the fact that, both now and in the past, Christian values brought to the democratic process are essential for a good and just social order.

This we must do not by simply wrapping our Bibles in the flag, but by showing our brothers and sisters in Christ that there are sound biblical reasons why we support the unique American experiment of separation of church and state. We must also, with humility and reason, demonstrate to our friends in civil society who reject the Scriptures that our biblical concerns express the highest human values and contribute principles to public policy by which people may flourish.

In so doing, we must consistently be diligent to expose the political illusion. Each of us must learn anew, if we had ever learned it before, to listen with healthy skepticism to the inflated rhetoric of the campaign trail. We need people ready to exercise what the underground grammarian Richard Mitchell has called "thoughtful discretion" when we listen to our foes, and yes, to our friends as well.

We Christians must also carefully define our objectives. Civil righteousness is a good end, and political power is an appropriate means to that end, but such power cannot bring in the kingdom or make people holy. We must be careful to say boldly with Paul: "I am not ashamed of the gospel, because it is the power of God for the salvation of everyone who believes. . . . For in the gospel a righteousness from God is revealed, a righteousness that is by faith from first to last" (Rom. 1:16–17).

Justice as the Objective

As the late Christian thinker Francis Schaeffer argued, the objective for the Christian is modeled in the very nature of God. We seek justice, not power. Because of who God is, "Power is not first, but justice is first in society and law. The prince may have the power to . . . rule, but he does not have the right to do so without justice." This means that Christians who serve in the political sphere have a special obligation to a higher King. Such persons should also heed Plato's words: "Only those who do not desire power are fit to hold it." This is radically opposed to the self-promoting nature of our political system. Yet it is also the call of Jesus Christ. He teaches that to lead we must serve (Matthew 20:25–28). Thus for the Christian, the call to political leadership is a call not to greater self-advancement, but to greater death to self in service to others.

In this service, we must never confuse power with authority. Power is the ability to accomplish one's ends or purposes in the world; authority is having not only the might, but also the right, to do so. Power is often maintained by force alone; authority arises from a moral foundation.

True authority comes not from political power, but from humble submission and obedience to the Word of God. Mother Teresa is the best living example: She spends her life in obedience to Christ, helping the powerless die with dignity, yet few people command more authority worldwide.

Fourth, we must be diligent to challenge and support our brothers and sisters in political office. All of us have the duty to bear one another's burdens, and servants of the Lord in politics have a particularly heavy burden to bear.

Actually, we have a double obligation to those who so serve: we are enjoined by the word to pray for one another, and we are commanded to pray for "kings and all who are in authority."

To our lasting benefit, we have a great pantheon of heroes to guide us in political service. William Wilberforce is a model for our times. He was the Christian member of the British Parliament who led the twenty-year fight against the slave trade, and ultimately secured the abolition of slavery itself in England. He is an example of what God may be pleased to do for a nation through the obedience of His servants.

Called to Obedience

Finally, one of the most powerful means we Christians have at our disposal to affect political life is through the church, not by making our congregations political precincts, as have both the

Right and the Left in recent elections, but by calling on the church to be the church.

In obedience to the lordship of Jesus Christ, we who follow him are called to be salt and light—salt rubbed into the meat as a preservative, and light shining on a hill in the midst of darkness.

When the church of Jesus Christ fulfills this high calling, Christians have the effect of preempting many of the problems that the state is eventually called upon to solve. Secular politics simply cannot compete with the body of Christ when it is empowered by the Holy Spirit in His service.

That is why, in those countries where a godless rule attempts to eradicate Christianity, it is Christian service that is forbidden. In the Soviet Union, for example, Christians are free to worship, and free to congregate in their church buildings, but their buildings, once glorious, are now not much more than ornate musuems. By law, Christians in the Soviet Union cannot have Christian schools or Christian service organizations, nor can they work for public justice.

It has been this way since the beginning. In ancient Rome, pagans were troubled and confused by the new Christian faith. Not that pagans were against religion, for across the empire a bizarre diversity of religious expression was flourishing under the tolerant hand of the Roman masters. No, religion was considered an acceptable and important aspect of culture. Therefore, as long as Christians fit the mold and allowed themselves to be defined by the society, they were accepted. It was when the church began to express its unique calling, refused to be defined by popular images, and proclaimed in word and deed that Christ is Lord, that it came into open conflict with the world.

Thus it has been from the beginning. Yet the early Christians had one great advantage over us: then it was clear that the surrounding culture was groping in the darkness of paganism, and that the culture should have no hand in defining the role of God's people in the world. But today, we have grown accustomed to thinking of ourselves as part of the "Christian West" and as a "Christian nation." That habit is hard to kick, because it has the narcotic effect of easing the painful reality of the stark contrast between twentieth century American culture and the calling of Christ to his church.

Yet we must kick that habit, if by serving heaven we are to be any earthly good. Our challenge is clear: we must reject the illusions, seductions, and false alternatives of the current political scene and reassert the ageless truth that Christ is Lord of lords and King of kings. With Athanasius, the great fourth century champion of the faith, we must stand for Christ *contra mundum*—"against the world."

In the very moment of our clearest opposition to the world, we will find that, as witnesses to the Truth and Life, we will have the inestimable privilege of helping to make Christ's invisible kingdom visible in the world. For, with Christ, we will "preach the gospel to the poor . . . proclaim release to the captives, and recovery of sight to the blind; set free those who are downtrodden, and proclaim the favorable year of the Lord" (Luke 4:18–19).

11. *The Powerful and the Powerless*

By JIM WALLIS

Focus

In Jim Wallis's view, "a totalitarian spirit fuels the engines of both Wall Street and the Kremlin." Wallis says that America's pursuit of "self-interested empire-building" causes much of the poverty and revolutionary violence throughout the world. A prominent leader of a new generation of "radical Evangelicals," Wallis believes that the U.S. government only pretends to support freedom movements while actually engaging in an "expansionist thrust" in foreign affairs. He writes that "the uncritical acceptance of the myth of 'the national interest' and 'national security' is essential in keeping the United States the number one nation."

Calling for redistribution of the world's wealth and political power, he argues that people in the undeveloped countries of the world are poor because residents of the United States are rich. Furthermore, the poverty of the poor is maintained by the economic and political systems of the United States.

Much of his criticism stems from a social and political analysis similar to Ronald Sider's (selection 7). Both believe that issues of wealth, poverty, and economic justice are central to the Judeo-Christian moral tradition, and that the God of the Jewish-Christian Scriptures cares especially about the poor and oppressed. "Nowhere in Scripture," writes

Wallis, "are the rights of the rich proclaimed; nowhere is God seen as the Savior and defender of the rich and their wealth."

He chides Evangelical churches for practicing "compassionless inactivity," and declares that Americans' "over-consumption is theft from the poor." He summons Christians to be "radically obedient" to the Gospel of Christ: "If our lives are secure, comfortable, and at home with wealth and power, we belong to the world rather than to Christ."

This analysis should be compared with that of Lloyd Billingsley (selection 12).

Jim Wallis is a founder and pastor of the Sojourners community in Washington, D. C., and editor of *Sojourners*. He has written *Agenda for Biblical People* and edited *Peacemakers: Christian Voices from the New Abolitionist Movement*.

THE DIVISIONS IN the world today are less along the lines of ideology than they are along the lines of power. Our times have seen a growing conflict generated by the disparity between the rich and poor of the world, between those who have power and those who do not. The central questions in the arenas of struggles for social justice concern the need for redistribution of wealth and power on a global scale.

The world's most powerful nations share a desire for economic and military domination that surfaces in startling structural and political similarities between the huge capitalist and socialist bureaucracies.

When the Soviet Union rolled its tanks into the streets of Prague and crushed the stirrings of independence in Czechoslovakia, the Soviets claimed an inherent right to prevent a country from slipping out of their orbit. That same doctrine operates at the heart of American foreign policy, as has been so brutally demonstrated in Vietnam and elsewhere in the Third World. When an insurgent social movement or a new government threatens to take a nation out of the United States' economic, political, and military orbit, the American government's often-claimed commitment to self-determination for other countries quickly shows itself to be without substance. When American policymakers believe that business, diplomatic, or strategic interests are threatened by a development in another country, the United States assumes the right to conspire unilaterally and act against that threat through economic reprisal, political subversion, assassination, paramilitary, or military operations. The same tactics are used in aggressively subverting "unfavorable" regimes and in creating circumstances in which American economic and political power is protected and promoted. Both American and Soviet powers have acted to create and maintain client regimes in other countries that exercise control through means of repression, terror, and torture.

A totalitarian spirit fuels the engines of both Wall Street and the Kremlin.

The Influence of Corporations

American policy is dominated by the vested interests of an increasingly concentrated corporate power structure that seeks greater control throughout the world with a coherent global strategy to help create and stabilize a system of "open societies" in which United States economic, political, and military interests can operate more or less freely. This Pax Americana is reminiscent of another "peace" from another time. Arnold Toynbee, the British historian, comments:

> America is today the leader of a world-wide anti-revolutionary movement in defense of vested interests. She now stands for what Rome stood for. Rome consistently supported the rich against the poor in all foreign communities that fell under her sway; and since the poor, so far, have always and everywhere been far more numerous than the rich, Rome's policy made for inequality, for injustice, and for the least happiness of the greatest number. America's decision to adopt Rome's role has been deliberate, if I have gauged it right. ("America and the World Revolution," quoted in David Horowitz, *Free World Colossus*, p. 15)

The causes of revolutionary war and violence are not primarily conspiracies and outside agitation, but are rooted in the economic and political institutions of the United States and other major powers, and in the values and attitudes of the people of the rich nations. Throughout its history, the United States has been characterized by a continuous expansionist thrust, first in striving for territorial acquisition and, more recently, in seeking economic and political control and domination. That same expansionist pattern has dominated the history of the other powerful nations of the modern world.

The expansionist thrust has always been represented as a noble effort to advance "freedom," "democracy," "civilization," or some other great value. The obvious questions that come to mind are: Freedom for whom and freedom for what? Who are the chief beneficiaries and who are the victims of these advances in "democracy" and "civilization"?

Cloaked in their own self-righteous rhetoric, the powerful nations in history have actually been engaged in self-interested empire building. A foreign policy designed to expand American profit and power in the world has never been affected by the changing of presidents and is a working assumption of both political parties. Concluding that "national security" comes only in dominating others, American leaders have created a society organized for war since 1945. We have watched the United States conduct military and paramilitary campaigns around the world. Less visible ways of intervention include the support of dictatorial regimes that protect American interests; the training of local military and police elites in the effective "control" of social revolution; and the use of terror, torture, assassination, and economic and political subversion.

The United States' enormous and far-flung commercial interests and worldwide deployment of military power have brought the growth of elaborate networks and systems of espionage and secret political offensives, of expanded research and development in methods of warfare and counterinsurgency, of huge public relations and propaganda campaigns designed for mass persuasion, of the militarization of science, and of the mobilization of the universities, all adding to the arsenal built to protect an empire.

Wealth and Power

The key concept is control. The rich nations have sought to create, on a global scale, those conditions and relationships that guarantee the protection and expansion of their economic and political power. By aggressive investment and trade, by maneuvering the weaker nations into dependent relationships, by use of financial arrangements, military agreements, and political alliances with local elites, the rich nations have forged an empire. It is an empire based upon the influence and control of the political economies of the nonindustrial nations rather than upon territorial conquest and is, therefore, "invisible," an empire without boundaries.

"We are the number one nation," said President Lyndon Johnson at a crucial point in the Vietnam War, "and we are going to stay the number one nation." He was merely articulating an honest and accurate definition of the doctrine of national interest as interpreted by American leaders and policymakers. Staying number one is a struggle for permanent victory that requires the United States to pursue its national interest at all costs.

The United States, being the richest and most powerful nation, becomes, as Martin Luther King charged, "the greatest purveyor of violence in the world." This happens by virtue of the necessity of protecting American wealth and power in the midst of the world's poor and exploited masses. A dependence upon violence in its many forms is inherent in being "number one," and the public's willingness to acquiesce when the call is sounded to support "the national interest" is crucial. The uncritical acceptance of the myth of "the national interest" and "national security" is essential in keeping the United States the number one nation.

The system of empire is based upon the consumer society. The constant pressure for an expanding Gross National Product (GNP) and rising standard of living justifies and requires commercial expansion and the use of political and military power to secure expanded openings for American businessmen around the world. Our ever-growing consumer society is thus at odds with world peace. An international economic system that keeps huge sectors of humanity at a subhuman level while permitting the minority to consume most of the world's resources can only result in conflict. Peace is possible only if the poor and weaker nations of the world are willing to accept the present distribution of wealth and power and the rules of the game as laid down by the United States and the other powerful nations. The alliance of multinational corporations and the military and political strength of the world's most powerful governments have forged the empire that upholds the consumer society.

We are finally coming to understand a discomforting but central fact of reality: the people of the nonindustrialized world are poor *because* we are rich; the poverty of the masses is maintained and perpetuated by our systems and institutions and by the way we live our lives. In other words, the oppressive conditions of life in the poor countries, like the causes of poverty and misery in our own land, are neither merely accidental nor because of the failures of the poor. Our throw-away culture of affluence and wasteful consumption fragments and privatizes our lives. Our consumer orientation lulls us into primary concern for ourselves, and into a passive acceptance of the suffering of others.

Hunger and disease due to hunger are today responsible for two-thirds of the deaths in the world each year. It is estimated that a child born in the United States today will consume, during a lifetime, twenty times as much as a child born in India, and will contribute fifty times as much pollution to the environment. Of every one hundred babies born in the world, forty will die before age six. Another forty are at risk of permanent physical and mental damage because of malnutrition. Only three out of that hundred will get the education and skills they need to perform creative and meaningful work. While those in the rich nations worry about the potential for violence in the rebellion of the poor against the status quo, they fail to recognize the violence inherent in established structures and relationships that inflict injustice and agony by relegating the poor to subhuman conditions of life.

We have learned much about the United States through the eyes of the disadvantaged, the black, brown, red, and poor white minorities locked in urban ghettos of human misery, in rat-infested tenements, and in rural prisons of poverty. Race and sex are still the basis for denying people their basic human rights, and class and color continue to be the primary factors in determining a person's share of justice, education, health, respect, income, and society's goods and services.

All of this is aggravated and intensified by the growing concentration of economic and political power in the hands of a few persons and institutions. Certain people, classes, and institutions possess an enormous and illegitimate amount of power that is exercised for their own benefit. This power is, at root, economic, and comes to dominate and corrupt the political process. In the United States, such power is centered in the small number of large corporations that shape the political economy. The decision-making of these large corporations is in the hands of the very few and the very rich.

'Free Market' an Illusion

To suppose that corporate decisions are subject to the forces of the "free market" or to a meaningful sense of public accountability is to engage in illusion. These multinational corporations have gained great power and are increasingly able to act unilaterally in national and international affairs. American society itself is organized according to the large corporate model, and corporate interests and profits dominate production, distribution, communication, information, education, technology, entertainment, and, of course, politics.

We confront a socio-economic-political system based on the dominance of the few over the many. The affluent life-style of the American people supports such a system at home and around the world. John Woolman, an early American Quaker, once said, "May we look upon our treasures, the furniture of our houses, and our garments, and try whether the seeds of war have nourishment in these our possessions."

Yet the Bible contains a mandate to protect the poor from the abuses of wealth and power. The prophets spoke of God's anger with the politics of oppressive affluence:

> O my people, your leaders mislead you,
> and confuse the course of your paths.
> The Lord has taken his place to contend,
> he stands to judge his people.
> The Lord enters into judgment
> with the elders and princes of his people:
> "It is you who have devoured the vineyard,
> the spoil of the poor is in your houses.
> What do you mean by crushing my people,
> by grinding the face of the poor?" says the Lord God of hosts.
> (Isa. 3:12–15).

The gospel is biased in favor of the poor and oppressed. It presents a call to the church—that body that is most dynamic when it is most a minority living in radical contradiction to the values of the world by its proclamation and demonstration of a whole new order called the kingdom of God. But our churches have yet to grasp that vision. Their lifestyle, social prestige, and relationships identify them with the elite power groups of our society, rather than with the poor and oppressed. Our Christian institutions are often dependent on parts of the American establishment that oppress the poor. To come to terms with the gospel will cost the churches a great deal.

The churches are faced with whether they will continue to align themselves with a world order that subordinates justice and peace to the interests of the American establishment. This choice must be made with the knowledge that such a world order is threatened by the counterviolence of those who are its victims. The consequence of a choice to align with the world order will be endless war, revolution, death, and destruction. Such an outcome is inevitable unless some of those who have benefited from the American world order withdraw their allegiance from it, resist its designs and demands, repudiate its basic assumptions and values, and begin to construct alternatives that will provide a new kind of leadership and direction in the wealthy nations. This mission is one of peace, reconciliation, evangelism, and prophetic ministry—a mission for the church.

God and the Poor

Issues of wealth, poverty, and econmic justice are central in the Bible. The sheer bulk of the biblical teaching about the rich and the poor is overwhelming. The Old Testament is filled with it. Jesus talks more about it than almost any other single issue. The apostles regard the relationship to money and the poor as a primary test of obedience to God. The people of God, in both the Old and New testaments, are seen as offering an *economic alternative* to the prevailing assumptions of the world that surrounds them.

Contrary to the dominant attitude of our own society, one's economic life and standard of living is not a private matter. It is a critical issue of faith and discipleship. Not only is the Bible's teaching on the rich and the poor striking in its quantity, it is uncomfortably plain and clear in its meaning. The Scriptures are not neutral on questions of economics. The God of the Bible is clearly and emphatically on the side of the poor and the exploited.

Throughout Scripture we find an insistence that a vital relationship to God will evidence itself in an active serving of social and political justice as witness to God's gift of life. The prophets warned that piety, proper religion, and ritual observance are inadequate. They demanded economic and political justice. Isaiah tells us that the fast in which God delights involves breaking the yoke of oppression, sharing our bread with the hungry, and bringing the homeless poor into our homes (Isaiah 58:5–7). Amos claims that worship and praise are not acceptable to God unless justice rolls down like waters and righteousness like an ever-flowing stream (Amos 5:21–24).

The coming of Jesus brings social revolution. The downtrodden were objects of Christ's compassion. When questioned if he was the "one to come" from God, Jesus offered proof of his messiahship by his ministry to the concrete needs of the suffering and afflicted (Matt. 11:5). Jesus also warns those who would call his name that they will be judged by how they respond to the hungry, the poor, the naked, the imprisoned, the sick, and the stranger. The parable of the Good Samaritan demonstrates that our responsibility for our neighbor extends to anyone in need, and leaps over the human barriers of race and class at personal cost of time, money, and danger. The apostles repeatedly claim that faith without works that demonstrate obedience is dead, and that the quality of our love for God is shown in our practical and sacrificial love for our brothers and sisters.

Nowhere in Scripture are the rights of the rich proclaimed; nowhere is God seen as the savior and defender of the rich and their wealth; nowhere are the poor exhorted to serve the needs of the rich and be poor for the sake of the wealthy. Throughout Scripture, however, the rights of the poor are proclaimed; God is revealed as their savior, deliverer, and avenger; and the rich are instructed to serve the poor and relinquish their wealth and power for the sake of the poor. Nowhere in Scripture is wealth praised or admired or the rich upheld and exalted over the poor. In many places in the Bible, however, the poor are blessed and uplifted, and the message of God's Word carries with it the hope of justice and liberation for the poor. Riches are seen in the Bible as, at best, a great spiritual danger and, most often, as a sign of sinful disobedience to God. Just because the rich are rich, it will be harder for them to enter into the kingdom than for a camel to pass through the eye of a needle. The gospel is preached to the poor, and the rich are told to sell what they have and give to the poor for the sake of the kingdom.

The Bible and Riches

The Bible makes clear that money and possessions are deeply spiritual concerns at the core of human experience and, perhaps, reveal more about an individual than any other aspect of a person's life. The danger of riches in the Old Testament is in the misuse of wealth and power in the oppression and exploitation of the poor. The earth and its fullness belong to God and are given for the life and development of all God's children. The Jewish tradition of Jubilee Year provided for a periodic redistribution of land and wealth that militated against the accumulation of riches. In the thunderings of the prophets, God was powerfully revealed as the God of the poor and dispossessed, pouring out his wrath upon the rich and powerful whose affluence crushed the poor and powerless.

In the New Testament, the teaching on wealth is intensified, and its possession is seen as a great spiritual danger. The possession of wealth twists and distorts people's priorities and values and is a crucial obstacle in their sensitivity to God. The New Testament condemns, not just improper attitudes toward wealth, but also the mere possession of undistributed wealth.

One of the very first tests of discipleship to Jesus Christ is a radical change in one's relationship to money and the possession of wealth. The demands of mammon are completely irreconcilable with a total commitment to God. Jesus says, "You cannot serve God and mammon." Notice that he does not suggest that you should not; he simply says that you cannot. He assumes that the will of God and the demands of mammon directly contradict each other, and loyalty must be given to one or to the other.

If Jesus was so concerned about the danger of money and possessions in a simple agrarian society, how much more do we, living in the most affluent nation the world has ever known, need to break radically with the power and authority of money and possessions in our lives. An affluent church witnesses to its radical dependence upon wealth, not upon God, and has almost nothing to say to the dispossessed majority of the globe.

We need to hear again the words of the New Testament applied with their full force to us. (cf. Luke 6:24–25; Matt. 19:24; Luke 14:33; Matt. 6:19–21; Matt. 6:24; Matt. 25:44, 45; Mark 4:7, 18–19;

Luke 12:15; 2 Cor. 8:13–14; Eph. 5:5, 6; 1 Tim. 6:8–10; James 2:14–17).

The "just comfortable" standard of living in the rich nations is a sharp contrast to the lives of the poor of the earth. We must begin to face the harsh reality that everything the Bible says about the rich applies to us. Our overconsumption is theft from the poor. No longer must our words put us on the side of the oppressed and our style of life put us on the side of the oppressors.

God did not give the Americans half the world's resources so that we could be good stewards of it; rather, the Americans have stolen those goods from the poor. Unless we are willing to stand with the oppressed by first breaking our attachment to wealth and comfort, all our talk of justice will be sheer hypocrisy. The stating of principles and good intentions, the denunciations of crying injustices, the endless declarations will lack any weight or moral authority apart from a deep awareness of our responsibility before God and our hungry neighbors.

It is well to remember that the mark of sacrificial giving in the New Testament is not in how much is given but, rather, in how much is left over after the giving is finished (Luke 21:1–4). We cannot give sacrifically and still remain wealthy. It is critical that we constantly heed the biblical warning against minimizing the cost of a visible, outward break with the power of money and possessions. An affluent church cannot say, "Gold and silver have I none," and neither can it say, "In the name of Jesus of Nazareth, walk!"

The Church: Called to Sacrifice

The church is the body of Christ. This dramatic biblical metaphor speaks of the powerful way the work of Christ has united us to him and to each other. It means that Christ is alive and present in the community and is head over the body. It means that the church is called to embody the presence of Christ in the world by obeying his words, reflecting his mind, and continuing his mission in the world by following the manner and style of his life, death, and resurrection. Jesus tells us that he came into the world not to be served, but to serve, and so it is with us. Our vocation is to serve men and women in his name. We are called, not to be conquerors, but to be a self-giving body whose leader was crucified on a cross and asks his followers to take up that same cross. We are called, not to accumulate wealth and influence, or to strive to manipulate power, but to empty ourselves as he did for the sake of others.

We are called to give a cup of cold water in his name, which will mean feeding the hungry, meeting the needs of the homeless and refugees, supporting the imprisoned, befriending the lonely, standing with the poor and the outcasts, and loving the unloved. This means confronting with our lives the institutional and root causes of the condition of the oppressed. The life that Christ gives is meant to be spread about, not hoarded for the private edification of believers. The compassion of Christ always resulted in action, and so must ours. John, the apostle, exhorts us:

> By this we know love, that he laid down his life for us; and we ought to lay down our lives for the brethren. But if any one has the world's goods and sees his brother in need, yet closes his heart against him, how does God's love abide in him? Little children, let us not love in word or speech but in deed and in truth.
>
> By this we shall know that we are of the truth, and reassure our hearts before him (1 John 3:16–19).

The cross of Christ is both the symbol of our atonement and the pattern for our discipleship. Today, many who name the name of Christ have removed themselves from human hurt and suffering to places of relative comfort and safety. Many have sought to protect themselves and their families from the poor masses for whom Christ showed primary concern. In affluent societies, our approach to social problems is to decrease their visibility. The migration patterns of Christians and their churches have again reflected the dominant social practice. The church's compassionless inactivity stems from being out of touch with the suffering of the poor and exploited. This modern isolation from human hurt is a major obstacle to being faithful to biblical mandates. How can we open our hearts and lives to those whom we have hardly ever seen, let alone ever known?

The biblical idea of love carries with it the deliberate extension of ourselves to others. The incarnation, the supreme act of God's love, required the Lord of Glory to plunge into the chaotic, violent, and rebellious human situation at tremendous cost (Philippians 2:6–11). But this act brought the salvation of the world. We cannot profess the name of Jesus without seeking to incarnate his pattern of self-emptying love and servanthood. This is not only an individual effort, but a corporate one undertaken by a body of people who have given themselves to Christ and his kingdom, to each other, and to serving in the midst of the broken world for which he died.

God entered the human situation as one of the poor and powerless. Thomas Merton, in his *Raids on the Unspeakable*, speaks of the meaning of the incarnation:

> Into this world, this demented inn, in which there is absolutely no room for Him at all, Christ has come uninvited. But because He cannot be at home in it, because he is out of place in it, his place is with those others for whom there is no room. His place is with those who do not belong, who are rejected by power because they are regarded as weak, those who are discredited, who are denied the status of persons, who are tortured, bombed, and exterminated. With those for whom there is no room, Christ is present in the world. He is mysteriously present in those for whom there seems to be nothing but the world at its worst. . . . It is in these that He hides Himself, for whom there is no room.

The gospel knows nothing of what sociologists call "upward mobility." In fact, the gospel of Jesus Christ calls us to the reverse, to a downward pilgrimage. Former attachments and securities in the false values of wealth and power are left behind as we are empowered by the Holy Spirit to seek first the kingdom. From an obscure birth in a dirty animal stable, to the crucifixion of a poor suffering servant who never had a place to lay his head, the gospel witnesses to God's identification with the poor and powerless. Such a life of identification will bring rejection from the world, and if one becomes too prominent, one might even be crucified. We may measure our obedience to the gospel by the degree of tension and conflict with the world that is present in our lives. If our lives are secure, comfortable, and at home with wealth and power, we belong to the world rather than to Christ.

'All Things in Common'

Our downward pilgrimage will drive us to community and is meant to take place in the context of a common shared life. The life of the early Christian fellowships, as seen in the Book of Acts and elsewhere in Scripture, presents the Christian life as a common life, the life of a people more than the life of individuals. Here were the ones who had known Jesus, walked with him, talked with him, listened to him, and lived with him for three years. They had seen him live, die, and rise from the dead. They were eyewitnesses to the gospel. They had both followed him and forsaken him. Their lives had been decisively and irrevocably changed by him. He had set their feet upon a new path, and they would never be the same. In response to his command, they gathered in an upper room to wait for the promised coming of the Spirit.

At the day of Pentecost, they were all in one place, waiting, when suddenly there came a sound like "a strong driving wind" and "they were all filled with the Holy Spirit." The consequence of the outpouring of the Spirit was a bold and mighty proclamation of the gospel, repentance on the part of many who saw and heard, and the establishment of a *common life* among the believers. (See Acts 2:42–47).

The coming of the Spirit resulted in a common life springing up among the early believers. (See Acts 4:32–35).

The holding of "all things in common" was not merely a futile experiment, nor did this practice end at Jerusalem. Rather, common life and sharing are shown throughout the New Testament and became the distinguishing mark of the early church. This shared common life contradicts the ordinary social value that the possession of money and property carries the inalienable right to use and dispose of those assets for one's own benefit. The doctrine of private property as the right to use all of one's material and other resources for one's own purposes is a ruling social axiom; however, this most basic economic assumption is decidedly not Christian. Rather, the descriptions of the Christian fellowships in Acts and elsewhere point to a common use and consumption of resources, assets, and gifts of the body. The key here is the common use according to need, rather than a particular form or legal status of common ownership.

The Spirit had shattered the normal assumptions of the economic order, and the early believers realized that the way of Christ militated against the private use and disposition of resources, and led to the sharing of all resources as needs arose in the community. Material resources, no less than spiritual gifts, were to be shared and freely given for the good of the body, and not for the personal gain and advantage of the one who possessed them. A whole new system of distribution had been created in God's new community, with each person in a process of giving and receiving according to ability and need.

The self-giving of the church, as the history of the early church testifies, happens within the body and also spreads out to any and all who are poor and in need. The people of God will always and everywhere follow the will of their God and the example of their Lord in serving the poor of the earth. In its life as a servant people, the church is guided by the Holy Spirit and energized by the love of Christ. Jesus Christ is the leader of the new community. In John 17, he prays for the new community:

> But now I am coming to thee; and these things I speak in the world, that they may have my joy fulfilled in themselves. I have given them thy word; and the world has hated them because they are not of the world, even as I am not of the world. I do not pray that thou shouldst take them out of the world, but that thou shouldst keep them from the evil one. They are not of the world, even as I am not of the world. Sanctify them in the truth; thy word is truth. As thou did send me into the world, so I have sent them into the world. And for their sake, I consecrate myself, that they may also be consecrated in truth. I do not pray for these only, but also for those who are to believe in me through their word, that they may all be one; even as thou, Father, art in me, and I in thee, that they also may be in us, so that the world may believe that thou hast sent me (John 17:13–21).

12. *Radical Evangelicals and the Politics of Compassion*

By Lloyd Billingsley

Focus Radical Evangelicals are both ideologically imbalanced and politically irresponsible in their approach to social issues, charges Lloyd Billingsley. The imbalance arises from a refusal to face the whole truth about the causes of poverty and oppression in America and the world. The irresponsibility derives from talk about "compassion" without an understanding of the world as it is. The radical Evangelicals' prophetic "compassion for the poor," is, according to Billingsley, notable for its selectivity.

Truth, not propaganda, is the prerequisite for responsible social witness, Billingsley asserts. He points to the arrogance of radical Evangelicals who are so eager to condemn the United States that they characterize the Vietnamese "boat people" as having fled their country to support a "consumer habit" imposed on them by the capitalistic West. "Denouncing the powers that be" is an easy enough exercise, says Billingsley, but Evangelicals who would be genuinely compassionate must first be unafraid to face the hard truths about totalitarian regimes.

Evangelical radicals are not only selective in their criticism: they condemn the status quo as evil owing to a romantic infatuation with all that is "socialist, anti-colonialist, and anti-imperialist." The author urges Christians to compare the treatment of the poor in the West with that in closed or totalitarian societies. The truths to be gleaned from such an examination may prove less rhetorically appealing than "denouncing the powers that be in the name of God," but radical Evangelicals, if they truly want to stand with the poor, must first be partisans of the truth.

Billingsley's views should be compared with those of Ronald Sider (selection 8) and Jim Wallis (selection 11).

Lloyd Billingsley is a novelist and the author of three non-fiction books, including *The Absence of Tyranny: Recovering Freedom in Our Time* (Multnomah, 1986).

THE POOR, SAY those on the Evangelical left, are the only ones who have the right to inscribe on their belt buckles, like German soldiers in 1914, the words *Gott mit uns*. Or, as these radical Evangelicals usually phrase it: God is on the side of the poor.

People are poor for various reasons, not for one only, but one would never guess this from reading radical Christian publications. For instance, people can be poor because of their own lack of discipline and initiative. A steady provider can develop an alcohol or cocaine habit and plunge himself and his family into poverty. This group gets no sympathy from the Bible at all. In fact, they earn God's judgment.

Other poor people are genuine victims who suffer from injury, disease, or catastrophes such as famine and earthquake. The people of God are commanded to help them, because God is moved with compassion for them.

Still others are poor because of economic exploitation. Slavery is a historical example of this; South African apartheid and the East Indian caste system are contemporary versions. The victims of such exploitation have rightful claim to biblical justice, too.

A final group are the voluntary poor, who willingly give up affluent careers to better serve God and their fellow human beings. With ministerial salaries what they are, pastors could almost be included in this group en masse. Missionaries are another obvious example.[1]

The radical Evangelicals, however, view poverty as almost exclusively the result of economic victimization. Somehow, they insist, Western structural mechanisms like an open market and universal sufferage discriminate against the poor; a controlled economy and one-party state such as that of Cuba is deemed by them as somehow liberating and beneficial. Radical Evangelicals assume that the free enterprise model is the exploiter. Large

---

corporations also receive the radicals' wrath in spite of the fact that, as Louis Fischer pointed out, Marxist governments are one huge corporation that controls *everything* and from which there is no escape, as there is from Nestle or Exxon. As Djilas shows, the capitalism that Marxists gripe about no longer exists, but the radical Evangelicals do not appear to have noticed. They are living in the past, nostalgic for the days of the dark satanic mills described by Charles Dickens and Karl Marx.

The exploitation model also begs the question of why living standards are higher in free economies than in state-controlled economies. People *flee* closed societies like mainland China for better conditions in free enterprise countries. When refugees leave poor countries such as Mexico or El Salvador, they most often go to the United States, not to socialist Nicaragua. Why is this, if capitalist, open-market, politically free countries are examples of exploitive structures? If socialist dictatorships are so desirable, why must they wall in their subjects? It bears repeating that even Hitler did not need such draconian measures.

Politics as Cure-all

The radical Evangelicals' economic exploitation explanation for poverty of course demands a political solution. It assumes that those groups that have risen out of poverty have done so by political means. There is little if any evidence for this, however, as Thomas Sowell shows in *The Economics and Politics of Race*. The overseas Chinese, the Italians in Brazil, the Irish and blacks in America, and the Jews in many countries have generally kept their distance from politics. They have bettered themselves economically, Sowell demonstrates, by hard work, thrift, and sacrifice. These disciplines can yield results only in an open economic system. If there is a political solution to poverty, it lies in the option for people to initiate their own economic activity.

The radical Evangelicals explain poverty in the lesser developed countries by echoing the Leninist explanation first advanced to show why—contrary to what Marx predicted—capitalist workers got wealthier instead of poorer. Lenin said, in effect, that capitalist bosses were exploiting poor countries and forestalling revolution at home by buying off their workers with high wages. Today, this explanation is called the North-South Economic Dialogue. It fails, however, to explain two things: why the lesser developed countries were poor in the first place, and why those countries that have had most contact with the allegedly imperialistic powers have higher standards of living. The theory is popular only because it advances an explanation of poverty based not on any inadequacies on the part of the lesser developed countries themselves, but only on moral deficiencies on the part of others. As Sowell writes:

> The enduring and fervent belief in imperialism as the cause of Third World poverty is difficult to understand in terms of empirical evidence. But this belief is much more readily understandable in terms of the high psychic and political cost of believing otherwise. These costs are high not only to some people in the Third World, but also to those in the West whose whole vision of the world depends upon seeing poverty as victimization and themselves as rescuers—both domestically and internationally. Many such people assume a stance of being partisans of the poor. But even to be an effective partisan of the poor, one must first be a partisan of the truth.[2]

There is in the radical Evangelicals' critique, too, a clear selectivity in the poor they choose to champion. There are certain poor groups who are in their view worthy of love and support—and then there are others that are not. Jacques Ellul, who radical Christians readily quote when he agrees with them, points out that groups like the Kurds, the Tibetans, and the monarchist Yemenites do not attract the attention of radical Christian groups. Why is this? Are they not as poor as American blacks or the Philippine underclasses? Why do radical Christians find them uninteresting? Ellul has a theory:

> Alas, the reason is simple. The interesting poor are those whose defense is in reality an attack against Europe, against capitalism, against the U.S.A. The uninteresting poor represent forces that are considered passé. Their struggle concerns only themselves. They are fighting not to destroy a capitalist or colonialist regime, but simply to survive as individuals, as a culture, a people. And that, of course, is not at all interesting, is it? But the choice violent Christians make has nothing to do with love of the poor. They choose to support this or that group or movement because it is socialist, anti-colonialist, anti-imperialist etc.[3]

To touch on the issue of labeling here, Ellul uses the term

"revolutionary Christians." Here, he substitutes "violent Christians."

Every issue of *Sojourners* and *The Other Side* magazines bears out this interesting/uninteresting distinction. They support, for the most part, the aristocratic poor who have advocates in the UN and among film stars, such groups as the PLO and SWAPO. They say nothing about the others. Hence, their call to aid the poor lacks credibility.

Is Poverty a Virtue?

Listening to the Evangelical Left, though, one wonders whether it is even desirable for any people to lift themselves out of poverty. The mindset of *Sojourners* and *The Other Side* reveals a tension between ameliorating conditions of the poor and exalting poverty as a virtue. Theoretically, once people lift themselves out of poverty, they become part of the materialist mainstream and thus fodder for broadsides to "be more concerned about the poor."

At the same time, the magazines declare that poverty is abominable, and they call God's wrath down on us for allowing it (even though Jesus Christ himself said the poor would always be with us). Radical Evangelicals also want us to believe that poverty is the only acceptable lifestyle for Christians. But one cannot have it both ways.

The radical Evangelical ethic that extols poverty as a virtue is a new version of the 1930s' intellectuals' deification of the proletariat. Arthur Koestler explained how eggheads like himself would willingly eschew their background and learning and lobotomize themselves just to be like Ivan Ivanov—the proto-typical poor worker. Everyone unproletarian was dismissed as bourgeois. Being proletarian can even become a question of wearing the right clothing. Malcolm Muggeridge has described Orwell as decked out in "proletarian fancy-dress." The call to holy poverty is the same sort of social descent.

Can it really be contended that North American and European Christians are not concerned about the poor? American Christians give billions each year in charitable donations. Groups like the Salvation Army have been on the scene at foreign and domestic disasters before anyone else: They are the ones who run missions for derelict alcoholics—a case of the uninteresting poor if there ever was one—not Greenpeace, the Socialist Workers Party, or the Sierra Club. What of the clinics, the counseling, and the hospitals founded by religious groups? What of the acceptance of refugees from countries as diverse as El Salvador and Vietnam?

Yet the March 1983 issue of *The Other Side* derided groups such as the Salvation Army for being "supportive of the political status quo," even though the Salvation Army also operates in Cuba and Nicaragua. In those countries, should the Salvation Army denounce the revolutionary status quo?

Government programs for the poor in the West have tended to be very generous. It has been said that the only budgets in the world larger than the American allocation for the Department of Health, Education and Welfare are the entire budget of the United States and the entire budget of the Soviet Union. In any case, it cannot be seriously maintained that Western governments do nothing about the poor. They even take in the poor created by their enemies, as demonstrated by the United States' acceptance of the last flotilla from Cuba, many of whose passengers were elderly and handicapped. Theoretically, the marvelous social services of the Cuban state should draw the poor from the four corners of the world.

When there have been earthquakes and natural catastrophes in various parts of the world, many Western nations have rushed material aid, medicine, and personnel to the scene. When Mount St. Helens devastates a huge portion of a state or when a tornado destroys 90 percent of a Wisconsin town, what Third World country constantly accusing the United States of being a grasping exploiter is there lending a hand? None. Western capitalistic nations, to their great credit, have continued to feed the hand that bites them. Some Third World leaders such as Julius Nyerere, whose country of Tanzania has received more aid than any other, have used transfers of funds to consolidate their own power, persecute their enemies, and continue economic experiments which have miserably failed.

All this is not to suggest that Western societies and their economic systems are perfect; but as the record shows, they tend to outperform their scientific socialist counterparts when it comes to providing for the poor.

None of us, especially those like myself who see a small role for government, should rest on our laurels. We need to be constantly exhorted to do more for the poor, within the church and without. God commands us to do so. Whether the Evangelical Left holds the moral qualifications to make this exhortation—along with its occasional appeal for donations for its own programs—remains to be seen.

When Jesus saw the multitudes, the Gospels tell us, he was "moved with compassion."[4] The face of the Savior must have had a way of radiating his inner feelings. In another place we are told that Jesus, beholding the rich young ruler, "loved him."[5]

Compassion is a beautiful word, but it is now so abased as to be barely usable. Politicians have been largely responsible for this. The late David Lewis of the Canadian New Democratic (socialist) party based his 1974 election platform on a call for a "Compassionate Canada," with the adjective in this case meaning, "More control by a government of its citizens' resources." The American Democratic party describes itself as "the party of compassion." The word in this connection has come to mean something like "the willingness of a representative to spend other people's money." Those unwilling to spend at acceptable levels are charged with "lacking compassion."

The 'Boat People': Whose Fault?

Jim Wallis outlined the radical Christian position on compassion in a September 1979 *Sojourners* editorial about Vietnamese refugees entitled "Compassion Not Politics for Refugees." Wallis conceded that the suffering of these people was "real," hardly an original revelation. He understated their perils, though, by neglecting to mention marauding Thai pirates who preyed on the refugees and sank their ships. He went on to say that it is important to "get the facts straight" and that the coverage of the boat people was "filled with inaccuracies, myths, misconceptions, and outright lies," though he neither mentioned nor refuted any of these with facts of his own. The situation, we are told, "is complex and highly politicized and does not lend itself to easy explanations."

The shift away from simple explanations represents a change for the radical Evangelicals. During the Vietnam War, it was very simple indeed: if you favored the American-South Vietnamese side, you were wrong; if you favored an American pullout and the victory of the North, you were right. It was simplicity itself. You were either part of the problem or part of the solution. But now easy explanations are eschewed, though Jim Wallis goes on to advance one himself.

Did the Vietnamese government, by any chance, have anything to do with this problem? Perhaps a bit. Their policies, wrote Wallis, were "harsh." One should pause a moment here and contemplate this adjective.

When the Reagan administration, a government elected by an overwhelming majority, put forth its 1980 budget, the cover of *Sojourners* thundered, "ASSAULT ON THE POOR." Its writers readily use pejorative terms such as "militant," "oppressive," "reactionary," and "right-wing" for those who disagree with them. But when a revolutionary government strips people who merely want to leave of all their belongings, extorts outlandish "exit fees," then shoves them off to sea in rusty tubs that barely float, all this merits the description "harsh," something one might say of an overbearing high school principal. What word would *Sojourners* use if West Germany sent its Turkish minority packing on rafts in the North Sea? It would probably not be "harsh." But there is more.

After this scolding, Wallis said the Vietnamese government "must take more responsibility for the orderly and safe exit of those who choose to leave." One looks for terms like "right" and "wrong" here, but the government simply must take "more responsibility," whatever that means. "In this respect," Wallis continues, "the revolution has become the regime and has begun to behave like governments everywhere." Really? Do governments everywhere do this kind of thing to potential emigrants? Does Iceland? Sweden? Belgium? Uruguay? As it happens, only socialist, revolutionary governments such as that of Vietnam have made crossing borders a tricky procedure, particularly on the way out.

It is not long before Wallis gets around to those who are, in his view, really responsible for the refugees—the United States, of course, even though the boat people problem happened after the American forces left—something that Wallis urged for years.

Slipped into all this is an amazing sentence about the refugees themselves that should be read over several times, preferably aloud, and as slowly as possible. It says a great deal about radical Evangelicals' compassion:

> Many of today's refugees were inoculated with a taste for a Western lifestyle during the war and are fleeing to support their consumer habit in other lands.

Western Values Caricatured

Notice the sweeping generality ("many") applied to those who were inoculated with this criminal taste for Western lifestyle. And what does Western lifestyle mean? A tendency toward democracy? Mickey Mouse T-shirts? Freedom of religion? A large welfare budget? Abundance of the necessities of life? What? The imagery is that of the addict, fleeing to support his habit. The conclusion is inescapable: many of the refugees to some degree *deserve* what they are getting. Their crime was to be "inoculated with Western lifestyle." This, *Sojourners* would have us believe, merits banishment in leaking boats.

Imagine this scenario: You are a Vietnamese refugee, drifting on a derelict freighter in the South China Sea. Water is low, food almost nonexistent. You have no medical supplies or resources of any sort. Speedboats appear, full of heavily armed Thai pirates who rape the younger women, take some prisoner, steal everything they can find, murder some people outright, then sink the ship. You are left treading water, the cries of the drowning ringing in your ears. Wouldn't it be comforting to know that in secure, faraway America, the editor of a radical Evangelical magazine, in an editorial about "compassion," is announcing to the world that you are a Western junkie, fleeing to support your consumer habit in other lands?

The November 1979 edition of *National Geographic* reported that Hong Kong officials picked up a pregnant woman and her child who were in two inner tubes being pushed through shark-infested waters by the woman's swimming husband. The consumer addiction of this group was indeed serious. Doubtless they were after that color television set denied them under socialism.

Wallis denounces then-Vice President Walter Mondale for calling the Vietnamese government callous and arrogant and ends his editorial with, "Our response to the refugees must be one of active concern for the refugees, not out of political self-interest, but out of the compassion of Christ." All in all, quite a performance.

Wallis's statement on the boat people is a piece of poltroonery that ranks with the most bigoted and vicious. It is similar to Anna Louise Strong dismissing the murder of kulaks on the grounds that Russia could get along without them, and explaining that Uncle Joe Stalin, after all, had only authorized what the people were already doing. The kulaks too, I suppose, in refusing collectivization, had thus inoculated themselves with the Western lifestyle. Then, too, it has the ring of *Pravda* statements about "rootless cosmopolitans" who have the nerve to leave the Soviet Union.

One wonders what, by these standards, constitutes an attack if Wallis's editorial, as claimed, expresses compassion. *Sojourners* does give us some clues. In February 1980, Danny Collum reviewed Bob Dylan's *Slow Train Coming* album. On one of the cuts, "Gonna Change My Way of Thinking," Dylan says he is going to "stop being influenced by fools." This was too much for Collum, who called it "accusatory" and "downright mean." One would almost think that Dylan was in the process of fleeing to support a consumer habit. Has the government of Vietnam ever been "downright mean"? Or just "harsh"?

Other questions arise: What of the Central American refugees pouring into the United States? Are they, too, fleeing to support a consumer habit? Should they stay at home and be happy in poverty? It hardly need be said what the implication is for those of us who live in the West.

Radicals and Compulsion

Compassion? When a radical Evangelical alludes to compassion, he really means compulsion. The *Sojourners'* attack on helpless refugees betrays a tunnel vision that is almost clinical. There is an ideological fungus on the political retina of radical Evangelicals that blinds them to the faults of the dour Stalinists who currently run Vietnam. Before they would make any negative statements about a revolutionary (good) government, they attack the moral integrity of the victims of that government. It is assumed that the Vietnamese who remain are bound to do what they are told, even forced labor, euphemistically described in other *Sojourners* articles as "participating in the building of a new society." In the meantime, for the radical Evangelicals, it is up onto Rocinante and off at a gallop to the next crusade on behalf of the downtrodden and oppressed through whose plight the United States can be denounced.

Michael Novak was once something of a radical Christian. As an antiwar activist, he even wrote speeches for George McGovern. When asked in an interview why he had changed his stance, he answered:

> One thing that encouraged me in the direction, in fact necessitated this direction, was the destructiveness of radical politics in foreign affairs. The terrible plight of the Cambodian people, the boat people of South Vietnam, and the extraordinary suffering of the people of Vietnam today, have led me to realize that those of us who called for the end of the war in Vietnam unwittingly did something terrible. We caused even more destruction and more suffering, and we are guilty of the consequences of our actions. The least we can do is to learn from such things.[6]

Here is a man who, facing the facts, admits that he was *wrong* about Vietnam. No such admission has been forthcoming from the radical Evangelicals. This is a bit surprising.

At other junctures in recent history, *Sojourners* has been strong on apologizing. In the wake of the Iranian hostage crisis, Wallis wrote an editorial entitled "We Could Just Ask Them to Forgive Us,"[7] even though it was the Iranians, not the Americans, who took the hostages. The piece ends, "If our national pride and arrogance prevail over our reason and compassion, we will indeed reap the whirlwind." To apologize for someone else's wrongdoing, then, is to show compassion, according to Wallis.

Perhaps the boat people deserve an apology for the things *Sojourners* has said about them; but, for now at least, being a radical Christian means never having to say you're sorry.

Not All Change Is Progress

Barely anything that appears in publications of the Evangalical Left challenges the assumption that change is progress. In their view, the worst possible action anyone can take, particularly a Christian, is to defend the status quo in any way. The changes that are urged are of a structural, institutional variety and will, we are told, lead to social justice.

What this "progressive" view lacks is an historical perspective. A status quo composed of a divine-right monarch, an arrogant aristocracy, an authoritarian church, and an all-powerful police force is one thing; a status quo of a government of freely elected officials, a free press, universal suffrage, an open market economy, generous welfare programs, public education, and a police force that must read one his rights before arrest, is something else. Yet the superstition of radical Evangelicals is that to challenge the sort of institutions that exist not only in the United States, but also in Canada, Lichtenstein, Belgium, and Holland is "progressive"; to hold that they are adequate is reactionary.

The test for anything is not whether it is progressive, but whether it is right. A preponderant government that simultaneously dominated and took care of everyone was what feudalism was all about. Free enterprise democracy constitutes an improvement on that model. To identify progress with an ever-increasing government that serves as a kind of omnipresent wet nurse is to endorse a return to a modern form of feudalism. André Gide used these very words of the Soviet Union: In the Soviet system, the arrogant landowner is replaced by the arrogant bureaucrat.

Evangelical radicals, like mainline liberals, are slow to recognize that good intentions are not enough, that government programs set up to eliminate poverty sometimes only create dependency, and that their main beneficiaries are often administrating bureaucrats. Yet it is the politician who most *talks* about poverty and social justice who attracts the support of the Evangelical Left. Curiously, many politicians of this description—Teddy Kennedy and Pierre Trudeau, for instance—are independently wealthy.

But a political candidate who is for free enterprise and business does not merit the support of the Evangelical Left because his *intention* is to help people make profits, regardless of what other benefits accrue to the community as a result of the increased economic activity.

In free societies, people have certain rights: life, liberty, and property, for instance. It is the role of government to guard these rights. The Evangelical Left confuses rights and goals. Living independent of government dole, in adequate circumstances, with enough surplus to help others, is an admirable goal, but no one can legitimately demand it as a right: It is the result of hard work—even, in many cases, of making a profit.

Of course, making a simple case for basic economic realities is less rhetorically appealing than denouncing the powers that be in the name of God. The truth is not always spectacular.

When it gets down to models of the kind of progressive societies radicals would have us emulate, the term "democratic socialism" emerges and Sweden invariably is named.

Yet Sweden is really a confiscatory, welfare-capitalist state. Democratic socialism as applied to, say, East Germany (German Democratic Republic) really means undemocratic socialism. It is hard to believe that people would voluntarily assent to the continued total control of their lives—especially control that resulted in reduced living standards. Democratic socialism—"socialism with a human face"—remains an illusion.

All governments have limits. No system can avoid the foibles of life. In Sweden, Denmark, and Holland, people smell bad, die young, go insane, have car accidents, contract terminal diseases, love each other, murder each other, and commit suicide much like the citizens of Brazil or Nepal.

There are no utopias. The advocacy of increased government control, far from being progressive, leads, as F. A. Hayek wrote, down the road to serfdom. One wonders, therefore, why radical Evangelicals lean so hard on political solutions.

Notes

1. R. C. Sproul, "Biblical Economics: Equity or Equality," in *Christianity Today,* March 5, 1982, p. 94.
2. Thomas Sowell, *The Economics and Politics of Race* (New York: Morrow, 1983), p. 229.
3. Jacques Ellul, *Violence* (New York: Seabury, 1969), p. 67.
4. Matthew 14:14.
5. Mark 10:21.
6. "Interview with Michael Novak" in *The Wittenburg Door,* November 1982, p. 24.
7. Jim Wallis, "We Could Just Ask Them to Forgive Us," in *Sojourners,* January 1980, p. 3.

13. The Moral Limits of Government

By Stephen Monsma

Focus

An Evangelical who has taught political science and served as a state legislator, Stephen Monsma believes that a "just society" is one marked by an order that maximizes individual freedom. "Under a just order, people will not find their lives totally predetermined and controlled by outside forces," he says. He defines justice as "respect for the basic freedoms and opportunities that are due every individual"; it can be maintained "only if a society's members accept certain obligations." The most "just" position on crucial political issues can be found only by carefully weighing the competing principles of individual freedom and social obligations.

The role of government is to prevent unjust policies or practices. Government, in Monsma's view, has "a God-given task of balancing freedom and obligations in such a way that it increases people's opportunities to live lives of praise to God and service to others."

Monsma draws a distinction between morality and justice. He says that some public policy issues are mistakenly classified as moral issues. He chides those who assume that the government has the authority, or even the obligation, to impose on all of society a standard of morality. Some Evangelicals are more concerned with "moral politics" than with justice. "Moral politics is, in essence, totalitarian. It seeks to control people, to force them to do good—or at least to force them to maintain the outward appearances of good behavior, since this is all moral politics can accomplish."

By contrast, Monsma calls for a politics of justice. He says justice is liberating and pluralistic, promotes freedom and opportunity, and does not foster "stifling conformity to someone's concept of moral behavior." The pursuit of justice, not morality, is the proper concern of government. "Morality is a matter of the heart. No law, no government, can control that. Justice is a matter of overt acts, and that is what government can and should control." Monsma's view can be usefully compared with those of Carl F. H. Henry (selection 5) and Ronald Nash (selection 7).

Stephen V. Monsma, a professor of political science at Pepperdine University, formerly taught at Calvin College, served eight years in the Michigan legislature and directed the Office of Operations Review for the Michigan Department of Social Services. Monsma is author of *American Politics, The Unraveling of America,* and *Pursuing Justice in a Sinful World* (Eerdmans, 1984).

IN TODAY'S WORLD, the general biblical call for government to promote justice and righteousness, and to oppose oppression and evil, can best be seen in terms of public or political justice. The concept of justice grows naturally out of broader biblical principles and can serve as a reliable—though not automatic or self-applying—guide for judging and reacting to specific issues in American politics.

To understand the meaning of political or public justice, the first principle is that men and women are created by God in His image to be free, loving, creative, and joyful beings whose lives praise God and serve others. This is humankind's God-given purpose. Unlike animals, we have been created by God to be freely choosing, morally responsible, and creative beings. The entire Bible teaches this—from the account of Adam and Eve in the Garden of Eden, to John's exhortation to Christians in the last chapter of Revelation to accept "the free gift of the water of life" (Rev. 22:17). Christ's summary of the greatest commandment—to love God above all and our neighbor as ourselves (Matt. 22:37–40)—supports this conclusion.

For human beings to be free to live lives of creative joy and love, society must be marked by a just order. Three terms are crucial here: "society," "order," and "just."

First, of course, is society: Human beings have been created by God to live with each other. We are social beings, and we need each other in order to develop into the thinking, choosing, communicating, and loving beings God intends us to be. It is only in community with others that we can become all that God wants us to be.

Second, for human beings to live together, society must be marked by order. "Order" refers to a situation in which human relationships and expectations are regularized by adherence to established rules, customs, and standards. Without this, all human relationships would be based on caprice and happenstance, chaos

---

Reprinted by permission of William B. Eerdmans Publishing Co. from *Pursuing Justice In A Sinful World* by Stephen Monsma, 1984.

would be king, and brute force law. For human society to exist at all, therefore, there must be some way to establish regular patterns of behavior. In an orderly world there is some way to determine what type of clothing is suitable for what occasions, on which side of the road cars should be driven, and whether or not punching someone in the nose is appropriate behavior. Customs, tradition, and law all play a part in bringing about order.

The Primacy of Order

If there is no social order, there can be no society, and if there is no society, human beings cannot be the loving, joyful, and creative beings God intends them to be.

Third, there can be a just order or an unjust order in society—and the distinction is crucial. Justice has traditionally been defined as the giving to all persons their due. The basic idea is that all people, as created in the image of God, possess certain rights that are their due, and that are theirs simply because they are human. The right to life itself, and the right to worship God freely, are examples. Of course, people often disagree on exactly what is due an individual, and thus what rights a society must respect if it is to have a just order. At the heart of the question must be that which is necessary or helpful in order for people to live the joyful, creative, and loving lives God intends for all his children. At the very least, then, a just order will protect basic freedoms and work to assure a broad range of opportunities for all.

This means that, under a just order, people will not find their lives totally predetermined and controlled by outside forces. An order imposed by a totalitarian government that dictates one's occupation, restricts one's travel, denies one freedom of religion, controls the upbringing of children, denies the freedom to speak or publish, and in numerous other ways controls private life, clearly violates justice. There is no freedom, and there is no opportunity to be a freely choosing, creative, and morally responsible individual. To be totally controlled is to be treated as less than human. Similarly, a person living in a primitive tribal society in which one's whole life and almost every act is circumscribed by extremely rigid traditions and taboos can also be denied the creative freedom God intends for all of us, even in the absence of formally enacted laws.

Closer to home, economic conditions and societal attitudes can also create an unjust order that denies people the basic freedom God intends for them. Take the case of a young black woman living in extreme poverty in an urban ghetto. There are no laws forbidding her to aspire to be the owner-operator of a small plant manufacturing component parts for computers. Indeed, she may be called by God to praise Him and serve others by pursuing this dream. But the order existing in American society conspires to raise almost insurmountable barriers to her achieving this goal. Racism and sexism make women and blacks less than fully welcomed in the manufacturing sector of the economy and surely not welcome as owners of high-tech businesses. Coming from a background of poverty, this woman will probably not be able to get the high quality education she would need to attain this goal. In all probability, the elementary schools and high schools in her neighborhood are low quality institutions that have profound disciplinary problems and offer little intellectual stimulation, and she may not be able to afford a college education.

The suffocating of freedom and opportunities—that is, an unjust order—can arise from societal attitudes, traditions, and structures as well as from unjust laws. Justice is not merely a negative concept—not only the absence of certain restraints on our activities—but a positive concept: the existence of actual opportunities that allow us to make morally responsible choices.

We need to discern two key social elements: (1) humankind's God-given purpose—to live loving, joyful, creative lives of praise and service—and, (2) a just order—societal customs, traditions, and laws that protect basic freedoms and assure a broad range of opportunities. These two elements are related, because it is the freedoms and opportunities assured by a just order that enable men and women to fulfill their God-given purpose.

Freedom Has Obligations

But an important point still needs to be made. Respect for the basic freedoms and opportunities that are due every individual—that is, justice—can be secured only if a society's members accept certain obligations. One's right to life is bought by another's accepting the obligation not to kill. Freedoms and opportunities are not free: their cost is the imposition of obligations on society. Working to establish a just order thus becomes the difficult task of deciding what freedoms to recognize and what opportunities to protect at the cost of imposing certain obligations. Is protecting the unborn child's right to life worth imposing on a pregnant woman the obligation to carry a fetus to term? Is my opportunity for a free college education worth imposing additional taxes on the rest of society? Is the opportunity to enjoy clean, clear streams worth imposing on both individuals and businesses the obligation not to pollute, even if that means certain manufactured goods will cost more or some people will lose their jobs? This is the appropriate way to frame every issue if a society is sincere about pursuing the goal of a just order.

The standard to be used in making these determinations is the goal of increasing the actual free range of choices available to all God's children to live as he intended them to: A just order thereby emerges.

But when confronted with specific, concrete political issues, how ought we determine the balance between freedoms or opportunities on the one hand, and obligations (which result in a just order) on the other? Two factors need to be considered in answering this question. The first is the seriousness to be attached to the freedoms and obligations at stake. Freedoms and obligations are not all equal: they can be ranked according to the degree to which they increase or diminish one's freedom and opportunities. Clearly, the right to life ranks much higher than the right to establish and run a manufacturing plant in the way that one thinks is most effective and efficient. Thus, if my manufacturing process results in toxic, carcinogenic chemicals contaminating others' water supply, it would clearly be just to enact a law that protects the public's health by requiring me to carefully dispose of the toxic waste. The relative importance of the competing freedoms and obligations is one crucial factor to be weighed in determining what is just.

A second factor is comparing the number of people who will win certain freedoms with the number who will be assigned corresponding obligations. If the freedoms and obligations being apportioned are roughly equal in importance, but many more people will find their freedoms restricted by additional obligations than will find their freedoms increased by additional opportunities, justice would dictate that the apportionment is not equitable.

It is often very difficult to determine in specific, concrete situations exactly what is just. To do so involves a process of balancing and weighing—a process that requires personal judgment and discretion. This task can be made more manageable, however, by considering both the importance of the freedoms and obligations at stake and the number of people who will be affected by the balance being shifted in one direction or another.

Achieving the balance between opportunities and obligations that results in a just order would be a natural, lighthearted, and joyous task if men and women were the perfect beings originally created by God. But something has gone tragically wrong in human affairs. Humankind is marked by sin and its bitter fruit, listed in Paul's epistle to the Galatians as "sexual immortality, impurity and debauchery; idolatry and witchcraft; hatred, discord, jealousy, fits of rage, selfish ambition, dissensions, factions and envy; drunkenness, orgies, and the like" (Galatians 5:19–21). The natural result of sin is that men and women demand more and more for themselves and recognize fewer and fewer obligations to others. The consequences include societies that constantly veer off the proper track and support unjust orders marked by exploitation of the poor, oppression of minority races, and destruction of the natural environment. More powerful societies take advantage of weaker societies. Disorder and injustices that would prevent people from living the joyful, loving, and creative lives God intends for all his children constantly threaten to become the prevailing condition of humankind.

It is because of this constant tendency of societies to succumb to unjust orders that God has established governments to oppose evil and to promote justice. In light of the nature of a just order, this means that government has the God-given task of balancing freedoms and obligations in such a way that it increases people's opportunities to live lives of praise to God and service to others. The sinfulness of the human heart makes this task both tremendously important and tremendously difficult. We must not underestimate either aspect of it.

Justice in the Political World

Christians should work for a more just order in society by supporting policy alternatives that strike a proper balance between freedoms and obligations. The problem is how to take this vision down into the swirling world of political issues and events and apply it thoughtfully and consistently.

In seeking justice, there is no magic formula. Two people who agree on using this standard to determine their positions on political issues may nevertheless arrive at opposite conclusions. Justice is not a magic formula leading irresistibly to preordained answers, but a standard applied to current, concrete issues in a creative process, rather than a mechanical one.

Two specific factors often lead people equally committed to following the standard of justice to arrive at different conclusions. The first is incomplete information. In the real world, one never operates on the basis of knowing all the facts. Usually, big chunks of information crucial to making a thoughtful, conscientious decision are missing completely or, at best, are fuzzy and in dispute. Almost every political issue must be decided in the face of missing information.

Second is the fact that one relevant value often clashes with another. Applying the standard of justice involves a weighing or balancing process. Freedoms and obligations are being apportioned. What values are at stake, and what weight they should be given, are often at the heart of political issues.

In sum, political issues are not resolved in a quiet, pristine, laboratory-like world where complete information is available and people have the time to carefully sort out and weigh the relevant values. Typically, information is incomplete, values clash, and time is short. Given these circumstances, it is hardly surprising that even people who start out with the same biblical standard sometimes end up disagreeing.

But even when they do disagree, their disagreement is on a much higher level—and therefore much has been gained—than those disagreements that occur because of false standards or selfish ambitions. Two politically involved people with the same biblical standard who are struggling over an issue are not like a couple of alley cats fighting and snarling over a scrap of food; they are more like two neighbors who disagree and try to work out a mutually satisfactory solution. Because the debate is on a much higher plane, the chances of a reasonable solution that will lead to creating a more just order are much greater than if the debate were based on fundamental disagreements about goals and purposes.

Moral Politics and Public Policy

Sometimes moral politics contradicts the politics of justice. Sometimes a distinction is made between moral issues, on which Christians are presumed to have something distinctive to offer, and morally neutral issues, on which Christians are presumed to have ideas neither more nor less noteworthy than anyone else's. In this view, public policy issues such as abortion, pornography, prayer in school, and gay rights are usually seen as moral issues, and presumably other issues are seen as morally neutral. Some would add such issues as poverty, nuclear disarmament, unemployment, and environmental pollution to the list of moral issues about which Christians should be deeply concerned.

In both cases, however, people seem to start out with the assumption that, if something is morally right and good, it is the proper role of government to impose it on all of society. The first group tends to latch onto personal ethics, and the second group onto social ethics; the first group runs into greater dangers, but both groups would be on firmer ground if they began by asking what is just instead of what is moral. The two questions are related, but they are distinct, and the distinction can make a huge difference. Christianity teaches us that government is to pursue justice, and thus Christians have a moral duty to pursue justice in the political realm. But this does not mean that all morality is justice. Christians must remember that they are called to hold certain private, personal standards of morality that have little to do with political justice.

Government is to pursue justice—not morality apart from justice. To the extent that justice and morality overlap, one can say that the justice-promoting activities of government also promote morality, but it is the pursuit of justice that is the controlling factor, not the pursuit of morality apart from justice.

The difficulty of government pursuing morality apart from justice is made apparent by the fact that no one can be forced to be moral, because morality is a matter of the heart, and governments can deal only with outward actions. Government can, for example, deter a man from killing his neighbor by threatening him with imprisonment or even death. But our Lord has told us that anyone who hates his neighbor has already committed murder in his heart. Thus government can stop an individual from acting out the dark hatred within his or her heart, but this involves no moral improvement in God's sight if the feeling that would motivate the deed is still there.

Similarly, when Christians have represented a majority of political power, they have often passed Sunday-observance laws that have closed stores, outlawed sporting events, and sometimes even required church attendance. Whatever one may think of such laws, let us be clear on one thing: they have little to do with morality. If "keeping the Sabbath day holy" means worshiping God in church, abstaining from commercial activities and sports, and devoting the day to spiritual growth and study, Sunday "blue laws" have little to do with true Sunday observance. The person who would have gone shopping or to a ball game on Sunday if such activities were not legally banned is likely to spend Sunday paying bills or playing pool in the basement—activities fully as commercial or recreational as the more public, but outlawed, ones. The government can even force a person to attend church, but it can force no one to worship God.

Morality is a matter of the heart, and no law, no government can control that. Justice is a matter of overt acts, and that is what government can and should control.

Justice and morality ask two quite different questions. Justice asks, "Does this issue involve questions of freedom and opportunity?" and "What position, on balance, would give more people greater freedom and opportunity to live fuller, more joyful, more creative lives?" Morality asks, "Does this issue involve questions of morally good behavior?"

Moral politics is, in essence, totalitarian. It seeks to control people, to force them to be good—or at least to force them to maintain the outward appearances of good behavior, because this is all moral politics can accomplish.

The politics of justice is liberating and pluralistic. It is liberating in the sense that it seeks greater freedom and opportunity, not stifling conformity to someone's concept of moral behavior. The result of this freedom is pluralism. Different individuals and groups will respond to their own faiths, whether those of Christianity, Judaism, humanism, or hedonism. God wills that all men and women love Him and obey His commandments, but He wills that this love and obedience be freely given to Him—not exacted from people through the power of law.

Pluralism and the Just Society

Some, given the freedom to choose, will not obey. This is inevitable in a pluralistic society in which some will pursue activities, form organizations, and express opinions contrary to those of Christians. There will be mosques as well as churches, nudist camps as well as Bible camps, hateful, racist literature as well as the writings of a C. S. Lewis or a Martin Luther King, Jr.

Yet justice with the resulting pluralism is not anarchic. It does not say that we all can do what we like irrespective of the impact on others. Justice recognizes that we live in society and that one person's actions can have a profound effect on others' freedoms—thus the importance of assuring rights and opportunities through the process of balancing freedom and obligations.

Consider, for example, religion in the public schools. The politics of justice opposes with equal fervor actions that would either mandate or outlaw prayers or other religious exercises in public schools. It therefore would oppose public prayers or other religious exercises as part of classroom activities, even though such activities are moral and even required by God. Christmas—or, for that matter, holidays of other religions—should not be observed. The differing religious backgrounds of students' families and justice's concern for the freedom of students and their families demand this much.

But the politics of justice also opposes some recent U.S. Supreme Court decisions that have outlawed the use of school facilities for voluntary religious activities outside normal school hours. Such politics would also allow the teaching of Christian and other religious views on such topics as the origins of the earth and humankind, obedience to government, and social problems. If such rights are not asserted, public schools can become the enemy of religion, stifling the freedom to act on one's religious beliefs that justice demands. There is in fact a danger that the public schools in the United States today, instead of being genuinely pluralistic, will teach a faith—some would say religion—that is outside of any recognized formal religion, but is based on a perceived consensual, materialistic, nontheistic "Americanism." But the public schools should be pluralistic institutions, not melting pots. They should allow for a colorful diversity of religious commitments, not promote a homogenized, secular faith.

In contrast, moral politics sees prayer as good and therefore something to be promoted or even required in public schools. It seeks—in its Christian manifestations—to make the public schools into Christian schools. After all, we are a "Christian nation," are we not? In some ways, we are, indeed, a Christian nation. I would to God we were much more deeply a Christian nation—that more of our people were obedient Christians, that our great universities, such as Yale, Harvard, and Princeton, reflected a Christian understanding of learning as they once did, and that our political leaders openly acknowledged Jesus Christ as Savior and Lord. But this is quite different from saying that our nation should be "Christian" by using political power to force nonChristians—including children in public schools who come from nonChristian families—to exhibit the outward signs of Christian belief. That is neither just nor Christian; it is totalitarian. And that is precisely where moral politics leads us.

Love as the Motive for Justice

But after distinguishing between moral politics and the politics of justice, there are some important ways to bring the two concepts close together. If by "moral politics" we mean politics based on Christian morality, that morality is summed up in the commands to love God above all and our neighbors as ourselves. The Bible testifies that this is, indeed, what lies at the heart of true Christian morality. The Christian political activist should be guided by this vision of morality. In the political world, love of God and neighbor must show itself in a passion for a more just order. One loves God and one's fellows, and therefore seeks justice for them.

How does one show love, for example, to prostitutes, many of whom have been led into this degrading means of making a living by an unjust, male-dominated society? The contention that most prostitutes freely chose this occupation is a thinly disguised fiction. Does one then show love to the prostitute by legalizing prostitution on the grounds that justice does not seek to impose a single moral standard of behavior on everyone, but instead allows for a variety of life-styles and moral choices? I think not. In a world of sexism, racism, exploitive pimps, and macho-influenced males, prostitution is usually nothing more than the ultimate in sexual exploitation and has nothing to do with the joyful, loving, creative life of which the Bible's vision of justice speaks.

The politics of justice—if it is motivated by a true love for all God's children and rests on a sophisticated vision of justice—will work, insistently and constantly, for a world of justice in which moral lives exhibiting love for God and humankind are made possible and encouraged. It allows an individual to live a moral life of love. Paradoxically, the politics of justice thereby attains, in a deeper and more profound sense, a higher level of morality than moral politics, with its direct pursuit of morality through the use of political power.

Justice is part of every issue. There are implications for justice in every issue. One of the problems with confusing morality with justice as the guiding principle of political action arises from the fact that "morality"—in the sense that clear Christian ethical issues are directly involved—is often not present in political issues. Thus, if morality were the standard, Christianity would not speak to many political issues.

But justice is present in all political issues. It is a more inclusive standard than morality. Political decisions by their very nature assign freedoms and obligations, benefits and costs in society. Political decisions do not have neutral effects: each decision has its winners and its losers. This is often true in a monetary sense, as when certain taxes are raised and others lowered, certain contracts are awarded, or more money is appropriated for one purpose and less for another. But there can also be winners and losers in terms of values or beliefs, as when schools are allowed or forbidden to offer classes in sex education, abortions are restricted or made more freely available, or reciting the pledge of allegiance is made mandatory at the start of each school day. In these examples—taken from actual political controversies—some financial advantages or disadvantages are part of the issue, but they are far outweighed (for most people involved) by the values or beliefs that are being affirmed or denied.

Justice means striking a balance between freedoms and obligations and doing so in a way that increases the opportunities available to all to live loving, joyful, and creative lives. Since political decisions consistently involve assigning freedoms and obligations, benefits and costs—thus creating a social order that is more just or less just—they consistently involve justice.

Justice will often be involved only indirectly, and specific decisions will often affect the level of justice present in society to a very small degree. Yet justice is there. The Christian political activist who is justice-oriented will constantly be alert for the implications for justice in public issues. For it is these small, incremental, often seemingly inconsequential steps toward or away from justice that determine the level of justice present in a society.

Individualism and Social Concerns

The politics of justice can contradict individualistic politics. One of the tendencies of many politically aware people that can lead to difficulties is that of seeing social and political issues almost totally in individualistic terms. An entirely appropriate emphasis on the importance of the individual can—and in the American experience frequently does—blind one to recognizing that individuals do not live, work, and play as separate beings. Instead, society is a whole made up of individuals grouped into innumerable organic associations. Individuals can fulfill their God-given purpose as thinking, willing, joyful, and creative beings only as parts of families, circles of friends, churches, synagogues, neighborhoods, work groups, clubs, unions, or other groupings. Very few human activities are done alone. Normally we eat, learn, work, play, and worship together. Usually we do so with people with whom we share, not a fleeting acquaintance, but a continuing relationship.

Therefore, in determining what is just in specific, concrete situations, one must be sensitive to how the options one faces will affect these groups or associations. Justice is not merely an individualistic concept; it recognizes the group dimension that is vital both to human well-being and to a just order.

The mainstream of American liberal thought often emphasizes individual rights in isolation from the rights or benefits the individual possesses as part of a group. As a result, justice is sometimes not promoted. For justice to be truly just, the freedoms and opportunities a person enjoys as part of a group or association must be recognized.

Should we, for example, require motorcyclists to wear safety helmets? By now it is clear that neither the Bible nor even the biblically based vision of justice I have developed offers a clearcut, obvious answer to that question. Yet what I have suggested speaks directly to the question. The "bikers" who oppose helmet laws are right: whether or not they should be required to wear helmets is a question of justice. The standard ought not to be what I personally believe would be the morally responsible thing for me to do if I were to ride a motorcycle. The question should be resolved by reference to freedoms and obligations that lead to opportunities for all God's children to lead joyful, loving, and creative lives of praise and service. And justice must weigh the impact that decision will have on families and other social groupings, not only how it will affect the individual.

But after all is said and done—whether it is the question of motorcyclists wearing helmets or weightier questions of racial discrimination, food for the hungry, or war and peace—Christians must make individual decisions on public issues. It is only through personal struggles with their own consciences—which have been informed by the teachings of the Bible, by their own understanding of the world, by the help of the church, and by the guidance of the Holy Spirit—that they can answer on what side of the constant stream of decisions flowing by them justice demands they should stand.

14. *Confusing Justice and Peace*

By DEAN CURRY

Focus

While some critics believe that radical Evangelicals confuse love and justice, Dean Curry suggests that they confuse justice and peace. In analyzing the purposes and ramifications of the 1973 "Chicago Declaration," an influential and widely publicized statement signed by many Evangelical leaders, Curry finds that many younger Evangelicals have rejected the social, economic, and political principles of American democracy in favor of a new version of pacifism—what he calls "shalom peace."

The Declaration was intended to challenge Evangelicals to greater concern for social justice in an "unjust American society," and was supported by many elder statesmen of the Evangelical movement. In Curry's view, however, it was fundamentally flawed. It suggested, for example, that social and political injustices in America and abroad were primarily the result of U.S. "economic and military might," but it made no reference to the injustices and brutality routinely perpetrated by totalitarian regimes.

Taking their cue from the Declaration, a new generation of radical Evangelicals now equates justice with a peace that is impossible to attain in a "fallen world." These radical Evangelicals refuse to acknowledge, says Curry, that there can be no justice apart from the freedoms best fostered in democratic societies. In espousing what they call "the politics of eternity," these radicals contribute to a profound misunderstanding of the necessary part the United States must play in world affairs. By rejecting—in the name of peace—the U.S. defense of freedom, these radicals may actually compound the injustices suffered by millions of people around the world.

Dean Curry is chairman of the Department of Political Science at Messiah College, and is the author, with Myron Augsburger, of *Nuclear Arms: Two Views on World Peace* (Word, 1987).

EVANGELICALS DO NOT have a rich history of scholarship—Biblical or otherwise—relating to war and peace. Historically, Evangelicals have borrowed from the dominant themes of the just war doctrine developed by the Roman Catholic Church and refined in the writings of Protestant ethicists such as Paul Ramsey.

Perhaps the most original contribution of the Protestant tradition to the theological reflection on war and peace came with the emergence of the various pacifist movements during the Reformation era. Since the emergence of the Evangelical movement earlier this century, however, the just war doctrine has provided the tenets by which Evangelicals have evaluated issues of war and peace. Until the present decade, Evangelical pacifism has been embraced by relatively obscure denominations such as the Mennonites that are both geographically and ethnically provincial.

With the advent of a more socially conscious Evangelicalism in the early 1970s, Evangelical attitudes toward war and peace began to change. In the larger sense of things, this reorientation was a reflection of a growing ideological polarization among Evangelicals generally. In many ways, the emergence of the "radical" or "young" Evangelicals under the institutional umbrella of organizations such as Evangelicals for Social Action was an event as important as the formation of the National Association of Evangelicals forty years earlier.

In the late 1960s and early 1970s, Evangelicals who had staunchly supported American military power and defense policies found themselves confronted with a growing number of "radical" Evangelicals who rejected many of the economic, social, and political premises of American society. It was not without significance that the first major publication to emerge from this "radical" Evangelicalism was entitled the *Post American,* a journal later renamed *Sojourners*.

Revised and reprinted with permission from the December 1984 issue of *Catholicism and Crisis, P.O. Box 1006, Notre Dame, Indiana, 46556.*

The 'Chicago Declaration'

What happened next paralleled the evolution of ideas in American society generally during the 1970s. Many individuals who had been associated with mainstream Evangelicalism during the 1940s, 1950s, and 1960s began to echo major themes of the social and political "radicals" of the late 1960s. The result was that Evangelical social action was increasingly based on the Biblical hermenutic, socio-economic critique, and political agenda of "radical" Evangelicals. This point of view was in many respects indistinguishable from the social and political critique of the secular Left in America.

This transformation imbued mainstream Evangelicalism with the ideology of what had previously been referred to as "radical." The transformation culminated in the "Chicago Declaration" of 1973. This was a landmark statement on Evangelical social responsibility in which mainstream Evangelicals such as Carl F. H. Henry, Vernon Grounds, and Frank Gaebelein joined such radical Evangelicals as Jim Wallis in declaring that "God requires justice (but) we have not proclaimed or demonstrated his justice to an unjust American society."

The Declaration's purpose was to "call . . . Evangelical Christians to demonstrate repentance in a Christian discipleship that confronts the social and political injustice of our nation." Christian discipleship, the Declaration insisted, required Evangelicals to ". . . challenge the misplaced trust of the nation in economic and military might—a proud trust that promotes a national pathology of war and violence which victimizes our neighbors at home and abroad."

With these words the leaders of Evangelicalism in America signaled a break with their tradition's general support of United States domestic and foreign policy. Though the Declaration is moderate in tone, the radical nature of its message is unambiguous. The Evangelical leaders who signed the "Chicago Declaration" were endorsing the proposition that American society is permeated with an injustice rooted in American social and economic structures. Furthermore, they were endorsing the proposition that the

United States uses its economic and military power to perpetuate injustice throughout the world. The message of the "Chicago Declaration" is clear: domestic and international injustices are the result of an inherent bellicosity in American economic and military structures; therefore, global justice is predicated upon the United States renouncing its use of power. Are there legitimate uses of American power? According to the Chicago Declaration, the answer is No, because American institutions are inherently unjust; accordingly, any use of American power is simply an attempt to further the interests of individuals and institutions that have a vested interest in the country's unjust structures.

In rejecting the traditional American consensus—liberal as well as conservative—with respect to the essential legitimacy of American socio-economic institutions, the Evangelical leaders who endorsed the "Chicago Declaration" were embracing a critique of American society and foreign policy derived directly from the New Left. In addition, in stating that "we proclaim no new gospel, but the gospel of the Lord Jesus Christ . . . (and) we endorse no political ideology . . . ," the signers of the "Chicago Declaration" were both theologically presumptuous and intellectually dishonest.

One hopes that most of the Evangelicals who signed the "Chicago Declaration" were not aware of the document's theological, social, and political implications. Over a decade later there is reason to believe that at least some of the signers would probably not endorse the document today. This is not to suggest, however, that the "Chicago Declaration" had little impact beyond the mid-1970s; the document formally established the critique, themes, and agenda which the Evangelical community, and especially the Evangelical leadership, has since regarded as both biblically and politically correct. Specifically, the Declaration established "peace and justice" as the central concern of Evangelical social mission. The concept of peace and justice embodied in the Declaration presupposes that American economic and foreign policy institutions are unjust.

It is both ironic and significant that, for many Evangelicals, "injustice" after the Chicago Declaration has been deemed a product of American society. Gone after 1973 was the historical

Evangelical concern about Marxism. Nowhere in the "Chicago Declaration" are the dangers of totalitarianism addressed.

'Peacemaking' and the Arms Race

This is the ideological context in which Evangelicalism's present preoccupation with war and peace was nurtured. Because "social justice" became the sine qua non of Christian responsibility, U.S. foreign and arms policies have become the focus of Evangelical political activism. These concerns dovetailed during the late 1970s with a resuscitated American peace movement which seized upon the production and deployment of a wide range of new weapons systems as a pretext for increased activism. "Peacemaking"—or opposition to nuclear weapons systems and strategies—became a priority for many influential Evangelicals.

In the spring of 1978, for example, nearly 200 Evangelical leaders issued a "Call to Faithfulness" and committed themselves to ". . . total abolition of nuclear weapons. We the signers of this declaration, commit ourselves to non-cooperation with our country's preparations for nuclear war . . . we commit ourselves to resist in the name of Jesus Christ."

Even more important than the Call was Billy Graham's 1979 announcement that he had changed his own views on nuclear weapons. Confessing that he had previously "confused the kingdom of God with the American way of life," Graham urged Evangelicals to reconsider their support for U.S. strategic policy.

By the early 1980s, influential Evangelicals such as Vernon Grounds, John R. W. Stott, and Ronald J. Sider were regularly speaking out against the arms race in general and U.S. arms policy in particular. In May of 1983, another landmark in the Evangelical debate over war and peace issues was established when over 1400 Evangelicals attended a conference on "The Church and Peacemaking in the Nuclear Age" in Pasadena. The conference committee represented a coalition of Evangelicals ranging from the Youth for Christ to the New Call for Peacemaking. The conference's claim to be the most significant event of its kind in the brief history of Evangelicalism in America was probably accurate. There was, to be sure, an effort on the part of the conference committee to elicit, as one organizer said, "a wide spectrum of opinion on questions of the nuclear arms race." In reality, however, the conference was dominated by the Evangelical "peace" activists who had championed the Chicago Declaration a decade before.

Where, then, does the Evangelical response to war and peace now stand? During the last fifteen years, many Evangelicals have reexamined their historical support for both the just war doctrine and U.S. foreign and arms policy. I have purposely used the word "many" to indicate the activities of some Evangelicals. For it is distressing to note that the Evangelical discourse on war and peace issues—particularly at Evangelical colleges and within Evangelical publications—gives little consideration to the wide range of viewpoints that are held by Evangelicals as a whole.

Evangelicals on War and Peace

In 1983, for example, the National Association of Evangelicals (NAE) commissioned the Gallup Organization to survey Evangelicals about their views on the nuclear arms race. The results of that survey are revealing. Of all the Evangelicals surveyed, seventy-seven per cent favored "an immediate verifiable freeze on the testing, production, and deployment of nuclear weapons." In holding this view, Evangelicals differed only slightly from the general public. When Evangelicals were asked if they believed that "a person can be a good Christian and still support the possession of nuclear weapons," however, fully eighty-five per cent answered Yes. Sixty-one per cent of the Evangelicals surveyed said they approved "of the way President Reagan is dealing with the nuclear arms situation."

In short, the results of the NAE/Gallup poll demonstrated that the vast majority of Evangelicals holds views on the war and peace issue significantly different from the Evangelical leadership. Certainly one must be cautious in interpreting opinion data; nevertheless, it is impossible not to be struck by the contrast between the views of the Evangelical worshipper in the pew, the Evangelical student in the classroom, or the reader of Evangelical publications, and the ideological commitment of many of the Evangelical leaders, teachers, writers, and preachers. When one perspective is presented without the consideration of material from other points of view—as is frequently done in the Evangelical college classroom and in Evangelical periodicals—a serious disservice has been done to honest, free intellectual inquiry.

Just War and Pacifism

In the Evangelical debate over war and peace issues, the legitimacy of both just war and pacifism traditions should be affirmed. The just war tradition seeks to be faithful to biblical ethics in the world in which we live—in what H. Richard Niebuhr called the "meanwhile" between the "already" and the "not yet" of God's perfect kingdom. Traditional pacifism serves to remind us where the "politics of this world" must be directed. The pacifist witness is purposely prophetic and points to the world to come. When the pacifist witness becomes confused with the "not yet" realities of the world in which we live, however, peace and justice issues will inevitably be distorted.

The past few years has seen "activist" pacifism gain wide acceptance among many Evangelicals. Unlike historical pacifism, which advocated nonviolence within the context of a theology of two kingdoms, activist pacifism accepts the ethics of Shalom—the ethic of perfect peace—as normative for policy-making in a fallen world. To seek to live one's own life according to what George Weigel calls the "politics of eternity" is certainly incumbent upon disciples of Jesus Christ. In a fallen world—a world of good and evil—however, the politics of eternity is a dangerous perspective from which to formulate public policy.

Ours is a world of imperfect peace and imperfect justice. Those whose calling is not to prophecy but to govern stand under the judgment of the ethics of God's perfect kingdom: they make choices knowing that they cannot create the best, most just, or perfectly peaceful world. By acknowledging the "already and not yet" dimensions of Christ's kingdom, those who are called to government can at best seek a better, more just, and more peaceful world.

It is perplexing that many Evangelical leaders, whose historic distinctions arise from their affirmation of the Judeo-Christian moral tradition, ignore the fundamental premise of their theology, namely, the all-pervasive nature of sin. In the fulfilled kingdom, perfect peace and perfect justice will reign together; swords will be beaten into plowshares, and the lion will lie down with the lamb. Until that future time, however, it is a grave moral error to equate justice with a peace that is impossible. Human history—particularly the history of the twentieth century—teaches that peace and justice are not unrelated concepts. The lesson of history is simple and immutable: there can be no peace apart from justice, and there can be no justice apart from freedom. Unfortunately, too many Evangelicals have, for whatever reasons, ignored the indisputable relationship between democracy, peace, and justice. Hitler, Stalin, Mao, and other totalitarian tyrants provide brutal evidence that there exists a type of "peace" that is far more unjust than many kinds of wars. Evangelicals who advocate the peace of Shalom as the absolute ethic upon which to base a national foreign policy have succumbed to a secular survivalist ethic, such as espoused by Jonathan Schell, that denies the transcendent values of freedom, human dignity, and protection of the innocent, which are more important than mere survival.

Equally disturbing is the corollary assumption that holds the socio-economic structures of all nations to be intrinsically evil to the same degree. This notion of the "moral equivalence" of all governments is attractive to many Evangelicals. But the assumption that all governments and their foreign policies are morally equivalent is one of the moral and intellectual tragedies of our time. The failure to make moral distinctions among governments can only mean, as Reinhold Niebuhr insisted, that a perverse preference is given to tyranny. There would be little to be concerned about if these notions were irrelevant, or confined to the academic community, but the reality is that many Evangelicals have adopted the "moral equivalent" assumptions. In doing so, they have blinded themselves to some of the greatest injustices in human history, and are tacitly giving support to those very forces which seek to destroy peace and justice.

The Paradox of Pursuing Peace

All Christians, and, indeed, all Americans, should welcome a socially-awakened Evangelicalism. It is disheartening, however, that the Evangelical engagement of the Biblical, moral, and strategic dimensions of war and peace issues has not reflected the balance, rigor, and spiritual humility that are the prerequisites of an effective Christian witness to the world.

The Evangelical experience has, unfortunately, closely mirrored the experience of most other religious groups which have sought to influence public opinion and policy. Evangelicals have followed the lead of many mainline Protestants and Catholics in moving away from their long-standing support of what John Courtney Murray called "the American proposition," and have embraced a set of counterpropositions which are likely to adversely affect American democracy.

Our God-mandated responsibility to build a more just and peaceful world requires that all Americans, including Evangelicals, reaffirm the importance of democratic values and institutions. As Richard John Neuhaus reminds us, democracy is both a gift and a task which God has given to our world.

At the same time, ours is a fallen world and we cannot escape the reality that we must usually choose between less than perfect options. We are to be faithful to our dual citizenship, heavenly and earthly. As citizens of the heavenly kingdom, we are called to be faithful to heavenly principles; as citizens of the earthly kingdom, we must face the limitations of our earthly responsibilities. This is part of the paradox of the Christian faith. Though we may take comfort in believing that some form of peace on earth is possible, we know that peace must, in the words of Cardinal John J. O'Connor, "be prayed for, worked for, negotiated for, and even, but as a last resort, fought for."

PART THREE

What Others Say

15. Fundamentalism: A Defensive Offensive

By NATHAN GLAZER

Focus Nathan Glazer seeks to assuage the concerns of those who think Fundamentalists want to impose a strict set of moral rules on American society. He suggests that the Fundamentalists' political resurgence in recent years testifies to the strength of liberal, not Fundamentalist, forces. The "great successes" of liberalism and secularism, achieved principally in Federal court rulings, have simply provoked Fundamentalists to reaction.

The reaction is defensive, not offensive, Glazer believes. Fundamentalists have undertaken what Glazer terms a "defensive offensive" because liberals—in their very success over the past generation—have forgotten that America is a many-cultured society, and that religion is an important component of many U.S. subcultures as well as of the larger culture.

The U.S. Supreme Court's rulings that banned school prayer (1962) and overthrew state laws against abortion-on-demand (1973) violated the religious convictions of a large segment of American society, Glazer observes. Despite these victories, liberals continue to press for imposition of a "cosmopolitan elite" worldview on the entire country, in utter disregard of the integrity of various subcultures—such as Fundamentalism.

In reaction to this drive for liberal hegemony, the

Fundamentalists have fought back to achieve balance and mutual respect in national affairs: "If we withdraw from imposing the views of the cosmopolitan elite on the whole country, we will find the new Fundamentalism returning to its modest role in the American kaleidoscope." This analysis should be compared with the views of Harvey Cox (selection 19) and Joseph Sobran (selection 26).

Nathan Glazer is a professor of education at Harvard University, an editor of *The Public Interest,* and the author of *Affirmative Discrimination, Ethnic Dilemmas,* and (with Daniel Patrick Moynihan) *Beyond the Melting Pot.*

WE ARE NOW buried in an avalanche of publicity and journalistic commentary, and even a moderate degree of analysis, regarding an upsurge of Fundamentalism. We have been told again and again about Fundamentalism's potential threat to civil liberties, to a healthy diversity of opinion, and to the hope that we can conduct public affairs free of the divisiveness of religious factionalism.

Of course, we have been plagued through most of our history by religious-based conflicts. Catholics, from the time when they increased in numbers in the United States owing to Irish and German immigration in the 1840s, often have been seen as a danger. They have been subjected to prejudice, and have felt forced to create their own distinctive institutions, particularly schools and colleges. In the regions where they were numerically dominant—in the cities and states of the Northeast—Catholics have been feared as a danger to diversity and secularism by Protestants and Jews. Jews have struggled with the anti-Semitism aroused by their ethnic and national differences, and with intolerance directed against their religion, its public practice, and the special arrangements in work, education, and dietary matters that its practice requires.

But these religious conflicts had seemed to be declining rapidly in intensity and significance in the 1960s and 1970s. The modernization of the Catholic Church, which created serious conflicts among Catholics, reduced conflict between Catholics and their non-Catholic neighbors. There had been fierce divisions between Catholics on the one hand, and Protestants and Jews on the other, during the 1930s, 1940s, and 1950s. Many of us were surprised and pleased to see divisive issues simply evaporate in the 1960s. Sadly, a distinctive Catholic culture also seemed rapidly to evaporate. Many Catholic schools closed because of the difficulty of financing in the absence of public funds; Catholic colleges became less and less distinctive, and less and less religious. Meanwhile, Catholic public opinion became more and more similar to the opinion of

---

Reprinted with permission of the author from *This World,* Number 2, Summer 1982 (c) The Institute for Educational Affairs, Inc.

other Americans of the same class and education. Two issues still remain even after the 1960s to divide Catholics from Protestants and Jews—support of parochial schools, and attitudes to abortion. But even these issues are today no longer distinctively *Catholic* issues, and certainly not as distinctively Catholic as they were twenty years ago. The Moral Majority is not Catholic, and those who support tuition tax credits and education vouchers, while they certainly include Catholics, have non-Catholics among their dominant voices. Christopher Jencks and Milton Friedman, the two fathers of education vouchers, from Left and Right, respectively; John Coons and Stephen Sugarman of the Law School of the University of California at Berkeley, who have indefatigably propagandized for education vouchers; and Senator Robert Packwood, of the Packwood-Moynihan tuition-tax-credit proposals, are not Catholic—or, if one or another of them may be, none is identified with Catholic causes.

It is hardly necessary to go through this recital to make the point that the new rising tide of religious issues has nothing to do with traditional Catholic/Protestant, or Jewish/Gentile splits and divisions: Rather, it pits Fundamentalist and resurgent traditional Protestantism against liberal Protestantism. Jews and Catholics, both traditional and liberal, are involved—but now not as representatives of embattled faiths, but as citizens, because major public issues have been raised. In terms of current conflicts involving religion, Jews, Catholics, and Protestants are no longer the principal combatants—the combatants are, rather, traditionalists against liberals of whatever religious background.

If some have been caught by surprise—including liberal journalists, such as Frances Fitzgerald, who rush to examine with concern the Moral Majority, its supporters and those it supports—that is because we have forgotten a great deal of American history. And perhaps even more important, we have ignored a great deal of existent and still potent American reality. This nation has been, if anything, a *religious* republic, and we are still, to a surprising degree for the modern, industrialized or post-industrialized world, a *religious* people. Ours is also, of course, a law-ridden republic and people. We are committed to elaborate legal processes to come to conclusions, and those conclusions are sometimes rather bizarre. And finally, paralleling our involvement in religion and our commitment to legal processes, we are committed to the market—to the free development of goods and services, which must inevitably undermine anything traditional in our society.

What has been happening in recent years is that law and the market have created a situation in which it was inevitable that the more religious elements of the population would react with anger and with vigor. They have done so, and put a fright into those who have forgotten our religious past, and are ignorant of the nature of the American people in the wide stretch of territory between Manhattan and Santa Monica.

Nationalizing Morality

It is worth pointing out, in case it has been forgotten, that intense religious-based beliefs have often directly inserted themselves, for good or ill, into American politics. We are reminded of this in Paul J. Weber's interesting article on religious lobbies in the first issue of *This World*. Weber points to two major movements in American life that were fueled primarily by religious sentiment. One was abolitionism. While this encompassed a much wider band of American opinion and power than that represented by the clergy of various Protestant denominations, Weber argues that "no other segment of the population pursued the issue with such intensity or tenaciousness. No other groups had the opportunity and facilities to raise consciousness to the extent religious groups did."

Weber's second example is more ambiguous, but still shows the power of religion in American public life: the temperance movement. Once again, not only religious groups were involved. There were "progressive" elements who saw in the wiping out of the saloon the salvation of the working man and his family. There was also more than a touch of anti-Catholicism, for Catholics in no way shared the fervor of Protestants, and in particular of the churches of the Protestant lower-middle classes, in opposing drink. But at the heart of the movement were religious groups. The manpower and womanpower, the contributions, and the publications, were animated primarily by a religious sentiment, rather than any pragmatic or rational analysis. This was also preeminently a "single-issue" movement, parallel to today's anti-abortion, pro-prayer, and other efforts. And it won. It resulted in the 18th Amendment banning drink, an astonishing victory, which eventually had to be repealed by yet another amendment to the Constitution.

What explains the recent resurgence of the Religious Right? It is worth looking at the issues that most agitate them, and asking what has made them issues. One was the Supreme Court decision *Roe* v. *Wade* of 1973 that thrust aside the abortion laws of fifty states. A second issue is the concern with a rising tide of nontraditional attitudes toward sexual and family roles, and the almost casual references to pre-marital sex, homosexuality, and drug use in television and the mass media. A third is the ban on school prayer. *In other words, it is the great successes of secular and liberal forces, principally operating through the specific agency of the courts, that has in large measure created the issues on which the Fundamentalists have managed to achieve what influence they have.*

This is perhaps a strong statement, but I believe I can defend it. Abortion was not a national issue until the Supreme Court, in *Roe* v. *Wade,* set national standards for state laws. Abortion did *not* become an issue because Fundamentalists wanted to *strengthen* prohibitions against abortion, but because liberals wanted to abolish them. Equal rights for women did *not* become an issue because Fundamentalists wanted to *limit* women's rights, but because the proposed Equal Rights Amendment raised fears, both rational and irrational, that all traditional distinctions between men's and women's roles would be overturned. (That these fears were not so irrational is evidenced by the litigation against a military draft for men only.) Pornography in the 1980s did *not* become an issue because Fundamentalists wanted to *ban* D. H. Lawrence, James Joyce, or even Henry Miller, but because, in the 1960s and 1970s, under-the-table pornography moved to the top of the newsstands. Prayer in the schools did *not* become an issue because Fundamentalists wanted to *introduce* new prayers or sectarian prayers, but because the Supreme Court ruled against all prayers. Freedom for religious schools became an issue *not* because of any legal effort to *expand* their scope, but because the Internal Revenue Service and various state authorities tried to impose restrictions on them that private schools had not faced before. (Only tuition tax credits, it can be argued, is a case of an aggressive attempt to overthrow an old arrangement—but tuition tax credits are less a concern of Fundamentalists than of Catholics and conservative Protestants and Jews.)

By now, perhaps it is hardly relevant who was the original initiator of these issues. But I rehearse this story to make a simple point that is much forgotten in the rising tide of fear: Dominant power—measured by money, access to the major media, influence, the opinion of our educated, moneyed, and powerful elites—still rests with the secular and liberal forces that created, through court action, the changes that have aroused Fundamentalism. What we are seeing is a defensive reaction of the conservative heartland, rather than an offensive that intends to or is capable of really upsetting the balance, or of driving the United States back to the nineteenth century or early twentieth century.

The two court decisions that have most sharply focused the anger of the heartland date back only to 1963—the school prayer decision, and 1973—the abortion decision. The court decisions that have made it so difficult for states to assist private (and religious) schools date back only to the early 1970s. The court decisions that have made it all but impossible for states, cities, and communities to control pornography do not go much further back.

A Defensive Offensive

We are in a strange political posture, indeed, one in which both liberals and Fundamentalists see themselves as embattled and endangered, in which both see themselves as playing a defensive role, as protecting some important value or institution against an attack which is upsetting a stable balance. It needs no argument to demonstrate that this is the posture of secular and liberal forces. I merely have to read my mail, which brings frequent appeals for contributions to protect, from the Moral Majority and others, the Constitution, the Supreme Court, and individual rights.

But I would argue that this is also the posture of the now-resurgent Fundamentalists. They may be on the offensive, but it is, if I may use the phrase, a "defensive offensive," meant to get us back to, at worst, the 1950s, and even that is beyond the hopes, or I would think the power, of Fundamentalist faith. This "defensive offensive" itself can be understood only as a response to what is seen as aggression—the aggression that banned prayer from the schools, or, most recently, the Ten Commandments from schoolhouse walls, that prevented states from expressing local opinion as to the legitimacy of abortion, and that, having driven religion out of the public schools, now is seeking to limit the schools that practice it, or to prevent any assistance to the private schools in which many parents—who want a religious atmosphere and education for their children—have sought refuge.

We are very far from the time when we might have legitimately feared the power of narrow-mindedness and bigotry as embodied in Fundamentalist and traditional religion. Not that there is not enough bigotry and narrow-mindedness to be found there, as elsewhere. But we must make a distinction between a powerful and self-confident movement that would hope to reshape America in its image, and a defensive one that wants to protect some enclaves for traditional religion. It is not easy to draw the line between one and the other, but what we face today is much more the second than the first.

First, in an organizational sense, the Fundamentalist movement is weaker than its opponents. It is sobering—and will be encouraging for liberals and secularists—to see how weak the major Fundamentalist, traditionalist, or conservative religious lobbies are in terms of money and manpower and prestige. Paul Weber has done yeoman service in trying to characterize the religious lobbies. He has located no less than seventy-four in Washington, of which twenty-seven are conservative Protestant. Of all seventy-four organizations, only nine had budgets of more than $1 million a year. Only three had staffs of more than thirty—and all three were liberal. The Fundamentalist lobbies are truly tiny, compared to many Washington lobbies.

Second, the conservative groups are for the most part quite new. The great majority were created in the 1970s. (This is yet another indication that they are defensive, and were launched against the social and legal changes of the 1960s and 1970s.) As is true of all new lobbying movements, probably many groups will not survive.

Third, the new conservative religious movements show less bias and bigotry against other religions or minority racial groups than did some religious groups in the past. They define as their enemies not Catholics, Jews, or Negroes, but secular liberals who have introduced changes which the Fundamentalists believe undermine religion and the family. Fundamentalists are not to be confused with the Ku Klux Klan or the American Protective Association. The new movement is perhaps the first major Fundamentalist Protestant movement that is not anti-Catholic. Indeed, it has many interests in common with Catholics, such as opposition to abortion and the concern for the independence of religious schools. Fundamentalism is not anti-Jewish, as evidenced in the interesting exchanges between Jerry Falwell and Prime Minister Begin of Israel. The movement is also not anti-black.

Indeed, whatever the inevitable caution, quite justified by history, with which Jews, Catholics, and blacks will view any white Protestant Fundamentalist movement, the present one is not based on religious or racial bigotry. One reason for this refusal to embrace bigotry is that Fundamentalist Protestantism is no longer dominant in the country, and therefore seeks allies everywhere—and allies can be found even among conservative Jews and blacks. In fact, blacks are still on the whole more religious than whites, and share, in a larger degree than white opinion generally, some of the positions of the Fundamentalist Protestant movements, such as opposition to abortion.

In any case, there is nothing in the issues embraced by Fundamentalist Protestants that is implicitly anti-Catholic, anti-Jewish, or anti-black, whatever the degree of these feelings that one may still find among some of the movement's supporters. Fundamentalists want to push the clock back, at worst, to the 1950s, and do not envisage pushing it back to a time when anti-Catholic, anti-Jewish, and anti-black sentiments were endemic and widely accepted. Fundamentalists know that a great deal has changed: but they are focusing on only some things, and nothing they say, nothing in their stands on issues, suggest that Catholics, Jews, or racial minorities would be anything less than full citizens in the ideal world they envisage.

Fourth, the new Fundamentalist movement expresses points of view and attitudes that the dominant mass media—the national newspapers, weeklies, and television networks—for the most part reject, and that dominant elites also reject. Evangelists' television audiences are much exaggerated; they do not appear on the television networks or the national newsmagazines—only their critics do. It is interesting to compare the attitudes on religion and religious issues of American public opinion generally and elite opinion, as we find in the important Connecticut Mutual Life Insurance Company-sponsored survey of American values. In this survey, 65 per cent of the public believed abortion to be morally wrong, but only 36 per cent of society's leaders. Seventy-one per cent of the public believed homosexuality to be morally wrong, but only 42 per cent of the leaders. Fifty-seven per cent of the public considered smoking marijuana to be wrong, but only 33 per cent of the leaders. If the surveyors had asked, a much greater percentage of the leaders probably would have supported the Supreme Court on prayer and aid to private schools than would the public.

Admittedly, one may draw various conclusions from this division between leaders and general public opinion. One may find the wave of the future in mass public opinion. But that is not generally the way lines of influence run. We are not in any danger of being overrun by a religious mob led by fanatical religious leaders.

The Counter-Revolution

But the strongest argument for seeing the new movement as defensive and with limited aims is that we saw in the 1960s and 1970s a real revolution, and that what we are seeing now is an attempt at a counter-revolution—but one which, like all counter-revolutions, will have to be satisfied to accept much of the change that has aroused it.

This revolution encompassed sex, dress, and drugs. One need recall only that in the late 1960s it was still possible for Harvard to debate passionately parietal rules—when boys could visit girls, and vice versa. The revolution encompassed women's roles: Twenty years ago, the proportion of women in medical and law schools was about 5 per cent; today it is around 30 per cent. The revolution encompassed the schools, once a place where traditional morality and religion were taught by teachers who were authoritative, and authoritarian—and were backed-up or disciplined by self-confident authorities. The driving forces of the revolution were two: The expanded reach of constitutional litigation, based on the model of civil rights litigation; and the power of the free market, in goods and ideas, to diffuse minority and unconventional models of behavior. The second faced a reduced resistance from community norms because of the power of the first.

But what both the legal revolutionaries and the marketing experts forgot is that we are not one culture, but many cultures. The once-dominant culture of middle America had been driven from television screens, mass magazines, universities, and opinion-molding circles. But it still existed. The Fundamentalists had suffered crushing defeats in the 1920s in their fight against revolution and modernism in the churches. They had been reduced to irrelevance in the Depression of the 1930s and the war against Nazism in the 1940s. In the family-building period of the 1950s, there had been little to arouse them. But the cultural revolution of the 1960s and 1970s did.

We are presently in a phase not dissimilar to that described by George M. Marsden in his interesting book, *Fundamentalism and American Culture: The Shaping of Twentieth Century Evangelicism, 1870–1925* (Oxford University Press, 1981). Marsden describes how what was the dominant intellectual and religious tendency of the 1870s was reduced to irrelevance—and anger—by the 1920s:

> The Fundamentalists' most alarming experience was that of finding themselves living in a culture that by the 1920s was openly turning away from God. "Christendom," remarked H. L. Mencken in 1924, "may be defined briefly as that part of the world in which, if any man stands up and solemnly swears he is a Christian, all the auditors will laugh." The "irreligion of the modern world," concurred Walter Lippman in his *Preface to Morals,* ". . . is radical to a degree for which there is, I think, no counterpart."

"The American Christians [Fundamentalists]," Marsden asserts, "underwent a remarkable transformation in their relationship to the culture. Respected 'evangelicals' in the 1870s, by the 1920s they had become a laughingstock, ideological strangers in their own land . . . The philosophical outlook that had graced

America's finest academic institutions came to be generally regarded as merely bizarre."

It all came crashing down in the Scopes trial in Dayton, Tennessee, in 1925. After that, Fundamentalism, insofar as the national mass media were concerned, went underground, though it still existed on a vast scale and represented the outlook on religion and life of a substantial section of the American population. In a second period of sexual license and of changing sex roles, and with a new expansion of the mass media and mass markets, now supported by the actions of an activist bar and a responsive Federal judiciary (neither of which we had in the 1920s), Fundamentalism reawakened, and reawakened, too, the dormant fear of theocracy. This fear is much exaggerated. It ignores the primarily defensive character of the new Fundamentalist movement. The aim of the new movement is basically to protect enclaves of literal, Fundamentalist faith and the practices that accompany it. It is in Arkansas, after all, that a state provision for equal time for creationism recently was attempted, not in New York, Illinois, or Texas.

The protection of enclaves is best accomplished, not by sweeping national decisions, but by practice, law, and custom adapted to the enormous variety of our country. The temperance movement, to take a revealing parallel, went too far when it imposed one section's view of drink on the rest of the country. But when that dispute was finally settled by the repeal of the 18th Amendment, it did not bother most people that in one section of the country or another, one could not get a drink on Sunday. In the same way, liberalism went too far when it imposed on the whole country the views of one part of the population regarding abortion, or school prayer, or support for religious schools, through major cases that led to sweeping Supreme Court decisions that set national standards. These major decisions made what should have been state and local issues, such as abortion and school prayer, national issues.

A Switch in Time

Is there a way out? I think there is. I am reminded of the Yoder decision of 1972, in which the Supreme Court ruled that the Amish of Wisconsin did not have to send their children to school past the age when they believe education is useful for them. It was not a simple decision. What of the rights of the children who may have wished to continue in school despite their parents' desire to protect them from secular influences past age fourteen? This was raised squarely in Justice Douglas's dissent. There are no simple solutions to conflict between overriding principles and minority practices, but this decision did create peace. Other decisions may have the same effect.

The battle lines are now drawn, as my mail pleading for contributions to protect free abortion, free television, and the rest daily reminds me. But I think that a few modest Supreme Court reversals would do wonders. One recalls that, in 1936, it seemed that nothing could change a conservative court but a radical increase in its size to change its complexion. But then there was the "switch in time that saved nine."

Is it possible to define the switches that are necessary to moderate Fundamentalist anger, and that may yet be acceptable to the cosmopolitan elite? I would like to suggest a theme for these switches: It is local option in morality, as we have local option in drink. Imagine the uproar if the Supreme Court were to take seriously an argument—it could be made by a decent constitutional lawyer—that restriction of drink in public places is as much an invasion of privacy, or restriction of free speech, or whatever other principle one wishes to find in the recess of the Bill of Rights, as prohibition on the use or sale or advertisement of contraceptive devices, or prohibition of abortion. There would be an uproar, and a painfully forged compromise would have been upset, and a new round of national conflict over morality opened. Local option, by states and communities, on such matters as abortion, Bible reading in schools (one can switch from one translation to the other, and add the Bhagavad Gita and the Koran as school composition changes), public assistance to private schools, and a number of other matters, could do wonders, and would simply and honestly reflect the reality that we are a diverse country. Nor would the Constitution be violated, even if undoubtedly many professors of constitutional law would be outraged. After all, the constitutional principles that permitted national prohibitions in these areas were found lurking in the Constitution only 180 years or so after it was adopted.

Marsden comments at one point in his study that both sides, it turned out, have been wrong in their hopes for the future. Fundamentalism is not an anachronistic remnant doomed to disappear rapidly, but neither is the world about to be saved, once and for all. Our policy must adapt to this reality. Fundamentalists must recognize that at least half of us are and will remain skeptical and unsaved; and secular liberals must accept the fact that their outlook will not gain universal acquiescence.

The arrangements that permit us to survive are those in which neither side imposes on the other its vision of the good society. Working out the details is not simple in a society in which there is no ruling elite, and any view, no matter how eccentric, may find itself law if it finds the right judge. But if we withdraw from imposing the views and beliefs of the cosmopolitan elite on the whole country, we will find the new Fundamentalism returning to its modest role in the American kaleidoscope.

16. *Who Put Morality in Politics?*

By George F. Will

Focus

Fundamentalists and Evangelicals did not start the current debate about morality and public policy—about Christianity and politics: the fight was started, in George Will's view, by proponents of a liberalism that has developed into "a doctrine of liberation." Fundamentalist and Evangelical Christians "have been provoked" by the aggressive use of government to reshape American moral life without due regard for the convictions of millions of American citizens.

"A culture abandoning restraints has produced among Evangelicals a heightened sense of their community, and of antagonism toward the national culture," writes Will. But he reminds us that the U.S. Supreme Court struck down states' laws against abortion-on-demand, sparking much of the Fundamentalist and Evangelical re-entry into national political affairs. It was "the forces that want subsidies for abortions" who supported the Supreme Court. "Yet we are told it is the Evangelicals who are aggressive about abortion."

The same irony arises on other issues, including social attitudes about homosexuality. Fundamentalists and Evangelicals did not seek to restrict homosexuals' "rights" until homosexuals began to use Federal government agencies not only to protect their "lifestyle" but to legitimize it at the expense of traditional mores.

"The ancient and Christian theories of government held that statecraft should be soulcraft; indeed, that government cannot avoid concerning itself with virtue." Today, Will observes, government "can concern itself with nurturing soybeans, but not virtue." Fundamentalists and Evangelicals who react against the contemporary theory of the Federal government's role are reacting against special interests that have attempted to put their own "morality in politics." Will's view may be usefully compared with those of Nathan Glazer (selection 15) and Grant Wacker (selection 22).

A nationally syndicated columnist, **George F. Will** is the author of several collections of essays including *The Morning After: American Successes and Excesses, 1981–1986* (The Free Press, 1986).

PLEAS FOR SOCIAL regeneration, laced with theology, have enlivened America's civic life since the days of Cotton Mather. There was a recent plea in Jimmy Carter's famous "malaise" speech. Carter noted a "crisis of the American spirit" and a "longing for meaning." He suggested, among other antidotes, a synthetic-fuels program. Eugene McCarthy recalls that Ike urged all Americans to spend the first Fourth of July of his Administration in prayer and penance, and on that day Ike went fishing in the morning, golfing in the afternoon, and played bridge in the evening.

But from the fractious Puritans on, religion often has had serious political consequences, and it may today. The conjunction of the civil-rights struggle, Vietnam, and Watergate convinced liberals that they had a "moral monopoly." But now Evangelical Christian groups, including one calling itself The Moral Majority, are plunging into politics. The public's preoccupation with the Evangelicals' finances reflects a preference for diving into the shallow end of every pool. More important than the question of who gets what is the question of why so many people are so aroused. The answer is: they have been provoked.

'The Therapeutic Ethic'

Many were first provoked by churches that seem to have suffered what Chesterton called "the dislocation of humility," humility not about ambition, but about conviction. Many churches have seemed reluctant, as Peter Berger says, "to make statements of faith unprotected by redeeming sociopolitical significance." But what began with the Evangelicals' belief that churches should save souls, not society, has become a movement convinced that society is jeopardizing souls and must be changed.

Public policy has become imbued with what is called "the therapeutic ethic," the idea that the morally and practically correct way to cope with aggressive or otherwise difficult people (or nations) is with social services that remove the causes of antisocial behavior. That idea seems fundamentally mistaken to Fundamentalist Christians who take seriously man's fallen condition. It has been said that Christianity is too optimistic about the universe and too pessimistic about this world, but given the record of this world, pessimism is realism. Christian pessimism often has led to political quietism, but many Evangelicals are anything but quiet.

As broad considerations of economic class lose their political importance, considerations of ethnicity, sex, culture, and religion are becoming more salient. Welfare-state answers to the basic questions about distributive justice have not calmed our politics. Quite different concerns, even more passionately fought over, have broadened the range of political argument. Americans have always been torn between two desires: for absence of restraint and for a sense of community. A culture abandoning restraints has produced among Evangelicals a heightened sense of their community, and of antagonism toward the national culture.

As the nation's social pyramid becomes steeper, those closer to the base than to the apex feel increasingly at the mercy of governing and media elites, and are increasingly insistent that those be elites of character as well as achievement. People measure fine character, in part, by shared values. In most societies, most of the time, the most basic values are not much thought about. If questioned, they elicit what sociologists have called "of course" statements, which express the community's "world-taken-for-granted." A dubious achievement of today's elites has been to help diminish the "world-taken-for-granted."

There has been a provocative widening of the unavoidable gaps between values expressed in public policies and values cleaved to by large segments of the public. Questions that touch the quick of our existence, such as the nature of life and the value of sex, recently did, but no longer do, elicit "of course" answers.

Don't blame Evangelicals for inflating abortion as a political issue. The Supreme Court did that by striking down fifty states' laws that expressed community judgments about the issue. Those who opposed those judgments got them overturned by fiat, not democratic persuasion. The forces that made that possible want subsidies for abortions, knowing that when you subsidize something you get more of it. Yet we are told it is the Evangelicals who are aggressive about abortion.

'Night Watchman' Theory

Evangelicals did not set out to alter social attitudes about homosexuality. Government has begun teaching, through many measures, that homosexual and heterosexual relations represent only different "preferences" (or, in the language of the 1980 Democratic platform, "orientations") among "life-styles." Militant homosexuals are responsible for this, and for making a hot political issue of government attempts to inculcate new attitudes.

The ancient and Christian theories of government held that statecraft should be soulcraft; indeed, that government cannot avoid concerning itself with virtue. Modern theory, however, involves government in unavoidable conflicts between theory and practice. The modern "night watchman" theory of government is that it exists only to protect persons and property. It can be ubiquitous and omniprovident regarding material things, but must be neutral regarding values. It can concern itself with nurturing soybeans, but not virtue.

American public philosophy asserts, untenably, that popular government presupposes especially virtuous citizens, yet cannot concern itself with the inner lives of its citizens. But the government does concern itself, emphatically in public education, but also in what it requires, encourages, proscribes, refuses to proscribe, and prevents being proscribed. As liberalism has become a doctrine of "liberation," it has spawned new "rights" in the name of which government has been empowered to promote certain values by stipulating behavior. Defenders of competing values are castigated for trying to "impose" their values. Evangelicals who are part of the reaction against this sometimes shoot wildly, but as Chesterton said, "Even a bad shot is dignified when he accepts a duel."

17. *Yale and the Moral Majority*

By WILLIAM F. BUCKLEY, JR.

Focus

In an address to incoming students, the president of Yale University, A. Bartlett Giamatti, launched a rhetorical attack on the Moral Majority. William F. Buckley, Jr., a Yale alumnus, rose to the organization's defense: "It is quaintly interesting that there isn't a single tenet of the Moral Majority (so far as I know) that hasn't officially been held by Yale University over a century or more of its life, and more or less unofficially since then. So what on earth excited Mr. Giamatti?"

Buckley answered his own query: President Giamatti and many other professed liberals were upset about what they discerned to be an "anger" within the Fundamentalist and Evangelical movement which led to formation of the Moral Majority. "But anger was officially cultivated, by Yale among other institutions, quite recently in the matter of such things as civil rights and the Vietnam War."

Buckley discerns a double-standard in the liberal assessment of the Evangelical and Fundamentalist political resurgence: "Civic action is regularly informed by theological insights. Thus we've had a group known as Clergy and Laity Concerned. They used to be Concerned About Vietnam, but lately they are just Concerned." Among their concerns is that conservative Christians have become as active as liberal Christians used to be.

"To be lectured against the perils of the Moral Majority on entering Yale is on the order of being lectured on the danger of bedbugs on entering a brothel," Buckley chides. "Mr. Giamatti should lecture the kids against the dangers of gonorrhea and gnosticism, and let the Moral Majority alone."

William F. Buckley, Jr., is the founding editor of *National Review,* a nationally syndicated columnist, host of the TV program "Firing Line," and the author of numerous books, both historical and fictional, including *God and Man at Yale* (1951).

WELL, THAT WAS A CLOSE ONE. The 1,267 members of the freshman class of Yale University have been warned against the Moral Majority by President A. Bartlett Giamatti. And what a speech it was: Jerry Falwell, head of the Moral Majority, is said to be quite a fulminator himself. He should go to Yale. To study under Bart Giamatti. Learn a thing or two about how one fulminates in the big leagues.

What's going on? To be lectured against the perils of the Moral Majority on entering Yale is on the order of being lectured on the danger of bedbugs on entering a brothel. What is it that exercised Mr. Giamatti, a man of great urbanity who has some lovely and incisive things to say about many issues?

Well, he says the Moral Majority are "peddlers of coercion" and that they have made "a radical assault" on pluralism, civil rights, and religious and political freedoms in the United States. How so?

Because they are "angry at change, rigid in the application of chauvinistic slogans, absolutist in morality." Thus, "they threaten through political pressure or public denunciation whoever dares to disagree with their authoritarian positions." Moreover, "they presume to know what God alone knows, which is when human life begins."

Enough.

On the latter point: How is it that the president of a distinguished and cosmopolitan university tells us that God alone knows when human life begins? If you penetrate this rhetorical formulation, you have a dimly obscured invitation to nescience. "God-alone-knows" is the safest way to say, "That-is-unknowable." Inasmuch as God is not invited to teach a regular course at Yale, Mr. Giamatti is saying in effect that the search for the answer to "When does life begin?" should be abandoned—because no one can tell.

Why not? If you grant the metaphorical extravagancies (Life Begins at Forty) you can indeed ask scientists to make sound judgments on when life begins. Or moralists. Or theologians. And in any case, the question is ultimately decided by civic action. But

Reprinted by permission of the author from *Right Reason*, Doubleday, 1985.

civic action is regularly informed by theological insights. Thus we've had for many years a group known as Clergy and Laity Concerned. They used to be Concerned About Vietnam, but lately they are just Concerned. That concern regularly focuses on the sins of everyone who wants America to be strong militarily, or wants to develop nuclear energy. These people are very big on denunciation, and it is interesting that Mr. Giamatti hasn't gone after them. Is it really his position that people reading the Bible are not free to enjoin its messages? Its messages as they read them?

Mr. Giamatti said he had no quarrel with the values of the Moral Majority, defined in the paraphrase by the *New York Times* as "love of country, a regard for the sanctity of life, the importance of the family, and high standards of personal conduct." But "the point is," said the president of Yale, "the rest of us hold to ideas of family, country, belief in God, in different ways. The right to differ, and to see things differently, is our concern." Well, so is it the concern of the Moral Majority. They are saying that certain values should govern Americans. Aren't we free to disagree? And why should they not say so, believing such values to be true? It is quaintly interesting that there isn't a single tenet of the Moral Majority (so far as I know) that hasn't officially been held by Yale University over a century or more of its life, and more or less unofficially since then. So what on earth excited Mr. Giamatti?

That the Moral Majority are "angry at change"? But anger was officially cultivated, by Yale among other institutions, quite recently in the matter of such things as civil rights and the Vietnam War. "And God said to Jonah, 'Doest thou well to be angry?' And he said, 'I do well to be angry, even unto death.' " Mr. Giamatti should lecture the kids against the dangers of gonorrhea and gnosticism, and let the Moral Majority alone.

18. *The Religious Right and Republicans*

By SIDNEY BLUMENTHAL

Focus

Though published two weeks before the 1984 presidential election, Sidney Blumenthal's analysis of the potentially disruptive influence of Fundamentalists and Evangelicals on the Republican Party has continued relevance. In 1984, Blumenthal predicted that the "Evangelical New Right," because of its uncompromising position on several social issues, especially abortion and school prayer, could split the Republican Party.

Blumenthal notes: "The Republicans are more sharply polarized over abortion than the Democrats." The polarization pits young libertarians against "social issue" conservatives. Many of the latter are Evangelicals who aligned with the Republican Party after the Democrats wed themselves to a broad liberal agenda. Blumenthal describes how, during the past two presidential campaigns, the Evangelical New Right was transformed from being an almost irrelevant fringe group into a centerpiece of the conservative movement. He credits Ronald Reagan with giving the Evangelical New Right the legitimacy it had sought for many years.

But the alliance between religion and politics within the Republican Party is a fragile one, Blumenthal believes, and he offers "a short history of the end of history, and maybe even of the G. O. P." Noting that many young Americans are libertarian,

Blumenthal says that a generational war could be triggered—spelling trouble for Republicans. A fracture within the Republican Party, however, might enhance the Evangelical movement: "The GOP may crack, but the New Right Evangelicals will flourish. That would be the ultimate fulfillment of 'social issue' conservatism. The divisions this sort of politics engender are inescapable. And the party that enacts sectarian doctrine into law in the attempt to regenerate a lost world will pay a steep political price." This essay may be usefully compared with that of Nathan Glazer (selection 15).

Sidney Blumenthal is a staff writer with *The Washington Post* and the author of *The Rise of the Counter-Establishment: From Conservative Ideology to Political Power* (Time Books, 1986).

"WE THANK YOU, Father, for the leadership of President Ronald Reagan." With this prayer of thanksgiving, the Reverend James Robison opened the 1984 Republican National Convention. Robison, a New Right evangelist with a syndicated television show based in Fort Worth, has met with the President frequently over the past years. In being allowed to bless the convention, Robison himself received the blessing of the Republican Party. He is a man of unequivocal opinions. He has said that an anti-Semite "is someone who hates Jews more than he's supposed to," and "The non-Christian can't understand spiritual things." After Robison draped Republican delegates with the mantle of divine election, the chosen party proceeded with its predestined agenda.

On the fourth night, the anointed President delivered his acceptance speech, and then bowed his head for the benediction, intoned by the convention's final speaker, the Reverend W. A. Criswell, pastor of First Baptist Church of Dallas. This was not Criswell's first campaign. In 1960 he was foremost among those assailing John F. Kennedy because Kennedy was a Catholic. "Can a Man be a Loyal Roman Catholic and a Good President of the United States?" was the title of a Criswell pamphlet. The answer, emphatically, was no. The Roman Catholic Church, he declared, was "a political tyranny." And Kennedy's election would "spell the death of a free church in a free state." Now, standing next to President Reagan, Criswell armed the Republicans with moral righteousness.

Robison's and Criswell's prominence at the Republican Convention was not a testament to the negligence of the convention's organizers. The Dallas affair was the most tightly controlled party event in years, scripted word for word from beginning to end, and approved by the White House, the Reagan-Bush Committee, and the Republican National Committee. Robison's and Criswell's elevation to the honored party pulpit was a testament to the rise of the Evangelical New Right. "It was not at all surprising," said Morton Blackwell, a former presidential assistant who served as

---

Reagan's liaison to the religious groups and the conservative movement through early 1984. "It made perfect sense."

On the morning of the convention's last day, Reagan attended a prayer breakfast, hosted by Criswell, at which he pronounced politics and religion "inseparable." Walter Mondale seized on Reagan's declaration by making the separation of church and state the first major issue of the campaign. The debate was abstract and philosophical. But the motivating force behind this controversy is something that is not abstract: the Evangelical New Right, a political elite that has been transformed in less than a decade from an almost irrelevant fringe into a centerpiece of the conservative movement. The New Right Evangelicals have a far-flung organizational and communications network, a uniquely compelling ideology, and thousands of trained, committed volunteers. Unlike other religionists, from Billy Graham to the Catholic bishops, who place some demarcation line between religion and politics, the New Right Evangelicals refuse to distinguish between the flag and the cross, a position encapsulated in their notion of America as a "Christian nation."

Because of the Evangelicals' centrality in conservative politics, the President, who considers himself at least as much a movement figure as a party leader, has been unwilling to distance himself from them. Throughout his first term, he briefed them, encouraged them, deployed White House resources to coordinate them, and thereby magnified them. This may not represent the establishment of religion, but it is certainly the cultivation of cults. Reagan used the Evangelical New Right apparatus to register millions of new voters. And on one issue—abortion, on which New Right Evangelicals have made an unlikely alliance with the Catholic hierarchy—the President has made a solid promise in exchange for their support. At private meetings at the White House with conservative militants he pledged to appoint Supreme Court Justices who will act to overturn *Roe* v. *Wade*. His pledge was reiterated by the Republican platform.

Looking Beyond the Reagan Years

Reagan regards the Evangelical New Right as an auxiliary force, a division of Christian soldiers in the conservative army. But their goals extend beyond his finite career. When he goes, they stay. As

Reagan has said: "You ain't seen nothing yet." The New Right Evangelicals can see past the second Reagan term to the Second Coming. They have a conception of history's end. The present is merely the period of pre-tribulation tribulations. What follows are the real troubles, then the Rapture, when the born-again are physically whisked up to heaven in time to avoid Armageddon, the ultimate battle between good (us) and evil (them, the evil empire), which will clear the air and usher in Christ's return. In preparing for the universal apocalypse, the movement Evangelicals are eagerly pursuing an ideological apocalypse. The business of soul winning has become the politics of takeover. The Evangelical New Right, for example, has systematically seized control of the leadership of the Southern Baptist Convention, the largest Protestant denomination, with more than 14 million members, altering long-held theological positions for political advantage. And state by state, from Minnesota to Texas, New Right Evangelicals are succeeding in taking over local Republican organizations. According to Gary Jarmin, director of the Evangelical New Right group Christian Voice, "The Republican party is a tool."

The appearance of the Reverends Robison, Criswell, and Jerry Falwell at the 1984 Republican Convention was a sign to New Right Evangelicals that the GOP is on the path of political salvation. Their ascending importance is due to the confluence of two long-term trends within the conservative movement: first, the effort of a splinter to move into the mainstream; and second, the effort by conservatives to capture for the Republican Party constituencies motivated by non-economic "social issues." The Democrats, at least since the New Deal, have been able, mainly by a common economic appeal, to unite a coalition of groups as diverse as rural Southern Baptists and urban northern Catholics. Perhaps, conservatives reasoned, it would be possible to undermine both the Democrats and moderate Republicans by shifting various groups into the GOP on a basis other than economics. As it turned out, the Evangelical New Right became the hard edge of the "social issue."

Goldwater Laid the Groundwork

In 1964, the managers of Barry Goldwater's presidential campaign believed that widespread backlash against the civil rights movement and the burgeoning youth culture could be mobilized on behalf of the Republican candidate. They produced a "documentary" half-hour film called *Choice* that featured a kaleidoscope of images, including rioting blacks, topless models, and nightclub denizens dancing the twist. A front group, Mothers for a Moral America, was created to act as the film's sponsor. The film's producer, Rus Walton, said its intent was to "take this latent anger and concern which now exists, build it up, and subtly turn and focus it."

In 1968, George Wallace, and to some extent Richard Nixon, sought to enlist "this latent anger." Kevin Phillips, a young aide to Nixon's campaign manager John Mitchell, saw the 1968 election returns as evidence of a profound political realignment, bred in great part by cultural hatred of Eastern liberalism. Phillips's 1969 book, *The Emerging Republican Majority,* was the first theoretical work on the "social issue." According to Phillips, a "populist revolt" of the recently arrived middle class, driven by resentment of the "mandarins of Establishment liberalism," had sustained Wallace and helped elect Nixon. By playing off ethnic, regional, and cultural polarizations, a new realignment could be forged. This kind of politics also happened to be ideally suited to Nixon's temperament.

On the surface, Phillips's analysis seemed to be an electoral strategy aimed at taking advantage of the harsh tensions of the 1960s and the growing geopolitical strength of the Sunbelt. But on a more immediate and effective level, he offered a factional strategy within the Republican Party for displacing Yankees in the interest of the conservative movement. *The Emerging Republican Majority* was less a party-building plan than an intra-party realignment strategy. Conservatives didn't just want to bring new groups into the party; through another door they sought to drive others out. And by enforcing party rules that tilt against the large states that are bastions of traditional Republican moderation, participation by Yankees and their potential allies could be reduced.

In 1970, another book on the "social issue" appeared: *The Real Majority,* by Richard Scammon and Ben Wattenberg. It argued that Democrats had been put on the defensive by the Republicans' manipulation of the "social issue," which they defined as the "more personally frightening aspects of disruptive change." They predicted that voters were moving to the left on economics and to the right on social issues. Therefore, they prescribed that Democratic politicians should appeal to the "unyoung, unpoor, and unblack" by seizing Nixon's thunder: when the going gets tough, the tough get going. Only then would Democrats recapture their straying partisans and thus the center.

The Real Majority was assiduously read by Nixon's political operatives, who tried to appropriate a strategy intended for Democratic usage. The point man for the Republican exploitation of the "social issue" in the 1970 midterm election was Vice President Spiro Agnew, who was well configured for this task: he was neither Catholic nor Baptist, but a border-state ethnic. He stumped the country, urging "workingmen" to join the "New Majority" against "the pampered prodigies of the radical liberals."

Republicans and Social Issues

After his 1972 landslide victory, Nixon toyed with the notion of changing the name of the Republican Party to the New Majority Party, a reflection of the realignment he was seeking. Watergate, however, intervened; Agnew pleaded *nolo contendere;* and the presidency fell to a traditional Republican, Gerald Ford. In 1980, after repeated attempts, Ronald Reagan, much more the conservative than either Nixon or Agnew, secured the GOP nomination. Some observers saw Reagan as the one who would use the "social issue" as the method to complete Nixon's work. As the Reagan administration assumed office in January 1981, the neoconservative essayist Norman Podhoretz, in a *Commentary* article entitled "The New American Majority," argued that Reagan's success was significantly due to a "wave of cultural disgust" at the "new culture" typified by "Gay Lib and abortion." Reagan was "perfect" to "reconstitute the new majority that Nixon had coaxed into emerging but had never had a chance to consolidate."

The Reagan political team, however, believed that the Republican Party risked its own destruction to the degree that the "social issue" became prominent. Senior White House aides embarked on a journey toward realignment by other means. They decided that, just as the Democratic coalition had unified around the economic issue, Republicans could do the same without the debilitating side effects of the "social issue." Moreover, there was little sentiment among the senior staff for a moral crusade, especially on abortion. Even Edwin Meese, the aide closest to the conservative movement, personally (and quietly) favored the pro-choice rather than the anti-abortion position, according to one of his colleagues.

A strategy of repressive tolerance was adopted toward the "social issue" and the constituencies aroused by it. According to a senior adviser, the strategy worked like this: the Evangelical New Right and its allies rallied followers around constitutional amendments on school prayer and abortion. The White House staff, fearing Republican fragmentation and the galvanizing of new opposition, offered insincere gestures of support while desiring continual frustration. With tacit White House agreement, Senate Majority Leader Howard Baker granted time for the various social issues to be ventilated. The bills lost and were sent back into limbo. Any White House aide who seriously tried to keep the "social issue" bills on the front burner also was sent into limbo. For example, Faith Whittlesey, director of the Office of Public Liaison, campaigned fervently for Evangelical New Right goals—even haranguing bewildered corporate executives on tuition tax credits—and quickly became a non-entity. In the meantime, Blackwell was assigned to maintain the constituency in a state of perpetual mobilization. The flaw in this strategy was that the White House served as an incubator for the movement it was trying to contain. Reagan never wholeheartedly cooperated with the containment strategy; he encouraged Evangelicals whenever he was given the chance, and to do so he created opportunities, especially photo opportunities, against the advice of his staff.

A New Form of Fundamentalism

Spokesmen for the Evangelical New Right invariably depict their movement as the spontaneously defensive response of traditional folk to the intrusive designs of a liberal elite. To be sure, certain Supreme Court decisions have stirred up a reaction. But New Right Evangelicals are not simply reacting to the jackboot march of liberalism. Their leadership has for years ambitiously, deliberately, and aggressively planned their rise to influence. This movement is not just another manifestation of historic populism, despite the frequent invocations of Andrew Jackson—who happened to be a radical and vigorous advocate of church-state separation. "Social issue" conservatism's claim to populism is based mostly on wishful history.

Nor is the Evangelical New Right in the mainline tradition of Evangelicalism itself. In the eighteenth century, Evangelicals believed adamantly that the realms of spirit and state were separate, a principal reason many Baptists fought in the Revolution. They associated the ecclesiastical establishment with the party of the rich and the well-born, an unholy alliance against the individual conscience. In the late nineteenth century, a new strain of Evangelicalism, which came to be called Fundamentalism, employed the revival technique to rally the faithful against a corrupting modern society. Fundamentalism stressed a literal interpretation of the Bible, conversion, and warfare against worldly trends. This warfare mainly took the form of separation from the evil world; withdrawal and abstinence was the way to purity. The Evangelical New Right is therefore an aberrant and relatively new form of Fundamentalism, and is rooted in anti-Catholicism.

In the 1950s, Carl McIntire was an obscure preacher who belonged to a religious denomination he himself had organized. He rode McCarthyism to fame and fortune by combining anti-Catholicism with anti-Communism. In Communism McIntire discovered an international conspiracy to match his conception of what he labeled "the harlot church." He also attacked mainline Protestant churches as "apostate, Communist, and modernist." In 1960 McIntire joined W. A. Criswell in the crusade against the papist Kennedy. The fervor of the cause didn't prevent McIntire's bright young apostle, Billy James Hargis, from splitting off to form his own group, the Christian Crusade. To McIntire's perspective, Hargis added the element of racial fear. In 1964 Hargis built a movement around a constitutional amendment to overturn the Supreme Court ruling on school prayer, an amendment endorsed by Barry Goldwater. McIntire and Hargis constructed empires of radio stations, seminaries, real estate holdings, publishing houses, and direct-mail operations—models for what was to come.

Among the myriad right-wing Fundamentalist groups roaming

the wilderness was the Christian Freedom Foundation (CFF), begun in 1950. Its goal was to train and elect "real Christians" to public office. In 1975 CFF's funding was assumed by Richard DeVos, president of Amway Corporation. (In the early 1980s DeVos became finance chairman of the Republican National Committee.) To propagate its ideas, CFF created Third Century Publishers, which issued *One Nation Under God,* by the former Goldwater operative Rus Walton. The book presented the notion of America as a "Christian Republic" based on "Christian principles" ranging from the elimination of taxes supporting public schools to the return of the gold standard.

The director of CFF was a voluble former sales marketing manager for Colgate Palmolive, Ed McAteer. To him, selling was akin to spreading the gospel. "We had truckloads of hair spray to sell," he says. "That's ideal training." McAteer had devoted his life to evangelism. He became a well-known layman on the circuit and attended international conferences. He knew virtually everyone, from the backwoods pastors to the television preachers. McAteer's contacts suggested to him the possible scope of the movement.

In 1976 McAteer left the CFF for a more promising job as field director of the Conservative Caucus, a new group that was part of the burgeoning New Right nexus. At its helm was Richard Viguerie, who had parlayed the George Wallace contributors list into a huge computerized direct-mail operation, and built a movement on single issue causes such as opposition to the Panama Canal Treaty. Viguerie's right-hand man, Howard Phillips, Conservative Caucus head, hired McAteer as his own right hand. "Ed was the most important person in making the religious right happen," says Phillips. "He took me around to meet a lot of people. His role was that of Johnny Appleseed." "I was crossbreeding," says McAteer.

The Moral Majority

In 1978, McAteer took Phillips to lunch at a motel outside Lynchburg, Virginia, to meet an unknown pastor, Jerry Falwell. They proposed a plan. Falwell should be the head of a new movement group that would draw in the religiously minded. Phillips even had a name: the Moral Majority. Falwell wasn't fully convinced. "There was skepticism from his people that there wasn't enough money," says Phillips. At the next meeting, however, Falwell was converted.

"McAteer didn't stop there," says Phillips. "There were more meetings." "I introduced everyone to everyone," crows McAteer. "I was introducing Phillips, I was introducing Viguerie." There were meetings, for example, with Pat Robertson, the oleaginous prophet of God, owner of the Christian Broadcasting Network, and chief of his own political outfit, the Freedom Council. Links were established with Christian Voice, a new group which pushed legislation to declare America a "Christian nation" and issued a "Biblical Scorecard" rating legislators on "Christian issues," such as funding for the U.S. Department of Education and support for a balanced budget amendment.

There followed meetings with James Robison. By 1980, McAteer was head of his very own organization, the Religious Roundtable, with Robison serving as vice president. The Roundtable rounded up thousands of Evangelical preachers for a convention in Dallas to be addressed by the Republican presidential candidate. But the group was little more than a letterhead. Robison, however, placed his personal staff and money at the Roundtable's disposal to organize the big event, an event Blackwell calls "a major turning point in the history of the United States."

"You can't endorse me," Ronald Reagan told the throng. "But I endorse you." His appearance gave the Evangelical New Right a legitimacy it had previously lacked. Without the sense that they had the approval of a major party's presidential candidate, many Evangelicals would not have been drawn into the network. "Vast numbers of religious leaders were considering whether to get involved," says Blackwell. "As a result of that meeting they decided to." The religious right was at that moment in a nascent stage, and the Roundtable gathering was like a movie lot façade. "There was no organizational context in 1980," admits Phillips. "It was largely rhetorical. But the Dallas meeting sent the message that there were a great many people who were greatly respected who were involved." McAteer's brilliant contrivance, pasted together at the last minute with crucial aid from Robison, created a stage setting for Reagan, whose "endorsement" was indispensable in turning appearance into reality. And he in turn appeared to dominate the social forces set in motion by the "social issue," trumping the born-again Carter.

A 'Battle for the Mind'

The New Right Evangelicals justified their spreading network by more than the imprimatur of Ronald Reagan. Every movement requires a theorist. If McAteer was the essential organizer and Falwell the publicist, then Tim LaHaye, a prolific author, played the role of popular philosopher. His 1980 book, *Battle for the Mind,* has sold more hardcover copies than *Megatrends*. He interprets American history according to the Book of Revelation. Most important, he names the enemy: secular humanism, our unacknowledged but official religion. "Secular humanism puts man at the center of all things," LaHaye explained to me. "It came to America by way of graduate schools. The guy who was the most influential was Robert Owen (the English utopian), who came to the conclusion that the American people were too religious to accept socialism. He and a group of transcendentalists, Unitarians, and atheists decided to make public education compulsory. That's when they brought in Horace Mann, the Unitarian. What Mann did for secular humanism in the nineteenth century, John Dewey did for the twentieth century. Now education is on a purely secular basis. And where do you get all your teachers? The Columbia University Teachers College. John Dewey was there. It is the strongest citadel of secular humanism in America. The total secularization of the public school system is only a small part of what will happen. They're almost in total control."

LaHaye's is a fusion conspiracy theory, which includes the Illuminati and the Trilateral Commission, but inexplicably omits the Masons. The secular humanists and their fellow travelers, he writes, number 275,000. They "control America"—the press, the government, the movies. (This last part works against Reagan, but it doesn't matter in such a grand theory.) America was founded as a "Christian nation," but our leaders and institutions are imposters. This makes sense because the Antichrist always assumes the guise of moral spokesman, which is one of the signs by which we can recognize him. LaHaye writes: "They label it democracy, but they mean humanism, in all its atheistic, amoral depravity." He aims at piety revealed by acts of faith. Public education, the "anti-God" fount of secular humanism, aims at critical intelligence revealed by acts of reasoning. We cannot re-enter the original covenant unless we are willing to be born again; those who do not are somehow false citizens. And America itself can be born again and enter sacred time through the institutions of the Evangelical New Right—a counterculture that will restore true doctrine. "This is," LaHaye says, "essentially what the President is saying."

LaHaye, a co-founder of Moral Majority, has in fact been a welcome guest at the White House. "I've heard secular humanism discussed with Reagan," says Blackwell. "I've heard him use the term. It was once discussed in the Cabinet Room. He responded affirmatively to the comments that were made." Better to nod, no doubt, than to nod off.

Blackwell, a former New Right operative employed by Viguerie, was the key contact for the movement Evangelicals in the White House. As he worked to develop support for the President, Blackwell helped coordinate the New Right leadership. He shepherded them regularly through the White House, helped shape their events to enhance the administration agenda, and circulated drafts of legislation. He contends that "we could do better if there had been repeated initiatives" on the various social issues. "The grass-roots groups can't get the full level of enthusiasm. They aren't about to activate their people unless there are public policy battles going on." Yet Blackwell, according to a senior adviser, understood that the "social issue" was secondary to the economic. He played the game, says this source, "to get the cadres trained."

When Sandra Day O'Connor was nominated for the Supreme Court, Blackwell wrote long memos to the President urgently conveying the sentiments of the anti-abortion activists. And he brought them in to meet with Reagan. O'Connor passed the anti-abortion test that Reagan himself administered. Only two more Supreme Court Justices are needed to overturn *Roe* v. *Wade*, and Blackwell is sure that the test will be applied again. "That's a cinch," he says. "The President himself brings it up in conversation, and when pro-life leaders met with him he promised it."

In his function as ambassador to the New Right, Blackwell

depended heavily on McAteer. "He'd call and ask if he should go to certain meetings," says McAteer. "I told him who was important and who wasn't. I'd tell him whom to see on what."

The Southern Baptist Convention

One of the subjects about which McAteer kept Blackwell informed was the conservative effort to wrest control of the Southern Baptist Convention (SBC) leadership. The SBC is the denomination that has historically supported a radical division between church and state because it was founded in rebellion against oppressive state religion. Baptists traditionally have placed their trust in the priesthood of the believer, not imposed dogma. From this theological tenet flowed SBC positions on abortion and school prayer. At the 1971 SBC convention, a resolution passed almost unanimously upholding the right of abortion if a mother was in any physical or emotional peril. And over a period of two decades, the SBC eight times affirmed support for the Supreme Court ruling that school prayer was unconstitutional. SBC convention delegates are "messengers," individuals proud of not being part of organized factions. But a small group of dedicated New Right Evangelicals has changed all this.

One of their nerve centers is the Criswell Center for Biblical Studies, housed in the First Baptist Church of Dallas, and led by Paige Patterson, a Criswell associate. "We got together fifteen or twenty people to redirect the denomination," he says. "First, we located all the conservatives we could. Second, we needed to counteract the one-sided information put out by the state Baptist newspapers. We started our own, the *Southern Baptist Advocate*. Third, we agreed to elect a solid conservative president. His appointive powers determine who goes on the boards and agencies." In 1979, the Evangelicals organized and financed enough messengers at the SBC convention to elect a president—Ed McAteer's home-town preacher, Adrian Rogers. (By now, Patterson was on the Roundtable board.) In 1980, the conservative faction elected Bailey Smith, who announced: "God does not hear the prayer of a Jew." In 1982, James Draper, a Criswell associate, was elected. At that convention, McAteer was adviser to the resolutions committee. "I pushed, I did," he says. "We got that abortion thing hammered out." Thus the SBC did a complete about-face on the issue. Then the SBC reversed its position on school prayer. "McAteer told me the convention was going to do that," says Blackwell. "We were delighted." At its 1984 convention, the SBC passed a resolution against the ordination of women as ministers becuase "God requires" their "submission." Then Charles Stanley, a Moral Majority board member who was recruited into the network by McAteer, was elected president.

Tactics similar to those used within the SBC are being used by Evangelicals within the Republican Party. "The Republican Party is going through a catharsis," says LaHaye. "It will become a magnet to conservative America." The force drawing people in is not one of nature; it's organized. "We've taken over the GOP in many areas," says Gary Jarmin of Christian Voice. "In Minnesota we've taken over more than half the party. At the Texas state convention in July 1984, Christian Voice brought in 1,500 delegates out of 5,000. This is a major change. We intend to use the Republican Party as a vehicle."

Mobilizing New Voters

John Buchanan, an eight-term moderate Republican Representative from Alabama, was among the first to be singed by the New Right Evangelicals' fire. In 1980, a group of about twenty-five people appeared in his office. "They introduced themselves as 'the Christians,' " says Buchanan. "They said, 'We're here to help elect those who support the Christians and defeat those against the Christians.' " Buchanan, a Southern Baptist minister, rejoined: "I'm a Christian myself." He recalls, "The first issue they brought up was the Department of Education, which they said was trying to destroy Christianity and establish the religion of secular humanism. I asked if that was an issue on which Christians could disagree. They said no." So "the Christians," mostly Moral Majority members, fielded a primary candidate against Buchanan, registered 5,000 new voters for the sparsely attended election, and unseated him. "The Republican party has abandoned its tradition and history, the principles of Lincoln," says Buchanan. "What was once a lunatic fringe has become a driving force in the party. They beat my brains out with Christian love."

But morality in one Congressional district is not enough. The Evangelical New Right played off the 1984 presidental campaign in order to expand its political machine, broaden its base, and prepare for the future. To that end, a new organization was set up—the American Coalition for Traditional Values (ACTV). On its board are the usual suspects: Falwell, McAteer, and all the recent presidents of the SBC. The chairman is LaHaye, and the field director is Jarmin. (To a degree, ACTV is filling the vacuum left by the partial disintegration of the Roundtable, which was damaged by McAteer's quixotic independent senate race in Tennessee.) The new group was officially launched on June 11, 1984, at a White House reception attended by Reagan and George Bush. On April 19, again lending his legitimacy to the movement, Reagan wrote LaHaye a letter in which he praised ACTV as having "the potential to speak to the millions of committed Christians" and thanked him for his "faithful patriotism." By Jarmin's estimate, 40,000 pastors were recruited to set up ACTV voter registration drives in their churches. "Within each church," says Jarmin, "we form a structure, identify who's registered and who isn't, put our literature through the pipeline. After we register you, we have to educate you."

At the 1984 Republican Convention, the President himself unveiled the Evangelical New Right worldview. He portrayed the movement as a defensive counter to liberal usurpers, those who are "secularizing our nation . . . intolerant of religion." His speech was not something novel. He had voiced the same opinions in March at the National Association of Evangelicals meeting, where he attacked those "who turned to a modern-day secularism." The Dallas sermon, however, aroused a furor. Suddenly, the tone seemed to shift. Reagan made more remarks, trying to clarify the previous ones. He declared that the "wall of separation" between church and state had been broken down by "irreligionists." He claimed that they "twist the concept of freedom of religion to mean freedom against religion." He complained that his Dallas utterance had been misunderstood, and in a sense it was: it was not generally understood that he was offering up his version of the secular humanism theory.

No matter how low Walter Mondale's standing in the polls, he rates high in the demonology of the Evangelical New Right. After all, his brother, Lester Mondale, a Unitarian minister, actually signed the 1933 manifesto of the American Humanist Association. This is no ordinary election, but a battle with the Beast itself. "Mondale admits he's a humanist!" exclaims LaHaye. "I've documented this! What he's said will be distributed to the millions of Christian people."

The Evangelical New Right sets its political revivals according to the electoral calendar. But while it rides Reagan's presidency, it runs it own race. Its fixation on the "social issue" disturbed younger members of the Reagan high command. They believe that the "social issue" is indeed becoming more salient. But now it's working against the "populist" scenario envisioned long ago. The "unyoung" of 1970 are a declining share of the electorate; those who were young in 1970 (and still are) are in the ascendance, even if they haven't elected one of their own as president yet. Although older voters may be responsive to "populism," the younger are strongly libertarian. Reagan's politicos fear that whatever mandate the President won may be eroded by "social issue" conservatism. "Younger voters are pro-choice on everything," says Robert Teeter, a pollster who was a key Reagan campaign strategist. "In terms of voting groups available to us, the New Deal is gone. 'We've got to have these new groups coming in. We can't take secondary issues and turn them off. It gets tough for whoever follows Reagan. The Republican Party can't institutionalize this. We can't live with it."

Abortion the Pivotal Issue

Reagan in his first term was able to postpone the reckoning over the "social issue" mostly because of his good luck with the economy. But by the containment strategy of constitutional amendments, so successful in his first term in holding off the righteous militants while exploiting their energy, Reagan trapped himself into a second-term crisis. He locked himself into a position where he must deliver. The amendments gambit will no longer suffice. And in moving from symbolism to substance, especially on abortion, he will almost certainly shatter the Republican Party.

The Republicans are more sharply polarized over abortion than the Democrats. According to the *Los Angeles Times*, 31 per cent of Republicans strongly oppose the anti-abortion amendment; 13 per cent somewhat oppose it; 6 per cent somewhat approve it; and 27 per cent strongly approve. Among delegates to the 1984 Republican Convention, only 32 per cent were in favor, according to NBC News. The traditional Republican constituencies are heavily opposed. The Harris poll records 71 per cent of the college educated opposed; 62 per cent of white Protestants; and, significantly, 68 per cent of Westerners. The West is the party's firm base, but with abortion criminalized by a Reagan-appointed Supreme Court, it could easily become shaky; it's the country's most libertarian region.

The GOP may crack, but the New Right Evangelicals will flourish. That would be the ultimate fulfillment of "social issue" conservatism. The divisions this sort of politics engenders are inescapable. And the party that enacts sectarian doctrine into law in the attempt to regenerate a lost world will pay a steep political price. The true believers would be neither surprised nor disappointed. They place the highest value on ideology, which they are certain foretells the fate of America and the Second Coming. They believe that their bursts of enthusiasm are bringing them closer to the end of time, but they are paradoxically promoting the movement which worships above all the god of worldly power.

19. Fundamentalism as an Ideology

By HARVEY COX

Focus

Contrary to popular misconceptions, Fundamentalism began among urban intellectuals. Only as it came to be embraced by "the smalltown and rural poor" did Fundamentalism come to be what even its adherents admit is a "redneck religion," argues Harvey Cox. Not merely a theology or even a subculture, Fundamentalism is, according to Cox, an ideology. As such, Fundamentalism "interprets and defends the perceived life interests of an identifiable social group." As a movement, Fundamentalism expresses "opposition to the powerful modern, liberal, capitalist world that [is] disrupting [the] traditional way of life."

Fundamentalists want to preserve not only the fundamentals of the Christian faith, but "a world in which these fundamentals would be more widely accepted and practiced. They want not only to 'keep the faith,' but to change the world so the faith can be kept more easily."

Cox doubts that Fundamentalists will be able to create such a society in America for three reasons: First, the "redneck" factor cannot be easily merged with the mainstream of American religious or public life; second, the Fundamentalists' belief that "the end of the age is near . . . produces a cynical sense of powerlessness" and makes it difficult for the movement as a whole to push for constructive social or political change; third, a tension is inherent in the Fundamentalists' use of technology—especially television, "a tradition-smashing phenomenon."

"What happens," Cox asks, "when a profoundly antimodernist attempt to reassert the primacy of traditional values utilizes a cultural form that is itself thoroughly modern and antitraditional?" He answers: "Jerry Falwell and other traditionalists who have embraced network television may have struck a mortal blow to exactly what they are trying to defend, the 'old time Gospel' and traditional religion."

Harvey Cox is a professor at Harvard Divinity School and the author of numerous articles and books, including *The Secular City* and *Religion in the Secular City*.

AMERICAN FUNDAMENTALISM IS a movement that began among urban intellectuals and was most keenly articulated by a Princeton scholar, Professor J. Gresham Machen. Why, then, did it come to find its home among rural white poor people and urban lower middle classes? The usual answer is that Fundamentalism is the religion of the uneducated, that accepting it was largely a matter of cultural deficiency. I do not agree with this thesis.

Fundamentalism is not only a theology and a subculture, but an ideology. It interprets and defends the perceived life interests of an identifiable social group. Jerry Falwell and Ed Hindson (using the familiar ploy by which blacks and gays and others have appropriated terms originally used as epithets against them) are largely correct to call Fundamentalism "redneck religion." This also means that Fundamentalism, like liberation theology, the religion of Native Americans, and some other theologies, is an antimodern ideology. For the smalltown and rural poor who appropriated it, Fundamentalism expressed their opposition to the powerful modern, liberal, and capitalist world that was disrupting their traditional way of life.

An ideology is a cluster of ideas and values that provides a class, nation, or some human group with a picture of the world that can guide and inspire corporate action. As an ideology, Fundamentalism contains an implicit image of what society should be. Fundamentalists not only insist on preserving the fundamentals of the faith, but envision a world in which these fundamentals would be more widely accepted and practiced. They want not only to "keep the faith," but to change the world so the faith can be kept more easily.

This requires a world in which science and philosophy play roles quite different from those they have today. When Fundamentalist scholars reject the modern idea that philosophy has little to say about worldviews, they are advocating not just a style of philosophy closer to the grand tradition of Plato, Aquinas, and Spinoza,

---

Reprinted by permission of Simon & Schuster, Inc. from *Religion in the Secular City*, 1984.

they are proposing a society in which philosophy would hold a more central role. When Fundamentalists bring infrared photographs of the Shroud of Turin into play, they express a confused yearning for a culture in which scientists and theologians would work together in a common intellectual enterprise.

Fundamentalists and Modernity

This vision of a common culture is held by nearly all the conservative and traditionalist critics of modernity. On the vital issue of how to achieve such a culture, however, Fundamentalism differs from both theologically conservative Evangelicalism and religious liberalism. Both of these accept, in varying measure, the modern reduction of the role of religion and theology. Though Evangelicals differ sharply from Liberals on what the content of the faith is, they tend to accept the modern world as the arena in which the theological task is to be done. The argument between Liberals and Evangelicals is about the message, not about the world. Fundamentalists, by contrast—as becomes paradoxically evident in their protestations about "separation from the world"—are more uncomfortable with the modern logos and more critical of it. Their idea of apologetics is not to translate the gospel into the mental categories of modernity, but to change modern mental categories so the gospel can be grasped. They are culture critics and political theologians despite themselves.

Their opposition to modernity places Fundamentalist theologians closer to liberation theologians than either would like to admit. Both refuse to accept the modern world or the "modern mind." Both speak from the context of social groups that have not benefited from the modern liberal ethos but have felt it a threat to their well-being. Both believe that the most pressing task of Christianity today is not the refinement and redefinition of doctrine—not translating the message into the world's terms—but bringing the world more into conformity with the message.

The fact that Fundamentalist and liberation theologians often come out on opposite ends of the political spectrum should not obscure this striking structural similarity between them. Karl Marx once said that, until his time, philosophers had merely interpreted the world but the need was to change it. One might say that Liberal and Evangelical theologians have tried to make the Christian message credible to the modern world. Fundamentalists and liberation theologians are not interested in interpreting; they do not want to speak to, and be heard by, the world so much as they want to change it. Can the form of traditional religion represented by Fundamentalism make a contribution to a postmodern Christianity? Its recent history raises some doubts.

There is something rather logical about American Fundamentalism's habit of swinging back and forth between withdrawal into a subculture and highly confrontational efforts to remake the whole of society. It stems from the belief that the whole world, not just some religious segment, should reflect its sacred source. This is a view of society that Paul Tillich once described as "theonomous" (as opposed to a "heteronomous" one in which religious values would have to be imposed). When one holds this view, it is impossible to settle for the marginal role to which religion has been relegated in the modern world. One either tries to change the whole society to bring it into conformity (thus risking heteronomy), or one retreats to a smaller, more manageable subculture where a kind of minitheonomy is possible.

Harold Berman of the Harvard Law School has written:

> It is supposed by some, especially intellectuals, that fundamental legal principles . . . can survive without any religious or quasireligious foundations on the basis of the proper political and economic controls and the philosophy of humanism. History, however, including current history, testifies otherwise. People will not give their allegiance to a political and economic system, and even less to a philosophy, unless it represents for them a higher, sacred truth.[1]

Fundamentalists in their own way support this theory of the relationship between religion and civil society. But will American Fundamentalists be able to help shape such a society in the future? There are three reasons why this seems unlikely.

The Influences of Culture

First, American Fundamentalism is at once theology, subculture, and ideology, but not all components have equal weight. "When I was a boy in Virginia," says Jerry Falwell, "in a redneck society, patriotism was just a part of life." To his credit, Falwell concedes that racism was also a part of that life, but he believes he has overcome it. His Thomas Road Baptist Church now has black members, and Falwell is proud that he has been attacked by the Ku Klux Klan as "an enemy of the white race."

But how many other values that Thomas Road Baptist Church and similar Fundamentalist churches stand for are derived from Christianity and how many derive from "redneck society"? Christians everywhere have to ask this question about their own cultures all the time. It springs from a recognition that, though culture must be the bearer of religion, biblical religion also judges and purifies cultural values. Are Fundamentalists ready to test the Christian bases of their nearly uncritical support of American foreign policy and the capitalist economic system? Are they willing to test these positions through careful study of the Bible and discussions with people who share the same faith but have a different culture?

There is evidence that some Fundamentalists are ready to enter such a dialogue, and to alter their positions on some social issues (not theological ones) if they are persuaded. But many are not ready for such conversations. They have lived in the Fundamentalist ghetto too long to want to emerge and converse.

The redneck ideology element in Fundamentalism makes the mixture of culture and theology more volatile. The poor rural workers of America have not always been as well disposed toward big businesses and corporate capitalism as the leaders of American Fundamentalism now seem to be. Falwell's friendly reference to the *Wall Street Journal* in his sermon would not have pleased the "great Fundamentalist" William Jennings Bryan, who stood in the courthouse in Dayton, Tennessee, long before Falwell did, but who also moved people to tears with his populist attacks on those who would crucify the working people of America on a "cross of gold." Some of Falwell's fellow Fundamentalists have accused him of betraying the cause, of becoming a "compromiser." Bryan not only defended the Bible from what he considered modernist attacks on it, but also stood up for the disprivileged rural and ordinary small-town people of America, the "moral majority" of his day, against the power of Wall Street and corporate wealth. He even resigned as Secretary of State when he could not in good conscience execute what his Christian conscience told him was a warlike and belligerent foreign policy.

Though Falwell claims Bryan's mantle, in many respects he has discarded Bryan's populist politics and become a supporter of the very people Bryan spent a lifetime combating. In American political Fundamentalism, we can trace the tension between the genuinely populist "poor redneck" tradition and the upwardly mobile pro-big business element. Which will eventually win?

If Bible study teachers in Fundamentalist churches continue to ponder the confrontation between Jesus and the "critics" he met in his day, like the Sadducees and the Herodians, they are bound to discover that these were not only "schools of thought" but political movements. The difficulty Jesus ran into with the Sadducees was not principally over doctrinal points. Rather, it arose from the clash between the property-owning, politically dominant classes the Sadducees represented and the landless rural poor and urban rabble who formed the majority of Jesus' movement.[2] If the "politics of Jesus," rather than some unlikely combination of Eastern Establishment and down-home booster politics, ever begins to predominate, as it already has on some occasions, then Fundamentalism would make quite a different impact on the national political scene.

Liberation theologians have generally not paid much attention to Fundamentalism. If they did, they would notice that the "redneck" element represents an ambiguous but not entirely negative dimension. Redneck politics in America has always been unpredictable, given to alternating spasms of red-clay rebelliousness and easy accommodation to demagoguery. But it has rarely for very long toadied to the modern equivalents of the Sadducees and Herodians. How much influence it will have in the current coming out of political Fundamentalism, and what that influence will be, remains to be seen.

End-of-the-Age Fatalism

My second reason for doubting whether Fundamentalism can succeed in making a contribution to a postmodern theology has to do with what might be called its "political apocalyptic" belief that the end of the age is near. This Christ-is-coming-soon eschatology not only discourages any kind of work for constructive change, but can produce a kind of overheated fatalism: if the big bang is going to come, then let it happen soon.

In Falwell's Lynchburg, Virginia, however, though they talk about the Lord's imminent return, they are planning for the long haul. Liberty Baptist College is now a university. Nearby, on Liberty Mountain, a retirement village is being built. Falwell's scheme for reuniting the scattered Fundamentalist tribes will require years of patient orchestration. No one seems to expect it to be all over soon.

Out in the byways, however, it is different. When the novelist A. G. Mojtabai went to Amarillo, Texas, to see how the town was responding to Bishop Leroy Matthiesen's plea to his people to consider not working for Pantex, a local plant where nuclear weapons are assembled, she found that the major religious opposition to the bishop came from the Reverend J. Alan Ford. Ford is minister of the Southwest Baptist Church (which claims to be "Amarillo's fastest growing church," with two thousand members) and the local leader of Moral Majority. Ford believes the biblical books of Daniel, Ezekiel, and Revelation tell us what will happen in the near future: ". . . a Russian invasion of Iran. Russia will press its advantage in the Middle East . . . Russia will go to war with Israel." It is all there in Revelation and in Ezekiel: we live in the last days.

Another minister in Amarillo, the Reverend Royce Elms, leader of a Pentecostal church, invited a visitor to examine Second Peter 3:10, which says that "the elements shall melt with fervent heat," and verse 12, "Wherein the heavens being on fire shall be dissolved." Elms comforts his people by assuring them that, though this catastrophe is imminent, there is also the Rapture: real Christians will be caught up into the air to meet the descending Lord. It will be instantaneous. "All through this, God is speaking through his word, telling us not to worry. If the Amarillo bomb dropped today, it wouldn't bother me one bit."[3]

In the regions and subcultures most influenced by Fundamentalism, this sense that we are in the last days, coupled with a kind of vertiginous fascination with the prospect, is widespread even among people who do not attend church. When I responded to the friendly query of a young couple I met in a restaurant in North Carolina about what I was doing "so far from home," and told them I was speaking at a local church in favor of the nuclear arms freeze, they smiled. I was wasting my time, they assured me. They never went to church themselves, they said, but they knew the world was going to end soon by an atomic war, because "that's what the Bible says." They then went back to sipping their beer and watching television.

After her trip to Amarillo, Mojtabai described it this way:

> The impression is unavoidable: some of the most ardent born and born-again Christians are writing Christianity off as something that didn't, couldn't work—at least, not in the First Coming. The conviction that mankind is bent on its own destruction, that goodness cannot succeed in a world so evil, the constant recourse to the Old Testament and to the most bellicose sections, the turning for betterment to the dire remedies offered by the book of Revelation, the only light left to the Second Coming—all this strangely negates the "good news" of the Gospels and the First Coming.[4]

This ominous fatalism is not only a far cry from that of the Bible and what most Christians have believed over the centuries, it is also a very different message from the one conveyed in the jovial, smiling atmosphere of Falwell's church. The trouble is that spreading the bad news of imminent nuclear war can become a self-fulfilling prophecy. When Fundamentalism ceases to proclaim the central kernel of the biblical message—that God calls human beings to repent and to change their evil ways, and that God's grace makes such repentance possible—then Fundamentalism forgoes any claim to being a Christian or even biblical theology. It has opted for a low-grade kismet, an it's-all-in-the-cards fatalism that produces a cynical sense of powerlessness. It has become a religious pathology.

Which of these two faces of the Fundamentalist tradition will eventually predominate—the one that calls the nation back to righteousness, or the one that closes the cyclone door and awaits the cataclysm? On the answer to this question hangs the future of Fundamentalism's capacity to speak a healing word and to influence the shape of the future. If its fatalistic side predominates, Fundamentalism may become one more factor in depriving us of any future at all.

The 'Gospel Glut' of the Airwaves

My third reason for doubting Fundamentalism's influence on post-modern Christianity is its recent romance with the electronic media. Fundamentalism is a highly traditional religious expression. Television is a tradition-smashing phenomenon. Yet rarely has any religious movement embraced an artifact of modernity as enthusiastically and as uncritically. The top regular religious television shows (Rex Humbard, Pat Robertson, Falwell, Oral Roberts) are all more or less Fundamentalist in orientation. Colleges and seminaries associated with the Fundamentalist movement have some of the finest television equipment available to students anywhere. It is generally acknowledged that Fundamentalist television is produced with a high level of technical competence. And this is only the beginning. Writing in the Evangelical periodical *Christianity Today,* Tom Bisset, general manager of the Baltimore station WRBS-FM, stated:

> The Christian world is about to be future-shocked by an invasion of space-age multiple delivery systems. . . . Much of the technological hardware is already in place. Cable and pay television have widened the public's viewing options. Two-way cable systems, where both parties can see and talk to each other, have been tested successfully. A nationwide Christian media counseling service beckons. Videocassette recorders and video-discs will soon make it possible for a local Christian bookstore to offer concerts, revival meetings, or teaching sessions—video and audio—for the price of a record. Low-power television, soon to be in use, and UHF/VHF translators, already in use, augment broadcasting's ever widening delivery system. . . .
>
> But even the wildest dreams would find it hard to anticipate what is coming in satellite and computer technology. Picture, if you will, a worldwide Christian satellite system pumping out 24 separate television signals and 24 separate FM signals to earth. That makes 48 new listening and viewing options available to anyone who is plugged into the right wire or who owns the necessary equipment. . . .
>
> Every conceivable audio and visual need will be covered. Every taste in music, every unique ministry, every interpretive

whim and wish—all can and will find their way to these highly specialized channels.[5]

Bisset fears a "gospel glut." What happens when a profoundly antimodernist attempt to reassert the primacy of traditional values utilizes a cultural form that is itself thoroughly modern and antitraditional? This is the tension between content and form, between message and medium, that occurs when Falwell's "Old Time Gospel Hour" goes over network television.

The German Jewish writer Walter Benjamin addressed this issue in an influential essay published in 1936, "The Work of Art in the Age of Mechanical Reproduction." Benjamin was writing about art, but his observation, as he himself said, is equally applicable to religion. He argued that the mechanical reproduction of any work of art profoundly alters its meaning, and makes it different in ways its reproducers can never anticipate. It was Benjamin's conviction that "the technique of reproduction detaches the reproduced object from the domain of tradition." This leads ultimately to "the liquidation of the traditional value of the cultural heritage"—or what Benjamin called the "decay of the aura."[6]

When one applies this analysis to religious phenomena, the change in meaning is particularly radical. For Benjamin, an essential feature of any work of art is the sense of distance and awe it elicits, a power he believed is also derived from the religious and spiritual purpose art originally served. It is this distance which gives it authority. Reproduction, in severing the object from its intended spiritual "location" and depriving it of its aura, at the same time robs it of its authority by making it too close, too available.

Falwell and other religious traditionalists who have embraced network color television—the ultimate form of modern mechanical reproduction—may have struck a mortal blow to exactly what they are trying to defend, which is the "old time Gospel" and traditional religion. The move from the revivalist's tent to the vacuum tube has vastly amplified the voices of defenders of tradition. At the same time, however, it has made them more dependent on the styles and assumptions inherent in the medium itself. This explains the none too subtle shift one feels at Thomas Road Baptist Church when the adult Bible study ends, the big lights go on, and the entire congregation suddenly becomes the cast of a nationwide network show. It is hard, despite Falwell's consummate skill at bridging the gap, not to feel that one has been pushed further into the modern world and moved a notch away from the "old time" antimodernist intent of the message.

Religious television moves toward entertainment. Falwell still appears behind the pulpit, but Pat Robertson uses a setting copied from late-night talk shows. On Roberton's "700 Club," a succession of splendidly dressed guests tell the audience how the Lord has brought them success, health, money, and power. The Gospel is reduced to a means of achieving the same modern secular goals the evangelist began by opposing.

The German social critic Jurgen Habermas sees a battle shaping up between what he calls "communicative life-worlds" and the more formally organized systems based on power and money steered by the media.[7] This is exactly the contradiction in which television-based political Fundamentalism finds itself today. In the contest between the system and traditional morality, Falwell and his followers fervently believe they are on the side of the angels. They believe that they are defending the old-time moral values against the invasion of modernity. But the technical and organizational means they have chosen to fight the battle may be destroying precisely the religious resources most needed to save traditional morality.

Television, mass computer mailings, and the latest marketing techniques are not neutral tools. Embedded in them are a set of attitudes and values that are inimical to traditional morality. They extend massification. As Habermas says, capitalist modernization transfers more and more "social material" from the "life-worlds" into realms of action controlled by large outside systems. This process previously left religion, education, and the family alone, and concentrated instead on more overtly economic sectors like banks and factories. Now, however, "the system's imperatives," says Habermas, "are attacking areas of action which are demonstrably unable to perform their own tasks if they are removed from communicatively structured areas of action."[8] Network television and computer mailings are not "communicatively structured areas of action." They are powerful anticommunicative forces, engaged in shoving more and more of those human activities which used to go on in small "life-worlds" into the insatiable maw of the modern system.

The contradiction between traditional religion and the mass media seems unavoidable. The deepest contradiction lies in the question of the nature of a genuine religious community. One real strength of the newly emerging Christian base communities in Latin America and elsewhere is that they foster the face-to-face groupings that human beings need so badly. The television evangelists do not. Despite their efforts to include viewers through letters, telephone calls, and a folksy style on camera, something essential is missing in a television congregation. By buying so heavily into the mass-media world, Fundamentalism may have unintentionally sold out to one of the most characteristic features of the very modern world that it wants to challenge. If the devil is a modernist, the television evangelists may have struck a deal with Lucifer himself, who always appears—so the Bible teaches—an an angel of light.

'Victories' Could Lead to Defeat

Just before I left Lynchburg, I stopped to visit the national headquarters of the Old Time Gospel Hour in a converted warehouse next to a supermarket. Inside, rows of volunteers take incoming calls on banks of telephones. The atmosphere is brisk, friendly, and efficient. Earlier in the day I was there, Falwell had appeared on network television talking about President Reagan's decision to seek an amendment to the United States Constitution that would permit voluntary prayers to be said in the classrooms of public schools. Falwell interviewed Senator Jesse Helms of North Carolina, a supporter of the amendment, and offered a "Kids Need to Pray" bumper sticker. He also asked viewers to call in their opinion on the subject to his toll-free number. The volunteers were receiving continuous calls, nearly all of them supporting the amendment. By calling and giving their names and addresses, of course, the callers were also supplying the Old Time Gospel Hour with thousands of prospective new donors. But some volunteers were also engaged in a kind of high-tech counseling. Typists sat at word processors sending out a stream of prewritten letters to troubled and questioning viewers all over the country. The age of mechanical reproduction, I thought, has come not just to art, but to prayer and the cure of souls.

In its nearly a century of life, American Fundamentalism has weathered many attacks. It has been a scandal to liberal intellectuals and a stumbling block to skeptics. But it has always been irascible, and full of a certain feisty vitality. Beaten back into its corner on many occasions, it has always emerged again, picking up stones to sling at the Goliath of modernism. But will the subtle whirr of computers and Nielsen ratings succeed where contempt, condescension, and even persecution have failed? Fundamentalists and other conservative Christians have something important to say to a world that has grown rightly sick of modernity. But there are very few people who want to live in a society in which the values of a particular subculture are unloaded onto all of us in the name of Jesus.

Fundamentalists have had a record of turning defeats into victories, and vice versa. When John T. Scopes was convicted for teaching evolution in Tennessee in 1925, it was a victory for Fundamentalism. It quickly became evident, however, that because of the immense publicity the case received, it had not been a victory at all, but a defeat. After the trial, Fundamentalists retreated again. Now, with television and computer mailings available, they smell a new victory, much bigger than the one they achieved at Dayton, Tennessee. But for some of the same reasons, this victory could turn into another defeat—perhaps this time for good.

Notes

1. Quoted in Carl F. H. Henry, "The Fundamentalist Phenomenon: The Ricochet of Silver Bullets," *Christianity Today* XXV, 15 (September 4, 1981), p. 30.

2. For recent descriptions of Jesus' relations to the political groupings of history, see *Jesus in His Time* (Philadelphia: Fortress Press, 1971), edited by Hans Jurgen Schultz, especially the essay by Paul Winter on "Sadducees and Pharisees."

3. A. G. Mojtabai, "Amarillo, the End of the Line," *Working Papers* IX, 4 (1982), p. 26.

4. Ibid., p. 28. For a best-selling statement of apocalyptic Fundamentalist eschatology, see Hal Lindsey and C. C. Carlson, *The Late Great Planet Earth* (Grand Rapids: Bantam, 1970).

5. Tom Bisset, "Religious Broadcasting Coming of Age," *Christianity Today* XXV (September 4, 1981), p. 30.

6. Walter Benjamin, *Illuminations* (1955 Suhrkamp Verlag, Frankfurt and London; translation, New York: Harcourt, Brace and World, 1968). See also Eugene Lunn, *Marxism and Modernism: An Historical Study of Lukacs, Brecht, Benjamin and Adorno* (Berkeley: University of California Press, 1982).

7. Jurgen Habermas, "Modernity vs. Postmodernity," *New German Critique* XXII (Winter 1981), p. 18.

8. Ibid., p. 18.

20. *Fundamentalism as a Social Phenomenon*

By MARTIN E. MARTY

Focus Martin E. Marty, one of America's leading historians of religion, criticizes those who condescendingly dismiss Fundamentalism as a quirky anachronism and underestimate the impact of this social phenomenon throughout the United States. Unlike members of "lackadaisical mainline churches who have to be cajoled into the pew," Fundamentalists, he observes, are "people who are religious [and] cannot help but be religious." Fundamentalists are "out to 'get saved,' " and so "cannot be beguiled out of their vision, distracted from their passion, or diverted from what consumes them."

Marty points out that such a religious seriousness strikes many "moderns" as quaint and, in some instances, dangerous. But it is neither. Marty finds the Fundamentalist resurgence in political affairs as in part a reaction to the "mixed offerings of modernity." In particular, he points to the crisis of values which has arisen within American culture. While Fundamentalists have for two generations occupied themselves with the private dimensions of their faith, they have reacted politically against a perceived threat to the moral foundations of American society and government.

Fundamentalists have become both visible and influential because of their ability to employ the tools of modernity—such as mass communications—against the moral effects of other aspects of modernity. Marty notes that Fundamentalists "have borrowed the technology of modernization with all its bewilderments and used it substantially to promote nostalgic and simplistic visions of the past as models for the future."

Marty stresses, too, that America is not "turning fundamentalist." Fundamentalism is newly influential in public affairs, but for continued effectiveness it must build coalitions, develop new leaders, and "make skillful uses of the edges that technology and dedication give it in close elections."

Martin E. Marty is Fairfax M. Cone Distinguished Professor of the History of Modern Christianity at the University of Chicago, a senior editor of *The Christian Century,* and author of *Modern American Religion: The Irony of It All, 1893–1919* (University of Chicago, 1987).

FUNDAMENTALISM, INVOLVING AS it does some ten to twenty million Americans,[1] is obviously a social phenomenon and demands interpretation as such. But the observer who isolates the social dimension has to take special care to be fair-minded—to give something of the participants' point of view. To descend on Fundamentalism from the outside with too many presuppositions about social movements may mean to lose the necessary sense of what animates the movement and inspires loyalty to it.

Fundamentalists for the most part would not see themselves as members of a "social phenomenon." Almost all observers have agreed with participants that Fundamentalism is in many respects a highly individualized version of Christian faith. The Fundamentalists for the most part are church members, but they are not "churchly" in a sacramental sense. They make little of an ontological reality that calls them to communal existence, a church that exists in the mind of God, or the structure of things before it manifests itself as voluntary local associations.

To the Fundamentalist, participation means being saved. It begins with a separation from the world in the form of being "born again," though there are Fundamentalists in, say, the Presbyterian tradition who find that term less congenial than do the majority in the Baptist traditions. From this separation follows a deeper desire to be separated also from sin and from half-faithful or even apostate people who call themselves Christians but who waver on certain fundamentals. The believer wants to be with Jesus in the Rapture, the millennial reign, and finally in the new heavens. The terms for the eschaton vary somewhat, but no one should ever forget the otherworldly or next-worldly dimension of this faith.

So it comes down to an individual search and a personal reception of grace. To take Fundamentalists seriously and to see their faith as a matter of integrity, we must, in any fair analysis of the social phenomenon, listen to the participants' description. In the deepest sense of the term, people who are religious cannot help but

Reprinted with permission by William B. Eerdmans Publishing Co. from *Evangelicalism and Modern America,* edited by George Marsden, 1984.

be religious. They cannot be beguiled out of their vision, distracted from their passion, or diverted from what consumes them. Members of lackadaisical mainline churches who have to be cajoled into the pew and seduced toward the tithe may forget the power of such engrossing religious appeals. But the Fundamentalist does not forget. He or she is out to "get saved," and little else matters.

Holding constantly to that understanding, however, the observer moves on. Fundamentalism, like all modern faiths—and this one is nothing if not modern, born in the face and challenge of modernity and taking advantage of its mixed technical offerings—involves the possibility that the believer will keep religion a "private affair."[2] Yet one will notice that the majority of the saved do form social organizations. The most powerful of these, of course, is the local church, which in the technical sense is the only church Fundamentalism knows. There are, however, voluntary extensions of this local reality: these take the form of clienteles for religious radio and television, power movements within moderate denominations like the Southern Baptist Convention, and constituencies that support Bible institutes, crusades, and publishing ventures.

A Space in the Social World

By this point of organization the individual Fundamentalist can no longer hide from the awareness that a social phenomenon has developed. Even as an ecclesial reality of a nominalist sort, Fundamentalist church life takes institutional form and thus takes up space in the world. Wary of receiving government aid and insisting, as Fundamentalists do, on separation of church and state, they still for the most part do accept tax exemption of properties used for specifically religious purposes. This exemption, which can be argued as a "right" of "good policy" or "public benefit," is a fiscal boon to American churches that far exceeds the subsidy that established churches receive in Europe. And, as tax-exempt by the public, churches enter the public realm.

The move from individuals' "being saved" to their being part of a social phenomenon goes far beyond the physical space of Fundamentalists' properties and the indirect public support through tax exemption. Fundamentalism wants to win converts, and this means moving door to door in public communities, passing out tracts in pluralist settings, and using air waves that are conceived as "belonging" to everyone. In this sense, in many parts of the country at least, nonfundamentalists become aware of the social dimensions of a voluntaryist religious vision.

A third stage of presence, however, moves Fundamentalism further in the public eye as a social phenomenon. This is its political aspiration. Most Fundamentalists do not see themselves as political, and their own witness about themselves has to be taken seriously. Through most of their history, most members have tended to be passive about connecting religion and politics. Their social class, often upper-lower or lower-middle, had kept them from the kinds of colleges, support funding, or aspiring that brings people to Congress or executive mansions. Intensely patriotic, they would vote or accept the call to military service, because Fundamentalist pacifism is extremely rare. They paid their taxes and probably had a lower crime and delinquency rate than the general public or some more relaxed religious forces could boast.

Fundamentalism as a social phenomenon has often been hard to isolate on the political level because voting tends to follow partisan and regional lines. Most Fundamentalists insist that they do not wish to organize political parties. Though many analysts see ties between theological and political "conservatism," that term itself is problematic when dealing with Fundamentalism. When the movement was born, it did not "conserve" much of what Roman Catholic, Eastern Orthodox, and mainline Protestant churches—which must make up nine-tenths of Christendom—would have regarded as the tradition worth preserving. It was quite radical in its primitivism, insisting that it was reproducing biblical-era belief and organization. More than it knew, the movement did draw on traditional thirteenth- and seventeenth-century scholasticism, Catholic and Protestant. Often in its more open Calvinist forms, it also paid respects to the sixteenth-century Protestant Reformation. But the movement makes no sense except as a very modern reaction to modernism,[3] a highly selective selection of the "fundamentals" of faith, a fresh patterning of the presumed "essences" of Christianity, one that makes little sense to the sacramental churches, whose "essentials" seldom come up. Fundamentalism in many senses, including the best ones, was not "conservative" but radical.

Yet the public and liberal religionists categorize the movement as theologically conservative and assume that this conservatism carries over symptomatically into politics. Certainly there are predispositions of this sort; yet examinations of voting records often show that Fundamentalists of the South and the Plains States allied themselves with populist movements that were anything but conservative. In the 1930s, true political conservatives often thought of the Tennessee Valley Authority as socialistic or communistic. Appalachian Fundamentalists, who wanted their farms electrified, voted for the program, whatever socialist images it carried. It would be a mistake to picture all Fundamentalists as political reactionaries at all times.

Defense and Aggression

Sometimes Fundamentalism as a social phenomenon shows up politically in a defensive way. Before the Democratic Convention of 1960, Fundamentalists and other Protestant conservatives sometimes made ephemeral common cause with the Protestant liberals to raise criticisms of Catholicism in American life in connection with the candidacy of John F. Kennedy.[4] They regularly hurry to Washington with the best of liberals to protect themselves from real or presumed intrusive threats on the part of the Internal Revenue Service or the Federal Communications Commission.[5] They may not see these defensive gestures as being political, bringing them into the zone of "social phenomena," but in the process of building coalitions and making alliances, testifying in Congress, lobbying, or seeking votes on specific issues, they have to be seen as far removed from individualist, nonpolitical life.

Beyond automatic participation in social life and defensiveness, much Fundamentalism has moved into more aggressive endeavors to be a social phenomenal presence. This occurs whenever its leaders, backed by visible followers, assert themselves in efforts to reshape social life in America. This is almost always done in the name of "morality" in putative distinction from, or even opposition to, "politics." Fundamentalists have cared deeply, as is their right, about gambling, alcoholic intemperance, and accessible pornography. These are, of course, moral issues: they are issues congenial to that strain of Protestantism that had long before become expert at dealing with individual "virtue" and "vice," as opposed to social and structural reworking of society.

The problem with keeping Fundamentalism an individual religiosity as opposed to a social phenomenon is that one cannot move far beyond simple personal voluntaryism without bumping into contravening political forces that have their own interests. The bumper sticker that says "Against Abortion?—Don't Have One!" illustrates an approach that would allow Fundamentalism to remain withdrawn from the political order and to be seen less as a social phenomenon. Studies in the summer of 1981 that revealed Fundamentalists to be represented almost as regularly in audiences of sexy-and-violent TV shows as was the general public might have inspired another set of bumper stickers: "Don't Like 'Em? Shut Them Off!" "Don't like intemperance? Don't drink." Let us take in good faith the Fundamentalist churches' claims that members do restrain themselves in the matters of abortion, pornography, and alcohol. They thus make a contribution to a moral America on their terms.

Legislated Morality

Fundamentalists would not be satisfied, however, with only that measure of contribution. Nine-tenths of America is not Fundamentalist, and if it continues in immoral practices, America will still not be "moral." So a moralist vision does and must move into politics again, let us keep insisting, in a process that is fully legitimate. Fundamentalism has its rights. It is at this point, however, that a blind spot develops, one that matches the blinders liberals wear when they sometimes say that Fundamentalists should not enter the political arena. To the Fundamentalist, religious liberal support of the civil rights or antiwar movements was political, not moral. Liberal opposition to capital punishment is political; Fundamentalist support of it is moral. Saving lives through poverty programs in the public sector is a political act; saving fetal life by prohibiting abortions is a moral venture. This distinction has not been compelling to any nonfundamentalist.

Fundamentalist leaders in 1980 and 1981 began to see the anomaly, indeed, the bad faith, implied in this distinction. The best known of them, evangelist Jerry Falwell, very frankly admitted that he had been "wrong" when he previously inerrantly followed his inerrant Bible in opposing clerical involvement in the politics of civil rights. He speaks with some measure of repentance for his old stand—perhaps prudently, possibly with deep conviction after a "conversion" and some measure of admiration for people like Martin Luther King, Jr.; perhaps it was a ploy, but here we should also grant the possibility of good faith, as a latter-day recognition of King's effort for human good. In either case, Falwell makes no secret of his having led part of Fundamentalism overtly into that moral-political realm.

To work for constitutional amendments, to seek passage of certain specific legislation, to attempt to prevent this or that international treaty—all these are marks not of individualist religiosity but of a social phenomenon of considerable power. The Fundamentalists' leaders justify their about-face on the grounds that America has grown so immoral that they must engage in a "teleological suspension of the ethical." Intemperance was and abortion is such a gross immorality in the sight of God, and such a hazard to the civil order, that one must take extraordinary means to address them as problems. Then one can lapse back into political passivity. This would mean that Fundamentalism is only *sometimes* a social phenomenon.

A Power Among Powers

Once the policy of separation, passivity, and even withdrawal is broken, however, much else follows. Today's Fundamentalist leadership has spotted a power vacuum and has enjoyed beginning to fill it. "How're ya goin' to keep 'em down on the farm after they've seen Paree?" How are you going to keep Fundamentalists off in individual religiosity after they have seen how easily they can effect some parts of their social vision? To seek power is not necessarily an evil: without power one cannot achieve good. But to seek power on present terms is to recognize that Fundamentalism, whatever its historic voice, today overtly seeks to be a social phenomenon with political dimensions.

If political Fundamentalism inconveniences other people—people who support the Panama Canal Treaty, abortion clinics, the Department of Education, or cocktail lounges—it has to understand that its jostling of the social fabric will inspire criticism and counterorganization. Legitimately wounded by a few unfair attacks on their rights as they intruded into the political order, some Fundamentalist leaders overstepped or showed naïveté by creating the suggestion that the idea of counteraction, even if only in the form of criticism, was always out of line. But there are no exempt spaces for people who enter the political order. Politics, however unready Fundamentalists may be to recognize it, is an order that involves conflict and compromise.[6] It is an assertion of power amidst other powers, an attempt to make moves that step on the toes of others who, thus alerted, stop wincing and start marching or arming or organizing. The social phenomenal character of Fundamentalism, then, has become patent. Attempts to disguise it are to be short-lived. Efforts to hold out against the move on the part of Fundamentalist minorities are not likely to protect the movement as a whole from a public perception that sees its social presence.

Fundamentalism, then, has become a political force among the forces, Politicians reckon with it as they do with labor unions and senior citizens' action agencies. Television critics regard it as a social phenomenon for its presence in "the electronic church." *Publishers Weekly* gives an accounting of its book sales. There is no place to hide, and the majority of Fundamentalist leadership does not wish to. Far, far removed seem the days when the individual search for salvation was the encompassing feature of Fundamentalism.

Seeing Fundamentalism as a social phenomenon today makes most sense when viewed against the past. Some years ago, in *Righteous Empire,* I made a distinction within Protestantism.[7] It had a "two-party" system, one termed "public" and the other "private." In 1857–58, at the time of the "laymen's revivals," whose social consequences Timothy Smith has so well chronicled in *Revivalism and Social Reform,*[8] one could view revivalists also as social movement leaders for reform, welfare, and political purposes. Before them, Charles Grandison Finney's generation of revivalists engaged themselves with issues that ranged from dueling to slavery.[9] But by 1908, when the old Federal Council of Churches was born, Fundamentalism was organized chiefly around certain more liberal social purposes and had left evangelism pretty well behind. By then, also, evangelists in the train of Dwight L. Moody through Billy Sunday, for all their casual and even sometimes forceful social comments, were seen as specialists in soul-saving—rescuing people from a world of shipwreck into salvationist lifeboats, to use Moody's celebrated metaphor.

Political Not Public

Has the picture now changed? In some respects, yes. Fundamentalism allows for development, indeed, development of doctrine, if one listens to the Falwell apologia, and what was once wrong can now become right, on biblical grounds—the only grounds Fundamentalists take seriously. But I believe that the public/private distinction remains appropriate, at least with respect to the evangelistic-evangelical tradition. The Fundamentalist move into politics in the 1980s is of a somewhat different character. Not to put too fine a point on it, its theological assumptions are now "political" but not "public." A public theology, as numbers of us have set out to define it, allows for the integrity of movements that are not conservative Protestant, Christian, or Jewish-Christian at all: God can work his "order" through the godless, in secular-pluralism. A public theology allows for a positive interpretation of that secular-pluralist order with its religious admixtures, even as it recognizes all the while the way the demonic pervades the orders of existence. The political theology of privatist Fundamentalism does not do so. It is born of separatists who do not regard nonfundamentalists with any positive ecumenical feelings. The Fundamentalist political scope may recognize Catholics and Jews or "traditional theists" as belonging in the civil order, but then insists that nontheists are outsiders, to be tolerated at best. Let it also be said that not all Fundamentalists have made the overt political move, and not all conservative Protestantism is Fundamentalist.

This public/political distinction is not a hard and fast one, and its nuances, now apparently fine, may easily elude us. Yet through the years, we shall need some handle to separate the two, for there are vastly different consequences in civil life. Admittedly, one can approach the subject in Humpty-Dumpty's way: "When I use a word, it means just what I choose it to mean—neither more nor less." And when one comes to study "public" in the *Oxford English Dictionary,* there is a growing sense of elusiveness: "The varieties of sense are numerous and pass into each other by many intermediate shades of meaning. The exact shade often depends upon the substantive qualified. . . ." Yet in thirty and more of the dictionary's definitions, the word "political" never appears to explain public. The first definition of "political" does need the word "public," however, which suggests that "political" in some ways can be a species of a genus called "public."

In the sense that I here use the word political, it refers to the activity by which interests—in this case, the Fundamentalists—seek their way, though they must finally compromise (or retreat) and be conciliated by receiving a share in power in proportion to their weight in the political community. Though politics is not exhausted by self-interest, it is moved chiefly by it. In the present case, the interest group seeks to protect its turf, to extend its mission, and to have its way at the expense of other ways.

At the same time, the public is pre-, para-, and post-political. It allows to other interests a full integrity. In its sphere, strangers meet and overcome their fears; conflict occurs and is to be resolved; life is given color, texture, drama, a festive air; mutual responsibility becomes evident, opinions are heard and countered; visions are tested. Crucial again in this second sense: religionists in the public sphere have a theological accounting of the validity of those who do not share their final outlook. Politically-minded church bodies need have a positive explanation of only their own and their allies' causes; all the rest may be neutral or negative. Thus it is that one can seek one's own way in politics without taking on a public mien, guise, or intention.[10]

The evangelists from Moody through Graham tried to "work" the private realm. When Billy Graham moved beyond it, as he did frequently in the 1950s through the 1970s, he saw this as casual extrusion from his calling as an evangelist or part of his responsibility as a citizen, without connecting the activity to his evangelism. Many evangelists are even less expressive than he was about positive political points. Their evangelism makes up a social phenomenon to them, but of a largely ecclesiastical character. That is, it takes up social space, but in the modern division of labor that space is sequestered in the bloc called "religion," not "culture comment," or "social impact," or "political pressure."

It is similar with Pentecostalists, who are also often confused with Fundamentalists. Taking rise early in this century, concurrently with Fundamentalism, Pentecostalism could make common cause with the scholastic-minded intransigents over against modernism. But the two movements made an uneasy partnership, because not all Pentecostalists accepted Fundamentalist-scholastic views of biblical inerrancy, and the Pentecostal claims of a kind of "enthusiasm" in connection with Spirit-baptism and speaking in tongues threatened many Fundamentalist dogmatists. Penetecostals may often have been populists, and they did their voting, but it has always been more difficult to get them into focus, not as a social phenomenon, but as a social movement with discernible political bents.

One could add other groups that are conservative but not part of the Fundamentalist social phenomena: black Protestant, whether Methodist or Baptist or Pentecostal; the Southern Baptist Convention, which has a Fundamentalist wing, but also has a quite separate history and existence; and conservative Reformed and Lutheran movements like the Christian Reformed Church and the Missouri Synod. These are examples of groups whose social-political careers differ widely from that of fundamentalism.

A Long Political Tendency

Fundamentalism, almost from the beginning, then, was more ready to be overtly political than were these cohort groups at the side. If we see Fundamentalism as a conservative Protestant force—born of reaction to liberal-modernism—that fused premillennialism with (Princeton-style arguments for) inerrancy, began to make a protostatement in *The Fundamentals,* got named in 1920, and was the aggressor in efforts to sway major denominations in the mid-1920s, we must realize that, even in the first generation,

Fundamentalism had a political posture. This was focused chiefly on the issues of Zionism. There were Protestant Fundamentalist Zionists in America before Jewish Zionism took hold. This derived from the peculiar reading of biblical prophecy which was popularized in the *Scofield Reference Bible* and which, in a series of prophetic biblical conferences, led to a virtual takeover of proto-Fundamentalism by dispensational premillennialists. Thus, as early as 1891, the tireless agitator William E. Blackstone gathered the names of over 400 prominent Americans and presented to President Harrison a petition asserting the political right of Jews to rebuild the nation of Israel.[11]

In the second generation, Fundamentalism was an organized force in the political realm, as was evident from its participation in the most celebrated religious event of the 1920s, the Scopes trial. This had to do with antievolution legislation and school book policy, and was thus overtly political. Through the 1930s the Fundamentalists were busy rebuilding their institutions after the denominational defeats around 1925. They did this very effectively through the war years, as various Fundamentalist fronts were organized around 1942.[12]

Then in the 1950s, during the Cold War era, Fundamentalists like Carl McIntire and Billy James Hargis, and any number of anti-Communist crusaders, began their program for a fortress America. Then as now, part of their chauvinism grew from the conviction that Falwell still announces: Even if the Second Coming *is* imminent, Christians are to "occupy until Christ comes," and they are to see America as a new Zion, its people as a chosen people. America must remain free, through Fundamentalist efforts, since it is the last training ground for evangelists who will rescue individuals elsewhere before the Rapture. This is far from a developed "public theology," but it is certainly a nationalist-political one.[13]

So the New Christian Right of the 1980s, which has Fundamentalism at its core, even as it picks up some Pentecostalists, Evangelicals, Southern Baptists, and conservative Protestants from confessional denominations, has precedent chiefly in the scholastic-millennial "hardline" tradition that took shape almost a century ago and was formally organized in the 1920s. What had been latent is now patent: the covert became overt, but there has been less switching and more "development" than spokesmen like Falwell allow for in their apologiae.

Why Social-Political Now?

If Fundamentalism is a social phenomenon with a political cast, and if it has been so in some ways from the beginning, it remains only to ask why it has become so visible, explicit, and belligerent now. The answer is too complex to be reduced to a few paragraphs, but several main features of a response to the question will throw light on the phenomenon today.

First, there is a worldwide reaction against many of the mixed offerings of modernity.[14] Fundamentalism, as part of it, both ministers to the victims of modernization and exploits them. Iran is the prototype. Technology and affluence swept the scene there, but the benefits were for the few. The shah's family, the Iranian elites who studied in America, and the oil shieks reaped the benefits. The rest of the population did not have its physical circumstances improved and only saw its traditions threatened. In reaction, ayatollahs preached the old scriptures, women returned to wearing the chador, and there was a fundamentalist-based religious revolution. Something similar is going on in numbers of underdeveloped nations. American Fundamentalists cannot be dismissed as a lower-class aspirant economic cohort, though some dimensions of social class are apparent in the movement. But it is clearly a force of resentment against "intellectuals," "elites," "the media," and the like—people who are at home with modernization and care little for presumed traditions.

Second, there is a worldwide movement, which we might call "tribalism," that is obvious in African nations, Israel, Iran, Lebanon, Ireland, the Asian subcontinent, and elsewhere.[15] In this movement, people retreat from modernity by withdrawing into their ethno-religio-cultural tribal bonds. This retreat was easier to begin in Lebanon, where there are spatial separations between such groups, than in America, where there is more intermixing. But in America, too, one might see Fundamentalism as the latest in the two-decade movement of groups, be they black, Chicano, Jewish, Catholic ethnic, homosexual, young, feminist, or whatever, to find and assert symbols. These symbols are designed to assure a group's power, place, and pride—over against the real or presumed threats of others. For example, there are not many blacks in formal Fundamentalism, though most blacks would be typed as belonging in the conservative revivalist tradition. Fundamentalists are visible as a social phenomenon because they are now getting their tribe together and finding ways to be assertive about their place.

Third, there was an ecological niche or cranny to be filled, a void that had room for a new growth. There has been, no one can deny, some sort of "value crisis" in America, a shift in understandings and practices having to do with family life, sexuality, and expression. Those who are devotees of pluralism, and who believe that transmittable values can emerge from public debate and conflict, somehow tolerate ambiguity and pick their way through the confusions of the decades. The Fundamentalists, however, can appeal to the impatient. Theirs is an almost Manichean world of black/white, God/Satan, Christ/Antichrist, Christian/"Secular-Humanist." On these terms, it is easy to invent and expose "conspiracies" of the forces against good—good America, good Fundamentalists. People who seek authoritarian solutions are likely to follow charismatic Fundamentalist leaders in such a time.

Finally, Fundamentalists, though they may lack a positive view of certain scientific and technological processes, are uninhibited in their use of the products. Radio, television, computers, direct-mail technology—all of which remain practically mysterious and inaccessible to mainline Christianity—seem made for the world of Fundamentalist splinter groups. Speakers on radio and television can portray clear choices with great simplicity. They have found ways to raise paracongregational funds to make possible opinion-surveying and pressure-grouping. They have "borrowed" the technology of modernization with all its bewilderments and used it to promote nostalgic and simplistic visions of the past as models for the future.

The Future

Will they win? The Fundamentalist message and pattern of meanings appeals to a rather definite class and personality type.

Fundamentalist leaders have contented themselves with making the most of their market potential within conservative Protestantism. America is not "turning Fundamentalist." It has become aware of Fundamentalism. Fundamentalists have seen a great growth in morale and visibility, and they will not soon slink away, but their interpretations, grounded in one kind of biblical inerrancy and premillennialism, are not the choice of the many.

This means that Fundamentalists have to build some coalitions, as they have done on the abortion front. It is also likely that some Fundamentalist leaders will adapt and modify to become more smooth, ingratiating, and palatable. They have begun to do this and, in the process, have already alienated huge sections of "non-political" Fundamentalism on one hand and "hyperfundamentalism" on the other. But the American *Danegeld* is too rich for these leaders not to be bought off, and the political lures are too strong for them to resist. Fundamentalist clienteles will also become ever more pluralistic. Their interests have to be met. Hence, for example, the exclusion of deadly tobacco from its usual place alongside deadly alcohol in the program. Fundamentalist leaders admit that they cannot make an antitobacco plank part of a crusade because too many followers smoke or make their living off raising and treating tobacco. Such waverings make Fundamentalism more compromising, more assimilable, and more capable of being conceived as one more element in the republic.

Only if the "formal system" should break down and the economic order collapse would it be likely that Fundamentalists could break out of their current cohort in the competitive market. If there has to be a whole new social contract some day, it is likely that there must be in it a state religion, compulsory in character, authoritarian in tone, and "traditional" in outlook. America would be "socialized," not in the name of Marx, but of Jesus, not in the name of Communism, but of Christian republicanism.[16] To mention all this is not to hint at a self-fulfilling prophecy, but to sketch the terms by which Fundamentalism could ever "win America" as a social phenomenon. Until then, it must pick its shots, build alliances, and make skillful use of the edges that technology and dedication give it in close American elections. Until then, Fundamentalists have to rely on the evocative power their often inaccurate images induce whenever they talk about the Jewish-Christian stipulations of the "Enlightened" founding fathers, or the "traditional theism" of once-Unitarian deistic public schools, as transmitters of the Founding Fathers' values.[17] Until then, Fundamentalists can also do their best service by making nonfundamentalists think about values and their transmission, pluralism and its problems, and American public faith and individual religiosity, in their always changing conjunctions.

Notes

1. There is no way, of course, to measure the number of Fundamentalists for these reasons: a) the distinction between Fundamentalist and Evangelical is too blurry; b) very few church bodies are constituted around the name Fundamentalism; c) many Fundamentalists are in church bodies that are not technically Fundamentalist; d) many people who might be classified as Fundamentalists are not necessarily to be located on any church rolls at all. Gallup polls of the late 1970s made some efforts to assess Evangelical sympathies, "Evangelical" and "born again" being terms the Gallup people used to encompass Fundamentalism as well. At that time, 60 per cent of the public claimed to be Protestants, 48 per cent of the Protestants claimed a "born again" experience, and 35 per cent of the Protestants considered themselves "Evangelical." It does not take much reckoning to find 10 million Americans out of this sector who could safely be described—or are self-described—as "Fundamentalist." See the *Gallup Opinion Index No. 145*, American Institute of Public Opinion, Princeton, N.J., 1978.

2. Many sociologists of religion have pointed to the phenomenon of privatization; the most systematic account is Thomas Luckmann, *The Invisible Religion* (New York: McMillan, 1967).

3. We now fortunately possess twin volumes that describe these polarities and parties: William R. Hutchison, *The Modernist Impulse in American Protestantism* (New York: Oxford University Press, paperback edition, 1982 [first published in 1976]) and George M. Marsden, *Fundamentalism and American Culture: The Shaping of Twentieth-Century Evangelicalism, 1870–1925* (New York: Oxford University Press, 1982 [first published in 1980]).

4. See Patricia Barrett, *Religious Liberty and the American Presidency* (New York: Herder and Herder, 1963).

5. In February 1981, an inclusive conference on this subject was held; proceedings are in Dean M. Kelley, editor, *Government Intervention in Religious Affairs* (New York: Pilgrim, 1982).

6. Definitions of politics on which I am here relying are elaborated upon in Bernard Crick, *In Defense of Politics* (Baltimore: Penguin, 1962), p. 15.

7. Martin E. Marty, *Righteous Empire: The Protestant Experience in America* (New York: Dial, 1970); see especially Chapter 17, "The Two-Party System," p. 177.

8. Timothy Smith, *Revivalism and Social Reform in Mid-Nineteenth Century America* (Nashville: Abingdon, 1957).

9. Donald W. Dayton, *Discovering an Evangelical Heritage* (New York: Harper and Row, 1976), is a popular account; see Chapter 2, pp. 15–24, on Finney.

10. Details of the concept of the public are in Parker J. Palmer, *The Company of Strangers: Christians and the Renewal of American Public Life* (San Francisco: Harper and Row, 1981).

11. See Timothy Weber, *Living in the Shadow of the Second Coming* (New York: Oxford University Press, 1981).

12. The first account of the second rise of Fundamentalism was Louis Gasper, *The Fundamentalist Movement* (The Hague: Mouton, 1963); see also Joel A. Carpenter, "Fundamentalist Institutions and the Rise of Evangelical Protestantism, 1929–1942," in *Church History 49* (March 1980), pp. 62–75.

13. Jerry Falwell, *Listen, America!* (New York: Bantam Books, 1981), outlines the program.

14. For a theoretical description of antimodernity in action, see John Murray Cuddihy, *The Ordeal of Civility* (New York: Basic, 1974), pp. 9–10.

15. An excellent description is Harold R. Isaacs, *Idols of the Tribe: Group Identity and Political Change* (New York: Harper and Row, 1975).

16. A doomsday scenario with a socialist tinge is in Robert L. Heilbroner, *Business Civilization in Decline* (New York: Norton, 1976), pp. 119–120.

17. A characteristic plea for "believers' rights" is to be found in Lynn R. Buzzard and Samuel Ericsson, *The Battle for Religious Liberty* (Elgin, Illinois: David C. Cook, 1982).

21. *Evangelicals Are Politically Diverse*

By Stuart Rothenberg

Focus

Stuart Rothenberg believes it would be a mistake to treat the Evangelical resurgence in politics as "a homogeneous religious and political force that is primed to take over the Republican Party and, ultimately, the country." The variety of groups within the movement and the voting patterns of Evangelicals in recent elections suggests that many journalists have "failed to take note of the diversity within the Evangelical community."

Rothenberg argues that non-Evangelicals must understand the distinctions between types of Evangelicals: "Anyone who lumps together charismatics [such as Pat Robertson], strict Fundamentalists [separatists], born agains, liberal Evangelicals, and radical Evangelicals, obviously does not understand Evangelicalism."

Rothenberg's focus is Pat Robertson, the charismatic TV preacher, host of the "700 Club," director of the Christian Broadcasting Network (CBN), president of CBN University, and a possible Republican candidate for President in 1988. Because of the diversity within the Evangelical community, Rothenberg notes that Robertson "will not hold a monopoly on the Evangelical vote any more than a Catholic candidate would over the so-called Catholic vote." He points out that Robertson has no easy task: "If Robertson does seek the Republican nomination, he will need to hold on to his Evangelical supporters, attract those Evangelicals who prefer a different candidate or who have not yet concerned themselves with politics, and appeal to the Non-Evangelical rank-and-file."

Stuart Rothenberg is editor of *The Political Report* newsletter of the Free Congress Foundation and author of *The Evangelical Voter* (Free Congress Foundation, 1984).

IN THEIR HASTE to cover the expected presidential candidacy of the Rev. Pat Robertson, journalists have made a serious error—they have failed to take note of the diversity within the Evangelical community. Articles regularly characterize Pat Robertson as the "Evangelical candidate" and treat the Evangelical community as a homogeneous religious and political force that is primed to take over the Republican Party and, ultimately, the country.

In fact, the "Evangelical community" includes a variety of approaches and groups, each with its own beliefs. Some leaders, such as Bob Jones, preach separation from non-Christians and criticize Evangelicals who work with Roman Catholics and Jews. Other Evangelicals, such as the Sojourners, see themselves as radical social and political reformers who work for "social justice" for the "underclass."

Major Differences

The term "Evangelical" is widely used but rarely defined. Generally, Evangelicals believe that Jesus Christ was both a real person and the Son of God, and that one must accept Jesus as one's personal savior to have eternal salvation. Beyond that, however, there are substantial differences among Evangelicals. These differences involve theology, denomination, style, and political orientation. Black Evangelicals, for example, are much more liberal in their political behavior than white Evangelicals.

To the non-Evangelical, distinctions between Evangelicals may seem trivial. But when strict Fundamentalist Bob Jones calls Fundamentalist Jerry Falwell "the most dangerous man in America," as he did, it becomes clear that sharp differences do exist. Anyone who lumps together charismatics, strict Fundamentalists (separatists), born agains, liberal Evangelicals, and radical Evangelicals obviously does not understand Evangelicalism.

Politically, Evangelicals cut across the spectrum. While more conservative than the population in general, their ranks also in-

---

Reprinted by permission of the author from the June 18, 1986, issue of the *Wall Street Journal*.

clude many liberals. A 1984 survey by the Free Congress Foundation's Institute for Government and Politics found that Evangelicals overwhelmingly support voluntary school prayer and oppose government funding of abortions, but also back the Equal Rights Amendment and support the availability of birth-control information in public schools. Evangelicals are also split on issues such as defense spending and the morality of abortion.

The diversity within the Evangelical community stems from religious and demographic differences. Those who say that religion is an extremely important part of their daily lives tend to be much more conservative than Evangelicals who say it is only somewhat important. Frequent church attendees, biblical literalists, and born-again Evangelicals also have different views from Evangelicals who rarely attend church, who believe that the Bible should not be taken literally, and who say they have not had a born-again experience.

When asked prior to the 1984 elections how important their religious views should be in determining their vote for President, only three out of ten Evangelicals polled said "extremely" or "very" important. However, more than half of those who were frequent church attendees, or who said that religion was "extremely important" in their lives, said that their religious views would be very important or extremely important in their decisions.

The all-too-prevalent stereotype that Evangelicals simply vote for the candidate selected by their minister is also amiss. About half of all Evangelicals say an endorsement by their clergyman would not enter into their decision, and only a small percentage say that they would vote for a candidate recommended to them by their preacher.

Traditionally Democratic, Evangelicals have been successfully wooed by Republicans, but they still constitute an important swing constituency in many elections, particularly in the South and border states. It was only a decade ago that a Democrat, born-again Christian Jimmy Carter, carried a majority of Evangelical voters.

Early indications are that Evangelical leaders are split on their choices for 1988 Republican and Democratic presidential candidates. Last April, the National Association of Evangelicals (NAE) asked a group of 110 denominational leaders, pastors, and lay persons who attended an NAE Washington briefing which candidates would make the best presidential nominees. Rep. Jack Kemp (R.-N.Y.) led the GOP field with 41 per cent, but other potential candidates, such as Sen. Bill Armstrong of Colorado (21 percent), Pat Robertson (15 per cent) and Vice President George Bush (12 per cent), had their share of supporters.

Among possible Democratic candidates, the NAE leaders selected Gary Hart (23 per cent), Rep. Richard Gephardt (22 percent), and Sen. Bill Bradley (16 per cent). Though Pat Robertson's showing was credible, it hardly indicates Evangelical bloc voting.

If he runs for President, Pat Robertson should do well among Evangelicals. But it is crucial to remember that his early supporters come primarily from a particular element of the Evangelical movement. They are probably more religious than many of their fellow Evangelicals, and they almost certainly are more likely to watch religious television programs. More important, they are politically active and generally conservative in their political beliefs and policy preferences. This makes them an important (but not dominant) force in GOP politics.

Pat Robertson will not hold a monopoly on the Evangelical vote any more than a Catholic candidate would over the so-called Catholic vote. But it is a mistake to portray him as a candidate whose support is automatically limited to the Evangelical community.

The importance of understanding Evangelicals as a social and political force is probably more apparent in the Spring 1986 Indiana primary than anywhere else. In covering the state's Fifth Congressional District primary, many reporters described State Sen. James Butcher as the "Evangelical candidate" in his race against state Treasurer Julian Ridlen. When Butcher won, those same reporters linked him with the Rev. Don Lynch, the upset winner in the Second District GOP primary. In both cases, journalists focused so heavily on the Evangelical label that they missed the real story.

Press Perceptions

Butcher had the support of a great many Evangelicals, and his views were certainly in tune with theirs. But he was much more than simply a "religious right" candidate. He was a veteran state legislator and civic leader who *happened* to have a strong following among Evangelicals. He ran as a conservative Republican acutely concerned with farm issues, not as an Evangelical Republican. Linking Butcher with someone like the Rev. Lynch, who had no political experience and was known solely as a moral issues candidate, tells us more about the perceptions of those covering the races than about the races themselves.

If Pat Robertson does seek the Republican presidential nomination, he will need to hold on to his Evangelical supporters, attract those Evangelicals who prefer a different candidate or who have not yet concerned themselves with politics, and appeal to the Non-Evangelical rank-and-file. That is no easy task. But if he continues to be regarded as "the Evangelical candidate," and if Evangelicals continue to be characterized as a homogeneous mass, most people will miss the real story.

22. *Searching for Norman Rockwell*

By Grant Wacker

Focus

Grant Wacker regards Evangelicalism as unique because of its "genuinely pastoral concern that tradition should still have a place in the modern world." More specifically, Wacker suggests that Evangelicalism promotes an America of "small towns, summer nights, and stable values."

Wacker believes that only a small segment of the larger Evangelical movement, what he calls the "Evangelical Right," is growing in numbers and influence. The Evangelical Right is defined by its "allegiance to a cluster of values derived from Victorian middle-class society. More precisely, [Evangelicals] are defined by [their] identification with the part of Victorian society whose ideals were represented by one hundred twenty million copies of the *McGuffey Reader*, and in later years sentimentally remembered in Norman Rockwell magazine covers."

Evangelicalism has been flourishing "just beneath the surface" of American culture, and "just outside the view of the press," for at least two decades. The movement was finally noticed in 1976, largely because of Jimmy Carter's avowal of having been "born again," a confession of faith that he readily acknowledged during his successful campaign for the presidency. Evangelicalism's key tenets include the affirmation of absolute moral principles, moral living, and traditional morality as the basis of public government.

The "arbiters of contemporary culture" who pose the greatest threat to these values include, according to Evangelicals, the mass media, television entertainers, public educational institutions, proponents of the "sexual revolution," secular humanists, and feminists. But the Evangelical Right is not alone in being concerned about the loss of moral values in society, Wacker insists. Many secular scholars also agree that "something has gone terribly wrong" in contemporary life.

Grant Wacker is an associate professor of religious studies at the University of North Carolina, Chapel Hill, and is the author of several studies of contemporary American religion.

IN THE DUSK OF the nineteenth century, Scottish churchman Marcus Dods remarked that he did not envy those who would carry the banner of Christianity in the twentieth century. "Yes, perhaps I do," he conceded, "but it will be a stiff fight." As it turned out, Dods's apprehensions were well founded, for one can scarcely doubt that throughout the Western world, and also in much of the non-Western world, the drumroll of secularization has set the cadence of twentieth-century history.[1]

The cultural diversity of the United States makes it difficult to know exactly when the old orthodoxies were displaced by the crippling doubts of modern life. Many historians believe that the scale started to wobble during the 1890s, then tipped decisively between the First and Second world wars. In any event, by 1980, polls showed that sixty-one million Americans were unchurched and that conventional belief was in disarray. In the preceding twenty years, the Protestant establishment—the American Baptist Church, the Christian Church (Disciples), the Lutheran Church in America, the Protestant Episcopal Church, the United Church of Christ, the United Methodist Church, and the United Presbyterian Church—had lost nearly four million members. Roman Catholics had lost hundreds of thousands of communicants and Jews had quit counting. As they neared the end of the century, the major religious groups necessarily entertained few illusions that in the foreseeable future they would grow at all, much less outpace the population. Hoping only to stop the decline, they seemed resigned—in words David Ignatow used in a different context—to "feel along the edges of life/for a way/that will lead to open land."[2]

Nonetheless, as the curtain opened on the 1980s the religious situation was not as grim as the media suggested and intellectuals hoped. In all parts of the nation, some churches were buzzing with a powerful resurgence of evangelical fervor. Theologically this new Evangelicalism, as it was called, looked like a dapper version of

Reprinted by permission of Mercer University Press from *The Evangelical Tradition In America*, edited by Leonard I. Sweet, 1984.

the frowzy Fundamentalism of the 1920s. But sociologically there was a big difference: it was almost fashionable.[3]

Actually, the movement had been flourishing just beneath the surface—or more precisely, outside the purview of the press—for at least twenty years. But in 1976—dubbed by *Time* and *Newsweek* as the Year of the Evangelical—the general public seemed suddenly to become aware of its existence. In that one year, Black Panther Eldridge Cleaver announced that he had had an old-fashioned religious conversion, Charles Colson's autobiography, *Born Again*, shot to the top of the book charts, and a strongly Evangelical Southern Baptist became President.[4] Soon it was no longer clear who the mainstream Protestants really were. In 1980, the annual circulation of Billy Graham's newspaper *Decision* topped twenty-four million, while the thoughtful and ever-so-sober *Christianity Today* outstripped its jaunty liberal rival, *Christian Century*, by five subscribers to one. Evangelical publishers were given access to a score of spectacularly successful titles. (Of course they were accustomed to success: each year between 1971 and 1974 they had marketed the best seller of the year—not to mention Hal Lindsay's 1970 blockbuster, *The Late Great Planet Earth*, which, next to the Bible, may have been the non-fiction best seller of all time.) Bill Bright's Campus Crusade for Christ, funded by high rollers like Nelson Bunker Hunt and T. Cullen Davis, rapidly moved toward its goal of raising a billion dollars to take the gospel to every person on the globe. Sixteen thousand Christian academies, proliferating at the rate of one a day, comprised a two-billion-dollar-a-year private education industry. At staunchly evangelical Wheaton College in Illinois, the number of National Merit Scholars and alumni with earned doctoral degrees rivaled the most prestigious colleges in the nation. Radio and television evangelists attracted millions. No one knows exactly how many millions, and it is clear that the number was smaller than commonly believed, but there is reliable evidence that the prime-time preachers drew a weekly audience of at least twenty million and garnered annual contributions exceeding a half-billion dollars.

Every index of membership and participation showed that most evangelical denominations were bursting at the doors. The Southern Baptist Convention lumbered past the thirteen million mark, and numerous smaller groups like the Assemblies of God posted decennial growth rates of thirty per cent of more. Perhaps most astonishing were the numerous polls showing that by 1980 at least thirty million Americans considered themselves "born again" evangelical Christians, and another twenty million styled themselves evangelical in belief and sympathy.[5]

Resurgence in the Sixties

After decades of relative quiet, why did Evangelicalism mushroom like this in the 1960s? Several scholars have suggested that external structural changes were a relevant factor. Reginald Bibby, for example, has shown that the birth rate rose faster among evangelical than among nonevangelical Protestants. Taking a very different line, Jeffrey Hadden has argued that the surge was powered by the movement's willingness to exploit the microelectronics revolution. Evangelicals, Hadden has noted, quickly adopted advanced computer technology that enabled them to target likely contributors and therefore move into the satellite and cable television market. Frances FitzGerald has pointed out that policy changes by networks and local radio and television stations enabled religious groups to buy air time. This particularly helped Evangelicals, who seem to have had fewer inhibitions about raising money through high-powered public appeals. Dean Hoge has discerned that the movement's growth may have been a by-product of demographic shifts. Although the evidence is murky, the tilt of the population into the South, where evangelical churches already predominated, may have especially benefited Evangelicals, simply because migrants tend to join more accessible churches.[6]

More commonly, though, Evangelical strength has been interpreted as a symptom of broad cultural changes. Dean Kelley, for example, has argued that churches that made strict demands and presented a distinctive theology flourished because they met an enduring need for ethical challenge and ultimate meaning. Mainstream churches asked little and gave little, and so watched their members walk away. Daniel Yankelovich has offered a variant of this argument, claiming that the heightened visibility of evangelical religion was a direct reaction to the heightened visibility of hedonistic life-styles in the 1960s and 1970s. Virginia Stem Owens, on the other hand, has insisted that Evangelicalism flourished precisely because it did not impose serious demands. She has suggested that the tension between evangelical ethics and the ethics of middle-class Americans may have been great enough to give the appearance of separation, but it was not sufficient to prevent substantial enjoyment of the material good life. Others, like J. Lawrence Burkholder, have charged that Evangelical success is partly the result of Evangelicals' willingness to give easy answers to difficult questions and to sanctify mundane aspirations by telling people exactly what they wanted to hear. For Theodore Roszak, Evangelical growth has been the result of a "hunger for wonders"—a reaction that quite predictably erupted in a culture devoted to an exclusively "science-based reality principle." More grandly, Jeremy Rifkin has proposed that, just as the sixteenth century disclosed an elective affinity between Protestantism and capitalism, the 1970s may have disclosed the beginnings of an elective affinity between Evangelical asceticism and postindustrial scarcity. In the end, though, Evangelicals themselves will be most persuaded by Martin E. Marty's judgment that they thrived because they clearly understood what the Puritans did not: that Godliness does not pass through the loins of Godly parents, but must be actively rekindled in the minds and hearts of each generation.[7]

Other scholars have offered other explanations, but this selection indicates that the explanations are extremely diverse and, to some extent, off target. The problem is that the premise has not been adequately examined. These and other thoughtful observers have invested considerable energy trying to account for Evangelical growth on the assumptions that Evangelicalism is, in fact, growing. I propose, rather, that what is growing is not Evangelicalism as a religious and theological movement, but rather a segment within Evangelicalism that is defined by its allegiance to a cluster of values derived from Victorian middle-class society. More precisely, it is defined by its identification with that part of Victorian society whose ideals were represented in 120,000,000 copies of the *McGuffey Reader*, and in later years sentimentally remembered in Norman Rockwell's magazine covers. I shall call this smaller, more overtly politicized segment the Evangelical Right, and the consensus it seeks (borrowing a term from George M. Marsden) Christian Civilization.[8]

By now there is nothing startling about the suggestion that there is a distinction between Evangelicalism in America and Evangelicalism for America. Scarcely anyone—that is, anyone outside the Evangelical camp—would doubt that the Evangelical label truly belongs to theologians like John Howard Yoder and Clark Pinnock, scholars like David O. Moberg and Timothy L. Smith, activists like Jim Wallis and John Alexander, public figures like Mark Hatfield and John Anderson, organizations like the Berkeley Christian Coalition and Koininia Farm, magazines like the *Wittenburg Door* and *Daughters of Sarah*, or denominations like the Christian Reformed Church and the Brethren in Christ. Yet for one reason or another, all have distanced themselves from the Christian Civilization clamor. When we assess the growth of this wing of Evangelicalism—which for lack of a better term we might call the Evangelical non-Right (it would be too much to call it the Evangelical Left)—it is clear that this wing is not measurably stronger now than it was ten or twenty or even fifty years ago.[9]

It is important to stress that the distinction between the Evangelical non-Right and the Evangelical Right is not invidious. Neither side has forged a theology free of ideological agendas, and neither has lived a faith free of cultural entanglements. It is just as important to stress that the distinction ignores the kaleidoscopic complexity of the movement. Nonetheless, the concept of an Evangelical Right, functionally defined by its commitment to the rebirth of Christian Civilization in America, is analytically useful. It illumines the fact that we have witnessed in the late 1970s and 1980s the rise of a particular kind of Evangelicalism with a particularly explicit set of social and cultural commitments. Beyond this, the distinction helps to unravel the knot in which clearly evangelical, sort-of-evangelical, and clearly nonevangelical groups—such as the Independent Fundamentalist Baptist Fellowship, the Coalition for Better Television, and the National Congressional Caucus—are entangled.[10]

The 'Christian Civilization' Thesis

A Christian Civilization is not so much a list of discrete ideals as a coherent world view—a way of seeing reality. But in order to understand this worldview, we first have to do what no partisan would do: dismantle it, block by block, piece by piece. It becomes evident, then, that there are several cornerstones. Fundamental, and buttressing all else, is the conviction that there are numerous moral absolutes that human beings do not create but discover. In this case, the problem is that modern culture is deceived by the opposite notion: that moral standards are forged within specific historical settings and thus wobble from one context to another. Despite this, Christian Civilization is grounded upon the conviction that some things never change.[11]

This outlook certainly is not restricted to the Evangelical Right. Even so modern a man as Harry Emerson Fosdick could make a trademark out of the phrase, "astronomies change while stars abide." But the Evangelical Right is distinguished by the range and diversity of the cultural forms that it considers absolute. Homer Duncan's widely circulated booklet, *Secular Humanism: The Most Dangerous Religion in America,* is unusually strident, but his point of view is typical.

> When we discard the Bible as our standard of absolute truth . . . we have no standard for determining moral values. The Bible says that murder is wrong, but nowadays many murderers are set free to kill again simply because the judge thinks they are mentally sick. Rapists are not accountable for their actions, so they are set free to ravish sweet little girls. . . . The Bible says that adultery and fornication are wrong, but since we have thrown away the Bible, college students and thousands of others live together with no restraint. The Bible pronounces the death penalty for homosexuality, but if the Equal Rights Amendment passes we will be compelled by law to send our children to homosexual teachers.[12]

The temper of Duncan's remarks suggests another difference between conventional notions of moral absolutes and those common within the Evangelical Right. Erling Jorstad has called it moral*ism*: the assumption that for every moral question there is one and only one morally correct answer. Jorstad's analysis is accurate as far as it goes, but moralism stems from an underlying presupposition that moral absolutes can be discerned with absolute clarity and certainty. Consider Paul Weyrich's admonition to campaign workers: "Ultimately everything can be reduced to right and wrong. Everything." Moralism also assumes that reality can be sliced down the middle. Thus Tim LaHaye characteristically asserts that everywhere in life there are "two basic lines of reasoning . . . atheistic humanism or Christianity. What this life is all about is *the battle for your mind:* whether you will live your life guided by man's wisdom (humanism) or God's wisdom (Christianity)." The world of the Evangelical Right is, in essence, a realm in which moral absolutes are strewn about like boulders on a desert. Yet they cast no shadows, making disagreements about their size and shape not legitimate differences of perception, but deliberate distortions of moral judgment.[13]

The second cornerstone of Christian Civilization is the conviction that moral absolutes ought to form the visible foundation of the laws that govern society. This means, quite simply, that norms and sanctions that regulate private conduct ought to regulate public conduct, too. On significant questions like abortion, public legal determinations ought to be no different than private moral judgments. Here again the Evangelical Right is hardly unique. Many thoughtful persons agree that morality—or what Richard John Neuhaus aptly terms "sacred points of reference"—ought to inform all aspects of public policy. But the Evangelical Right is distinguished by its insistence that the primary question is not *whether* society's laws will express a particular moral code, but whose. The point is that laws, and for that matter public policies, always reflect a society's ultimate values. Thus law is "inescapably religious," argues R. J. Rushdoony, a leading architect of the Christian Civilization ideal, because law "establishes in practical fashion the ultimate concerns of a culture." In the worldview of the Evangelical Right, no law or public policy is morally neutral—and to claim otherwise is naive if not deliberately dishonest.[14]

The third cornerstone of Christian Civilization is the conviction that the moral absolutes that undergird—or that ought to undergird—society's laws are commonly revealed in nature, and explicitly revealed in the Bible. Moreover, the moral values disclosed in nature and the Bible are precisely the values that until recently have been highly esteemed in Judeo-Christian culture. That this is true is obvious in the Declaration of Independence and Constitution of the United States. "Our Founding Fathers were not all Christians," Jerry Falwell admits, "but they were guided by biblical principles. They developed a nation predicated on Holy Writ."[15]

Not surprisingly, this perceived identity of natural, biblical, Western, and republican values bristles with ramifications for contemporary society. Perhaps most consequential is a severe narrowing of the American tradition of religious pluralism. Although partisans of the Evangelical Right often assert that Christian Civilization can embrace healthy diversity, thoughtful spokesmen like Harold O. J. Brown acknowledge that pluralism is feasible only within a consensus of biblically grounded, traditional values. Recent attempts by the Evangelical Right to ban *Ms.* magazine from public libraries, or to press for laws prohibiting unmarried couples from renting motel rooms, or to push for federal funding of programs to promote teenage chastity, are powerful reminders that, in a Christian Civilization, the boundaries of permissible behavior are tightly drawn. Donald Howard, founder of the influential Accelerated Christian Education program, puts it plainly: "Legislation against apparent and obvious evil . . . [is] what will happen when Jesus Christ reigns."[16]

The confluence of natural, biblical, Western, and republican values also means that, in a Christian Civilization, government's role is to foster conventional virtues such as the preservation of unborn life, and to restrain vices like homosexuality. Government's role is also not to tinker with the operations of a free market economy. The Evangelical Right has never developed a systematic rationale for the latter position—which political scientist Michael Lienesch aptly calls a "supply-side theory of salvation"—but that is beside the point. The fact is that in a Christian Civilization, government, no less than church or family, is squarely responsible for the cultivation of moral fiber.[17] Yet it scarcely needs to be said that this has not been the reigning political philosophy during the past half-century. In this period, as columnist George F. Will has observed, an influential minority of Americans have come to believe that government is to be "ubiquitous and omniprovident regarding material things, but . . . neutral regarding values. It can concern itself with nurturing soybeans, but not virtue." To the Evangelical Right, the result is literal craziness—an incomprehensible inversion of values. Philosopher Michael Novak makes the point well: "Children in our public schools are to be allowed sex education but not prayer. Can it be true that prayer is more dangerous to the schools than sex?" This abdication of responsibility for moral nurture by government at all levels is perceived to be as much a cause as a symptom of the nation's perceived deterioration. Indeed, it is just this notion—that government has a pastoral role—that explains why many conservatives like William Safire and Barry Goldwater have distanced themselves from the Evangelical Right: they have perceived, quite correctly, that the movement is fired by an interventionist rather than libertarian vision of society.[18]

These, then, are the cornerstones of Christian Civilization: belief that there are moral absolutes that any honest person can rightly discern; that these moral absolutes ought to be reflected not only in a Christian's private life, but also in a society's fundamental laws; and, that the preservation of moral absolutes is the proper task of government.

The Media and American Life

Perched atop these cornerstones, the Evangelical Right believes it is easy to see how the arbiters of contemporary culture have led America astray. In the eyes of the Evangelical Right, newspapers, magazines, radio, and television undermine Christian Civilization not so much by direct attack as by unintentional distortion and intentional snideness and caricature. Journalists who spend more time in New York than in Peoria, and who rarely know what it means to earn a living with callused hands, meet a payroll, or run a business in a maze of entangling government regulations, persistently skew the news toward the interests of a liberal state. More insidious is television entertainment. In the world of the soap opera and sitcom, the mores of Hollywood parade as the mores of middle-class America. Sex in Hollywood, as columnist Dick Dabney noted, is usually extramarital and God frequently is an epithet or an anthropological reference to a being still believed in through some parts of the South. In the media, religious conviction emerges as fanaticism, self-discipline as prudery, and sharing one's faith as zealotry. Conservative Christians end up as hayseeds who think that Bach is a beer and Haydn a quarterback for the Rams.[19]

The Evangelical Right has a point. Donald E. Wildmon, leader of the Coalition for Better Television, justifiably complains that though millions of Americans profess Christianity, pray before meals, and every Sunday morning pack up the kids for church, these scenes are never enacted on television. According to one study, ninety-four per cent of the references to sexual intercourse on daytime soap operas in a given testing period involved unmarried partners. Indeed, many so-called secularists would agree with television critic Ben Stein's judgment that television "lowers educational achievement, encourages violence, generates lassitude and paints a wildly untrue and distorted picture of American life."[20]

Still more serious in the mind of the Evangelical Right is the belief that America's educational institutions are harming the souls of its youth. Several issues are involved here. Most obvious is the growing commitment in high schools and colleges—including church colleges—to the use of critical, historical, and empirical methods in the humanities and behavioral sciences. The result, inevitably, has been a greater willingness by students as well as teachers to reexamine inherited traditions. Incompetent teachers, classroom crime, and peer domination are not new. What is new is the assumption that nothing is assumable. And this is the heart of what the Evangelical Right means by "secular humanism": a determination to question moral truths that the Bible and great men of all ages have never dreamed of doubting. But secular humanism does not stop there. A series of pamphlets on Christian scholarship published by Bob Jones University (*The Christian Teaching of English, The Christian Teaching of History,* and so forth) charges that "modern unbelief in the possibility of being sure about anything produces an attitude of relativism in interpreting and evaluating literature." The final product of this "irresponsible and pernicious" tendency is the notion that "all interpretations are equally valid, that there are no right or wrong interpretations." Thus, argues Francis Schaeffer, who probably qualifies as the official intellectual of the Evangelical Right, secular humanism boils down to "the absolute insistence that there is no absolute."[21]

The Role of Public Schools

Less obvious but equally nettlesome to the Evangelical Right is what it perceives as the perennial mediocrity of the public schools—a mediocrity supposedly perpetuated by intellectual laziness in professional schools of education. Within the movement is a deep suspicion that children are being shortchanged with the jargon of "interpersonal dynamics" and "self-image enhancement," and being denied, as one partisan bitterly put it, the "substance of scholarship . . . history, long division, and Spanish." Closely related is a perception that social science textbooks and supplementary reading texts in history and English make extraordinary efforts to legitimate the values of urban Jews, alienated intellectuals, militant blacks, radical feminists—everyone, in short, except the millions of lower middle-class whites whose taxes support public schools. The Evangelical Right is acutely aware that in these books, as elsewhere, the only ethnic stereotype one can freely use as a slur is WASP or redneck. "In all their exoduses and liberation plots," complained one such WASP, "I'm the Pharaoh."[22]

To partisans of the Evangelical Right a still more pernicious deception is the claim that modern education is value-free when it is perfectly clear to them that it is not. Sex education is a good example. The Evangelical Right is not, as a rule, opposed to human reproduction education in a biology class. What it resists is sex education in a health or ethics class where behavior traditionally considered immoral is portrayed in ostensibly value-free terms as normal or, at worst, unusual. Seventh-grade textbooks, which suggest that, from a cross-cultural perspective, conventional Christian sexual ethics are "irregular," or textbooks that describe homosexuality, incest, masochism, and nymphomania with the clinical impartiality of a survey of table manners, are constant reminders to the Evangelical Right that public education is anything but value-free. Another irritant is the omnipresence of the evolutionary hypothesis in high school and college textbooks. Although leaders of the Evangelical Right bravely maintain that creation is scientifically credible, the real thrust of their argument is the contention that evolution, no less than creation, presupposes a particular metaphysics. It is simply disingenuous, they insist, to purport that methodological agnosticism has no relation to substantive agnosticism. They admit that there may be an analytic distinction between the how and the why, between process and meaning, but for actual human beings, and especially for honest adolescents, these issues are not easily separated. In this regard, the honest outsider can hardly disagree. When leading scientists like Carl Sagan and Theodosius Dobzhansky boast on television and in popular magazines that evolutionary cosmology *is* the metaphysics of the modern world, all Americans are reminded that science and religion mix all too well.[23]

So, in the eyes of the Evangelical Right the nation's schools grievously threaten Christian Civilization. Secular humanism permeates instructional content, and fraudulence twists instructional method. Schools are infected by a disease more difficult to extirpate because it is more difficult to pin down. It afflicts the nation as a whole, but shows up most clearly in the educational system. This disease is America's inability to produce great men and great leaders of men. Thus Jerry Falwell characteristically warns that the United States is facing a "vacuum of leadership"—especially by men. The lack of "male leadership in our families is affecting male leadership in our churches, and it is affecting male leadership in our society." To persons like Falwell it is clear that, along with drugs that cloud the mind and secular humanism that rots the soul, America's youth have been saturated with social attitudes that soften the backbone. They have grown up in a society "void of discipline and character-building," an environment that teaches them "to believe that the world owes them a living whether they work or not."[24]

This deep-running fear of moral weakness is the key to understanding the rapid growth of the manliness syndrome in the academies and colleges of the Evangelical Right—the high premium placed upon "hard-hitting" sermons, short haircuts, cold showers, and winning (not just competing) in rigorous contact sports. In a milieu in which born-again generals and professional athletes are not so much admired as venerated, it is understandable that Falwell would assure his hearers that Jesus was "not a sissy," that the monthly *Christian Athlete* would headline "Jesus the Competitor," or that Concerned Women for America would excoriate gender-integrated gym classes where boys, who formerly played basketball and football, "are now having dancing, instead."[25]

The symbols are ludicrous, but the underlying concerns are not. The literature of the Evangelical Right often resembles the old-fashioned jeremiad. Some of it, such as the materials published by Rus Walton's Plymouth Rock Foundation, is fiercely ideological. Yet books like Francis Schaeffer's *A Christian Manifesto,* John W. Whitehead's *The Second American Revolution,* or Peter Marshall and David Manuel's *The Light and the Glory*—all of which try to prove that America has strayed from its Protestant origins—reflect deep bewilderment about the reasons for the faltering of the American Dream. They convey the hurt of a disillusioned love for America as much as they expose the naiveté of the Evangelical Right's understanding of early American history. Once again, however, the Evangelical Right is not alone. Critics who are not naive have discerned similar shadows: for social historian Christopher Lasch, it is the culture of narcissism; for intellectual historian Robert Nisbet, it is the twilight of authority; for cultural historian Giles Gunn, it is the myth of historical entitlement; for sociologist Daniel Bell, it is the presumption of economic entitlement; for journalist Lance Morrow, it is the illusion of the discontinuous self. For all of these writers, something has gone terribly wrong. An earthquake seems to have buckled the spiritual landscape so that moral accountability has shifted from the individual to society in every part of modern life.[26]

'Humanists' and the Family

In the perspective of the Evangelical Right, though, the arbiters of contemporary culture who pose the most deadly threat to Christian Civilization are not media folk or educators, but the enemies of the traditional, patriarchal, nuclear family. What the historian sees as a cluster of closely related cultural changes, the Evangelical Right experiences as a finely tuned conspiracy, coordinated by a master blueprint of international scope. To the members of the Evangelical Right, the *Attack on the Family,* as James Robison describes it, or *The Battle for the Family,* as Tim LaHaye describes it, is so perfectly orchestrated that it could not be anything except the handiwork of the Antichrist.[27] Leaders of the Evangelical Right consider the general loosening of sexual restraints to be the most conspicuous manifestation of the Antichrist's determination to destroy the family. No-fault divorce, abortion-on-demand, civil rights for homosexuals, and sexual freedom for teenagers seem to them to have become staples of American life. They point to polls that show a million couples living together and two-thirds of the population cheerfully winking at such arrangements. Across the land, Tim LaHaye grouses, secular humanists have opened the floodgates to "adultery, fornication, perversion, abomination, and just plain *sin*." When it is clear that humanists are determined to crush "every vestige of the responsible, moral behavior that distinguished man from animals," he asks, is it surprising that a movement like the Evangelical Right has come into existence to take a stand for old-fashioned family values?[28]

Perhaps not, but many observers do find it surprising that the Evangelical Right should exhibit such fascination with the sexual revolution. Its fear of homosexuals, its preoccupation with the dangers of pornography, its misperception of rape as an act of lust rather than violence, its racially tinged opposition to birth-control clinics and over-the-counter sales of birth-control devices, and, above all, its appetite for sex manuals for Christian couples, suggest that the new liberation stirs a murky well of libidinous fears and passions within the Evangelical Right as much as it violates the rules of comportment in Christian Civilization.[29]

In addition to the so-called sexual revolution, the Evangelical Right sees a general threat to the family in feminism, and saw a very particular threat in the proposed Equal Rights Amendment. Feminism arouses a storm of fear within the Evangelical Right which outsiders find difficult to understand, much less take seriously. Although the causes of the fear are complex, historians Donald G. and Jane DeHart Mathews have persuasively argued that much of it grows from distrust of the deregulated adult male. In its heart of hearts, the Evangelical Right, they note, believes that feminism will liberate men rather than women from conventional expectations. Under all the noisy rhetoric about states' rights and unisex toilets runs a silent but desperately serious question: If the adult male is no longer compelled by law to protect and provide for his family, is there any reason to believe that he will corral his marauding impulses?[30] Thus Evangelical antifeminists like James Robison firmly believe that the feminist movement will inevitably turn women into "objects for exploitation or

. . . resources to be 'used.' " Nowhere are the Evangelical Right's fears and frustrations more revealingly focused than in a provision of the proposed Family Protection Act of 1981 that *requires* overseas military personnel to send a prescribed portion of their paychecks home to their spouses each month. Indeed, journalist Frances FitzGerald, after an extended visit to Jerry Falwell's Thomas Road Baptist Church in Lynchburg, Virginia, concluded that women might well have invented the church:

> The prohibitions [mainly] fall on traditional male vices such as drinking, smoking, running around, and paying no heed to the children. To tell "Dad" that he made all the decisions would be a small price to pay to get the father of your children to become a respectable middle class citizen.[31]

Even so, the most lethal threat to the family, in the judgment of the Evangelical Right, is neither the sexual revolution nor feminism, but the awful truth that the established institutions of American society have determined to keep parents from controlling the values of their adolescent children. Although television evangelists are usually too upbeat to say it explicitly, the literature of the Evangelical Right leaves a haunting impression that the rawest nerve of all is parents' fear that their kids will grow up to scorn them. A prospectus advertising Blair Adams and Joel Stein's three-volume history of American education—entitled, significantly, *Education as Religious War: A Historical Perspective on the Paganizing of America*—articulates the brokenheartedness that shadows countless articles and letters-to-the-editor:

> Millions of parents know the sadness and despair of rejection by the offspring of their own loins. Their children either openly or secretly hold their ideas in contempt. . . . Parents . . . see their children drawn into a whole culture, or rather anticulture, which the parents recognize to be destructive and harmful. Yet there seems to be nothing that they can do.[32]

Ironically, the Evangelical Right has no qualms about using these same established institutions—notably schools and government—to reinforce the authority of the family. One of the principal aims of the Family Protection Act, for example, is to buttress parents' legal ability to oversee the lives and values of their adolescent children. Nonetheless, for countless parents desperate measures are needed in desperate times. In the final analysis, the force that really propels the Evangelical Right is not preachers, bankrollers, or hucksters, but the ordinary mothers and fathers who believe, as columnist Dick Dabney phrased it, that America is gripped by a disease that has "undermined the character of the young" by teaching children that they are animals and therefore are "justified in living as amorally as animals." In the minds of these angry, bewildered parents, it is an "inward philosophical disease . . . that [has] gone down so deep into the nation's bones that it would take some kind of miracle to cure it."[33]

Intergenerational conflict is not new, but two factors seem to have made the current situation peculiar, if not unique, in American history. One is the ambivalence Americans have come to feel toward some of their most basic values. Polls show that, on issues such as premarital celibacy, attitudes changed fundamentally in the 1960s and 1970s, while on issues such as marital chastity and the normativeness of the traditional family unit, there was little alteration. Thus the apparent tension between generations is to some extent a tension within generations and, undoubtedly, within individuals as well. The other factor is that there is a large measure of truth in the Evangelical Right's charge that the "reality-defining agencies" of contemporary society are committed to a scientific and historical—or what they call a secular humanistic—view of life. The grip of the scientific and historical worldview is symbolized by *United States* v. *Seeger*. In this 1965 decision, the United States Supreme Court ruled that, though a person may be an atheist in the ordinary meaning of the term, a belief held by that person may be considered religious, and thus constitutionally protected if it "occupies a place in the life of its possessor parallel to that filled by the orthodox belief in God." One need not be a partisan of the Evangelical Right in order to see that when one of the main "reality-defining agencies" of modern life finds it more useful to write about religion in functional rather than in substantive terms, something akin to a cultural continental divide has been crossed.[34]

Origins of Evangelicalism's Ideals

These, then, are the forces which, in the eyes of the Evangelical Right, have conspired to destroy Christian Civilization: the media, the schools, and the foes of the family. Still, an important question remains: Why are Evangelicals so powerfully attracted to the Christian Civilization ideal in the first place? Although many Catholics, Mormons, Jews, and others are sympathetic, the real loyalists are the Evangelicals. Yet if Evangelicalism is essentially a religious and theological system, why are Evangelicals so prone to identify their faith with a social ideal so firmly rooted in Victorian middle class culture?

Historical reasons first come to mind. The simplest and in some ways most compelling answer is that Victorian culture is ineradicably encoded in the genes of evangelical religion. Since the late 1950s, when professional historians started seriously to explore the Evangelical tradition, it has been increasingly evident that Evangelicals perennially have felt an irresistible attraction to the early-to-mid-nineteenth-century milieu in which they were born. American Protestants have always been inclined to identify God's purposes with American destiny, but scholars like Ernest Lee Tuveson and Robert Handy have convincingly shown that Evangelicals have gone much further by identifying God's purposes with *evangelical* destiny, and both of these with a particular stage in the development of American culture.[35] Beyond this, from the 1830s (if not earlier) through the 1930s, Evangelicals were strongly disposed to consider themselves the moral custodians of the culture. The antislavery and temperance crusades on both sides of the Atlantic are proof enough of that. But the more important point—as major studies like Paul Boyer's examination of urban reform, or George Marsden's exploration of Fundamentalist origins amply demonstrate—is that Evangelicals considered themselves the moral custodians of the culture in direct proportion to the degree that they felt alienated from it. As they felt less and less at home, they struggled with greater determination to make America safe for Christian Civilization. In the long perspective of nineteenth- and twentieth-century history, the spectacle of contemporary Evangelicals leaping into the public arena is not a bit curious. What is curious is the relative quiet of the 1940s and 1950s.[36]

There are also sociological reasons why Evangelicals have been eager to lead the crusade for Christian Civilization. Here we have to be unusually careful. There is no question that Evangelicals *tend* to fall into the lower middle class and *tend* to vote as WASPS ordinarily vote. Despite the general accuracy of this categorization, however, there are many exceptions. The large bloc of black Evangelicals, the relatively rapid vertical mobility of blue-collar Evangelicals, the liberal-to-radical politics of "new" or "young" Evangelicals, and old-line pacifist Evangelicals are only a few of the problems that defy the conventional sociological categorizations.[37] Scholars as diverse as Peter Berger, Daniel Patrick Moynihan, and Martin E. Marty, however, have discerned in American society the outline of a group that goes by various names but is often called the New Class. The New Class, they argue, is composed of persons who procure information, exchange ideas, and manipulate the organs of communication—in short, writers, artists, intellectuals, teachers, professors, bureaucrats, advertisers, and so forth. The New Class is, in other words, the class that generates the symbols that define social reality. The Old Class, by contrast, is composed of persons who produce, market, and maintain goods and services—farmers, blue-collar workers, technicians, business people, sales people, and many in the service professions. Clearly the New Class, which generally coincides with the ascribed enemies of Christian Civilization, has a vested interest in the preservation of what might be called modern civilization: a strong welfare state and an absence of restraint in matters of thought, communication, and life-style. The Old Class, which embraces most Evangelicals, has just as clear a vested interest in the preservation of Christian Civilization: a strong concern for the cultivation of morality, and an absence of restraint in matters of economic exchange.[38]

Finally, there are cultural reasons why Evangelicals are so powerfully attracted to the Victorian values embodied in the Christian Civilization ideal. Nostalgia is a big part of it. Norman Rockwell's America probably never existed, but until the 1960s it was reasonable to suppose that it might have. Then everything went wrong. Small towns, summer nights, and stable values became not so much an elusive memory as a bitter hoax. By 1970, a leading historian of American religion could plausibly assert that the nation had passed into a "post-Puritan, post-Protestant, post-Christian, post-modern, and even post-historical" era. For many thoughtful Americans, he later judged, the dominant feeling had come to be, in Yeats's words, "all coherence gone."[39]

Still, the arteries that link Evangelicalism and the Victorian Christian Civilization ideal run deeper than nostalgia. Here Donald G. and Jane DeHart Mathews's analysis of the continuities between religious and cultural Fundamentalism (which closely correspond to what I have termed theological Evangelicalism on one side and the Evangelical Right on the other) is particularly illuminating. They argue that religious and cultural fundamentalists tend to think in the same way. For both, historical process and cultural pluralism are ignored or denied, social reality is fractured by a Manichean faultline that divides absolute good from absolute evil, and public discourse is structured to avoid moral discriminations so that abortion and genocide, or nudity and pornography, or honest doubt and destructive criticism, all come out very much the same. Further, what is most important for both, holiness is defined as purity: the maintenance of time-hallowed boundaries. Holiness is therefore "keeping distinct the categories of creation." To attack the "anomalies of women-who-want-to-be-men and men-who-refuse-to-be-men, therefore, is part of the process that purges society of its impurities."[40]

Yet having said all this, it is important to remember that the forces that prod Evangelicals to identify with a particular cultural outlook are also the forces that keep Evangelicalism from lapsing into irrelevance. The Evangelical Right represents, in other words, cultural captivity, but it also represents cultural awareness—a genuinely pastoral concern that tradition should still have a place in the modern world. Still more pertinently, the Evangelical Right represents an awareness that this age, like all ages, "is standing in the need of prayer." The question is whether a message that owes more to the old-fashioned gospel of the nineteenth century than it does to the transforming gospel of the first century will do much good. But, as Evangelicals declare, grace has always been amazing.

Notes

1. Dods quoted without citation in Charles W. Gilkey, "Preaching: The Recovery of the Word," in Arnold S. Nash, editor, *Protestant Thought in the Twentieth Century: Whence and Wither?* (New York: Macmillan, 1951), p. 220. For secular-

ization, see Peter L. Berger, *The Homeless Mind: Modernization and Consciousness* (New York: Random House, 1973).

2. Old orthodoxies displaced, see Henry F. May, *The End of American Innocence: A Study of the First Years of Our Own Time* (Chicago: Quadrangle Paperbacks, 1959); of the unchurched, see George Gallup, Jr., and David Poling, *The Search for America's Faith* (Nashville: Abingdon, 1980), p. 80; of polls, see "The *Christianity Today*-Gallup Poll: An Overview," in *Christianity Today,* December 21, 1979, p. 1668; of the Protestant Establishment, see *Yearbook of American and Canadian Churches 1981* (Nashville: Abingdon, 1981), and David A. Roozen and Jackson W. Carroll, "Recent Trends in Church Membership and Participation," in Dean R. Hoge and David A. Roozen, editors, *Understanding Church Growth and Decline: 1950-1978* (New York: Pilgrim Press, 1979), pp. 22-28; of Catholic decline, see James Hennessey, S.J., *American Catholics: A History of the Roman Catholic Community in the United States* (New York: Oxford, 1981), chapter 21; of Jewish decline, see Nathan Glazer, "Jewish Loyalties," in *Wilson Quarterly 5* (1981), pp. 134–145; of Ignatow, see epigraph to his *Rescue the Dead,* quoted in Giles Gunn, editor, *New World Metaphysics: Readings on the Religions Meaning of the American Experience* (New York: Oxford, 1981), p. 405.

3. See Winthrop S. Hudson, *Religion in America* (New York: Scribner's, 1981), chapter 17. For general news accounts, see Kenneth L. Woodward, "Born Again!" in *Newsweek,* October 25, 1976, pp. 68–78; "Back to that Oldtime Religion," in *Time,* December 26, 1977, pp. 52–58; James Mann, "A Global Surge of Old-Time Religion," in *U.S. News and World Report,* April 27, 1981, pp. 38–40. For extensive treatments, see Donald G. Bloesch, *The Evangelical Renaissance* (Grand Rapids: Eerdmans, 1973); Richard Quebedeaux, *The Worldly Evangelicals* (San Francisco: Harper and Row, 1978); John D. Woodbridge, *The Gospel in America: Themes in the Story of America's Evangelicals* (Grand Rapids: Zondervan, 1979); and Ed Dobson, *The Fundamentalist Phenomenon: The Resurgence of Conservative Christianity* (Garden City, New Jersey: Doubleday, 1981).

4. On Evangelical background, see George Marsden, *Fundamentalism and American Culture: The Shaping of Twentieth-Century Evangelicalism, 1870–1925* (New York: Oxford, 1980), and Joel Carpenter, "A Shelter in the Time of Storm: Fundamentalist Institutions and the Rise of Evangelical Protestants, 1919–1942," in *Church History,* Vol. 49 (1980), pp. 62–75. See also, Kenneth Woodward, "Born Again!" in *Newsweek,* October 25, 1976, pp. 68–78; "Back to that Oldtime Religion," *Time,* December 26, 1977, pp. 52–58. On Eldridge Cleaver, see *Time,* December 26, 1977. On Charles Colson, see Gary C. Wharton, "The Continuing Phenomenon of the Religious Best Seller," in *Publisher's Weekly,* March 14, 1977, pp. 82–83.

5. See, for example, "All That and Billy Graham Too," in *Time,* September 22, 1980, p. 83; and Harold Lindsell, "The Decline of a Church and Its Culture," in *Christianity Today,* July 17, 1981, pp. 931–934.

6. Reginald W. Bibby, "Why Conservative Churches Really Are Growing: Kelley Revisited," in *Journal for the Scientific Study of Religion, 17* (1978), pp. 134, 136; and Jeffrey K. Hadden, "Soul Saving via Video," in *Christian Century,* May 28, 1980, pp. 609–610.

7. Dean M. Kelley, *Why Conservative Churches Are Growing: A Study in the*

Sociology of Religion (New York: Harper and Row, 1972), pp. 39–42, 52–53, 84, 131; Virginia Stem Owens, *The Total Image: Or Selling Jesus in the Modern Age* (Grand Rapids: Eerdmans, 1980); Martin E. Marty, "The Marks and Misses of a Magazine," in *Christianity Today,* July 17, 1981, p. 947.

8. For the nature of Victorian culture in America, see Daniel Walker Howe, editor, *American Quarterly,* Vol. 27 (1975). For the concept of a Christian civilization, see Mark Thomas Connelly, *The Response to Prostitution in the Progressive Era* (Chapel Hill: University of North Carolina Press, 1980), pp. 8–10.

9. See Robert D. Linder, "The Resurgence of Evangelical Social Concern, 1925–1975," in David F. Wells and John D. Woodbridge, editors, *The Evangelicals* (Nashville: Abingdon, 1975), pp. 189–210; Richard Quebedeaux, *The Young Evangelicals* (New York: Harper and Row, 1974); Robert E. Webber, *The Moral Majority: Right or Wrong?* (Westchester, Illinois: Cornerstone Books, 1981), pp. 119–182; and Martin E. Marty, *A Nation of Behavers* (Chicago: University of Chicago Press, 1976). For evidence that the Evangelical non-Right is not growing, see Norris Magnusson, *Salvation in the Slums: Evangelical Social Work, 1865–1920* (Metuchen, New Jersey: Scarecrow Press, 1977).

10. See Erling Jorstad, "The New Christian Right," in *Theology Today,* Vol. 38 (1981), pp. 193–200; and James E. Wood, Jr., "Religion, Fundamentalism and the New Right," in *Journal of Church and State,* Vol. 23 (1981), pp. 409–421.

11. See Jerry Falwell, "Future-Word: An Agenda for the Eighties," in Ed Dobson, *Fundamentalist Phenomenon,* pp. 186–223 (reprinted in this anthology).

12. Harry Emerson Fosdick, *The Living of These Days: An Autobiography* (New York: Harper and Brothers, 1956), p. 230. On widespread belief in absolutes in America, see Jackson W. Carroll, *Religion in America: 1950 to the Present* (San Francisco: Harper and Row, 1979), pp. 29–33.

13. See Bill Keller, "Lobbying for Christ: Evangelical Conservatives Move from Pews to Polls," in *Congressional Quarterly Weekly,* September 6, 1980, p. 2630; and Tim LaHaye, *The Battle for the Mind* (Old Tappan, New Jersey: Revell, 1980), p. 9.

14. Richard John Neuhaus, quoted without citation in Shriver, *The Bible Vote: Religion and the New Right* (New York: Pilgrim Press, 1981) p. 45; and R. J. Rushdoony as quoted in John W. Whitehead and John Conlan, "The Establishment of the Religion of Secular Humanism and Its First Amendment Implications," in *Texas Tech Law Review,* Vol. 10 (1078), p. 20.

15. See Falwell, *Listen America!* (New York: Bantam/Doubleday, 1981), p. 25.

16. For typical (and typically ambivalent) assertions of the value of pluralism, see Jerry Falwell as interviewed in *Christianity Today,* September 4, 1981, p. 1097; and Harold O. J. Brown, "The Road to Theocracy?" in *National Review,* October 31, 1980, pp. 1328–1329.

17. For the moral role of government, see William A. Rusher, "Goldwater and the Religious Right," in *Moral Majority Report,* October 19, 1981, p. 7. The economic theories of the Evangelical Right are assayed in Michael Lienesch, "The Paradoxical Politics of the Religious Right," in *Soundings,* Vol. 66 (1983), pp. 70–99.

18. See George F. Will's essay, "Who Put Morality in Politics," in this anthology; Michael Novak, "Prayer, Education," in *National Review,* October 17, 1980, p. 1270; and "Goldwater Blasts New Right," in *Time,* September 28,

1981, p. 27. Alan Crawford sharply distinguishes what he calls traditional, New Right, and hearth-and-home styles of conservatism in his *Thunder on the Right: The 'New Right' and the Politics of Resentment* (New York: Pantheon Books, 1980), pp. 7, 34–39, 148–162. Models of political organization and behavior within the Evangelical Right are astutely analyzed in Michael Lienesch, "Right-Wing Religion: Christian Conservatism as a Political Movement," in *Political Science Quarterly,* Vol. 97 (1982), pp. 403–425. See also John C. Bennett, "Assessing the Concerns of the Religious Right," in *Christian Century,* October 14, 1981, pp. 1018–1022.

19. On the Evangelical Right's perception of the media, see Falwell, *Listen America!,* p. 104, 117, 164–170; and LaHaye, *The Battle for the Mind,* pp. 147–148. See also Nick Thimmesch, "Lear," in *Moral Majority Report,* July 20, 1981, p. 7.

20. Donald E. Wildmon, "Let's Get Religion in the Picture," in *Christianity Today,* February 19, 1982, p. 11; and Ben Stein, "The War to Clean Up TV," in *Saturday Review,* February 1981, pp. 23–27.

21. Bob Jones University pamphlets quoted in Wray Herbert, "Fundamentalism vs. Humanism," in *Humanities Report,* September 1981, p. 8. For secular humanism as the denial of moral absolutes in schools, see Onalee McGraw, *Secular Humanism and the Schools* (Washington, D.C.: Heritage Foundation, 1976), pp. 4–7; David Cook, *Christianity Confronts Communism, Humanism, Materialism, Existentialism* (Wheaton, Illinois: Tyndale House, 1981); and Kenneth L. Woodward, "The Right's New Bogeyman," in *Newsweek,* July 6, 1981, pp. 48–50.

22. Quotation from Falwell, *Listen America!,* p. 184. See also Walter E. Williams, "Public Schools Promote Mediocrity," in *Moral Majority Report,* September 21, 1981, p. 14. "WASP values excluded" quotation is from Martin E. Marty, *Context,* July 15, 1980. I am indebted to Jim W. Jones of the Fort Worth *Star Telegram* for discussion of this issue.

23. For deceptions in sex education, see Duncan, *Secular Humanism,* pp. 21–24; Falwell, *Listen, America!,* pp. 122–27, 179; LaHaye, *Battle for the Mind,* p. 212; Reo M. Christenson, "Clarifying 'Values Clarification' for the Innocent," in *Christianity Today,* April 10, 1981, pp. 501–504; James Robison, *Attack on the Family* (Wheaton, Illinois: Tyndale House, 1980) pp. 87–97; and the series of articles in *Moral Majority Report,* May 18, 1981, p. 7. For teaching of evolution, see Whitehead and Conlan, "Establishment . . . Of Secular Humanism," pp. 47–57; LaHaye, *Battle for the Mind,* pp. 60–68; the transcript of nationally televised debate between Duane Gish, Institute for Creation Research, and Russell F. Doolittle, Department of Chemistry, University of California at San Diego, at Liberty Baptist College, Lynchburg, Virginia, October 13, 1981; and Theodosius Dobzhansky, "Changing Man," *Science,* January 27, 1967, pp. 409–415. For the cultural significance of creationism, see the excellent analyses by Dorothy Nelkin, "The Science-Textbook Controversies," in *Scientific American,* April 1976, p. 39, and Ronald L. Numbers, "Creationism in 20th-Century America," in *Science* (1982), pp. 538–544. More generally, see Charles S. Blinderman, "Unnatural Selection: Creationism and Evolutionism," in the *Journal of Church and State,* No. 24 (1982), pp. 73–86.

24. Falwell, *Listen, America!,* pp. 15–16. See also Robison, *Attack on the Family,* pp. 21–23. For a larger perspective on the underlying issue, see Leonard

I. Sweet, "The Epic of Billy Graham," in *Theology Today,* No. 37 (1980), pp. 90–92.

25. For the manliness syndrome, see FitzGerald, "A Disciplined, Charging Army," pp. 78, 96; Quebedeaux, *Worldly Evangelicals,* pp. 74–76, and Jerry Sholes, *Give Me That Prime-Time Religion: An Insider's Report on the Oral Roberts Evangelistic Association* (New York: Hawthorne Books, 1979). Also, Falwell, as quoted in "Politicizing the Word," *Time,* October 1, 1979, p. 68. Concerned women are quoted in LaHaye, *Battle for the Mind,* p. 151.

26. Plymouth Rock Foundation book lists, "FAC-Sheets," cassettes, etc., Marlborough, New Hampshire. Best known is Rus Walton's *One Nation Under God.* See also Francis Schaeffer, *A Christian Manifesto* (Westchester, Illinois: Crossway Books, 1981); John W. Whitehead, *The Second American Revolution* (Elgin, Illinois: David C. Cook, 1982); Marshall and Manuel, *The Light and the Glory.* For a thoughtful critique of this outlook, see Ronald A. Wells, "Francis Schaeffer's Jeremiad," in *Reformed Journal,* May 1982, pp. 16–20; Christopher Lasch, *The Culture of Narcissism: American Life in an Age of Diminishing Expectations* (New York: W. W. Norton, 1978); Robert A. Nisbet, *The Twilight of Authority* (New York: Oxford, 1975); Giles Gunn, *New World Metaphysics,* p. 405; Daniel Bell, discussed without citation in Martin E. Marty, *The Public Church: Mainline-Evangelical-Catholic* (New York: Crossroad, 1981), p. 29; and Lance Morrow, "What Does an Oath Mean?" in *Time,* August 24, 1981, p. 70. More generally, see Godfrey Hodgson, *America in Our Time: From World War II to Nixon* (New York: Random House, 1976).

27. On the perception of an international antifamily conspiracy, see LaHaye, *Battle for the Mind,* pp. 110, 143–44; Robison, *Attack on the Family,* p. 7; Falwell, *Listen, America!,* pp. 112–16; David A. Noebel, *Rock 'n Roll: A Prerevolutionary Form of Cultural Subversion* (Manitou Springs, Colorado: Summit Ministries, 1980). Virtually every concern of the Evangelical Right is exhibited in LaHaye's *The Battle for the Family,* (Old Tappan, New Jersey: Revell, 1982). The vituperativeness of this volume is reminiscent of the publications of Gerald L. K. Smith and Gerald Winrod in the 1930s.

28. On changing sexual mores, see Yankelovich, *New Rules,* pp. 93–96, and "Black and White, Unwed All Over," in *Time,* November 9, 1981, p. 67; and LaHaye, *Battle for the Mind,* pp. 64–65.

29. The Evangelical Right's preoccupation with sexual issues is particularly evident in LaHaye's *Battle for the Family* and Robison's *Attack on the Family.* See also any issue of *Moral Majority Report,* particularly the issue of July 20, 1981. For an analysis of homosexuality and the Evangelical Right, see Quebedeaux, *Worldly Evangelicals,* pp. 128–31; Robert K. Johnston, *Evangelicals at an Impasse: Biblical Authority in Practice* (Atlanta: John Knox Press, 1979), Chapter 5; and Tom Minnery, "Homosexuals Can Change," in *Christianity Today,* February 6, 1981, pp. 172–77. More broadly, see Quebedeaux, *Worldly Evangelicals,* pp. 77–78, 126–28; and Robert M. Price, "Ye Must Be Porn Again (Some Trends in Evangelical Books on Sex)," in *Wittenburg Door,* April–May 1981, pp. 28–30.

30. Donald G. Matthews and Jane DeHart Mathews, "The Cultural Politics of ERA's Defeat," in *OAH Newsletter,* November 1982, pp. 13–15. See also George Gilder, interview, *Playboy,* August 1981, p. 94.

31. Robison, *Attack on the Family,* p. 23. The Family Protection Act is

discussed in Deryl M. Edwards, "Jepsen, Laxalt, Smith Say Americans Want to Strengthen Family," in *Moral Majority Report,* July 20, 1981, p. 10; and FitzGerald, "A Disciplined, Charging Army," p. 74. See also Phyllis Schlafly, "How to Clean Up America," in Falwell, *Clean Up America,* p. 24.

32. Falwell, *Listen, America!,* p. 78; LaHaye, *Battle for the Mind,* p. 64; Robison, *Attack on the Family,* p. 133; and Blair Adams and Joel Stein, *Education as Religious War,* pp. 1, 3. Discussions of sexual permissiveness are almost always framed in terms of teenage, not adult, deviance from traditional norms. See Glen C. Griffin, "Children . . . Being Rocked by Audio Pornography," in *Moral Majority Report,* April 1981, p. 15.

33. Dick Dabney, *"God's . . . Network,"* p. 35. See also James M. Wall, "What Future for the New Right?" in *Christian Century,* November 25, 1981, pp. 1219–1220; and more broadly, Christopher Lasch, *Haven in a Heartless World: The Family Besieged* (New York: Basic Books, 1979).

34. For value ambivalences, see Daniel Yankelovich, *New Rules,* pp. 93–96, 103, and Gallup and Poling, *America's Faith,* pp. 43–44. For "reality defining agencies" and the Seeger decision, see Whitehead and Conlan, "Establishment . . . Of Secular Humanism," pp. 1, 5, 13–14.

35. Ernest Lee Tuveson, *Redeemer Nation: The Idea of America's Millennial Role* (Chicago: University of Chicago Press, 1968). Robert T. Handy, *A Christian America: Protestant Hopes and Historical Realities* (New York: Oxford, 1971). See also Marsden, *Fundamentalism,* Chapter 3 and pp. 204–205; and, for a cross-cultural perspective, Hartmut Lehmann, "Piety and Nationalism: The Relationship of Protestant Revivalism and National Renewal in Nineteenth Century Germany," in *Church History,* No. 51 (1982), pp. 39–53.

36. Marsden, *Fundamentalism,* and Paul Boyer, *Urban Masses and Moral Order in America,* 1820–1920 (Cambridge: Harvard University Press, 1978). See also Richard V. Pierard, *The Unequal Yoke: Evangelical Christianity and Political Conservatism* (Philadelphia: Lippincott, 1970), and James Fulton Maclear, " 'The True American Union' of Church and State: The Reconstruction of the Theocratic Tradition," in *Church History,* No. 28 (1959), pp. 53–59.

37. For the social position, cultural attitudes, and political habits of Evangelicals in general, see the summary of the literature in John Wilson, *Religion in American Society: The Effective Presence* (Englewood Cliffs, New Jersey: Prentice-Hall, 1978), pp. 349–353. For the extraordinary complications involved in constructing a social-cultural-political profile of the typical Evangelical, see John Stephen Hendricks, "Religious and Political Fundamentalism: The Links between Alienation and Ideology," (Ph.D. dissertation, University of Michigan, 1977). For a close-grained profile of Evangelical voting behavior in the 1980 general election that also underscores the risk of sociological generalizations, see Seymour Martin Lipset and Earl Raab, "The Election and the Evangelicals," in *Commentary,* March 1981, pp. 25–31, and George Gallup, "Evangelicals Not Monolithic in Views on Key Issues," reprinted in the Chapel Hill *Newspaper,* September 8, 1980, p. 2B.

38. See the articles, especially that by Peter Berger, in B. Bruce-Briggs, editor, *The New Class?,* (New Brunswick: Transaction Books, 1979). See also Martin E. Marty, "Interpreting American Pluralism," in Carroll, *Religion in America,* p. 89; James Davison Hunter, "The New Class and the Young Evangelicals," in *Review*

of Religious Research, No. 22 (1980), pp. 155–69; and Robert Wuthnow, "The Current Moral Climate," in *Theology Today,* No. 36 (1979), pp. 249–250.

39. See, for example, Richard L. McCormick, "Ethno-Cultural Interpretations of Nineteenth-Century Voting Behavior," in *Political Science Quarterly,* No. 89 (1974), pp. 351–377. Quotations are from Sydney E. Ahlstrom, "The Radical Turn in Theology and Ethics: Why It Occurred in the 1960s," in *Annals of the American Academy of Political and Social Science,* No. 387 (1970), pp. 1–13, reprinted in John M. Mulder and John F. Wilson, editors, *Religion in America: Interpretive Essays* (Englewood Cliffs, New Jersey: Prentice-Hall, 1978) p. 445; and Ahlstrom, "The Traumatic Years: American Religion and Culture in the '60s and '70s," in *Theology Today,* No. 36 (1979), p. 522.

40. Mathews, "Cultural Politics." For the interpenetration of religious and cultural symbols, see Joseph Gusfield, *Symbolic Crusade: Status Politics and the American Temperance Movement* (Urbana: University of Illinois Press, 1969), and Giles Gunn, editor's introduction, *New World Metaphysics*. For splitting the world into absolute good or evil, see Marsden, *Fundamentalism,* pp. 223-224, and Luther P. Gerlach and Virginia H. Hine, *People, Power, Change: Movements of Social Transformation* (Indianapolis: Bobbs-Merrill, 1972), Chapter 6. For the integral relation between religion and boundaries, see Catherine L. Albanese, *America: Religions and Religion* (Belmong, California: Wadsworth, 1981), pp. 3–5, 12–13. See also Fredrik Barth, *Ethnic Groups and Boundaries: The Social Organization of Culture Difference* (Boston: Little, Brown and Co., 1969).

23. *Evangelicals and Catholics: A New Ecumenism*

By GEORGE WEIGEL

Focus

An intriguing development in the continuing debate about the role of religion in American life is the "new ecumenism" that unites many Protestant Evangelicals and Roman Catholics. In exploring the origin of this new cooperation, George Weigel suggests that Catholics and Evangelicals can generate "fresh thinking about the right relationship of religiously-based values and public policy."

Weigel finds new bonds between members of traditions separated since the Reformation in "a shared perception that the systematic effort to strip American public policy discourse of any relationship to the religiously-based values of the American people portends disaster for the American experiment." That experiment, Weigel says, is based on "a set of claims about the nature of the human person and about his or her relationship to society and to the state." Catholics and Evangelicals share a "common love for the American proposition [that] places them in a distinctive position to be the agents of a reconsecration of the American experiment."

To define the new "axis of ecumenical dialogue," Weigel recommends that Catholics and Evangelicals "begin a common theological and ethical exploration of the complex problem of war and peace, security and freedom in the modern world, . . . a social ethic adequate to thinking through the international threats of both war and totalitarianism," and "the relationship between peace-making as a moral responsibility and political task, and the moral claims of human freedom, especially religious liberty.

"American Evangelicals and American Catholics have much to learn from each other and much to teach each other." By working together, they can serve the national interest in "the present testing of the American proposition."

George Weigel is president of the James Madison Foundation in Washington, D. C., and the author of *Tranquillitas Ordinis: The Present Failure and Future Promise of American Catholic Thought on War and Peace* (Oxford University Press, 1987).

THE GREAT CHURCH and State Debate of 1984, which was really a debate over the place of religiously-based values in the American public policy arena, may have simmered down since the elections, but it is far from settled. In fact, it can never be settled with finality, for America, as Lincoln affirmed at Gettysburg, is a "proposition." Prior to the constitutional mechanics of government, America is a set of claims about the nature of the human person, and about his or her relationship to society and state. These claims are tested in each generation.

The testing of the American proposition today requires, I think, a new axis of ecumenical dialogue. The main participants will be American Roman Catholics and American Evangelical Protestants.

Why the need for a new ecumenism? And why Catholics and Evangelicals? After all, for the first three centuries of our national experience—from the days of the Pilgrims and John Winthrop—the churches of the Protestant mainline—Congregationalist, Episcopalian, Presbyterian, and Methodist—were the chief shapers of our moral and cultural life. For the past fifty years, though, these churches have largely forsaken the task of culture-formation; some mainline church leaders have not only acquiesced in, but contributed to, their churches' cultural "dis-establishment." This seemed clear during the Great Church and State Debate of 1984, in which it was not the churches of the mainline, but Catholics and Evangelicals, who were forcing the issues, defining the terms of debate over the meaning of the American proposition, and providing the moral and cultural leadership role that was once assumed to be the mainline's prerogative.

Social, Political, and Theological Bonds

Thus, the "new ecumenism" has arisen almost by accident. It is not the product of theological seminars in major universities; it is the result of a shared perception that the systematic effort to strip American public policy discourse of any relationship to the reli-

Reprinted by permission from the July/August 1985 issue of *Eternity* magazine.

giously-based values of the American people portends disaster for the American experiment. The ironic view of history has something to be said for it: Norman Lear may seem an odd matchmaker for Catholics and Evangelicals, but his People for the American Way and similar groups have accomplished just that.

The new ecumenism is a potentially volatile mixture. The older ecumenism—with its praiseworthy concern for doctrinal questions of baptism, Eucharist, ministry, polity, and authority in the church—was perhaps a bit less volatile because culturally it was more comfortable. Evangelicals and Catholics, on the other hand, are going to have to take some time to get used to each other. Both traditions have biases and prejudices that must be faced and overcome. But the two traditions share a basis for common reflection and common work in meeting this generation's test of the American proposition.

There is theological ground for dialogue. American Catholics and nonfundamentalist American Evangelicals are both what we might call (painting here with a wide brush) theological centrists. Neither accepts the secularization hypothesis that human beings have somehow outgrown their need for religion, for a transcendent point of reference for life, and for a belief that a fuller truth and a more complete love bound the world. Neither Catholics nor Evangelicals are sectarians; neither believes in a church set absolutely against the world, or declines responsibility for ordering the human community.

Both traditions are committed to a biblically-rooted faith, and both reject the kind of narrow biblicism often practiced by both the left and right in public policy debates—the kind of biblicism that ransacks the Scripture to locate prooftexts in support of previously-determined political judgments. Both traditions have supported independent higher education in America, a sign that both Catholics and Evangelicals affirm the compatibility of faith and human reason. Both traditions explore the hints and traces of the Potter's hand that we discern in His creation.

No doubt there are important theological tensions between Catholics and Evangelicals, but there is ample ground on which to build the needed conversation.

There are also demographic reasons for the new ecumenism.

Catholics and Evangelicals share a similar position in American political culture. Evangelicals are the new kids on the block; Catholics got on the block just a generation ago. The Evangelical experience—of a community coming in from the political and cultural wilderness after the great divisions of the 1920s—is similar to the experience of Catholics in America for the past 160 years. Both traditions thus share a common freshness in their apprehension of the American experiment and their responsibility for helping shape it; both traditions share a common gratitude for, and excitement about, the possibilities of this "new thing amidst the ages," as the Great Seal of the United States describes America. The cynicism and lack of nerve so often encountered in more established American cultural elites is refreshingly absent from the larger parts of both the Catholic and Evangelical communities.

All of this puts Catholics and Evangelicals in an interesting position, one in which both can be prophetic and transformational in the American experiment. Martin Luther King, Jr., said that "whom you would change, you must first love." That stance is common to both American Catholics and American Evangelicals. The two traditions are neither cheerleaders nor cynics; their common love for the American proposition places them in a distinctive position to be the agents of a reconsecration of the American experiment and a rebirth of freedom for all. The new ecumenism can generate fresh thought about the right relationship of religiously-based values and public policy.

Facing War and Peace Issues

Nowhere is the need for fresh thought more urgent than in facing the questions of war and peace. Religious peace activism has insisted, quite correctly, that these are questions of profound moral importance. Strategic and political judgment require moral judgment. *Realpolitik,* or politics conducted purely in the interest of power, cuts across the grain of the American proposition and experiment, and religious peace activism has reminded us of this fact.

But peace activists have adopted pagan imagery and language drawn from such figures as Helen Caldicott and Carl Sagan. The peace movement has fixed on questions of weaponry to such an extent that it has neglected to think through the larger contextual question of how the world is going to create institutions that will permit us to resolve inevitable conflicts without the use or threat of mass violence.

The peace movement has also often failed to take adequate measure of the threat posed by Soviet power and purpose, and has taught Americans that human rights concerns (even the problem of religious persecution in the USSR) can be addressed apart from arms control and disarmament issues. Religious peace activism, so single-mindedly focused on changing American foreign policy, rarely addresses the much more significant and difficult question of how America might work to change Soviet policy.

All of these teachings are presented with moral fervor, and many are packaged as if they were clear imperatives drawn from the Sermon on the Mount.

Here then, the new ecumenism has a unique opportunity to reshape a central debate over the relationship of religiously-based values and American public policy.

The new ecumenism should begin a common theological and ethical exploration of the complex problem of war and peace, security and freedom in the modern world. Such an exploration would bring the remarkable accomplishments of twentieth century biblical scholarship to bear on this issue, not in the form of proof-texts for preferred policy positions, but as material for moral reflection on the ethical and political complexities faced by individuals who are citizens of a free society and members of the ecumenical church.

Four Areas for Reflection

Common biblical and theological reflection on the moral problem of peace and freedom should focus on at least four areas. The first is eschatology. Ours is the first generation, as Pope John Paul II said at Hiroshima in 1982, that must make a conscious choice for the future. That responsibility can lead to survivalism, or it can lead to a new vision of human maturity. Such a choice will be based on how well we understand the relationship between the kingdom that remains to come and the possibilities of the human condition revealed in the resurrection. There is much to be explored here.

The second area for common reflection is in the creation of a social ethic adequate to thinking through the international threats of both war and totalitarianism. How do we relate the moral claims of the New Testament to foreign policy choices? What is the contemporary meaning of Romans 13 and its injunction for Christians to obey public authority? What is the relationship between norms of the gospel and moral norms that are derived from human reason? How can just war theory and pacifism both be honored without indulging in impossible attempts to find a theoretical "middle ground" between them. There is much material for common reflection here, particularly since Evangelicals lack a fully-formed social ethic and the intellectual elites of American Catholicism have spent considerable time over the past generation abandoning the social-ethical heritage that was theirs. A great task of ecumenical reclamation and renewal suggests itself here.

The third area for common reflection is the relationship between peace-making as a moral responsibility and political task, and the moral claims of human freedom, especially religious liberty. Many religious peace activists wish to divide these issues, presumably out of concern that the USSR not be "upset" and therefore be disagreeable in negotiating arms reductions. But the sundering of peace and freedom is both morally unsound and politically unwise. It is morally unsound because it is irresponsible to abandon persecuted brothers and sisters in Christ; it is politically unwise because there is little likelihood of making progress on mutual disarmament with an adversary that violates the solemn obligations it assumed by adhering to the Charter of the United Nations, the Universal Declaration of Human Rights, and the Helsinki Accords. The conjunction of peace and freedom is not easy to achieve. Pursuing both goals simultaneously requires political imagination and dexterity. But the pursuit of these linked goals is also a question of moral will. Forging that will is a common task for the new ecumenism's theological dialogue.

Finally, there are ecclesiological issues to be sorted out. Both American Protestantism and American Catholicism are sorely tempted today by the vision of a "partisan church" in which the correctness of social analysis and political position define one's right relationship to the church community. Mainline Protestant and, increasingly, Roman Catholic, leadership are drawn into the public arena in highly predictable, patterned ways; so, too, are some on the Religious New Right. Nonfundamentalist Evangelicals and a significant number of Catholics are dissatisfied with the notion of a partisan church, whether its partisanship be exercised in favor of Ronald Reagan or (much more likely) the left wing of the Democratic Party. Evangelicals and Catholics can—or at least could—share a different position: that the church's primary public role in the debate about foreign policy is not to be another protagonist in existing arguments, but to be the principal agent shaping the moral horizon against which a wiser debate could form to address both peace and freedom. Steps in this direction are now underway in the National Association of Evangelicals' "Peace, Freedom, and Security Studies" project.

The old ecumenism is not to be abandoned amidst these new developments. Its accomplishments in theological understanding and growth should be celebrated. But a new ecumenism is needed to meet the present testing of the American proposition. The new ecumenism, largely Catholic and Evangelical, but also drawing on Lutheran and some mainline currents of thought, could take as its first task the radical alteration of the contours of the moral debate on war and peace, security and freedom in American society. These are issues central to the identity and purpose of the American experiment; they are among the gravest issues on which the American proposition is being tested. American Evangelicals and American Catholics have much to learn from each other and much to teach each other. Both traditions wish to take an increasing share of responsibility for the future of the American experiment. The time to get to work together is at hand.

24. *Religious Belief and the Constitutional Order*

By WILLIAM J. BENNETT

Focus Secretary of Education William J. Bennett argues that the "American experience cannot be understood without reference to the Judeo-Christian tradition," and that "the First Amendment was not intended to result in the complete exclusion of religion from public life." The framers of the Constitution, though they differed in religious convictions, were united in affirming "the importance of religion as an aid and a friend to the Constitutional order."

Bennett explores the relationship between religious convictions and political liberties. He suggests that "religion deepens politics" because religion produces the civic virtues that enable a society to become democratic. Religion also provides a "frame of reference for the claims that transcend everyday life." These include manners and morals in the home, school, and community, and national responsibilities towards other countries.

Bennett specifically points out the role of religion in promoting tolerance of different viewpoints. Paradoxically, most Americans with strong religious convictions have great respect for the convictions of other Americans. Furthermore, Bennett points out that the Constitution's framers discerned a direct link between commonly-shared values and individual rights. They believed that "complete neutrality between particular religious beliefs can and should coexist with public acknowledgement of general religious values." Bennett therefore criticizes both religious and secular attempts to set aside the Constitution's premise of "a consensus of shared values."

To protect religious liberty, the framers sought to "outlaw religious establishments and to moderate religious passions," while recognizing that "religious values require public acknowledgement, common defense, and mutual respect."

William J. Bennett is the U.S. Secretary of Education.

AS WE COMMEMORATE the bicentennial of the United States Constitution in 1987, and focus on the moral and philosophical underpinnings of the document, we should rediscover that the Constitution reflects and supports the constitution of the American people.

I have studied the Constitution as a student of philosophy and as a student of law, so I am confident when I say that it is time to retrieve the Constitution from the lawyers. For the Constitution belongs to all of us. It was written not only to protect our legal rights, but to express our common values. We cannot understand ourselves as individuals without understanding the ideas that "constitute" us as a people.

As the emblem of our national values, the Constitution reflects three distinct and related elements of our common culture: the Judeo-Christian ethic, the democratic ethic, and the work ethic. In fact, the process that produced the Constitution has itself been ascribed to all three of these ethics. To Walt Whitman, the Constitution was the product of divine inspiration. He called it a "bible of the free" for the modern world. To John Quincy Adams, the Constitution was the product of democratic compromise. He said that it was "extorted from the grinding necessity of a reluctant nation." To William Gladstone, the Constitution was the product of hard work. He called it "the greatest work ever struck off at a given time by the brain and purpose of man."

In appraising the role of religious belief in American democracy, I confess that I sympathize with the religious beliefs of the overwhelming majority of the American people. My upbringing, my experience, and my study have made me sympathetic to religious beliefs. As a friend of religion, I am often struck in my encounters with the academic community by the fact that my support of religion seems to inspire the deepest bewilderment and suspicion.

Of course, it is not only members of the academy who disagree with me. I once spoke to the Knights of Columbus on the relation-

---

Adapted from a speech given by the author for the 1986 Paine Lectures at the University of Missouri-Columbia on September 17, 1986.

ship of our political and social order to religious belief. I stated my position clearly: that the American experience cannot be understood without reference to the Judeo-Christian tradition, and that the First Amendment was not intended to result in the complete exclusion of that tradition from public life. For saying this, I was attacked as an "Ayatollah." It was suggested that merely broaching the subject of religion in public life was an incitement to "Khomeinism and Kahaneism." It was also suggested that I considered myself a messenger "heaven-sent to silence the heathen."

I have described this line of attack as a *reductio ad Khomeini*. It ignores my reaffirmation of this nation's commitment to the principles of tolerance and equal rights for all—for the non-believer as well as for the believer. With its fear of religious intolerance, the attack denies the fundamental strength of the American people—a people at once deeply religious and deeply tolerant. And the attack betrays a misconception that it is somehow improper for public officials in America to speak publicly and positively about the role of religion in American life.

The Founders and Religion

As we prepare for the bicentennial of the Constitution, we need to take a serious look at the historical record. The Founders discussed the role of religion in democracy calmly and frankly. We need to follow their lead and reclaim their legacy. There are those who argue that it is impossible in the twentieth century to gauge the intent of the Founders in the eighteenth century. I disagree. On the question of religion and the Constitution, the Framers' intent is explicit and history is clear. It is true that the Framers of the Constitution were themselves divided by a rich diversity of religious allegiances and personal convictions. But virtually all of them were united by a common belief in the importance of religion as an aid and a friend to the Constitutional order. As the Frenchman Alexis de Tocqueville observed, "I do not know whether all Americans have a sincere faith in their religion—for who can search the human heart?—but I am certain that they hold it to be indispensable to the maintenance of republican institutions."

From devout churchgoers to rationalizing deists, the Founders spoke with one voice about the importance of religion in civic life.

George Washington, a Virginia Episcopalian, warned in his Farewell Address: "Of all the dispositions and habits which lead to political prosperity, religion and morality are indispensable supports. And let us with caution indulge the supposition that morality can be maintained without religion." John Adams, a Massachusetts Unitarian, agreed in no uncertain terms: "Our Constitution was made only for a moral and religious people. It is wholly inadequate to the government of any other." James Madison of Virginia, an Episcopalian, insisted that, "He who would be a citizen in civil society must first be considered a subject of the divine governor of nature." And even Thomas Jefferson agreed. Jefferson, the deist who was always skeptical of sectarianism in any form, asked, "Can the liberties of a nation be thought secure . . . when we have removed their only firm basis, a conviction in the minds of the people that these liberties are the gift of God?" Religion, Jefferson concluded, should be regarded as "a supplement to law in the government of men," and as "the alpha and omega of the moral law."

From Sam Adams to Patrick Henry to Benjamin Franklin to Alexander Hamilton, all of the Founders intended religion to provide a moral anchor for the American people's liberty in democracy. Yet all the Founders would be puzzled were they to return to America today, because they would find, among certain elite circles in the academy and the media, a fastidious disdain for the public expression of religious values—a disdain that clashes directly with the Founders' vision of religion as a friend of civic life. This is why, on the bicentennial of the Constitution, it is not enough merely to identify the intent of the Founders, it is also necessary actively to defend the intent of the Founders.

The first question we should ask ourselves is: Why did the Founders see a connection between religious values and political liberty? Tocqueville, as always, points to an answer: "Liberty regards religion . . . as the safeguard of morality, and morality as the best security of law and the surest pledge of the duration of freedom. Religion promotes self-restraint, in the rulers and the ruled, and mitigates the individualist tendencies that atomize society." In short, Tocqueville concluded, "religion is much more needed in democratic republics than in any others."

But it is not necessary to go back to Tocqueville and his *Democracy in America* to understand the connections between religion and liberty in our democracy. It's simply a matter of common sense: Our commitment to liberty of conscience—including the freedom to believe or not to believe—follows, in good part from the respect for religion felt by the majority of Americans. It is ironic that anyone who appeals today to religious values runs the risk of being called "divisive," or attacked as an enemy of pluralism. For the readiness of most Americans to defend tolerance and equality does not derive only from an abstract allegiance to Enlightenment ideals, but from a concrete allegiance to the Judeo-Christian moral tradition.

Religious Values Nurture Virtue

The connection between religion and liberty is one reason that the Founders considered religion to be indispensable to our democracy. There are many more reasons. One is that, at its best, religion deepens politics. Religion is a wellspring of the civic virtues that democracy requires to flourish. Religion promotes hard work and individual responsibility, and it lifts each citizen outside of himself and inspires concern for community and country. At the same time, religion offers a sense of purpose and a frame of reference for the claims that transcend everyday politics—claims like our collective responsibility to foster liberty around the globe, and to be kind, good, decent, and forgiving in our homes, our schools, and our communities.

A second reason is that religion promotes tolerance. This seems like a paradox. After all, religion is about absolute truth, and does not the search for absolute truth lead to absolutism and to intolerance? Not necessarily—and, in America, thankfully, not very often. At its most sectarian, religion can, indeed, be used in the service of intolerance. When religion is "kindled into enthusiasm," as Madison warned, it may "itself become a motive to persecution and oppression." But more often than not in America, religion has had the opposite effect. As an example, I would refer to the striking way different schools receive me when I speak. I remember starting off a speech at a Baptist college—known for its enthusiasm—by stipulating that I spoke as a Roman Catholic. The audience was at first surprised by my frankness, but quickly settled down and courteously listened to what I had to say. Many even liked it. On the other hand, some in the so-called "enlightened" universities—aggressively secular, perhaps even intolerantly so—are more likely to greet me as an "ayatollah" or to shout down speakers with whom they disagree. Paradoxically, then, strongly held religious convictions seem to foster respect for the convictions of others.

I think President Reagan put it well when he told an ecumenical prayer breakfast: "Our government needs the church because those humble enough to admit they are sinners can bring to democracy the tolerance it requires in order to survive." I think the President was right. I also think that his proposition cuts both ways: Just as religion moderates the potentially divisive tendencies of democracy, a properly functioning democracy moderates the potentially divisive tendencies of religion. When religion is excluded from public life, religious people can become resentful, extremist, and sectarian. But when religion is included in public life, and is subject to public scrutiny, religious people tend to speak in a language that all sects and all citizens can understand. As Jefferson wrote to Madison, "by bringing the sects together . . . we shall soften their asperities, liberalize and neutralize their prejudices, and make the general religion a religion of peace, reason, and morality."

Tolerance and Equal Justice

Jefferson was right. In a free democracy, where much depends on broad public sentiment, religious groups must soften their asperities, and find that they must pursue their ends by appealing to a consensus of shared, not particularized, values. This has been true throughout American history, and it is true today.

The question of tolerance also points to a protection at the very heart of the Constitution: equal justice under law, for non-believers as well as for believers. When Patrick Henry proposed a tax for the "annual support of the Christian religion," Madison successfully opposed it on these grounds: "Whilst we assert for ourselves a freedom to . . . observe the religion which we believe to be of divine origin, we cannot deny an equal freedom to those whose minds have not yet yielded to the evidence which has convinced us." And Jefferson agreed. In his Virginia Statute for Religious Freedom, Jefferson argued: "No man shall be compelled to frequent or support any religious worship place, or ministry whatsoever."

This is an important point. Absolute freedom of conscience is the first of our freedoms. The American people are irrevocably committed to equal rights for all. No one can, or should, be forced in America to assent to any particular religious belief, or even to the general religious beliefs derived from the Judeo-Christian tradition and embedded in our common culture. At the same time, however, religious beliefs do deserve, at all times, common acknowledgment, mutual respect, and public encouragement. We tend to forget that the Founders saw no conflict between our individual rights and our common values. In their minds, complete neutrality between particular religious beliefs can and should coexist with public acknowledgment of general religious values.

This is not merely a question of constitutional principle, though it is that. It is also a question of civic health. My point is not simply that children who go to church are less likely to take drugs, or that empirical studies show an inverse relation between religious belief and teenage pregnancy, although both are true. My point is that we are coming to recognize again the extent to which many of our social problems require for their solution the nurture and improvement of character. For many Americans—for most Americans—religion is an important part of the development of character. That is not to say that religious faith is necessary for sound character. But that it can help, and that it has helped many, who can doubt? And so, as we move toward a national consensus that, in dealing with social problems, we must improve the character of our citizenry—of ourselves—we should not, out of a misplaced fastidiousness, spurn the vast resources of ethical precept and practice that are inspired and reinforced by religious belief.

Balancing Religious and Political Priorities

In effect, we need a reconstitution of the consensus of the Founders. All of them were comfortable with a public role for religion—as long as there was no preference for one sect over another. To Jefferson, religion was an essential element of education. His "Act for Establishing Elementary Schools" in Virginia permitted religious activity in the classroom—as long it was not "inconsistent with the tenets of any religious sect or denomination."

The first United States Congresses also saw nothing unconstitutional about some governmental support of religious values. The first three U.S. Congresses authorized chaplaincies for the Congress, the Army, and the Navy. The same Congress that adopted the First Amendment also adopted the Northwest Ordinance, which reads: "Religion, morality, and knowledge, being necessary to good government and the happiness of mankind, schools and the means of learning shall forever be encouraged." If that Congress had meant to forbid all cooperation between government and the church, why did it call on the states "to promote religious and moral education"?

On the occasion of the bicentennial of the Constitution, then, we need to learn again from the wisdom of the Founders. They knew that it is never easy to maintain neutrality between sects. They knew that the preservation of equal rights requires political sensitivity and legal vigilance. But they also knew that, for the sake of liberty, government should acknowledge the religious beliefs on which democracy depends—not one single belief, but belief in general.

History records few other examples of nations that have managed to maintain the delicate balance between religious faith and political tolerance. In the twentieth century, we have seen both atheistic Communism and religious fanaticism degenerate into tyranny. The Founding Fathers pledged their lives to avoid tyranny in any form. The real genius of the Constitution they fashioned lies in the balance it strikes between unity and diversity, and between religious liberty and political equality, to the mutual benefit of both religion and politics.

To maintain that balance is no easy task. In America today, we face misunderstandings from both ends of the spectrum—from secularists on one side, and from sectarians on the other. There is a secularist orthodoxy that seeks to eradicate all signs of religion from public life. With a reckless disregard for both American history and the American people, some secularists are not content to pursue government neutrality among beliefs, or even government protection of non-belief; instead, they seek to vanquish religion altogether. But as former Supreme Court Justice Potter Stewart pointed out, the banishment of religion does not represent neutrality between religion and secularism, because the conduct of public institutions without any acknowledgment of religion is secularism.

Schoolbooks and America's Religious Heritage

In my speech to the Knights of Columbus, I offered my opinion that the U.S. Supreme Court in recent years has failed to reflect sufficiently on the relationship between our religious faith and our political order. The court itself has acknowledged the lack of "clarity and predictability" in its decisions. But the court does not bear sole responsibility for the shunting aside of religion in American public life. As a recent study by New York University Professor Paul Vitz found, the overwhelming majority of elementary and high school textbooks goes to extraordinary lengths to avoid any references to religion.

In a representative item from Vitz's study, one sixth-grade reading book includes a story called "Zlateh the Goat," by Nobel laureate Isaac Bashevis Singer. In the story, a boy named Aaron is told to take Zlateh, the family goat, to a butcher in the next village to be sold. On the way, Aaron and Zlateh get caught in a three-day blizzard and are lost in the snow. At this point, Singer writes, "Aaron began to pray to God for himself and for the innocent animal." But in the reading book, this has been changed to: "Aaron began to pray for himself and for the innocent animal." Later, after Aaron and Zlateh have found shelter in a haystack, Singer writes, "Thank God that in the hay it was not cold." But in the school book, this has been changed to: "Thank goodness that in the hay it was not cold."

This example of the expunging of religion from American public life would be funny if it were not so serious. Has the very mention of God's name in public become not just an offense, but some sort of political sin? Among orthodox Jews, it has always been considered a religious blasphemy to write the name of God in full. Well, have we come to the point where, in school textbooks, it is now considered a secular blasphemy to write the name of God, even if omitting His name does violence to the original text? Have we come to the point where it is now considered a secular blasphemy to acknowledge the name of God at all? Have we come, in some bizarre way, full circle: from scrupulous piety to fastidious disdain?

The main conclusion of Professor Vitz's study is that many of our high school textbooks go to extreme lengths to ignore the role of religion in American history. In case after case, his study points to exclusions, misrepresentations, and distortions that range from the silly to the outrageous. One world history book, for example, ignores the Protestant Reformation. An American history textbook defines pilgrims as "people who make long trips." Another defines Fundamentalists as rural people who "follow the values or traditions of an earlier period." Still another textbook lists three hundred important events in American history, but only three of the three hundred have anything to do with religion.

Soon after Professor Vitz's conclusions were released, Americans United for the Separation of Church and State conducted its own study of textbooks. This is a group hardly sympathetic to the religious lobby, but it, too, agreed that "most high school social studies and civics textbooks completely ignore religious liberty, and give little or no consideration to the religious clauses of the First Amendment." Then Norman Lear's People for the American Way also endorsed the findings. Finally, the *Washington Post* published an op-ed piece entitled, "A Liberal Case for Religion in School."

The Whole Truth of U.S. History

Today, almost two centuries after the signing of the United States Constitution, we need to make a pledge to one another: Let us pledge simply to tell our children the truth—the whole truth—about our history. The story of America is the story of the highest aspirations and proudest accomplishments of mankind. It is impossible to understand those aspirations and accomplishments without understanding the religious roots from which they sprang. We must tell our children about the Puritans who founded a "shining city" with the sacred mission of being a beacon unto the nations and a community of saints in a New Jerusalem. We should tell our children about Jefferson and Franklin, who proposed that the Great Seal of the United States depict Moses leading the chosen people from the Wilderness to the Promised Land. We should tell our children about Abraham Lincoln, who saw the Civil War as "a punishment inflicted upon us for our presumptuous sins to the end that the whole people might be redeemed." And we should tell our children about the Reverend Martin Luther King, Jr., who carried the "gospel of freedom" to the mountaintop, and who wrote a letter to the world from Birmingham Jail: "When these disinherited children of God sat down at lunch counters," he wrote, "they were in reality standing up for what is best in the American Dream and for the most sacred values in our Judeo-Christian heritage."

In recent years, we have shown a reluctance to tell the whole truth about American history. We have excluded our religious history from our textbooks, and we have excluded religious values from our public life. For doing this we have paid a double price: First, in our efforts to deny religious values in the name of religious liberty, we have threatened the very toleration that it affirms. As John Locke reminds us: "Those that by their atheism undermine and destroy all religion, can have no pretence of religion whereupon to challenge the privilege of toleration." Second, we have created, in the words of Richard John Neuhaus, something like a "naked public square." We now seem to be unable to celebrate in public the common values that most of us still affirm in private. And so our politics, deprived of religion, has threatened to become short-sighted and self-interested. As we should have expected, religious people—excluded from politics—have threatened to become resentful, extremist, and sectarian.

Religious Zealots Misread the Past

Ironically, those who seek to exclude religion from politics may end by inciting the dangers they fear. For there are some whose vision of America yields nothing in dogmatic certainty to the opposing vision of the secularists, and who, no less than the secularists, misunderstand the character of our constitutional order. There are those in America today who believe, like Samuel

Adams, that America should be a "Christian Sparta." They properly deserve the name "sectarian" rather than "religious." For, though, they sometimes speak in the name of religion in general, they would promote their own particular brand of religion into a favored position in public life. Not content to bring religious values into the public square, they would deny the government's constitutional obligation to be neutral among particular religious communities.

Like their secular antagonists, these religious zealots suffer from a misreading of history. If the secularists assert—wrongly—that the Founders meant to exclude all public support of religion, then the sectarians assert—wrongly—that the Constitution was designed, first and foremost, "to perpetuate a Christian order." One sectarian scholar even argues that Christianity was the primary cause of the American revolution. He calls for a "Christian historiography and a Christian revisionism" to foster a "return to the Protestant restoration of feudalism." A sectarian newspaper columnist insists that the Founders intended that all schoolchildren should be taught to acknowledge the divinity of Jesus Christ.

This is bad scholarship and dangerous politics. In the days of the Puritans, Massachusetts may, indeed, have been an intolerant Calvinist theocracy. But as the "church covenant" evolved into a "half-way covenant," so the Calvinist theocracy gave way to a constitutional democracy. By 1787, the Founders were determined at all costs to prevent the national government from establishing any form of religious orthodoxy. In July of 1986, Americans celebrated the one hundredth anniversary of the Statue of Liberty. Throughout those one hundred years, Protestants, Catholics, Jews, Buddhists, Muslims, and many of other religious faiths, have flocked from all over the globe to the "shining city on a hill." All, in their turn, have come to find their own peace in this land of religious liberty.

Like the Founders, we must remain vigilant against those who would disturb that peace. A public figure recently said that Christians feel more strongly about love of country, love of God, and support for the traditional family than do non-Christians. This sort of invidious sectarianism must be denounced in the strongest terms. The vibrant families and warm patriotism of millions upon millions of non-Christian and non-religious Americans give it the lie. Its narrowness would have disappointed the Founders, and its intolerance clashes with the best traditions of our democracy.

The same public figure was on much firmer ground when he later observed: "I don't think we should invest any candidate with the mantle of God." This point is crucial. On the one hand, religion should never be excluded from public debate. But, on the other hand, religion should never be used as a kind of divine trump card to foreclose further debate. Those who claim that their religious faith gives them a monopoly on political truth make democratic discourse difficult. Disagree with me and you're damned, they seem to suggest. In doing so, they insult the common sense and tolerant spirit of the American people.

In America, the roots of religious liberty and political equality are long and deep. On August 17, 1790, in the first years of our constitutional government, the Hebrew Congregation of Newport, Rhode Island, wrote to President George Washington to express thanks that the government of the United States gives "to bigotry no sanction, to persecution no assistance." This was President Washington's reply:

> The Citizens of the United States of America have a right to applaud themselves for having given to mankind examples of an enlarged and liberal policy, a policy worthy of imitation. All possess alike liberty of conscience and immunities of citizenship. It is now no more that toleration is spoken of, as if it was by the indulgence of one class of people, that another enjoyed the exercise of their inherent natural rights.

And President Washington added, in beautiful words:

> May the children of the Stock of Abraham, who dwell in this land, continue to merit and enjoy the good will of the other inhabitants, while every one shall sit in safety under his own vine and fig tree, and there shall be none to make him afraid.

So, to those today who make others afraid by calling America a "Christian nation," this is my reply: You are wrong. Sam Adams was wrong. We are not a "Christian Sparta," but Justice William Douglas was right when he said, "We are a religious people." We are indeed the most religious free people on earth. A recent survey showed that, though 76 per cent of the British, 62 per cent of the

French, and 79 per cent of the Japanese said they believe in God, fully 95 per cent of Americans said they do. It is noteworthy that, in each case, a similar percentage said they were willing to die for their countries. For the virtues that inspire patriotism—hard work, self-discipline, perseverance, industry, respect for family, for learning, and for country—are intimately linked with and strengthened by religious values. In short, the democratic ethic and the work ethic flourish in the context of the Judeo-Christian moral tradition from which they take their original shape and their continued vitality.

'Civil Religion': An American Treasure

Let me be clear: The virtues of self-discipline, love of learning, and respect for family are by no means limited to the Judeo-Christian tradition, or to any religious tradition. My point is that, in America, our civic virtues are inseparable from our common values. And values such as courage, kindness, honesty, and discipline are, to a large degree, common to almost all religious traditions. But it is the Judeo-Christian moral tradition that has given birth to our free political institutions; and, it is the Judeo-Christian moral tradition that has shaped our national ideals. Though we should never forget the contributions of a host of people from other religions and cultures who have come to our shores in search of freedom and opportunity, we should acknowledge that freedom and opportunity have flourished here in a political and social context shaped by the Judeo-Christian moral tradition.

In a book entitled *The Vietnamese Gulag*, a recent immigrant, Doan Van Toai, describes his escape to America after years of being confined to a Communist prison. Toai marvels at the liberty of our society—and at our license to take it for granted. "Perhaps," he tells us, "it is the immigrants' function from generation to generation to remind [Americans] of what a treasure it is they own."

One of the treasures of America is the treasure that Tocqueville called the "civil religion," and that Jefferson called the "general religion." This is the national creed that distills values common to all sects, in all religions, from all cultures. Neither Tocqueville nor Jefferson could have anticipated the variety of faiths that would eventually find a home in America—more than three hundred denominations at last count. Much divides each of these denominations from the others—small questions of doctrine and large questions of revelation. But what is agreed upon is important: It has content and power. It infuses American life with a sense of transcendence. All profit from it, although none is forced to assent to it. And, as the Founders predicted, the constitutional order depends on it.

This, then, is the first lesson of the bicentennial of the Constitution. To protect religious liberty, the Founders sought to outlaw religious establishments and to moderate religious passions. At the same time, they recognized that religious values require public acknowledgment, common defense, and mutual respect. And nothing has happened in the past two hundred years to suggest that Washington, Madison, Adams, and Jefferson were wrong. All of them envisioned a federal government neutral between religions in particular, but sympathetic with religion in general. For they knew that to be indifferent to the vitality of religious belief is to be indifferent to the vitality of our constitutional order—and of our Constitution. On the occasion of the Constitution's bicentennial, let us keep faith with our Constitution—the greatest political document ever struck off by the hand of man.

25. *Televangelism and Politics*

By JEFFREY K. HADDEN

Focus

As the most visible exponents of the New Christian Right, TV preachers—"televangelists"—will continue to play a leading role, says Jeffrey Hadden, in "one of the most important social movements of the century." Focusing on media response to the political influence of the New Christian Right since the 1980 presidential election, Hadden assesses televangelism as a movement potentially "of the order and magnitude of the revolution that Martin Luther symbolized."

Though he thinks the secular media initially overestimated—grossly so—the New Christian Right's impact in the 1980 and 1984 presidential elections, Hadden believes the movement shows several signs of long-term vitality. These include access to a vast nationwide audience through radio and television networks; financial support from radio listeners and television viewers; organization, including nationwide agencies; legitimacy, based on the Christian Right's conviction that Almighty God has blessed the movement; and demographics, that is, trends pointing to an older and more conservative American population.

"If we are experiencing the dawning of a new (conservative) era, the New Christian Right is destined to play a major role in shaping its character," Hadden writes. Much of that role will derive from the movement's "unrestricted access to mass media." But "whatever the outcome, one important fact has been almost completely missed by the media and intellectuals: the 'kooky' Fundamentalists that secular intellectual elites thought had disappeared after the Scopes Trial have already defined much of the agenda of this society for the foreseeable future, and therefore shaped the direction of American culture as we rush toward the twenty-first century."

Jeffrey K. Hadden is a professor of sociology at the University of Virginia and co-author (with Charles E. Swann) of *Prime Time Preachers* (Addison-Wesley, 1981).

WHILE RELIGIOUS BROADCASTING has been with us for many years, it was not until the 1980s that most Americans became aware of the phenomenon which Ben Armstrong has called the "electric church." Armstrong, executive director of National Religious Broadcasters (NRB), sees the electronic church as having "launched a revolution as dramatic as the revolution that began when Martin Luther nailed his ninety-five theses to the cathedral door at Wittenburg."

This may sound like trade association boosterism, but it would be a mistake to dismiss it as such. Armstrong's assessment of religious broadcasting is based on the belief that modern communications technology has provided an important tool for the fulfillment of the Scriptures. Evangelicals believe that Christ's greatest commandment was "Go yet into all the world, and preach the gospel to every creature" (Mark 16:15). Electronic communication, some Evangelicals believe, is literally a gift from God which makes possible the fulfillment of this Great Commission.

It is not the success of "televangelists" in preaching the Gospel message, however, that has made the electronic church controversial. Rather, it is that a few of those who preside over electronic pulpits have used airwaves as a means of transforming America politically. It was this shift in attitude toward politics by a few Evangelical and Fundamentalist preachers that made electronic pulpits controversial during the early 1980s.

Politically minded televangelists first became publicly visible in early 1980. A "Washington for Jesus" rally in April, which drew nearly 250,000 participants, listed a dozen television ministers and religious broadcast executives as sponsors. Though rally leaders disavowed any political agenda, opponents argued that no one assembles a quarter of a million people on the Washington Mall, and dispatches representatives to visit members of Congress, unless there is a political message to be sent.

By late summer, Jerry Falwell, who bolted the "Washington for

---

Reprinted by permission of Mercer University Press from *New Christian Politics,* edited by David G. Bromley and Anson Shupe, 1984.

Jesus'' rally because it was not explicitly political, had emerged from the pack of television preachers as the leader of born-again politics. He made various boastful predictions about the role his Moral Majority and other religious political groups would play in the next election, and this boasting won him cover stories in *Newsweek* and *U.S. News and World Report,* as well as many television appearances.

By the 1980 elections in November, the corralling of 1600 Pennsylvania Avenue by a one-time movie actor was not totally unexpected. Ronald Reagan, though long associated with the right wing of the Republican Party, was not considered a sufficient threat to excuse the liabilities amassed by Jimmy Carter's administration. What was not expected on that first Tuesday of November, however, was the virtual annihilation of the liberal leadership running for reelection to Congress.

Falwell, whose name had become practically a household word during the campaign, wasted no time in stepping forward in the name of his Moral Majority to claim responsibility for conservatives' political victories. Several defeated Congressmen and Senators agreed with Falwell's assessment. To sanctify this ''truth'' that born-again politicians had suddenly become a force to be reckoned with in American politics, pollster Louis Harris reported that the Moral Majority was responsible for the margin of victory in the presidential election. Harris made a blunder in his operational definition of ''moral majority'' that deserves to go down in the annals of polling alongside the famous 1948 *Chicago Tribune* poll that gave Thomas Dewey a victory over Harry Truman. But hardly anyone noticed.

Media attention continued to focus on Falwell in the months following the 1980 elections. Falwell's every move and utterance seemed to be newsworthy. During this period, the media also discovered that there were actors and organizations other than Falwell and the Moral Majority in this right-wing religiopolitical movement. Not until it became apparent that conservatives would not make similarly dramatic gains in Congress in 1982 did the story of the New Christian Right fade from page one.

By the middle 1980s, the widespread fear of the New Christian Right which dominated liberal sentiment only a short time ago was replaced by a complacency and a belief that the power of the New Christian Right had been exaggerated. The importance of this new political force, however, is not properly assessed by measuring its demonstrable impact on the 1980 and 1982 elections.

The New Christian Right is one of the most important social movements of this century. It may even signal a revolution of the order and magnitude of the revolution that Martin Luther's nailing of his ninety-five theses to the cathedral door in Wittenburg symbolized. The politically minded televangelists have been, and will continue to be, critical to this unfolding social movement.

The religiously based social movement is aligned with, but independent of, the conservative groups that helped sweep liberals from Congress and elected Ronald Reagan to the presidency in 1980 and 1984. It will be some years before we know whether this surge of conservatism is the beginning of a new era in American history, or merely an aberration from the liberal tradition of the past half-century.

If we are experiencing the dawning of a new era, the New Christian Right is destined to play a major role in shaping its character. The reason is that Evangelicals, who lean politically to the right, have developed unprecedented access to mass media. No other special interest group, except the interest of selling the products of our free enterprise system, has ever had so much unrestricted access to mass media.

Media Bias and the New Christian Right

The mass media constitute a lens through which we are afforded glimpses of what is happening in the world beyond our immediate experience. The world is constantly filled with events beyond our firsthand experience. What we know about this world is largely determined by the decisions of reporters and editors who define what is news, and by commentators who decide what is worthy of analytical treatment.

We may perceive the media, or certain segments of the media, to be biased in particular ways. But they substantially define what is important beyond our immediate firsthand experience by their selection of materials that are "newsworthy." This is not the place to raise anew all the knotty questions surrounding the issue of objectivity and bias in news reporting. The importance of this fact is that neither news reporters nor commentators were prepared for the religiopolitical story which began unfolding in early 1980. The result has been an unending flow of reflexive reporting which reveals more about reporters' values than about the phenomenon under examination.

Few reporters have been as open about their bias as *Village Voice* reporter Teresa Carpenter. In a cover story about Jerry Falwell, she readily admitted that she was inclined to view him as a "sophisticated snake oil salesman." This bias, to use her words, resulted from the fact that "whenever I step within a ten-foot radius of a fundamental minister my reason clouds over." This bias is perhaps to be expected in a publication like the *Village Voice,* which consciously and systematically slants news to fit the bias of its liberal readership. The more serious bias is that of the reporter who honestly believes he or she is being fair and balanced when, in fact, strongly negative attitudes toward the subject matter permit the subtle intrusion of slovenly work habits into the collecting and sorting of information.

The liberal political bias of journalists has been suspected for a long time. A study of their values conducted by Robert Lichter and Stanley Rothman published in *Public Opinion* in 1981 documents the suspicion. Eighty-one per cent of the media personnel surveyed voted for Carter over Ford, and an identical proportion earlier picked McGovern over Nixon. In 1964, ninety-six per cent of media personnel surveyed selected Johnson over Goldwater. On the religion profile presented by Lichter and Rothman, half of the media members surveyed reported no religious affiliation. Eighty-six per cent reported that they seldom attend religious services, and only eight per cent said they regularly attend church or synagogue services.

That the large majority of reporters is not in tune with either the political or religious values being espoused by television preachers is only part of the problem in reporting a story of this magnitude. Equally important is that the media reporters lack the cultural knowledge of conservative religious traditions in America which is necessary to understand what is happening. In fact, a large proportion knew almost nothing about religion at all, and few have any prior experience in reporting religion.

These observations about the media became apparent at the National Affairs Briefing in Dallas in August 1980, the first major event of the New Christian Right to be extensively covered by the media. Of the 250 or so reporters sent to cover that event, only about ten were religion writers. The event, highlighted by candidate Ronald Reagan's appearance, was significant, but it took on much greater significance as a result of the coverage it received.

The large majority of reporters present had never seen a Fundamentalist preacher hold an audience spellbound. It was an awesome and frightening experience for them. They took the political rhetoric more seriously than did most of the hearers, and they uncritically accepted the speakers' exaggerated claims of political strength. Their reporting of this event legitimized the move of a few televangelists into politics, and set the alarmist tone that followed for nearly two years.

Most editors would not knowingly send a male chauvinist to cover an ERA rally, a KKK sympathizer to a civil rights demonstration, or a food editor to cover a prize fight. But the average reporter covering preachers-turned-politicians was as mismatched for the task as these examples. The reporters lacked knowledge and were possessed of a sufficiently negative bias to render them inadequately prepared for the assignment. As a result, much of the reporting about the rise of the religious right has been a quagmire, shifting and yielding to the latest and most persuasive arguments.

Shifting Interpretations

There have been four distinct periods and moods in media coverage of the New Christian Right. Each period can be seen as reflecting the presuppositions of the mass media, commensurate with the knowledge in their possession at the time.

The first period is one of discovery and alarm. The Washington for Jesus rally in April 1980 might have passed unnoticed had it not been for the cadre of Washington-based, liberal church leaders who clamored until a few reporters paid attention. Media consciousness of the involvement of conservative Christians in politics increased several-fold when Falwell and his Moral Majority showed up in force at the National Republican Convention in July in Detroit. A few weeks later, in August, the 250 media representatives were in Dallas to watch several leading televangelists share the podium with Ronald Reagan at a two-day meeting called the National Affairs Briefing.

The outcome of the 1980 elections, plus the attribution of responsibility to the New Christian Right, intensified a sense of alarm. The left responded with a countermobilization of resources. Established organizations like the American Civil Liberties Union (ACLU) and Common Cause mobilized their constituencies. New organizations such as People for the American Way and Americans for Common Sense sprang into existence with the explicit purpose of doing battle with the New Christian Right.

A second period of response focused on an assessment of resources. It commenced as the media began to discover that many of the New Christian Right's claims were exaggerated. Falwell, in particular, had conned the press. He didn't have twenty-five to fifty million viewers of "The Old-Time Gospel Hour" as he had claimed, but only about 1.5 million. Neither did the Moral Majority have four million members, as claimed. When Falwell first claimed four million members in the Moral Majority, the organization scarcely had a membership at all. While there was an embryonic organization, the Moral Majority consisted essentially of a mailing list that was only about one-tenth as large as the membership figure Falwell boasted.

Simple arithmetic made it clear that the Moral Majority could not register and influence millions of voters. Post-election polls showed that only a small minority of Americans considered itself sympathetic to Moral Majority leadership. Moreover, when Moral Majority sympathizers were asked for their views on specific issues important to Moral Majority leaders, very large proportions disagreed with the leadership.

The truth is that Falwell had for months made fools of the press—it was purely and simply a case of the country boy taking the city sophisticates for a ride. Few people admit that someone else has gotten the better of them, and media analysts of the "Falwell phenomenon" were no exception.

Several developments helped sustain the myth of the mighty legions of religious fanatics on the right. First of all, several of the new organizations on the left would have lost their very raison d'etre if the New Christian Right were not really the ogre the opponents were describing. People for the American Way (PWA) was especially effective in keeping alive the message of danger on the right. The PWA produced a couple of television specials, ran full-page newspaper advertisements, created a publication series, and set up a system to monitor the political televangelists.

Also, warnings of the "American Ayatollahs" hit the bookstores. Titles like *Holy Terror* (Conway and Siegelman, 1981), *God's Bullies* (Young, 1981) and *Religious Pied Pipers* (Cooper, 1981) served as stern reminders that the Fundamentalists were taking over the country.

Even with all this publicity, the story of New Christian Right and the Moral Majority would probably have gone away except that Falwell refused to fade like a morning glory in the noonday sun. The more publicity he got, the more he seemed to thrive on it, even if the coverage were unfavorable, which much of it was. By midsummer of 1981, Falwell was receiving phone calls from Ronald Reagan and Menachim Begin asking for his support. He sassed the President and got away with it, and a few days later led a delegation of television preachers to Blair House to meet with the prime minister of Israel. A man who can command the attention of heads of state must have a power base somewhere.

Understandably, the media were reluctant to let go of a good story. As long as there was only a trickle of evidence challenging Falwell's claims, the myth of the mighty man from Lynchburg could be sustained. Gradually, however, the evidence challenging Falwell's made-up facts mounted; as it did, a new story emerged.

The third phase of media coverage of the New Christian Right was characterized by the debunking and dismissal of Falwell and, with him, the Moral Majority and other New Christian Right organizations. Utilizing statistics assembled by social scientists and survey analysts, the media began to write stories discrediting Falwell. Initially the reports were cautious. It was easier to suggest that the Moral Majority train was running out of steam than to admit that it had been powered all along by uncritical media acceptance of Falwell's claims. But in May 1983, National Public Radio reporter Tina Rosenberg pronounced that the Moral Majority was now yesterday's news, and the organization never was anything more than a media hype. She explained that "Falwell wants attention, liberals want an ogre, the press wants a good story. Whenever all parties want the same thing, they tend to get it whether they deserve it or not."

Rosenberg's article was not so much a revelation to reporters who had been pondering the shaky evidence of Falwell's power for a long time as a capstone to an emerging wisdom among Washington-based political writers.

Long before the Rosenberg article appeared, many reporters had already shifted their attention to The National Conservative Political Action Committee (NCPAC) as the real ogre on the right. When the right wing candidates failed to make further inroads by knocking off more liberals and moderates in the 1982 elections, the media gave NCPAC the same ceremonial burial they had earlier given Falwell and the Moral Majority. In fact, they didn't even wait for the elections. By June 1982, the *Washington Post* reported that NCPAC would have a more difficult time defeating liberals in 1982 because liberals and moderates had now had time to prepare strategies to counter NCPAC's hard-hitting, negative advertising campaigns. A few days later the *New York Times* chimed in with the same theme.

The results of the 1982 elections confirmed the media's predictions. It had been a good story, but the party was over. The only thing wrong with this assessment of the rise and fall of the New Christian Right is that it doesn't bear much relationship to what really happened between the discovery of the phenomenon in 1980 and the pronouncement of its demise in 1982. This is because the media have consistently failed to distinguish between the New Right and the New Christian Right. The two groups are not the same in terms of origins, constituencies, or goals.

The power base of the New Right is substantially secular and finds its focus in economic interests. The power base of the New Christian Right is sentiment and ideology, which are only partially religious in character. The coalition of the two groups on the right finds its strength in the organizational skills of the former and the potential of the latter to mobilize a broader base of support than is possible among the network of special interest groups affiliated with the New Right.

Leaders of both groups agree that New Right leaders were instrumental in encouraging Falwell to create the Moral Majority. Much to their chagrin, however, they had virtually nothing to do with the creation or the development of Moral Majority strategies and tactics. Falwell is an independent Baptist, and he does things his own way.

Only gradually did the latent coalition become a working coalition. The press largely missed this important fact. Weeks, even months, after the 1980 elections, major New Right organizations, for example, NCPAC, Conservative Caucus, Heritage Foundation, RAVCO, plus their most eminent personalities, were treated by many representatives of the press as merely part of Falwell's Moral Majority following.

Eventually, most reporters learned this was not the case. But many then adopted the alternative view that Falwell and the entire cadre of political activists of the religious right were merely puppets of the New Right. This view is not correct, but it has played an important role in the debunking of Falwell and his fellow televangelists as significant actors on the political scene.

The media have now gone on to other "more interesting" stories. But what is most interesting is that Falwell hasn't disappeared at all. Rather, he has become a taken-for-granted actor on the scene. The frequency with which his presence is noted, but taken for granted without derogatory comment, is evidence of the media's having moved beyond the debunking and dismissal phase.

One expects Falwell to be a regular guest at the Reagan White House. He hasn't quite replaced Billy Graham in Americans' consciousness as the pastor of presidents, but no one else can lay better claim to being the pastor of the current occupant of the White House.

When Richard Viguerie uses his direct-mail network to invite a few thousand of his conservative friends to a Fourth-of-July picnic, who does the *Washington Post* select out of the crowd to feature on page one of the style section? Falwell, of course. And who has appeared on the Phil Donahue Show more than any other person? Falwell. Falwell is no longer a novelty in American life. Just like Ronald Reagan, he is hardly loved by liberals, but his presence on the political scene cannot be denied.

More important than the fact that Falwell's presence is no longer a novelty is the taken-for-grantedness of his fellow Fundamentalists and Evangelicals in the political news. By the midpoint of his first term, President Reagan had addressed the National Religious Broadcasters on four occasions. He used an address before the National Association of Evangelicals to reaffirm his conviction that the Soviets are evil, and to rally support in opposition to the nuclear freeze movement. While Evangelicals and Fundamentalists are enjoying unprecedented access to the presidency and the White House, theological moderates and liberals have been virtually locked out. No president during this century has so completely snubbed the established religious leadership of this country.

Part of the reason for this change is that Reagan is the White House incumbent. But such an attitude is predicated on the assumption that Reagan is an anomalous president, an assumption widely shared by the liberal press. So, the presuppositions of the media continue to slant their understanding of the religious right's remarkable rise to social and political respectability.

But what of the future of the New Christian Right on the political scene? Is its influence and respectability tied to the fortunes of Reagan and his possible successor? Will the televangelists play a significant role in shaping conservative Christian politics?

Future Political Influence

In *The Emerging Order,* Jeremy Rifkin argued that "the evangelical community is amassing a base of potential power that dwarfs every other competing interest in American society today." Rifkin's conclusion is based on his assessment of Evangelicals' access to mass media. Their television broadcasting, he believes, will provide the foundation for the infrastructure to "build a total Christian community." Rifkin hopes that this force will address issues, such as the environment, which liberals claim are critical to the well-being of mankind.

In *Prime Time Preachers,* Charles Swann and I substantially agreed with Rifkin's assessment of the potential power base. We were less sanguine about the prospects that this emerging political force would address issues considered of importance to liberals, although we did not rule out the possibility of changing political agendas with the rise to power.

Forecasting has always been a precarious business, but there are several reasons to believe that televangelists will play an important role in shaping America's future.

Media personalities come and go. Jerry Falwell has a lot of talent, but it is not certain that he will be the central figure of the New Christian Right ten or twenty years from now. All social movements need charismatic leaders, but it takes more than leadership to produce a movement.

After fifty years of elaborating upon the combinations and permutations of liberal democratic philosophy, Americans are reassessing their values and government. This reassessment has to do with the role of government in our lives—what it may and may not do, what it should and should not do, and what it must and must not do. These concerns create a mosaic that crisscrosses traditional liberal-conservative positions. It is likely that the resolution of many of these issues will not be easily labeled as liberal or conservative. Still, it seems likely that many issues will be resolved in terms more compatible with a conservative than a liberal philosophy.

In the terms of sociological analysis, there are five structural properties possessed by the New Christian Right that give it an edge over the New Right and every other competing interest group in the attempt to reshape America. The first is access to the media. No other interest group has ever possessed so much access to media for promoting an ideological perspective than do Christian religious broadcasters. Furthermore, as direct mail research has made abundantly clear, it is not the size of the audience that is critical, but the confluence of interests between what is promoted and the receiver of the message. Those who like what they hear from Jerry Falwell, Pat Robertson, or James Kennedy will likely end up on mailing lists that will provide them with printed material which will reinforce their commitment to the cause. Politically oriented televangelists are already speaking to far larger audiences than did Martin Luther King, Jr., when he was the unchallenged leader of the civil rights movement.

Though many Evangelicals and Fundamentalists have been taught that religion and politics don't mix, there is a natural affinity between conservative theology and conservative politics. To date, only a small portion of radio and television broadcasters has endeavored to politicize audiences. But the warm reception conservative political speakers have received at annual conventions of the National Religious Broadcasters suggests that the latent political consciousness is ready and waiting to be mobilized.

The second structural property of the New Christian Right is finances. Social movements can be launched by voluntary labor, but to become effective agents of social change, they need money. Televangelists could not survive without converting audience response into financial contributions to pay for broadcasting time. It takes over a million dollars a week to fund Falwell's "Old-Time Gospel Hour" and various Liberty University projects he promotes on the air. He can't afford to lose these contributions to the Moral Majority, but he has the technical skills required to raise significant sums of money for his political activities. So do other politically minded televangelists.

Third, there is the New Christian Right's organization. No political organization, however popular its ideas with a potential constituency, can be built overnight. The claims of organizational strength made by the Moral Majority, Christian Voice, and other politically oriented religious groups in 1980 were unreal, and only political novices would have tried to get away with such claims. But in the several years since these organizations gained national visibility, they have begun to acquire the skills essential for organizational development. This is so, in large measure, because of the interorganizational alliances between New Christian Right and New Right organizations. To the extent that the New Right and the New Christian Right coalition can be held together, the latter will benefit significantly from the organizational skills of the former.

Fourth is the process of legitimacy. All social movement organizations struggle for the right to claim that God is on their side. No social movement of any consequence has succeeded without making a convincing case for the claim that its goals and the will of God are the same. Not everyone has to believe a movement's claims, obviously, but in the absence of persuasive God-talk, many otherwise sympathetic bystanders will not be transformed into movement constituents.

The American labor movement, for example, successfully borrowed gospel tunes and superimposed labor folk lyrics. Those tunes and lyrics carried the "gospel truth" to the common man in a way that was more authentic than the pious rhetoric of J. P. Morgan. During the civil rights movement, the lyrics of liberation and faith were often the same, and key leaders were in fact men of God. As one ranking Southern Senator is alleged to have said: "There wouldn't have been a civil rights movement if a bunch of damned preachers hadn't of gotten the idea that segregation was a moral issue." In claiming life, liberty, country, and family as causes, the New Christian Right and its allies have obtained good symbols of divine sanction.

The New Christian Right's fifth property pertains to demographics. America is on the threshold of a demographic revolution which will reshape the character of our society for as far into the future as anyone can imagine. Simply put, Americans are growing older. Fewer and fewer people die young and more and more live longer. The demographic reality portends a more conservative America. First, as individuals become older, they tend to accept a religious worldview. Second, older people tend to hold more conservative or orthodox religious views. Third, there is a close connection between conservative religious views and conservative political views.

Thus, as America becomes older, it will also become more conservative. Those who believe that the current wave of conservatism is an aberration from the long established progressive trend in America need to study the implication of this gradual aging process.

The precise character of the conservatism which will come with our aging remains to be seen. The special and economic interests of the New Right are probably too narrow to command the loyalty of a majority of Americans. Whatever the outcome, one important fact has been almost completely missed by the media and intellectuals: The "kooky Fundamendalists" that secular intellectual elites thought had disappeared after the Scopes Trial have already defined much of the agenda of this society for the foreseeable future, and therefore shaped the direction of American culture as we rush toward the twenty-first century.

NOTES

1. Ben Armstrong, *The Electric Church* (Nashville: Thomas Nelson, 1979), p. 10.
2. Jeremy Rifkin, *The Emerging Order* (New York: G. P. Putnam's Sons, 1979), p. 105.
3. Ibid., p. 114.
4. Jeffrey K. Hadden and Charles Swann, *Prime Time Preachers: The Rising Power of Televangelism* (Reading, Massachusetts: Addison-Wesley, 1981).

26. *Secular Humanism and The American Way*

By Joseph Sobran

Focus

Fundamentalists and Evangelicals are not alone in their belief that a new form of aggressive "secular humanism" informs the public policy debate in America. Joseph Sobran, a Roman Catholic, argues that the traditional concept of a "wall of separation" between church and state has been transformed by the American Civil Liberties Union (ACLU) into a doctrine calling for the exclusion of religious values from public life. It is not the Fundamentalists and Evangelicals, but the liberals, argues Sobran, who posit a single, militant "American Way."

The ACLU exhibits an "impulse toward total secularization" in viewing religion as "an irrational force, capable, when it interferes in secular life . . . of producing great harm." Because a liberal, secular bias has come to dominate public affairs, Fundamentalists and Evangelicals—indeed, all religious Americans—are forced to play "political games under rules laid down by their adversaries."

Sobran sees this situation leading to the "divinization of political man." Americans are allowing the state to become "a de facto god." In such circumstances, there is no transcendent, let alone divine, authority, because "all authority, all social order, all human relations claiming divine sanction must be treated as fictions, and probably mischievous fictions at that—else we violate the separation of church and state."

Sobran is encouraged that "conservative forces are becoming far more sophisticated about the real motives and *modus operandi* of their adversaries." But he believes that religious individuals and groups need "a footing on which to stand as we say 'No' to the all-swallowing state." Such a footing requires that religious Americans "speak in the language of the Divine, in spite of all the taboos imposed by a false secularization." Sobran's view should be compared with the views of Richard John Neuhaus (selection 1) and Nathan Glazer (selection 15).

Joseph Sobran is a nationally syndicated columnist, a senior editor of *National Review,* and author of *Single Issues* (Human Life Press, 1983).

WE HEAR ENDLESSLY of the importance of "compassion" and "understanding," and it is not at all to dispute the importance of these things to observe that they are far more difficult to achieve than their frequent and facile invocation would lead us to think. Compassion is easy to work up for a moment, when one reads, for instance, a news story about a little boy battered to death by his mother and her lover; it is harder to sustain for a constantly complaining relative.

As for understanding, people can live together and yet talk at cross-purposes for years on end. Deciphering language whose meaning seems clear, especially when it comes from people who seem innocent of all subtlety, can be hard. It can be especially hard when you already despise them and judge them to be far below yourself in intellectual caliber. All the more reason to make the effort, beginning with the self-reminder that an effort may in fact be necessary.

These ruminations began one day when, my children being out of the house for a few days, I pondered Jean-Paul Sartre's remark that "hell is other people." Sartre was, in my judgment, a profound fool, and I began to wonder, nonetheless, what he would have meant by that. He chose to regard other people as hellish; he chose not to have children, his paramour, Simone de Beauvoir, having made a point of saying publicly that she had had an abortion. What a pair. They had ruled out the great experiences celebrated by Shakespeare, the real risks of living in others; they had chosen, on doctrinaire principle, to be like Lear in Act I, aborting their progeny instead of investing themselves in a new life, imposing raw will on others and insisting that this infernal choice epitomized the human condition. The Lear of Act V was presumably guilty, in their eyes, of bad faith.

But were they so odd? I had just taken my children to the latest James Bond movie, the only film in town that didn't seem to feature Bo Derek in a bubble bath, and it struck me that Bond's

Reprinted with permission from the Fall, 1982 *Human Life Review* (© 1982 by the Human Life Foundation, Inc., New York, NY).

world was much like theirs, for all its *haut bourgeois* sheen: a world of mayhem, where lust was "liberated" from lasting union and the encumbrance of children. We had had to sit through not only the helicopter and submarine and ski-slope adventures, which was, after all what we'd come for, but the inevitable, PG-level lechery; parental guidance now casually includes allowing children to be shown that "sex," as we call it, need not be cursed with issue.

The New Hypocrisy

At what point did it suddenly go without saying that this is life? When did the dirty joke cease being a joke, and become a lifestyle? It is one thing to take a controversial position, but another to pretend it's not even controversial. This is the new hypocrisy: the suppression of any admission that there can be two points of view, even as we pretend we are somewhat daring in taking one of them. Suddenly we find a new constitution in effect, when we can't even recall having taken a vote, much less held a debate.

The press has been full of scornful articles on Fundamentalists who attack what they call "secular humanism." The articles put the phrase between quotation marks, deriding the very idea that there is such a *thing* as secular humanism; they contrive to make the idea sound like a lunatic fantasy, akin to delusions that fluoridated water is a Communist conspiracy.

Well, we need not call the phenomenon "secular humanism" (though men like Leo Pfeffer—not the Jerry Falwells—coined the phrase, applying it to themselves). But it is disingenuous to deny that there is such a phenomenon at all.

One very subtle and effective technique of evading debate is to pretend that there can really be nothing to argue about. Part of this technique is the refusal to accept any opponent's label for one's own position. The moment one admits having a special position, that position becomes vulnerable. Much more adroit to represent the attribution of any definable position to an opponent's *gaucherie*.

And it is true that a label like "secular humanism" can become a catch-all for whatever we disapprove of. Still, it is unlikely that even the coarsest Bible-thumper is expressing a disapproval only of something whose existence is confined to his imagination. If his perception is crude or distorted, we ought to acknowledge, in all fairness, that he nonetheless perceives *something;* and we ought to take the trouble to define it accurately.

The people the Fundamentalists call secular humanists like to say that they "avoid labels," and ordinarily they are no doubt eager to do so; as if to suggest that they are nothing but a random collection of individualists whose essence is so very refined that the words have not yet been coined that can capture it. But this may be too self-flattering, and too self-serving. When it suits their purposes, they *can* find labels for themselves. One of the targets of Moral Majority wrath, TV producer Norman Lear, has formed an organization called People for the American Way.

As a rule, liberals (to use a label not quite out of use) scorn the arrogance of anyone who posits a single "American Way." If conservatives do so, liberals are quick to speak of McCarthyism and intolerance. Likewise the liberal priest Robert Drinan, in his inaugural speech as president of the Americans for Democratic Action, called the Moral Majority and its ilk "enemies of this country"—a piece of invective not permitted to those enemies. As so often happens, those who demand tolerance for themselves turn out less willing, once they find a safe perch, to extend tolerance to others.

Is Anything Intolerable?

This is only natural, and natural in a sense that need not suggest the baseness of fallen nature. The Anglican Richard Baxter once laid down the rule, "Tolerate the tolerable," implying, as Samuel Johnson observed, that there must also be a category of things not tolerable. The question becomes: What view of life is the liberal side upholding under which the Moral Majority must be deemed intolerable?

The question is complicated by the fact that Drinan, like Falwell, is a clergyman, and therefore presumably not a "secular humanist." Or is it that simple? While he was in Congress, Drinan fought extraordinarily hard, even vituperatively, for legal abortion and even for federal funding for abortions, subordinating the doctrines of his religion to the imperatives of "a woman's choice." Can it be that a Catholic priest would willingly pave the way for the killing of unborn human beings, each of whom has not only a moral right to live, but an immortal soul?

Perhaps. Drinan can always take the familiar line (I expect he did take it) that he is "personally opposed" to abortion even as he fought for the *civil* right of a woman to "control her own body." We may even lay aside, though not fail to note, the amazing disparity of passion between his political commitment to abortion and his moral opposition to the actual performance of the act.

Even so, the question nags: How can a merely *legal* right to do an admittedly evil thing (for this is what "personally opposed" must mean) impose such a *moral* imperative to tolerate, and subsidize, the evil thing itself? One might passionately favor states' rights, under the federal system, to the extent of opposing a federal anti-lynch law; but surely, in that case, one would feel obliged, as vehemently as possible, to make clear one's moral abhorrence of lynching. The people in Congress and elsewhere who "personally oppose" abortion do nothing of the kind. It is fair to infer—actually it is silly to doubt—that their expressed opposition to abortion is only formalistic.

Put otherwise, it is nearly impossible to imagine any of them trying to discourage a woman, on moral grounds, from making the choice they have struggled to legalize. None of them has audibly laid down moral criteria for abortion. None of them has confronted the simple physical agony suffered by the child in late abortions. None of them expressed revulsion at the acts, perhaps homicidal even under the loose guidelines of the Supreme Court, committed by Doctors Kenneth Edelin and William Waddill.

We can hardly believe, in the face of such evidence, that the term "pro-abortion" is less apt than the term "pro-choice." They may pretend merely to be engaged in sharply distinguishing the moral and legal realism; but if that were true, they would make the distinction in practice, not just in verbal *formulae* which have no practical consequences.

Put in broader terms, it is clear that for at least many of them, there is no effective distinction between these realms. They identify the moral and legal realms as thoroughly, at least in their practical conduct and emotional experience, as any Prohibitionist who ever thought that what is intrinsically immoral must be made illegal, and that whatever is legally tolerated must be considered as having a moral sanction.

In sociological terms, the modernizing process is thought to consist largely in "differentiating" categories of human action. One of the basic modern differentiations has been the separation of church and state; and pro-abortionists claim the sanction of the modernizing principle by asserting that legalizing abortion is only a way of extending the church-state distinction. In the words of the American Civil Liberties Union (ACLU), which has fought against the Hyde Amendment on constitutional grounds, limitations on abortion serve "no secular purpose"—a phrase and a principle earlier laid down by the Supreme Court.

Some Things Are Sacred

But the modernizing principle, perhaps perfectly valid in itself, is fraudulently invoked if it is used to mean an illicit secularization of all of life, including what ought to belong to the sacred. In a sense, the modernizing principle can be said to derive from the words of Christ: "Render unto Caesar the things that are Caesar's, and unto God the things that are God's." St. Augustine himself elaborated the distinction, differentiating the earthly and heavenly cities.

But no Christian has ever admitted, and until recently few American liberals have ever held, that this distinction requires us, *qua* citizens of the earthly city, to act as if the heavenly city were less real than the one we presently inhabit. This has changed. In Europe it began to change with the French Revolution, in which social anticlericalism was wildly mixed with hatred of religion—with, ultimately, the hatred of God explicitly avowed by Sartre in recent times. The Russian Revolution, among others, set out to abolish religion altogether, with no pretense of merely separating the secular and sacred realms: for Communism, the state comprehends all of human existence.

But in the American tradition, such claims by the secular have never been officially adopted. Nor are they today, but they have been furtively advanced, under color of separationism. And now we find them being ever more boldly, if confusedly, advanced, still under the aegis of keeping church and state separate.

Pursuant to its suit against the Hyde Amendment, the ACLU inspected Congressman Henry Hyde's mail and offered its heavy component of religious expressions as evidence that the Hyde Amendment—to limit federal funding of abortions—was illicitly motivated by non-secular purposes. An ACLU agent even testified that he had followed Hyde to mass and observed him receiving Communion—a further taint on the Amendment. This could only be considered evidence that the Amendment was unconstitutional if specifically religious motives are somehow forbidden by the Constitution to influence public policy. This is a historically novel doctrine: Sunday "blue laws" are only one sign that the American people have never understood their polity and its theoretical basis as the ACLU understands them. (The ACLU has also sued to force Catholic hospitals to make their facilities available for the performance of abortions.)

Another sign of the new understanding appeared in the election of 1980, when liberal columnists like Anthony Lewis of the *New York Times* accused clergymen like Falwell and Cardinal Medeiros of Boston of *violating the Constitution* in taking political positions. Several conservatives quickly replied that this charge had never been thrown at the many clergymen who had taken liberal positions on war, civil rights, and nuclear energy. But the more fundamental point was that the liberals were implicitly interpreting the constitutional command that "Congress shall make no law respecting an establishment of religion" as, in effect, an actual abridgment of the clergy's own "free exercise" of religion. Lewis, to his credit, admitted that this was true, and retracted the charge. The remarkable thing was that he had made it at all, a fact that bespoke the impulse toward total secularization we are concerned with here.

Again, when it appeared that a Mormon federal appeals judge, Marion Callister, might be called on to rule on the constitutionality of the deadline extension for ratification of the Equal Rights Amendment (ERA), liberals like the columnist Ellen Goodman demanded that Callister be disqualified—because the Mormon Church officially opposes ERA. This was too much for Leo Pfeffer, the nation's foremost avowed secular humanist: In a splendidly impartial display of principal, he wrote a letter to the *New York Times* in defense of Callister, pointing out that his disqualification would amount to an unconstitutional "religious test" for public office.

These are only a few examples of the steadily-growing claims of all-out secularizers for the exclusion of all religious influence from American public life. We may also mention the growing boldness of purely secular agencies, like the *Times*, in demanding the reform of churches along secular lines: they think nothing of campaigning for the ordination of women or denouncing ecclesiastical disciplines by churches against their own members, or calling on the churches to alter doctrinal positions on moral issues like birth control. As long as they can find (and publicize) one dissident member of a faith, they see nothing amiss in their leaping into the fray on his (or her) side. The affair of Sonia Johnson, the excommunicated Mormon feminist, is a case in point: Mrs. Johnson enjoyed highly sympathetic media coverage, it meaning nothing to the media, apparently, that this was the internal affair of an institution with doctrines and organization of its own. Again and again we encounter the implicit demand that the churches reform themselves on lines stipulated by secularist forces.

What 'Secular Humanists' Believe

At this point the Moral Majoritarian may innocently feel that the case is pretty well closed: the secular humanists consistently show their tremendous arrogance. But putting it this way may be premature. What is it that these secular humanists, to call them that, feel, deep in their hearts, that they are doing?

Making all allowances for hypocrisy, we must still remember that the most destructive people may be quite sincere. In any case, the people we are discussing don't call themselves secular humanists, and don't even think of themselves as such. They are not conscious of dishonestly promoting a special creed; they are not conscious of holding such a creed at all. I know of no evidence whatever that they talk among themselves in a dialect very different from the one they use in public. That must tell us something. How do they see themselves?

I venture to say that they think of themselves not as scheming atheists, but, precisely, as upholders of the American Way. When they cite the First Amendment, they mean it—at least as they grasp the import of the First Amendment. The simplest explanation is that they think of it as containing the radiant essence of the Constitution, and of our basic political premises.

They think of religion as an irrational force, capable, when it interferes in secular life (and they assume that its influence is properly described, on the whole, as interference), of producing great harm. At the very least, they feel that it consists in claiming a special "pipeline to God" and a "monopoly on Truth" that renders rational social discourse next to impossible. We can converse fruitfully with each other, they feel, only if we confine our public discourse to premises we can all accept—which means that anything purporting to be divine revelation has no place in that discourse. They acknowledge that the Judeo-Christian tradition contains many excellent things, which can, of course, be held without subscribing to that tradition as a whole, or on its own terms.

This is the key, I think. They feel that there is a moral consensus about matters like murder, theft, charity, and the like, and that we can all peaceably agree on these regardless of how we regard the tradition as a whole. They therefore welcome the political utterances of the clergy—so long as, and only so long as, these are confined to areas of consensus between Christians and non-Christians.

Liberals Control the 'Consensus'

But of course there is a catch here, and they don't notice it. Their notion of "consensus" is reductive, in a way particularly convenient to them. It means that the area of agreement is defined almost exclusively by themselves. If they reject a certain part of the Judeo-Christian tradition, then religious people are forbidden to bring that part into public discourse. In fact, religious people must behave within the secular arena as if that part didn't exist. To behave otherwise is to impose the views of a minority on everyone. The views of the majority, by definition, are those views acceptable to liberals, "secular humanists," or whatever we are to call them: they are a recognizable body, almost a sect, even if we hardly know what to call them.

Religious people, in other words, are required to play the political game by rules laid down by their adversaries. And this, the most fundamental rule of all, is supposed to have been the first and original principle of the Republic. That is the meaning of the constant appeal to the First Amendment. But—a critically important fact—this Amendment is not itself subject to amending. It is supposed to have exactly the kind of dogmatic status which Christians claim for divine revelation. Its origin is never fully explained; it (in its liberal interpretation) is simply posited as the condition of all possible political existence—and, as the claims of politics expand to include all human life, of all human existence on earth. (If there is any other dimension of human existence, it is not to be considered.)

In this way, the liberal/secular humanist ground rules seem to those who accept them unquestioningly to supply the basis for all manner of further claims on other institutions. Discussion of the sacred and *its* claims are, ironically, foreclosed *by the First Amendment itself*. That is why liberals, as Basile Uddo has remarked in a splendid essay on the American Civil Liberties Union, can unblushingly ban religious expression from public institutions, establishing new forms of virtual censorship—in addition to the proscriptions against religion in politics I mentioned earlier.

The repercussions are enormous. They affect all institutions, public as well as private. I have already mentioned the casual demand that religious bodies abide by secular standards: if this can be required, it should be an easy matter to require as much of institutions that straddle the secular and the sacred. If human life itself must not be regarded as sacred, if the family must not be understood as of divine institution, then there is nothing to stop the political order from washing over its banks to reform these, too, redefining them at its convenience. Property and wealth, of course, are politically up for grabs. Public education need observe no restraints except against prayer and Christmas carols; there is no reason to regard sex education as beyond its province, since neither religious nor parental authority in these matters need be regarded as inviolable.

Politics, in short, loses all its old limitations, and, subject only to the taboo on religion, becomes the arena within which all human destiny is worked out. The state becomes a *de facto* god. No other human relations—certainly not those of the family—can claim priority over those of state and citizen. What with newly posited children's and women's rights, the state may even assume the power of interfering in family relations, ostensibly to protect one citizen against the arbitrary action of another.

Inevitably this means that there is no authority above man himself. Practically, it means the divinization of political man, man acting through the state. All authority, all social order, all human relations claiming divine sanction, must be treated as fictions, and probably mischievous fictions at that—else we violate the separation of church and state.

'The Desire To Be God'

Man, Sartre tells us, is himself "the desire to be God." Under the liberal regime this is never openly admitted, and can't be. But it comes to the same thing. We are getting the ideology of the French Revolution under the guise and forms of the American tradition.

I repeat, there is no reason to suppose all this is a diabolically conscious process, cunningly disguised by its avatars. There is every reason to accept their protestations that they believe they merely represent "the American Way." Norman Lear can use his television sit-coms to propagandize for sexual liberation, abortion, and democratic socialism without feeling that he is doing anything any reasonable person would deem controversial. But his "reasonable person" is Jerry Falwell's "secular humanist." They are talking about the same thing, and merely disagreeing over labels—though "merely" is hardly the word for a disagreement that issues from radically different philosophic frameworks.

Lear might well contend that his framework enjoys more intellectual respectability than Falwell's—and so, in a sense, it would. The very word "intellectual" has taken on a special coloration: it refers almost exclusively to the "secular humanists" themselves, those who make it a principle never to advert to divine authority in their public life. For them, man achieved his independence with the Enlightenment, and Harold Rosenberg's ironic phrase "the herd of independent minds" has an enormous resonance. To be an intellectual, in the current sense, is not necessarily to have any *personal* intellectual distinction at all: it is merely to belong to the party, or "herd," that rejects traditional religion and seeks humanistic authority.

And how are such intellectuals to deal with non-intellectuals, that is, the religious? By force. It may be disguised; indeed, for purposes of liberal decorum it usually is. But since there is no reasoning with people who reject the "First Amendment" premises of rational discourse, the political prescriptions of the enlightened—abortion, say, or racial busing—may have to be imposed by fiat, with whatever compulsion is feasible and necessary. The judiciary—custodian of the secular humanist ground rules—has served as a theocratic priesthood which, in the name of the American Constitution, has successfully circumvented popular politics to realize much of the liberal agenda. By such devices has the party of the New American Way managed to read its opponents out of the American polity.

But this is changing. Conservative forces are becoming far more sophisticated about the real motives and *modus operandi* of their adversaries. The very outcry over "secular humanism" on both sides shows that conservatives have caught the scent.

The Family Under Attack

Religious, philosophic, and metaphysical questions are all important, but the real battleground is the family—the level at which most people are directly touched. The family's weakened status could never have been simply imposed from above. To a great extent, alas, it springs from popular demand. Fornication, adultery, and abortion are nothing new, nor was their popularity ever confined to judges. But these old sins are now being institutionalized as "rights," and more and more people sense that what once appeared as attractive options are now forming part of a new, malign political order in which the reality of the family must crumble before the reality of sheer state power. What was once the sanctuary of private affection now falls under the domain of raw force. The French secularist tradition that begot Sartre has been more lucid about this than the gentler Anglo-Saxon tradition under which the abolition of man (to use C. S. Lewis's phrase) took on the aspect of liberal modernization.

Sartre said boldly that every man is alone, and that society is agglutinated by terror. Our society is a long way from the totalitarian systems Sartre delighted in, but it has its own uneasiness. We are beginning to realize that the humanitarian claims of "compassion," under which the state claims more and more of our substance, mask an order based on compulsion, and therefore fear—if only the fear of agencies like the Internal Revenue Service and those acronymic organs of state "social welfare."

At the moment it is awkward to dispute the universalist claims of "compassion" in the name of the more concrete and humble loves of the family. The conservative forever finds himself in the position of King Lear's daughter Cordelia—condemned for hardheartedness for refusing to enter a competition of extravagant professions. In an age that denies man's nature (because it suppresses the mention of God), we are expected to join the new political creation that will improve the handiwork of the Creator by subjecting it to larger and larger organization, driven by what Robert Frost called "that tenderer-than-thou collectivistic regimenting love with which the modern world is being swept."

'We Are Under God'

In the last analysis we must have a footing on which to stand as we say No to the all-swallowing state. Such a footing requires us simply to speak in the language of the Divine, in spite of all the taboos imposed by a false secularization. The word "godless" has been deliberately made to sound quaint and out of place in political discourse, for the very reason that it is most apposite. Terms like "secular humanism" are similarly forbidden (if only by ridicule) for the very good reason that they effectively identify, if only approximately, the specific outlook we are up against.

We must insist that we are all mere men, not gods; even collectively we are not God, nor are we God in our political representatives. We are *under* God. We are His creatures, his frail, sinful creatures, made to love each other in simple though difficult ways: as husbands and wives, parents and children, neighbors among neighbors, friends among friends, and, yes, citizens among citizens, in all relations recognizing that we stand under judgment. If we try to be more than mere men, we will only become less, the order of love and justice giving way to the order of sheer arbitrary power. Whoever tries to change the social fabric in which we are knitted together by God will only lead us into chaos. Within the social order God made us for, we can have contentment and occasional joy. Outside it, only lust, greed, fear, and despair.

Those to whom this view of things sounds impossibly backward are what are meant by the phrase "secular humanists." It is worth noticing that they have their own kind of fear: they describe their adversaries not only demeaningly, as "reactionaries," but as actually "dangerous." As they should: for those who still belong to the order of love actually pose a fatal menace to the New American Way. The secular humanists deplore any talk of a "Communist menace," because they look on Communism as an essentially rational (though no doubt occasionally brutal) social principle, akin somehow to their own, and therefore eligible for "dialogue" and "negotiation." After all, Communism never adverts to the supernatural. It is only a variant of secular humanism, which is why secular humanists remain far more scandalized by religious wars and persecutions than by the continuing oppressions (including the persecution of religion) of the Communist regimes.

This is why the secular humanists have resisted distinguishing between authoritarian and totalitarian regimes: even to recognize the difference—including the unique totalitarian feature of armed borders, at which people are shot for trying to escape—is automatically to admit the special monstrosity, to ordinary people, of states that assume the status of divinities. The furtive sympathy of many "liberals" for Communism is alternately hotly denied and openly expressed, according to the change of seasons. Stalin, Mao, and Castro have all had their vogues, with American professors and senators returning from brief visits to exult that "they have much to teach us." What they ultimately have to teach us is what depths godless man can sink to. That those are exalted as heights tells us all we really need to know about the godless men of our own society.

In the current debates over "secular humanism," "creationism," "the separation of church and state," and so forth, the precise words have no final importance. But in the field of God and man, society and the world, they serve to alert us to certain decisive alignments, whose membership on both sides I hope I have described and analyzed accurately enough, without concealing my own partiality to the side I think is finally in the right, even if it sometimes seems to be losing the immediate arguments or simply swinging at the air. In fact the very deficit of obvious intellectual firepower on the "Moral Majority" side seems to me to testify to its valor; when men like the Reverend Falwell risk ridicule and disgrace, along with bitter vilification, I am reminded principally of the wisdom of the God he and I adore, Who has revealed that the last shall be first, and that He has chosen the foolish things of this world to confound the wise.

Bibliography

Part One: Background and Origins

Books

Askew, Thomas A., and Spellman, Peter W. *The Churches and the American Experience*. Grand Rapids: Baker Book House, 1984.

Bloesch, Donald. *The Evangelical Renaissance*. Grand Rapids: Eerdmans, 1973.

Frank, Douglas W. *Less Than Conquerors: How Evangelicals Entered the Twentieth Century*. Grand Rapids: Eerdmans, 1986.

Hunter, James Davison. *American Evangelicalism*. New Brunswick, N.J.: Rutgers University Press, 1983.

Hunter, James Davison. *Evangelicals: The Coming Generation*. Chicago: The University of Chicago Press, 1987.

Kantzer, Kenneth S., ed. *Evangelical Roots*. Nashville: Thomas Nelson Publishers, 1978.

Machen, J. Gresham. *Christianity and Liberalism*. New York: MacMillan, 1923. Reprint. Grand Rapids: Eerdmans, 1979.

Mardsen, George, ed. *Evangelicalism and Modern America*. Grand Rapids: Eerdmans, 1984.

Mardsen, George. *Fundamentalism and American Culture*. Oxford, England: Oxford University Press, 1980.

Noll, Mark A.; Hatch, Nathan O.; and Mardsen, George M., et al. *Eerdmans' Handbook to Christianity in America*. Grand Rapids: Eerdmans, 1983.

Noll, Mark A.; Hatch, Nathan O.; and Mardsen, George M. *Search for Christian America*. Westchester, Ill.: Crossway Books, 1983.

Neuhaus, Richard John. *The Naked Public Square*. Grand Rapids: Eerdmans, 1984.

Quebedeaux, Richard. *The Worldly Evangelicals*. New York: Harper and Row, 1978.

Quebedeaux, Richard. *The Young Evangelicals*. New York: Harper and Row, 1974.

Reichley, A. James. *Religion in American Public Life*. Washington: The Brookings Institution, 1985.

Sandeen, Ernest. *The Roots of Fundamentalism: British and American Millenarianism 1800–1930*. Chicago: University of Chicago, 1970.

Stone, Ronald H., ed. *Reformed Faith and Politics*. Washington: University Press of America, 1983.

Sweet, Leonard I., ed. *The Evangelical Tradition in America*. Macon: Mercer University Press, 1984.

Wells, David, and Woodbridge, John, eds. *The Evangelicals*. Grand Rapids: Baker, 1977.

Woodbridge, John; Noll, Mark; and Hatch, Nathan. *The Gospel in America: Themes in the Story of America's Evangelicals*. Grand Rapids: Zondervan, 1979.

Articles

Hatch, Nathan O. "Evangelicalism as a Democratic Movement." *The Reformed Journal,* October 1984.

Hunter, James Davison. "Operationalizing Evangelicalism: A Review, Critique, and Proposal." *Sociological Analysis 42,* 1982.

Marty, Martin E. "Religion in America Since Mid-Century." *Daedalus,* Winter 1982.

Murphy, Cullen. "Protestantism and the Evangelicals." *The Wilson Quarterly,* Autumn 1981.

Sweet, Leonard I. "The 1960s: The Crises of Liberal Christianity and the Public Emergence of Evangelicalism." In *Evangelicalism and Modern America,* George Marsden, ed., Grand Rapids: Eerdmans, 1984.

Wacker, Grant. "Uneasy in Zion: Evangelicals in Postmodern Society." In *Evangelicalism and Modern Society,* George Marsden, ed., Grand Rapids: Eerdmans, 1984.

Part Two: Speaking For Themselves

Books

Billingsley, Lloyd. *The Generation That Knew Not Josef*. Portland, Oreg.: Multnomah Press, 1985.

Bloesch, Donald G. *The Future of Evangelical Christianity*. Garden City, N.Y.: Doubleday and Company, Inc., 1983.

Curry, Dean C. *Evangelicals and the Bishops' Pastoral Letter*. Grand Rapids: Eerdmans, 1984.

Dobson, Edward. *In Search of Unity: An Appeal to Fundamentalists and Evangelicals*. Nashville: Thomas Nelson Publishers, 1985.

Eidsmore, John. *God and Caesar*. Westchester, Ill.: Crossway Books, 1984.

Falwell, Jerry. *Listen America!* New York: Doubleday and Company, Inc., 1980.

Falwell, Jerry; Dobson, Ed; and Hindson, Ed. *The Fundamentalist Phenomenon.* (Second Edition) Grand Rapids: Baker Book House, 1986.

Henry, Carl F. H. *Confessions of a Theologian.* Waco: Word Books, 1986.

Henry, Carl F. H. *The Christian Mindset in a Secular Society.* Portland, Oreg.: Multnomah Press, 1984.

Herbert, Jerry S., ed. *America, Christian or Secular?* Portland, Oreg.: Multnomah Press, 1984.

Johnston, Robert. *Evangelicals At an Impasse.* Atlanta: John Knox, 1979.

LaHaye, Tim. *The Battle for the Mind.* Old Tappan, N.J.: Fleming H. Revell Company, 1980.

Marshall, Paul. *Thine Is the Kingdom.* Grand Rapids: Eerdmans, 1986.

Monsma, Stephen V. *Pursuing Justice In a Sinful World.* Grand Rapids: Eerdmans, 1984.

Mouw, Richard J. *Politics and the Biblical Drama.* Grand Rapids: Eerdmans, 1976.

Nash, Ronald H. *Social Justice and the Christian Church.* Milford, Mich.: Mott Media, Inc., 1983.

Schaeffer, Francis A. *A Christian Manifesto.* Westchester, Ill.: Crossway Books, 1981.

Schaeffer, Francis A. *The Great Evangelical Disaster.* Westchester, Ill.: Crossway Books, 1984.

Schlossberg, Herbert. *Idols For Destruction.* Nashville: Thomas Nelson Publishers, 1983.

Sider, Ronald J., ed. *The Chicago Declaration.* Carol Stream, Ill.: Creation House, 1974.

Skillen, James W., ed. *Confessing Christ and Doing Politics.* Washington: Association for Public Justice Education Fund, 1982.

Wallis, Jim. *The Call to Conversion.* San Francisco: Harper and Row, 1981.

Webber, Robert. *The Church in the World.* Grand Rapids: Zondervan, 1986.

Webber, Robert. *The Moral Majority: Right or Wrong?* Westchester, Ill.: Cornerstone, 1981.

Whitehead, John W. *The Second American Revolution.* Elgin, Ill.: David C. Cook Publishing Company, 1982.

Wolterstorff, Nicholas. *Until Justice and Peace Embrace.* Grand Rapids: Eerdmans, 1983.

ARTICLES

Billingsley, Lloyd. "First Church of Christ Socialist." *National Review,* October 28, 1983.

Carpenter, Joel. "The Fundamentalist Leaven and the Rise of an Evangelical United Front." *The Evangelical Tradition in America,* Leonard I. Sweet, Macon: Mercer University Press, 1984.

Clouse, Robert. "The New Christian Right, America, and the Kingdom of God." *Christian Scholar's Review 13,* 1983.

Henry, Carl F. H. "The Fundamentalist Phenomenon: The Ricochet of Silver Bullets." *Christianity Today,* September 4, 1981.

Hunter, James Davison. "The New Class and the Young Evangelicals." *Review of Religious Research,* December 1980.

Marsden, George. "The New Fundamentalism." *The Reformed Journal,* February 1982.

Mouw, Richard. "New Alignments." *Against the World for the World,* Peter Berger and Richard Neuhaus, eds. New York: Seabury, 1976.

Pierard, Richard V. "Religion and the New Right in Contemporary Politics." *Religion and Politics,* James E. Woods, Jr., ed. Waco: Baylor University Press, 1983.

Smidt, Corwin. "Evangelicals and the 1984 Election: Continuity or Change?" Paper presented at the Annual Meeting of the Society for the Scientific Study of Religion, Savannah, 1985.

Smith, Timothy L. "The Evangelical Kaleidoscope and the Call to Christian Unity." *Mid Stream: An Ecumenical Journal,* July/October 1983.

Part Three: What Others Say

Books

Cox, Harvey. *Religion In The Secular City.* New York: Simon and Schuster, 1984.

Douglas, Mary, and Tipton, Steven M., eds. *Religion and America.* Boston: Beacon Press, 1982.

D'Souza, Dinesh. *Falwell: Before the Millennium.* Chicago: Regnery Gateway, 1984.

Fowler, Robert Booth. *A New Engagement.* Grand Rapids: Eerdmans, 1982.

Goldberg, George. *Reconsecrating America.* Grand Rapids: Eerdmans, 1984.

Griffith, Carol Friedley, ed. *Christianity and Politics.* Washington: Ethics and Public Policy Center, 1981.

Hitchcock, James. *What Is Secular Humanism?* Ann Arbor: Servant Books, 1982.

Horn, Carl, ed. *Whose Values?* Ann Arbor: Servant Books, 1985.

Liebman, Robert C., and Wuthnow, Robert. *The New Christian Right.* New York: Aldine Publishing Company, 1983.

Rothenberg, Stuart, and Newport, Frank. *The Evangelical Voter.* Washington: Free Congress Research and Education Foundation, 1984.

Sobran, Joseph. *Single Issues.* New York: Human Life Press, 1983.

ARTICLES

Berger, Peter. "From the Crisis of Religion to the Crisis of Secularity." in *Religion and America,* Mary Douglas and Steven M. Tipton, eds. Boston: Beacon Press, 1982.

Bethell, Tom. "Sojourning." *Catholicism in Crisis,* February, April, June 1984.

Briggs, Kenneth A. "Evangelicals Turning to Politics: Fear Moral Slide Imperils Nation." *The New York Times,* August 19, 1980.

Brookhiser, Richard. "Theocracy in America: Campaign '84 Revisited." *The American Spectator,* August 1985.

D'Souza, Dinesh. "A Student Editor's Experience." *National Review,* November 12, 1982.

D'Souza, Dinesh. "Jerry Falwell's Renaissance." *Policy Review,* Winter 1984.

Fitgerald, Francis. "A Reporter At Large: A Disciplined, Charging Army." *The New Yorker,* May 18, 1981.

Hunter, James Davison. "Religion and Political Civility: The Coming Generation of American Evangelicals." *Journal for the Scientific Study of Religion,* 1984.

Krauthammer, Charles. "America's Holy War." *The New Republic,* April 9, 1984.

Krauthammer, Charles. "The Church-State Debate." *The New Republic,* September 17–24, 1984.

Lipset, Seymour Martin, and Raad, Earl. "The Election and the Evangelicals." *Commentary,* March 1981.

Marty, Martin E. "Insiders Look at Fundamentalism." *The Christian Century,* November 18, 1981.

Ostling, Richard N. "Jerry Falwell's Crusade." *Time,* September 2, 1985.

Ostling, Richard N. "Power, Glory—and Politics." *Time,* February 17, 1986.

Sobran, Joseph. "Beyond the Moral Majority." *Center Journal,* Winter 1981.

Wall, James M. "What Future for the New Right?" *The Christian Century,* November 25, 1981.

Index of Names